Czech (& Central European)
Yearbook of Arbitration®

Czech (& Central European) Yearbook of Arbitration®

Volume IV

2014

Independence and Impartiality of Arbitrators

Editors

Alexander J. Bělohlávek

Professor
at the VŠB TU
in Ostrava
Czech Republic

Naděžda Rozehnalová

Professor
at the Masaryk University
in Brno
Czech Republic

Filip Černý

Dr. Iur.
Charles University
in Prague
Czech Republic

JURIS

Questions About This Publication

For assistance with shipments, billing or other customer service matters,
please call our Customer Services Department at:
1-631-350-2100

To obtain a copy of this book, call our Sales Department:
1-631-351-5430
Fax: 1-631-351-5712

Toll Free Order Line:
1-800-887-4064 (United States & Canada)
See our web page about this book:
www.arbitrationlaw.com

Printed in the United States of America.
ISBN 978-1-937518-39-4
ISSN 2157-9490

JurisNet, LLC
71 New Street
Huntington, New York 11743 U.S.A.
www.arbitrationlaw.com

The title *Czech (& Central European) Yearbook of Arbitration*® as well as
the logo appearing on the cover are protected by EU trademark law.

Typeset in the U.S.A. by Juris Publishing, Inc.

Address for correspondence & manuscripts
Czech (& Central European) Yearbook of Arbitration®
Jana Zajíce 32, Praha 7, 170 00, Czech Republic
www.czechyearbook.org

Editorial support
František Halfar, Jan Halfar, Lenka Němečková, Karel Nohava

Impressum

Institutions Participating in the CYArb® Project

Academic Institutions

University of West Bohemia in Pilsen, Czech Republic
Faculty of Law, Department of International Law &
Department of Constitutional Law
[*Západočeská univerzita v Plzni, Právnická fakulta.*
Katedra mezinárodního práva & Katedra ústavního práva]

Masaryk University (Brno, Czech Republic)
Faculty of Law, Department of International and European Law
[*Masarykova univerzita v Brně, Právnická fakulta,*
Katedra mezinárodního a evropského práva]

Pavol Jozef Šafárik University in Košice, Slovak Republic
Faculty of Law, Department of Commercial Law and Business Law
[*Právnická fakulta UPJŠ, Košice, Slovensko. Katedra obchodného a*
hospodárskeho práva]

VŠB – TU Ostrava, Czech Republic
Faculty of Economics, Department of Law
[*VŠB – TU Ostrava, Ekonomická fakulta, Katedra práva*]

Institute of State and Law of the Academy of Sciences of the Czech Republic, v.v.i.
[*Ústav státu a práva Akademie věd ČR, v.v.i.*]

Non-academic Institutions Participating in the CYArb® Project

International Arbitral Centre
of the Austrian Federal Economic Chamber
[*Wiener Internationaler Schiedsgericht (VIAC), Vienna*]

Court of International Commercial Arbitration Attached
to the Chamber of Commerce and Industry of Romania
[*Curtea de Arbitraj Comercial Internaţional de pe lângă Camera de Comerţ şi Industrie a României, Bucharest*]

Arbitration Court Attached to the Hungarian Chamber
of Commerce and Industry
[*A Magyar Kereskedelmi és Iparkamara mellett szervezett Választottbíróság, Budapest*]

Arbitration Court Attached to the Economic Chamber
of the Czech Republic and Agricultural Chamber of the Czech Republic
[*Rozhodčí soud při Hospodářské komoře České republiky a Agrární komoře České republiky, Prague*]

Arbitration Court Attached to the Czech-Moravian Commodity
Exchange Kladno
[*Rozhodčí soud při Českomoravské komoditní burze Kladno (Czech Republic)*]

ICC National Committee Czech Republic
[*ICC Národní výbor Česká republika*]

The Court of Arbitration at the Polish Chamber of Commerce in Warsaw
[*Sąd Arbitrażowy przy Krajowej Izbie Gospodarczej w Warszawie*]

Slovak Academy of Sciences, Institute of State and Law, Slovak Republic
[*Slovenská akadémia vied, Ústav štátu a práva. Bratislava, Slovensko*]

| | |

Proofreading and translation support provided by: Agentura SPĚVÁČEK, s.r.o., Prague, Czech Republic, and Pamela Lewis, USA.

Contents

Czech (& Central European) Yearbook of Arbitration

All contributions in this book are subject to academic review.

List of Abbreviations

AAA	American Arbitration Association
ABA	American Bar Association
ADR	Alternative dispute resolution
ARIAS UK	United Kingdom AIDA Insurance and Reinsurance Arbitration Society
CAM	Chamber of Arbitration of Milan
CEFAREA	French Reinsurance and Insurance Arbitration Centre
CESL	Common European Sales Law
CPC	Czech Code Procedure Civil
DAB	Dispute Adjudication Board
DCFR	*Draft Common Frame of Reference*
DIS	Deutsche Institution für Schiedsgerichtsbarkeit
DRB	Dispute Resolution Board
ECHR	European Convention on Human Rights
FIDIC	International Federation of Consulting Engineers
GCCP	German Code of Civil Procedure
GDDKiA	General Directorate of National Roads and Motorways
IBA	International Bar Association
ICAC	International Commercial Arbitration Court
ICC	International Chamber of Commerce
ICSID	International Centre for Settlement of Investment Disputes
ICT	Information and communication technology
JRPRRD	Joint Resolution, LLC Procedures for the Resolution of US Reinsurance Disputes
LCIA	London Court of International Arbitration
NYC	New York Convention of 1958
RIDSP	Resolution of Intra-Industry US Reinsurance and Insurance Disputes Supplementary Procedures

SCC	Stockholm Chamber of Commerce
SCCI	Slovak Chamber of Commerce and Industry
UMA	Uniform Mediation Act
UNCITRAL	United Nations Commission on International Trade Law
VIAC	Vienna International Arbitral Centre
WIPO	World Intellectual Property Organization

Articles

Czech (& Central European) Yearbook of Arbitration

Czech (& Central European) Yearbook of Arbitration

Jaroslav Valerievich Antonov

Legal Mechanisms of E-justice for Ensuring Independence and Impartiality of Arbitrators in Light of International Practice

Key words:
E-democracy | legal mechanisms | e-justice | impartiality and independence of arbitrators | transparency | accountability | access to justice | electronic workflow | remote interaction | openness of information | legal practice.

Abstract | *E-democracy is becoming an increasingly important trend in the world of legal and political practice. In 2009, the European Council identified the role and place of e-democracy as a means to strengthen the existing system of democracy by increasing public participation and ensuring access to the democratic process. Likewise, the Council of Europe has highlighted the e-justice system as one of the important areas of e-democracy. E-justice involves the creation of a transparent, accountable and independent judiciary based on electronic workflow. Questions the impartiality and independence of the arbitrators are key to any adjudication, including arbitration. Ensuring a fair and independent proceeding is often seen as a factor in increasing the attractiveness of investment by business, as impartial and independent judicial proceeding gives confidence in the future. This paper evaluates the legal perspectives of e-justice in ensuring the impartiality and independence of the arbitrators based on international experience and legal positions of the European Court of Human Rights.*

Jaroslav Valerievich Antonov is a practicing lawyer. He is also a lecturer in the Department of Constitutional Law of the North-west Institute of the Russian Presidential Academy of National Economy and Public Administration.
e-mail: reoverclock@gmail.com

| | |

I. Introduction

1.01. E-democracy is a new course of development of democratic institutions. Its adoption is advocated by the Council of Europe, which has expressed the idea that e-democracy should help the democratic process, contribute to the strengthening of democratic tendencies, and aid in the transparency and legitimacy of governments. At the same time, the administrative role of the state should not be challenged or questioned.[1]

1.02. According to the Council of Europe, the wide democratic participation of individuals and groups ensures great transparency and accountability of democratic institutions and processes, and allows citizens in other democratic forms (voting, deliberation, discussions, society initiatives and other) to benefit from society.[2]

1.03. In its Recommendations, the Council of Europe stated that it is important to ensure that e-democracy is a supplement to traditional democratic processes, rather than excluding them. E-Democracy should expand the opportunities for citizens to participate in political processes, and contribute to the implementation of each of the rights guaranteed by Article 10 of the European Convention 'On the Protection of Human Rights' for the good of every person and the democratic culture of each society.[3]

1.04. The key characteristics of e-democracy are the participation of citizens in political life, the transparency of government functions and the legitimacy and accountability of the government.

1.05. The legitimacy is a key characteristic of arbitration because people should be assured of the objectivity of the arbitration. The accountability and transparency are necessary characteristics for ensuring high level of legitimacy.

1.06. The Council of Europe notes that e-democracy includes e-parliament, e-legislation, e-justice, e-mediation, e-environment, e-elections, e-referendum initiative electronic, e-voting, e-consultation, e-petitions,

---

[1] Recommendation CM/Rec(2009)1 of the Committee of Ministers to member states on electronic democracy (e-democracy)available at: http://www.coe.int/t/dgap/democracy/Activities/GGIS/CAHDE/2009/RecCM2009_1_and_Accomp_Docs/Recommendation%20CM_Rec_2009_1E_FINAL_PDF.pdf (accessed on 30 September 2013).

[2] DANIEL MEDIMOREC; PETER PARYCEK; JUDITH SCHOSSBÖCK, VITALIZING DEMOCRACY THROUGH E-PARTICIPATION AND OPEN GOVERNMENT: AN AUSTRIAN AND EASTERN EUROPEAN PERSPECTIVE, Bertelsmann Stiftung 14 (2011).

[3] Recommendation CM/Rec(2007)11 of the Committee of Ministers to member states on promoting freedom of expression and information in the new information and communications environment, available at: https://wcd.coe.int/ViewDoc.jsp?id=1188541 (accessed on 30 September 2013).

e-campaign, electronic polling, and electronic surveying. It uses e-participation, e-deliberation and electronic forums.[4]

1.07. Of these the form of e-democracy that may be used to ensure the proper working of arbitrators is e-justice.

1.08. According to the position of the Council of Europe, e-justice is the use of information and communication technology (ICT) in the administration of justice by all stakeholders in the judiciary in order to enhance the efficiency and quality of public services provided to individuals and legal entities. It includes an electronic communication and data exchange, as well as access to arbitration information. The implementation of e-justice can be applied with e-participation, e-mail and electronic discussion forums.

1.09. E-participation can provide more easy way to realize right for arbitration protection by simplifying the procedures of filing claims by interested parties. E-mail can provide a more effective exchange of documentation between arbitration and interested parties. Electronic discussion forums can help to identify optimal decisions and instruments for system of e-judiciary by using the wide society discussion.

1.10. Just as the judicial system is a key component of democracy, e-justice is the most important aspect of e-democracy, and its main goal is to improve the efficiency of the judicial system and the quality of justice. Access to justice is one of the vital aspects of access to democratic institutions and processes.

1.11. E-justice should improve the quality of legal services to individuals and organizations through the use of ICTs to accelerate the proceedings, to improve the overall quality of services and to increase transparency.

1.12. The Council of Europe also notes that e-justice should provide convenient access to legal and judicial information for the public, including representatives of business, legal practitioners, the judiciary, while observing and respecting the rights and freedoms of citizens.

1.13. E-justice should include the development of information systems on the status of cases in an online format, informative websites for arbitration tribunals, national and international internet portals for judicial information, the use of video conferencing systems, and methods and standards for the electronic exchange of information.

1.14. Within the framework of e-justice, a particular emphasis is placed on the widespread use of electronic data, including cross-border exchange, which will allow the judiciary to work effectively.[5]

---

[4]   *Ibid.*

1.15. It should be noted that the framework of e-justice is not about the transfer of legal rights to users on the Internet, as this would undermine the principles of a traditional democratic system. Rather, e-justice offers new resources for individuals and organizations. These include the opportunities to get information about the administration of justice and legal procedures on a website, opportunities for starting certain types of legal proceedings using electronic applications, the ability to follow proceedings by accessing the latest relevant information in the Internet, and the ability to pay the legal costs and expenses through online banking.

1.16. It also needs to provide comprehensive, high-quality legal opportunities for individuals and organizations to exercise their right to effective judicial protection, and deliberately and effectively apply the guarantees provided for in the framework of the judicial system.

1.17. E-justice can also facilitate the efficient review of cases involving citizens and organizations in different countries.[6] System of E-justice must ensure electronic workflow, electronic information, electronic remote instituting proceedings and filing documents. All interested parties in the system of e-justice can also realize their rights in the full electronic procedure.

1.18. According to the position of Council of Europe, the e-justice is one of the parts of the system of e-democracy. Therefore, e-justice has the same features as the e-democracy. Thus, we can note the following beneficial legal mechanisms of e-justice:
— access to information;
— remote interaction;
— available online system of judgments;
— international acceptance of judicial decisions;
— electronic workflow;
— electronic remote instituting proceedings and filing of documents;
— electronic information;
— electronic consulting.

1.19. At the same time, e-justice is implemented in the following areas:
— educational;
— professional support of working;
— access and convenience to the judicial system for all citizens and organizations;

---

5   Recommendation CM/Rec(2009)1 of the Committee of Ministers to member states on electronic democracy (e-democracy), available at: http://www.coe.int/t/dgap/democracy/ Activities/GGIS/CAHDE/2009/RecCM2009 1 and Accomp Docs/Recommendation%20 CM Rec 2009 1E FINAL PDF.pdf (accessed on 30 September 2013).
6   *Ibid.*

    — transparency of judicial work;

    — accountability of the judiciary.

1.20. The implementation of e-justice, in the context of the legal mechanisms, contributes to the implementation of the judicial function in a transparent manner. This transparency of information results in new opportunities for ensuring independence and impartiality of arbitrators.

1.21. Some have argued that every service that provides information in electronic form associated with the judicial system, and allows the electronic exchange of judicial information through ICT, can be defined as the e-justice.[7] The main criterion for distinguishing e-justice from the electronic exchange of judicial information or electronic communication however is a real increase in the efficiency of the administration of justice in terms of accessibility and transparency.

II. E-justice in the International Legal Practice

1.22. Perhaps the most ambitious project for introducing the e-justice is within the European Union.[8] The development of e-justice is a key element in the modernization of the judicial system. The Council of Bars and Law Societies of Europe considers that the main objective of e-justice is to improve the efficiency of justice across Europe for EU citizens, with priority given to the introduction of e-signatures and e-identification.

1.23. Delays in resolving litigation and adjudication have a number of negative effects.[9] The idea of the state's inability to deliver justice quickly and effectively can cause distrust in state institutions, undermining the social and political structure and the international prestige of the country.

1.24. At the national level in Europe several projects have been implemented to improve the quality of justice information. These provide information on the Internet that relate to legal systems, legislation and case law. Systems have been introduced for the exchange of information by electronic means between the parties of a case and the

---

[7] E-Justice, Law and Internet foundation, available at: http://www.netlaw.bg/l_en/?s=19&i=6 (accessed on 30 September 2013).

[8] Dragos Calin, *E-Justice in the European Union.* Romanian Academy – Center for European Legal Studies, Legal Research Institute, 1 REVISTA FORUMUL JUDECATORILOR 212 (2010), available at: http://papers.ssrn.com/sol3/papers.cfm?abstract_id=1889134 (accessed on 30 September 2013).

[9] First Implementation Paper for CCBE e-Justice Strategy, Council of Bars and Law Societies of Europe, available at: http://www.ccbe.eu/fileadmin/user_upload/NTC document/EN_First_Implementat1_1231836210.pdf (accessed on 30 September 2013).

arbitration tribunal in which the case is being tried. In some instances fully electronic procedures were utilized, such as video conferencing.[10]

1.25. According to the document 'Towards a European e-Justice: Strategy' of May 30, 2008 e-justice, including criminal and civil proceedings, has a dual purpose. On the one hand, it aims to create a European portal to facilitate access to justice for citizens and businesses across Europe. On the other hand, it is aimed at strengthening legal cooperation on the basis of the existing legal instruments.[11]

1.26. Access for individuals and legal entity to justice in Europe was aided by the creation of an e-justice portal for individuals and legal entities that can facilitate their access to the justice system.[12]

1.27. The scope of the e-justice portal has been revealed in a number of scenarios. Firstly, it has contribute to access to information. Ignorance of the rules in other Member States is one of the main factors that hinder people to assert their rights in another EU country. The portal provides information for European citizens in their own language about the judicial system and proceedings procedures throughout the EU. The portal allows anyone to find the answers to questions of jurisdiction, in accordance with the laws of each country, as well as providing detailed information on the financing and execution of arbitration tribunal decisions, which is especially important for ensuring the independence and impartiality of arbitrators. Secondly the e-justice portal fosters effective judicial cooperation.

1.28. Mediation is also facilitated by the e-justice portal. Mediation is a structured process in which two or more parties to the dispute, through negotiations involving an experienced mediator, resolve a dispute through the use of a general agreement. Mediation provides a cost-effective and less risky dispute resolution as a mediator helps the parties to reach a middle ground and there is no absolute winner or loser.

1.29. The e-justice portal encourages the use of videoconferencing, including for remote arbitration hearings. This can provide the easy distant access for justice and also new ways for effective society and state control.

1.30. The enforcement of arbitration decisions is a benefit of the e-justice portal. It has developed a mechanism for the transfer of information

---

[10] Communication from the Commission to the Council, the European Parliament and the European Economic and Social Committee, Towards a European e-Justice Strategy, available at: http://eur-lex.europa.eu/LexUriServ/LexUriServ.do?uri=COM:2008:0329: FIN:EN:PDF (accessed on 30 September 2013).

[11] E-Justice, Council of Bars and Law Societies of Europe. available at: http://www.ccbe.eu/index.php?id=333 (accessed on 30 September 2013).

[12] Ibid.

between Member States to assist in the enforcement of judgments and the implementation the European orders of execution.

1.31. Finally the portal assists in translations. Legal actions are carried out almost exclusively in the native language and the use of a foreign language is only marginally allowed. High-quality and adequate translation are important for an independent and impartial investigation. In this connection, the portal has an organized system of automatic translation and, if necessary, a professional translation.[13]

1.32. To implement a transparent and efficient exchange of legal documents, as well as to improve cross-border access of citizens and organizations to legal means in Europe in 2013, a project was launched called CODEX. CODEX provides a digital method of legal information exchange between Member States. Thus overly bureaucratic procedures and the extraneous documents can to be eliminated in legal exchanges between EU countries.

1.33. The project has the following objectives:
— the implementation of e-justice in the EU in compliance with the principle of subsidiarity;
— the achievement of interoperability between existing national judicial systems;
— the creation of conditions for cooperation and teamwork of all member states in order to realize a more efficient judicial system in Europe;
— improving the efficiency of processing a larger number of cross-border processes, especially in civil, criminal and commercial cases;
— the modernization of the judicial system in Europe.[14]

1.34. In a subsequent work, the 'European E-Justice Action Plan', set out three basic functions for the European e-justice system. These have a key influence on the impartiality and independence of arbitrators.
1) They should free up access to information in the field of justice.
2) They should dematerialize the proceedings. This is the replacement of the 'physical' relationship between the parties with an 'electronic' relationship in the proceedings and mediation;
3) They should strengthen the relationship with the judiciary, establishing strong links through video conferencing and special electronic networks.[15]

---

[13] Legal notice, available at: https://e-justice.europa.eu/contentMaximisation.do?plang= en&legalnotice=1 (accessed on 30 September 2013).
[14] "Towards cross-border e-Justice" – e-CODEX in Rome, available at: http://www.e-codex.eu/news-and-media/news/single-view/article/towards-cross-border-e-justice-e-codex-in-rome.html (accessed on 30 September 2013).

Czech (& Central European) Yearbook of Arbitration

1.35. It should be noted that I considered the most notable international projects of e-justice. There are several reasons for this. International projects are primarily aimed at harmonization and standardization of the judicial system. Also, e-justice is almost always aimed at cross-border cooperation. Additionally, businesses more often expand beyond national borders, and that international cross-border aspect, creates a special urgency and broad prospects for application. It should be noted that national e-justice projects are generally prevalent in almost all the countries of Europe and beyond, including Germany, Russia, France, UK, Czech Republic, Spain, Italy, Belgium, USA, Canada, Ireland, Poland, Uzbekistan, Australia, etc and some of arbitration problems that tie with national jurisdiction can be solved on the national level. [16] For example, Russian e-justice system is a state system and it is used in the states tribunals.

1.36. Automation System proceedings allows to solve one of the main tasks of informational support tribunal – automation of processes passing a tribunal case in arbitration and the creation of full-text electronic banking judicial decisions taken by this tribunal.[17]

1.37. Electronic workflow system designed to automate processes general office work and the transition to a paperless environment and as a consequence of the creation of an entity controlled electronic workflow system. It can help exclude various abuses due to the inability to fully trace the movement of paper documents in the proceedings.[18]

1.38. In the Russian system of e-justice given for users the opportunity of filing a claim and the required documents in electronic form, viewing data on proceedings, the opportunity to reference the basis of judgments in electronic form. The system also provides the option

---

[15] European e-Justice action plan, Council of the European Union, available at: http://register.consilium.europa.eu/pdf/en/08/st15/st15315.en08.pdf (accessed on 30 September 2013).

[16] National e-justice projects, available at: http://www.justiz.de/index.php; http://www.arbitr.ru/e-justice/; http://legifrance.gouv.fr; http://www.justice.gov.uk/; http://portal.justice.cz; http://www.poderjudicial.es; http://www.giustizia.it/giustizia/; http://www.juridat.be/; http://www.nycourts.gov/; http://www.lsuc.on.ca/index.aspx; http://www.courts.ie/; http://novojustice.com/polands-e-court; http://soliqinfo.uz/ru/2013/08/23/rus-e-lektronnoe-sudoproizvodstvo-mif-ili-real-nost/; http://soliqinfo.uz/ru/2013/08/23/rus-e-lektronnoe-sudoproizvodstvo-mif-ili-real-nost/; http://www.courts.qld.gov.au/information-for-lawyers/search-civil-files-ecourts (accessed on 30 September 2013).

[17] E-justice, Supreme Commercial Court of the Russian Federation, available at: http://www.arbitr.ru/e-justice/doc/23390.html (accessed on 30 September 2013).

[18] E-justice, Supreme Commercial Court of the Russian Federation, available at: http://www.arbitr.ru/e-justice/doc/23409.html (accessed on 30 September 2013).

"electronic guard", which allows tracking information about interesting cases and in case of any changes it sends e-mail notification. [19]

1.39. To ensure transparency the system of e-justice provided opportunities live video about proceedings on the Internet, as well as obligatory audio records of proceedings. [20]

1.40. In France, the system of e-justice is considered from the perspective of a national system of electronic communication between arbiters, advocates and all stakeholders using digital signature and a fully electronic workflow. This allows to optimize and to monitor the documentation, as well as the possibility of remote communication. However, for this have actual accessibility of this system in all processes. [21]

1.41. Thus, electronic technologies allow controlling proceedings and documentation and it can really help for ensuring accountability and transparency of arbitration.

1.42. In addition to e-justice projects, there is also a new form of justice in the form of electronic arbitration tribunal. These have spread not only in private (commercial) legal practice, but also in some countries, such as India. It is important to distinguish these electronic arbitration tribunals from the concepts of e-justice of state courts previously described. Electronic arbitration tribunal belong to private arbitration and are not government or public arbitration and because of that it must have independence proceedings and own e-justice system for protection of interests parties. However, the system of e-justice of electronic arbitration tribunal must based on principles previously described

1.43. Since electronic arbitration tribunals involve a fully remote interaction and a fully electronic workflow, such a practice can have a significant impact on the independence and impartiality of arbitrators. The main risks of infringement of impartiality and independence are associated with no transparent personal contacts and interaction between parties. The system of e-justice can help to make these contacts more transparent and accountable.

1.44. The first electronic arbitration tribunal was established in the Netherlands in 2011. This electronic arbitration tribunal is an online

---

[19] Supreme Commercial Court of the Russian Federation, available at: https://my.arbitr.ru/ (accessed on 30 September 2013)

[20] Arbitration Procedure Code of the Russian Federation No. 95-FZ of 29.07.2002; par. 6 art. 155

[21] E-Justice in France: The e-Barreau Experience, Socila Science Research Network, available at: http://papers.ssrn.com/sol3/papers.cfm?abstract_id=1763270 (accessed on 30 September 2013)

court for civil disputes, with the proceedings designed to take 8 weeks and with an affordable price. This is a special tribunal which passed sentence independently. The sentences have the same legal effect as a judgment of state arbitration.

1.45. Transparency of the process is achieved by online document sharing on an adversarial basis, and through access to information on the professional education and experience of the electronic arbitrators.[22]

1.46. This Electronic arbitration tribunal for the first time fully integrates the legal field of ICT and provides the most effective access to justice.[23]

1.47. In India, there is also an electronic tribunal, which began operating in 2013.[24] Of particular note is the fact that a regular hearing cannot take place at all, unless one of the parties has expressed their desire to have it. Thus, it may be a completely independent and impartial proceeding, in so far as the personal contact is completely eliminated. In case of disagreement with the decision of the arbitration, there is a provision for an electronic appeal. Consideration of the case in the first instance takes 6 weeks, in the second instance 4 weeks.[25]

1.48. Similar arbitration tribunals work successfully in the UK, Canada, USA, Australia, China, Singapore, New Zealand, Netherlands, France, Switzerland, Spain, and Sweden.[26]

1.49. At the same time, in Quezon City in the Philippines, the electronic arbitration tribunal is the state tribunal. However, this arbitration tribunal is not fully online, despite the stated objective of ensuring the quality of justice within a reasonable time, and instant search of information for arbiters and tribunal employees. This system is more of an element of the system of e-justice, as it does not involve consideration of cases by fully using the internet.[27]

1.50. Thus e-justice is different from the e-arbitration, in that the implementation of e-justice is not intended to change the traditional

---

[22] E-court, available at: https://www.e-court.nl/ (accessed on 30 September 2013).

[23] The first online private court, Innovating Justice, available at: http://www.innovatingjustice.com/innovations/e-court-the-first-online-private-court?view_content=details (accessed on 30 September 2013).

[24] E-court India, available at: http://e-court.in/ (accessed on 30 September 2013).

[25] E-court India, e-Court provides a uniform litigation process throughout India, available at: https://e-court.in/how_it_works/how.php (accessed on 30 September 2013).

[26] E-courts, available at: https://e-court.im/;https://e-court.ca/; https://e-court.us/; https://ecourt-au.com/; https://e-court.cn/; https://e-court.sg/; https://e-court.co.nz/; https://e-court.co.nl/; https://ecourt.fr/; https://e-court.ch/; https://e-court.es/; https://e-court.se/ (accessed on 30 September 2013).

[27] Sereno: 'e-Court' to enhance transparency in justice system, Inquirer.net, available at: http://newsinfo.inquirer.net/426537/sereno-e-court-to-enhance-transparency-in-justice-system (accessed on 30 September 2013).

procedure of the proceedings. Rather, it involves the creation of an open, friendly and accessible system of complete information on the administration of justice and the judiciary. Likewise, it integrates information systems and implements the electronic document. Conversely, within e-arbitration review takes place remotely and some steps can be changed or completely missed (e.g. the hearing).

1.51. The electronic (online) arbitration is thus characterized by remote justice, electronic evidence, e-participation and electronic workflow.

III. Impartiality and Independence in the Systems of Arbitration

1.52. Similarly to the e-justice system, an electronic arbitration tribunal has a tangible positive impact on ensuring of the independence and impartiality of arbitrators.

1.53. One of the features that distinguish arbitration from other methods of dispute resolution is the proposition that the parties are free to choose their 'tribunal'. It is recognized that when choosing the arbitrators, it must be taken into account that the arbitrators must be independent and impartial. The lack of independence and impartiality may be grounds for disqualification of an arbitrator by a party, so the independence and impartiality of arbitrators must be clear.

1.54. In international arbitration, in accordance with established legal practice, one to three arbitrators should participate in the proceedings. Thus, if the parties cannot agree on the nomination of the one arbitrator the appointing authority selects the appropriate arbitrator. If the arbitral tribunal shall consist of three arbitrators, each party shall appoint one arbitrator. The third arbitrator shall be chosen either by the appointing authority or on a bilateral reciprocal basis by the arbitrators appointed by the parties, unless the parties agree otherwise. This is reflected in the rules of arbitration of international organizations such as the ICC, LCIA, and UNCITRAL.[28]

---

[28] ICC Rules of Arbitration, International Chamber of Commerce, available at: http://www.iccwbo.org/products-and-services/arbitration-and-adr/arbitration/icc-rules-of-arbitration/ (accessed on 30 September 2013); LCIA Arbitration Rules, The London Court of International Arbitration, available at: http://www.lcia.org/Dispute Resolution Services/LCIA Arbitration Rules.aspx (accessed on 30 September 2013); UNCITRAL Arbitration Rules, available at: http://www.uncitral.org/pdf/english/texts/arbitration/arb-rules-revised/arb-rules-revised-2010-e.pdf (accessed on 30 September 2013).

III.1. The Principle of Independence and Impartiality

1.55. The fundamental principle in international commercial arbitration is that an arbitrator must be and remain impartial and independent for the duration of the proceedings. This requirement is enshrined in most national laws, international conventions and rules and arbitration rules.

1.56. It should be noted that the notion of 'independence and impartiality' in the rules are not clearly defined. This is due to the fact that it is extremely difficult to determine the quality and the exhaustive list of indicators of independence and impartiality of arbitrators. In legal practice, one can determine independence and impartiality in the way that 'independence' is generally perceived as the particular situation of fact or law that is objectively verifiable, while 'impartial' is always a mental and subjective state.

1.57. In this regard, it is assumed that it is much easier to identify a lack of independence of the arbitrator, than to provide proof of partiality. Partiality of an arbitrator cannot usually be identified by their behaviour, so communication with one of the parties can be established based on external sources.

1.58. The ICC decided not to establish special rules for determining independence and impartiality, as there were fears that rules would be too strict. Stephen Bond, former Secretary General of the tribunal, has stated that one of the main signs of the lack of independence as a 'close, significant, recent and proven relationship' between the party and the alleged arbitrator.[29]

III.2. Disclosure

1.59. To be suitable for use in a particular case, a prospective arbitrator must disclose all facts and circumstances which are likely to be considered grounds for disqualification.

III.3. Partiality

1.60. The concept is a requirement of impartiality of the arbitrator and is treated as a benefit in the context of the relationship between one of the parties and the arbitrator with respect to the subject matter of the dispute. Central to this concept is the assumption that a partial arbitrator is not valid and cannot operate properly. This is due to the fact that they are predisposed to one side and partial to another. Thus, the 'partial' is an abstract concept, which primarily includes a state of mind.

---

[29] YVES DERAINS, ERIC A. SCHWARTZ, A GUIDE TO THE ICC RULES OF ARBITRATION, The Hague: Kluwer Law International 120 (2005).

III.4. The Consequences of Partiality

1.61. In the event that the partiality of the arbitrator may be proved, it is possible for the parties to declare the removal of an arbitrator in accordance with the procedure written in the regulations of the arbitration.

1.62. There should be full confidence among all parties that the arbitrators are impartial. Perhaps if this factor is not decisive for the determination of impartiality, without a doubt, it is still of decisive importance.

III.5. An Ongoing Financial or Professional Relationship with One of the Parties to the Dispute

1.63. The issue of financial or professional relationships is probably the biggest obstacle to impartiality.

III.6. Financial or Professional Relationship with One of the Parties to a Dispute

1.64. If a relationship with one of the parties ended with the dispute, assessing independence and impartiality will of course differ from the estimates of each party, which would be given in the case where the relationship would continue after the dispute has arisen. [30]

III.7. Procedural Violations

1.65. One commonly identified problem is that during the proceedings one of the parties is of the opinion that the arbitrator has lost impartiality in relation to one of the parties, without giving them a chance to realize their procedural rights.[31]

1.66. In principle, all of the above problems in ensuring impartiality and independence are associated with the absence of public information about the arbitrators, including their business connections, previous and current work, or other data or circumstances that may be relevant to the case beyond participating in the arbitration proceedings,. It is likely that the need to increase the level of control, including the possibility of reducing the personal influence of the parties to an arbitrator can be aided by the introduction of a fully electronic workflow that will minimize the 'human factor', along with the formation of uniform and clear standards for determining the independence and impartiality of arbitrators. It is an objective problem that can be addressed by national and international e-justice systems.

---

[30] Arbitrators, Out-Law.com, available at: http://www.out-law.com/en/topics/projects--construction/international-arbitration/arbitrators/ (accessed on 30 September 2013).

[31] *Ibid.*

1.67. The e-justice in fact must ensure full electronic procedure of realization rights of interested parties.

1.68. The national e-justice system must base on principles of transparency, legitimacy, accountability.

1.69. The Council of Europe states some instruments of realization of e-justice system:

1) access to information;
2) remote interaction;
3) available online system of judgments;
4) international acceptance of judicial decisions;
5) electronic workflow;
6) electronic remote instituting proceedings and filing of documents;
7) electronic information;
8) electronic consulting.[32]

1.70. For example in Russia e-justice system realizes some of these instruments. It is access to the information, electronic workflow, electronic remote instituting proceedings and filing of documents, electronic information.

IV. Problems of Ensuring the Independence and Impartiality of Arbitrators in the Arbitration

1.71. There are a number of problems of ensuring the independence and impartiality of arbitrators in the commercial arbitration because arbitration tribunals are usually formed within certain organizations, and these organizations have a direct impact on the course of the arbitration.[33]

1.72. Many of the permanent arbitral tribunals have either a definite or 'semi-definite'[34] list of arbitrators. This list is approved by the organization that organizes the arbitration. As a rule, the arbitral tribunal shall be constituted from the list. Thus, there is potential for the appointment of arbitrators who have personal or financial relationship with this organization.

---

[32] Recommendation CM/Rec(2009)1 of the Committee of Ministers to member states on electronic democracy (e-democracy), available at: http://www.coe.int/t/dgap/democracy/Activities/GGIS/CAHDE/2009/RecCM2009 1 and Accomp Docs/Recommendation%20 CM Rec 2009 1E FINAL PDF.pdf (accessed on 30 September 2013).

[33] Obespechenie bespristrastnosti tretejskih sudej v sudebno-arbitrazhnoj praktike i v zakonodatel'stve, available at: http://zakon.ru/Blogs/OneBlog/6612 (accessed on 30 September 2013).

[34] Under the semi definite list, the parties may choose arbitrators that are not included in the list of arbitrators, and the chairman of the arbitral tribunal or the single arbitrator shall be appointed or chosen only from the approved list of arbitrators.

1.73. There has been at least one case where the arbitrator, who expressed a dissenting opinion when deciding, was then removed from the list of arbitrators of a permanent arbitral tribunal at the Chamber of Commerce of one of the countries of Eastern Europe. Another case involved a situation where the arbitrator was removed from the list due to disagreements with the chairman of the Arbitration tribunal.[35]

1.74. It should also be noted that, according to some authors, being on the list of arbitrators, brings the hope of participating in the proceedings and obtaining a material reward. Although this is a fair expectation, there can be a question about the advisability of such lists at all. This could put the entire existing system of arbitration in doubt. In this case, a decisive influence on this fact does not seem to be able to provide even the centralization and internationalization of the lists in international commercial arbitration. It is possible that the positive trend will be observed in the case of the existence of open lists of arbitrators. Thus, it is obvious that the most effective system in this case would be a system of e-justice because it can help optimize this process by electronic workflow and increase accountability and transparency. But in this case I consider that this problem cannot to decide completely in any case because the list of arbitrators must to be confidential.

1.75. The ability to choose their own arbitrators, enshrined in the rules of most arbitration does not preclude the possibility of the influence of the parent organization of the arbitral tribunal on the final list of arbitrators by using it financial and political mechanisms because arbitral tribunal actually belongs to this organization

1.76. In the arbitration of the ICC, the parties shall agree on the de facto name of a single arbitrator in about 20 % of cases and in relation to the chairman of the arbitration (in a case three arbitrators) – in 60 % of cases.[36]

1.77. In principle, it should be recognized that the criteria on which the compiled lists of arbitrators are constructed are usually unknown. Usually, an organization involved draws up a list by taking into account the rotation of the various interests. It is likely that this process will affect the openness of information about arbitrators and proceedings on the implementation of justice. The openness of information can provide the actual information for parties about arbitration and interactive distant communication can ensure effective and timely react in the case any unlikely changes

---

[35] *Supra* note 33.
[36] *Ibid.*

1.78. The parent organization of the arbitral tribunal considers the challenges to an arbitrator which is usually due to a lack or loss of independence or impartiality.

1.79. There is no assurance that an organization which is itself included in a list of arbitrators, will impartially react to the arguments of the dependence of the arbitrator on the organization.[37]

1.80. This opinion has a foundation, and in some cases can be justified. However, following this logic one should recognize that any organization that is involved in the organization of the tribunal could potentially be biased and partial because it may have an influence on the work of that tribunal. At the same time, it is clear that the openness of information and documents managed in electronic form will help to decide such problems with greater accountability and greater objectivity.

1.81. For example, in Russia e-justice system ensure the way for all interested parties for checking and control their personal proceedings documentation. It should be note that all information and documents workflow is checked in the system of e-justice. In the conflict all documents workflow can to be controlled.

1.82. An organization, which was created for the arbitration, shall pay the fees of the arbitrators. In the case where there is no clear and transparent system for determining the fees of the arbitrator, there is the possibility of direct influence.[38] An important aspect of this is the way in which work is funded by the secretariat of the permanent arbitration tribunal.[39]

1.83. This problem, involving classified information on the fees of the arbitrators is, apparently, a private trade secret. At the same time, these processes are quite an obvious influence on the formation of arbitral awards. In this sense, the construction of an e-justice system should provide the mechanisms to control specialized arbitrators payment by authorized international entities which must ensure the secrecy information about arbitrators on the one hand and on another hand it must have some ways for control in this case. At the same time, it is inconceivable that the right guaranteed by international legal acts of the right to privacy and business secrets would be violated.

1.84. None of the permanent tribunals of arbitration in Russia are actually able to have a completely independent e-mail system. Thus, e-mail arbitration is provided and regulated by the agency that founds the

---

[37] *Ibid.*
[38] *Ibid.*
[39] *Ibid.*

arbitration.[40]It is clear that this situation leads to the formation of direct information based arbitration from parent organizations. At the same time, it is obvious that the formation of the modern system of arbitration should be based on the principles of electronic document management software which should be administered by a specialized national and/or supranational authority. It seems that this problem is also facing the e-justice system and can only be solved by the formation of a national and eventually international e-justice system with uniform and clear principles and conditions.

1.85. There is an arguable opinion that a considerable place in the selection of the arbitral tribunal has to do with its reputation. This is formed from the information not only about the 'fair hearing' from the parties involved in the proceedings, but also information on how to organize the arbitration tribunal, where 'competent' experts are included in the lists of arbitrators, and information about what pressure these individuals have experienced in cases41 .However, by its nature independence can only be fully established by persons who are really disinterested in the outcome of the arbitration case. Of course, conflict between the two parties over the process of formation of the arbitrators is, without a doubt, a positive effect. In practice the parties are often not equal to each other. This is especially true since the arbitral tribunals formed by large organizations.[42] In this case, the examination of commercial disputes in contracts with such organizations is carried out in the arbitration tribunals established by them. It is clear that the balance of interests in this case will be dismissed, or at least the potential to be partial in favour of the interests of the parent organization of the arbitration is murky. It is quite clear that there is a need for a transparent and understandable system of arbitral tribunals on the basis of legal principles and ideas underlying the system of e-justice.

V. The Jurisprudence of the European Court of Human Rights on Issues of Impartiality and Independence of Arbitrators

1.86. International commercial arbitrations take only a small part of the total number of arbitration cases. The larger part of arbitration takes place in

---

[40] *Ibid.*

[41] V. V. Hvalej, *O nezavisimosti arbitrazhnyh institucij voobshhe i Rossijskoj Arbitrazhnoj Associacii v chastnosti*, available at: http://arbitrations.ru/files/articles/uploaded/Khvalei_RAA_Tretsud.pdf. (accessed on 30 September 2013).

[42] In Russia it is arbitration in an open joint stock company 'Gazprom', available at: http://www.gazprom.ru/about/arbitral/ (accessed on 30 September 2013).

the framework of national arbitration tribunals where there is a wide choice of options for the selection of arbiters and the rules of arbitration including choice of law. This is because the proceeding is held under the laws of the particular state in accordance with the rules of national jurisdiction.

1.87. Since the rules of arbitration cases and the principles for determining the impartiality and independence are somewhat different from the rules applicable to the arbitration tribunals, as well as the fact that the order of consideration of arbitration cases in each state is unique, it is reasonable to consider the content of the principles of independence and impartiality of arbitrators on the basis of decisions by the European Court of Human Rights - the major European supranational judicial body.

1.88. The Court notes that in order to determine whether the tribunal be considered 'independent' for the purposes of Article 6 § 1 of the Convention, the following criteria should serve as a guide:
1) the appointment of its members and their term of office;
2) the existence of guarantees against outside pressures;
3) enough evidence to provide an appearance of independence of the tribunal.[43]

V.1. Interaction of Other Branches of Government and Intervention in the Activities of the Arbitral Tribunal

1.89. The concept of the separation of powers between the executive and the judiciary is particularly important in the framework of the decisions of the tribunal,[44] although the provisions of Article 6 and any other provisions of the Convention do not oblige the States to comply with any theoretical constitutional views on the validity of interaction between the two branches. The Court must verify whether the requirements of the Convention were fulfilled.

1.90. According to its approach set out in the case of *Sovtransavto Holding* v *Ukraine*,[45] the tribunal finds that it does not matter whether the interference impact is actually on the course of the proceedings. Based on the separation of the executive and legislative branches of government, intervention shows a lack of respect for the independence of the judiciary and suggested doubts about the independence and impartiality of the tribunal.

---

[43] *Findlay* v *the United Kingdom* (dec.), No. 22107/93, 25 February 1997.
[44] *Henryk Urban and Ryszard Urban* v *Poland* (dec.), No. 23614/08, 30 November 2010.
[45] *Sovtransavto holding* v *Ukraine* (dec.), No. 48553/99, 25 July 2002.

1.91. The Court emphasizes in this regard that the amount of the State's obligations to ensure 'the independence and impartiality of the tribunal' in accordance with Article 6 § 1 of the Convention is not limited only by the scope of the judicial system. This also implies the obligations of the executive, legislative, and any other body of the state, regardless of its level, to respect and comply with the decisions of tribunal, even if they do not agree with them. Thus, for the government to ensure respect and maintain the authority of tribunal is a necessary condition for public confidence in the tribunal and, in general, for the rule of law. To do this, the constitutional guarantees of independence and impartiality of the judiciary must be provided. They also need to be effectively incorporated into routine administrative attitudes and practices.

1.92. The Court also notes that the independence and impartiality of the judiciary, if examined as a whole, requires that individual arbiters be free from undue influence – not only on the part of the judiciary, but also from inside.[46] The lack of sufficient safeguards to ensure the independence of arbiters in the judicial system and, in particular, from its judicial management[47] may lead to the conclusion that the doubts about the independence and impartiality of the tribunal are objectively justified.[48]

1.93. The Court notes that the appointment of arbiters of the executive branch is acceptable provided that the designated entities are free from the influence or pressure in the performance of their judicial functions.[49]

VI. Conclusion

1.94. Almost all of the problems of ensuring the impartiality and independence with arbitrators of national arbitral tribunals, of international commercial arbitration, of state arbitration and arbitration assessors are associated with the absence or lack of transparency and accountability of the proceedings. Specifically, they lack a common information base and open data for monitoring the independence and impartiality of the process by competent national authorities.

1.95. Often, the lack of independence and impartiality of arbitrators is due to the violation of the right of access to justice, as the European Court of

---

[46]   *Parlov-Tkalčić* v *Croatia* (dec.), No. 24810/06, 22 December 2009.
[47]   *Ibid.*
[48]   *Agrokompleks* v *Ukraine* (dec.), No. 23465/03, 6 October 2011.
[49]   *Flux* v *Moldova* No. 31001/03, § 27, 3 July 2007.

Human Rights. Lack of transparency of the proceedings may eventually lead to the emergence of informal networks of arbitrators and the emergence of a personal interest in the case. The e-justice system is intended to solve this problem, as it is characterized by transparency, accessibility and accountability. Its implementation at the national and international level would, without a doubt, contribute to the independence and impartiality of arbitrators.

| | |

Summaries

FRA   [*Les instruments juridiques de la cyberjustice garantissant l'indépendance et l'impartialité des arbitres à la lumière de la pratique internationale*]

La cyberdémocratie prend progressivement de plus en plus d'importance dans le monde des pratiques juridiques et politiques. Le Conseil de l'Europe a défini en 2009 la fonction et la place de la cyberdémocratie, la décrivant comme un moyen de renforcer le système démocratique existant en y faisant participer l'opinion publique et en lui assurant un accès aux processus démocratiques. Le Conseil de l'Europe a en même temps souligné que la cyberjustice constituait un élément important de la cyberdémocratie. Il s'agit de la constitution d'un système transparent, prédictible et indépendant de règlement des litiges fondé sur des procédures de travail électroniques. La problématique de l'indépendance et de l'impartialité des procédures de jugement est une question centrale de tous les jugements, y compris des décisions arbitrales. On considère souvent que la garantie d'une procédure juste et indépendante constitue un facteur attractif pour l'investissement, car un règlement indépendant et impartial des litiges fonde la confiance dans le futur. On évalue ici les perspectives juridiques de la cyberjustice pour garantir une impartialité et une indépendance des arbitres qui seraient fondées sur les expériences internationales et les avis exprimés par la Cour européenne des droits de l'homme.

CZE   [*Právní nástroje E-justice zajišťující nezávislost a nestrannost rozhodců ve světle mezinárodní praxe*]

E-demokracie nabývá postupně na svém významu ve světě právní a politické praxe. V roce 2009 definovala Rada Evropy úlohu a postavení e-domokracie jako prostředku posilování existujícího systému demokracie prostřednictvím účasti veřejnosti a zajištěním přístupu k demokratickým procesům. Rada Evropy rovněž zdůraznila, že elektronický justiční systém představuje významnou součást e-

demokracie. E-justice se týká vytváření transparentního, předvidatelného a nezávislého systému rozhodování sporů založeného na elektronických pracovních postupech. Problematika nestrannosti a nezávislosti rozhodovacích procesů představuje klíčovou otázku při každém rozhodování, včetně rozhodčího řízení. Zajištění spravedlivého a nezávislého řízení se často považuje za faktor ovlivňující atraktivitu pro investice ze strany podnikatelů, neboť nestranné a nezávislé rozhodování sporů zakládá důvěru v budoucí vývoj. Tento článek hodnotí právní perspektivy e-justice při zajišťování nestrannosti a nezávislosti rozhodců založené na mezinárodních zkušenostech a názorech vyjadřovaných Evropským soudem pro lidská práva.

| | |

POL   [*Narzędzia prawne portalu e-sprawiedliwość gwarantujące niezawisłość i bezstronność arbitrów w świetle praktyki międzynarodowej*]

Portal e-sprawiedliwość, powstały w wyniku elektronicznej wymiany dokumentów, charakteryzuje przejrzystość, przewidywalność i otwartość w zakresie udzielania informacji. Niniejszy artykuł zajmuje się wpływem perspektyw systemu e-sprawiedliwość na bezstronność i niezawisłość arbitrów.

DEU   [***Die Rechtsinstrumente der E-Justiz als Garant der Unabhängigkeit und Unparteilichkeit der Schiedsrichter im Lichte der internationalen Praxis***]

E-Justiz zeichnet sich aus durch Transparenz, Berechenbarkeit und Offenheit bei der Bereitstellung von Auskünften und ist das Ergebnis des elektronischen Austauschs von Schriftsätzen. Dieser Aufsatz befasst sich mit dem Einfluss, den die Perspektiven der E-Justiz auf die Unparteilichkeit und Unabhängigkeit von Schiedsrichtern genommen haben.

RUS   [*Правовые инструменты электронного правосудия для обеспечения независимости и беспристрастности арбитров в свете международной практики*]

Существуют различные формы и правовые механизмы электронной демократии. В их число входит электронное правосудие. Электронное правосудие характеризуется прозрачностью, подотчетностью, открытостью информации, обеспечением электронного документооборота. Автор рассматривает в данной работе перспективы влияния электронного правосудия на обеспечение беспристрастности и независимости арбитров.

ESP *[Instrumentos jurídicos de la justicia electrónica para garantizar la independencia e imparcialidad de los árbitros a la luz de la práctica internacional]*

La justicia electrónica se caracteriza por la transparencia, la previsibilidad y la apertura respecto a la facilitación de información, y es el resultado del intercambio electrónico de documentos. El artículo versa sobre la influencia de las perspectivas de la justicia electrónica en la imparcialidad e independencia de los árbitros.

| | |

Alina Mioara Cobuz Bagnaru
Liability of Arbitrators

Key words:
Impartiality and Independence | New Romanian Code of Civil Procedure | Arbitrators' Liability under New ICC Rules | American Arbitration Association Rules | ICSID Regulation | Commercial Arbitration Rules of the Japan Commercial Arbitration Association | Romanian Law | Court of International Commercial Arbitration and the Rules of Procedure of the Chamber of Arbitration of the Bucharest Stock Exchange | Rules of Arbitral Procedure of the Court of International Commercial Arbitration under the Chamber of Commerce and Industry of Romania

Abstract | *The article addresses the notion of liability of arbitrators from an academic perspective, by focusing on various arbitration regulations. Also, the article focuses on the notions of independence, neutrality and impartiality of arbitrators, which should characterize arbitrators during the entire arbitration proceedings in which they were appointed. The replacement of arbitrators during the proceedings is allowed as a result of incompliance with the previously mentioned notions. Furthermore, given the amendments to arbitration regulations, the notion of liability of arbitrators was tackled from the perspective of new amendments in the arbitration field.*

However, irrespective of the dynamics of such notions in arbitration regulations, the liability of arbitrators is great and is becoming more and more complicated, following an increase in the popularity of arbitration and the increased trust in this form of dispute settlement, as an alternative to state justice. Given the high level of complexity of the topic and the author's intention to provide an accurate view, the author has compared various arbitration rules and the corresponding regulations setting measure to this notion.

Dr. Alina Mioara Cobuz Bagnaru - Attorney-at-law, PhD, Member of the Bucharest Bar, Founding Member of Cobuz si Asociatii, Arbitrator with the Bucharest Stock Exchange, FINBAN mediator, Member in European Court of Arbitration.
e-mail: alina@cobuz.ro

| | |

I. Introduction

2.01. Arbitration has become a preferred manner of dispute settlement, which parties are resorting to more and more frequently. The advantages of arbitration include that it is confidential and as part of the arbitration proceedings, parties get to appoint their own arbitrator. However, the arbitrators' appointment by the parties does not imply that they act as party representatives. A party-appointed arbitrator acts similarly to a judge. Hence, an arbitrator is awarded a provisional mandate which is valid throughout the duration of the arbitration. The mandate ceases upon the issuance of the final award.

2.02. In other words, within the arbitration proceedings, arbitrators are not the parties' lawyers. Instead, they remain impartial, independent and neutral for the entire arbitration proceedings, irrespective of having been appointed by the parties.

2.03. On the other hand, if the parties identify any breaches of the arbitrators' responsibilities during the proceedings, they may challenge or replace the arbitrators. There is also the possibility for arbitrators to reject their appointment, based on considerations actually related to their incompatibility with the case in question.

2.04. It is important to clarify the meanings of impartiality and independence, the definitions of which imply both a subtle distinction and an interrelation.

2.05. There are various opinions[1] which accord a connection between impartiality and pre-judgment. However, impartiality and pre-judgment are two different concepts. If we refer to the New Romanian Code of Civil Procedure, pre-judgment is a case of impartiality. In the German version of the institution of challenge, it becomes difficult to classify a situation implying a weak concept of impartiality combined with the breach of other requirements imposed by the rule of law or state standards.

2.06. Another example can be identified in the Code of Ethics for Arbitrators in Commercial Disputes developed by the American Bar Association (ABA). This Code basically designed an ethical source to guide arbitrators and make them liable for their behaviour during the arbitration proceedings. Arbitrators have both a public responsibility and a responsibility towards the parties to the dispute. This Code introduces further notions like the presumption of neutrality. The

---

[1] N.A. When these various opinions were considered to give the examples in the Introduction, I took into account those systems of law also containing some definitions of the concepts of impartiality and independence, which are not further tackled in the subsequent sections.

concept of neutrality includes the two notions of independence and impartiality as working standards in the arbitration proceedings. As a basis for the presumption of neutrality, arbitrators are bound to determine whether their competence is valid

2.07. All this involvement of arbitrators in the validation procedure, including the statements of independence and impartiality, represent not only the high morals which each of the arbitrators needs to be characterized by, but also the kind of flexibility which arbitrators enjoy during their selection procedure. All these are regulated by various standards which set up and confirm trust in the arbitration proceedings.[2]

II. Arbitrators' Liability as Set Forth by Various International Arbitration Rules

II.1. Arbitrators' Liability under the ICC Rules

2.08. The new International Chamber of Commerce (ICC) Rules[3] provide rules concerning the appointment, replacement and challenge of arbitrators.

2.09. Article 11(1) of the ICC Rules General Provisions provides the following: 'Every arbitrator must be and remain impartial and independent of the parties involved in the arbitration.'

2.10. Before appointment or confirmation,[4] a potential arbitrator must sign a statement of acceptance, availability, impartiality and independence.[5] The potential arbitrator must reveal to the Secretariat, in writing, any facts or circumstances which might give rise to doubts concerning the arbitrator's independence in the eyes of the parties, as well as any circumstances which might give rise to reasonable doubts concerning the arbitrator's impartiality. The ICC Secretariat must make such information available to the parties in writing and establish a limit for any observations from the parties.

2.11. Compared to Article 7(2) of the ICC Rules, which referred merely to 'a statement of independence', Article 11(2) of the new ICC Rules provides the need for the arbitrators to fill out a complete statement titled 'the statement of acceptance, availability, impartiality and independence'.

---

[2]   Elizabeth Shampnoi, JD, Vice President of the New York region for the American Arbitration Association.

[3]   Rules of Arbitration of the International Chamber of Commerce, in force as of 1 January 2012.

[4]   Art. 11(2) of the new ICC Rules.

[5]   In practice, a potential ICC arbitrator must make all disclosures and statements set forth at Art. 11(2) in one single document titled the statement of acceptance, availability, impartiality and independence ('the Statement').

2.12. An arbitrator[6] must immediately inform the Secretariat and the parties in writing on any facts or circumstances similar to those described in Article 11(2) of the ICC Regulation concerning the arbitrator's impartiality or independence which might occur during arbitration.[7]

2.13. Decisions made[8] by a court concerning the appointment, confirmation, challenge or replacement of an arbitrator are final and the reasons substantiating such decision are not shown. Upon accepting their appointment to act, arbitrators undertake to complete their responsibilities in compliance with these Rules.[9]

2.14. The challenge of arbitrators must be made pursuant to Article 14 of the new ICC Rules. This Rule requires that the challenge of an arbitrator, for an alleged lack of impartiality, for reasons of independence or for different other reasons, must be made by submitting to the Secretariat a written statement mentioning the facts and circumstances on which the challenge is based. In order for the challenge to be allowed, it must be submitted by the party within 30 days following their receipt of the notification on the appointment or confirmation of the arbitrator, or within 30 days following the date when the party which requested the challenge was informed on the facts and circumstances on which the challenge is based, if such date is subsequent to the receipt of notification. The court decides upon its admissibility and, at the same time, on the merits of a challenge, as applicable, after the Secretariat has provided the interested arbitrator, the other parties and any other members of the arbitral tribunal with the opportunity to make any written comments within a reasonable time period. Such comments are sent to the parties and the arbitrators.

2.15. Replacement of the arbitrators must be made in compliance with Article 15 of the new ICC Rules. This Rule requires that an arbitrator be replaced in case of death, acceptance by a court of the arbitrator's resignation a challenge or on the request from all parties. An arbitrator may also be replaced on a court's own initiative when it decides that the arbitrator is prevented *de iure* or *de facto* from fulfilling their functions as arbitrator or when the arbitrator fails to fulfill such functions pursuant to the determined rules or within the set time limits.

---

[6] Art. 11(3) of the new ICC Rules.

[7] Arbitrators must make a realistic appraisal of their workload; otherwise, they risk becoming unable to fulfill their tasks as set forth at Art. 22 and 24 of the ICC Rules of Arbitration, by causing delays in the proceedings and particularly in the release of the arbitral award. There were cases when an excessive workload led to the resignation of the arbitrator or led a court to remove the arbitrator pursuant to Art. 11(2) of the 1998 Rules.

[8] Art. 11(4) of the new ICC Rules.

[9] Art. 11(5) of the new ICC Rules.

2.16. When an arbitrator is replaced, the court decides, at its own discretion, whether comments should follow, and the arbitral tribunal determines if and to what extent the previous proceedings must be repeated before the reconstitution of the arbitral tribunal. Subsequent to the conclusion of the proceedings, instead of replacing a deceased arbitrator or an arbitrator who has been removed by a court pursuant to Article 15(1) or 15(2), a court may decide, whenever it deems necessary, that the remaining arbitrators should continue arbitration. In order to make such decision, the court considers the opinions of the remaining arbitrators and the parties and other issues it might deem adequate in such circumstances.

II.2. Arbitrators' Liability under the UNCITRAL Arbitration Rules

2.17. The United Nations Commission on International Trade Law (UNCITRAL) Arbitration Rules, as revised in 2010, Articles 11- 13 – 'Disclosures by and Challenge of Arbitrators' set forth the following concerning an arbitrator's liability:

2.18. If someone is approached in view of their potential appointment as arbitrator, such person shall disclose any circumstances which might generate reasonable doubt concerning their impartiality or independence. Following their appointment and during the arbitration proceedings, arbitrators shall, from time to time and without delay, disclose to the parties and to the other arbitrators all circumstances of this kind, except when they have already made such disclosure.[10]

2.19. Any arbitrator may be challenged when there are such circumstances which generate reasonable doubts concerning the arbitrator's impartiality or independence. A party may challenge the arbitrator they appointed only for reasons they become aware of following the arbitrator's appointment. When an arbitrator does not act or finds themself *de jure* or *de facto* unable to fulfill their functions, the procedure for the challenge of an arbitrator set forth at Article 13[11] is applied.

2.20. A party which intends to challenge an arbitrator sends a notification about the challenge within 15 days following their notification of the appointment of the challenged arbitrator or within 15 days following the respective party's becoming aware of the circumstances mentioned at Articles 11 and 12.[12] Notification of the challenge must be sent to all

---

[10] Art. 11 of the UNCITRAL Arbitration Rules.
[11] Art. 12 of the UNCITRAL Arbitration Rules.
[12] Art. 13 of the UNCITRAL Arbitration Rules.

other parties, the challenged arbitrator and to the other arbitrators. If an arbitrator is challenged by one party, all parties may agree to the challenge. Also, following the challenge, the arbitrator may withdraw from their office. In neither case does this mean acceptance of the validity of the grounds for the challenge. If within 15 days following the date of notification of the challenge not all parties agree on the challenge or the challenged arbitrator does not withdraw, the challenging party may choose to pursue it. In such case, within 30 days following the notification of the challenge, they must seek a decision on the challenge from the appointing authority.

2.21.   Article 14 of the UNCITRAL Arbitration Rules – Replacement of an Arbitrator provides details on the procedure for the replacement of an arbitrator.

2.22.   Subject to paragraph 2, in any case when the arbitrator needs to be replaced during the proceedings, a substitute arbitrator is appointed or selected, according to the procedure set forth at Articles 8 through 11 applicable to the appointment or selection of a replaced arbitrator. Such procedure is applied even when during the proceedings for the arbitrator to be replaced one party has not exerted its right to appoint or take part in the appointment. The appointing authority, upon the request of a party in light of the exceptional circumstances of the case, may find that it would be reasonable for one party to be deprived of their right to appoint a substitute arbitrator, after providing the parties and the remaining arbitrators with the opportunity to express their opinions. The appointing authority then may: (a) appoint the substitute arbitrator or (b) following the conclusion of the hearing, authorize the other arbitrators to continue the arbitration and make a decision or an award.

2.23.   A very important part of these Rules is the provision from Article 15 which refers to resuming hearings upon the replacement of an arbitrator. When an arbitrator is replaced, the proceedings are resumed when the replaced arbitrator has ceased to fulfill their functions, unless the arbitral tribunal decides otherwise.[13] Except for intentional wrongdoing, the parties waive, to the fullest extent allowed by the applicable law, any claim against arbitrators, the appointing authority and any person appointed by the arbitral tribunal based on any act or omission related to arbitration.[14]

[13]   Art. 15 of the UNCITRAL Arbitration Rules.
[14]   Art. 16 of the UNCITRAL Arbitration Rules.

II.3. Arbitrators' Liability under the American Arbitration Association Rules

2.24. Pursuant to the Arbitration Rules of the American Arbitration Association (AAA) – International Dispute Resolution Procedures (Including Mediation and Arbitration Rules), as amended and effective 1 June 2009, arbitrators acting pursuant to these Rules must be impartial and independent.

2.25. Before accepting an appointment, a potential arbitrator must disclose to the administrator any circumstances which might generate reasonable doubts concerning their impartiality or independence. If at any time during the arbitration proceedings new situations occur which could generate such doubts, the arbitrator must immediately disclose such circumstances to the parties and to the administrator.

2.26. A party may challenge any arbitrator every time such circumstances exist which give rise to reasonable doubts concerning the arbitrator's impartiality or independence. The party wishing to challenge an arbitrator must submit a notification concerning the arbitrator's challenge within 15 days following receipt of the arbitrator's appointment or within 15 days following the time when circumstances which give rise to the challenge become known to the party.[15] Upon receiving such challenge, the administrator notifies the other party of the challenge.

2.27. When the arbitrator is challenged by one party, the other parties may agree to accept the challenge. In case of the existence of an agreement, the arbitrator must withdraw. In absence of such an agreement, the challenged arbitrator may withdraw from their duty. In neither case does withdrawal mean that the arbitrator accepts the validity of the grounds of the challenge.

2.28. If one arbitrator withdraws after being challenged, when the administrator supports the challenge or determines that there are sufficient reasons for accepting the resignation of an arbitrator or when an arbitrator dies, a substitute arbitrator is appointed pursuant to Article 6, unless the parties agree otherwise.[16]

2.29. When one arbitrator of a three-member arbitral tribunal does not participate in the arbitration due to reasons other than those set forth at Article 10, the other two arbitrators have the exclusive power to continue the proceedings. They are able to formulate any decision or award, notwithstanding the failure to attend by the third arbitrator. When deciding whether to continue the arbitration proceedings or to make any decision, ruling or award despite the failure of the third

---

[15] Art. 8 of the AAA International Arbitration Rules.
[16] Art. 10 of the AAA International Arbitration Rules.

arbitrator to attend, the other two arbitrators consider the stage of the arbitration, the reason (if any) expressed by the third arbitrator who fails to participate and any other issues deemed appropriate under the circumstances of the case. When the other two arbitrators decide not to continue arbitration without participation of the third one, based on evidence deemed satisfactory by the administrator, the latter declares the seat vacant and appoints a substitute arbitrator, pursuant to the provisions of Article 6, unless the parties agree otherwise.[17]

II.4. Arbitrators' Liability under the ICSID Regulation

2.30. Pursuant to the Rules of Procedure for the Arbitration Proceedings (Arbitration Rules) under the International Centre for Settlement of Investment Disputes (ICSID) Convention, Regulations and Rules,[18] an arbitral tribunal is deemed constituted and the proceedings are deemed to have started on the date when the General Secretariat informs the parties on the acceptance of the appointment by all arbitrators.

2.31. Arbitrators need to make a statement by which they undertake not to accept any direction or compensation in relation to the proceedings from any source other than the one set forth by the Convention on the Settlement of Investment Disputes between States and the Nationals of Other States and the Rules and Regulations drawn up under it.

2.32. Arbitrators to the ICSID proceedings make a statement about their professional and business relations,[19] past or present, with the parties and any other circumstances so as not to reflect any doubt on the reliability of the arbitrators' independent judgement. Arbitrators not signing such a statement before the end of the first tribunal meeting are deemed to have quit.

2.33. At any time before the constitution of the arbitral tribunal, any party may replace an arbitrator appointed by it and the parties may jointly agree to replace any arbitrator. The replacement procedure must comply with Rules 1, 5 and 6.[20]

---

[17] Art. 11 of the AAA International Arbitration Rules.

[18] ICSID Convention, Regulations and Rules, effective 15 April 2006, International Centre for Settlement of Investment Disputes.

[19] Starting with the first session of the tribunal, each ICSID arbitrator is required to give a signed statement asserting their own independence and agree to maintain the confidentiality of the proceedings (Arbitration Rule 6). The ICSID amended Rule 6(2) in 2006, by requiring arbitrators to disclose their professional, business and other types of relations with the parties as well as any other circumstances which might place doubt on the reliability of their independent judgment in the eyes of either party. The amendment is part of an ongoing obligation to disclose, maintained during the entire arbitration proceedings.

[20] Rule 7 – Replacement of Arbitrators, ICSID Convention, Regulation and Rules.

2.34. The party proposing the disqualification of an arbitrator pursuant to Article 57 of the Convention must promptly submit its proposal to the Secretary-General with their reasons before the proceedings are declared closed.[21]

2.35. The Secretary-General must promptly submit the proposal to the members of the tribunal and, if related to a sole arbitrator or the majority of the arbitral tribunal members, the Chair of the Administrative Council notifies the other party of the proposal. The arbitrator whom the proposal concerns may immediately provide clarification to the arbitral tribunal or to the Chair, as applicable. Except when the proposal concerns a majority of members of the arbitral tribunal, the other members must immediately review and cast their votes on the proposal in absence of the arbitrator in question. When the members are equally distributed, they must immediately inform the Chair, through the Secretary-General, on the proposal or any clarification provided by the arbitrator in question or concerning the lack of a decision.

2.36. When the Chair must rule on a proposal to disqualify an arbitrator, they must make a decision within 30 days following the receipt of the proposal. During such time, the arbitration proceedings are suspended until a decision is made on the proposal.

2.37. The Secretary-General must immediately inform the parties and, if applicable, the Chair of the Administrative Council of the disqualification, decease, incapacity or resignation of an arbitrator and, if applicable, of the tribunal's approval of the resignation.[22] From the perspective of arbitration practice under the ICSID Rules, since January 2010, the parties had challenged arbitrators in 26 registered ICSID cases.

2.38. The reasons for challenging an arbitrator under the ICSID procedure is based on three criteria: relations with the parties,[23] relations with the parties' counsel or their law firms[24] and/or involvement in other arbitrations raising similar issues.[25]

---

[21] Rule 9 – Disqualification of Arbitrators, ICSID Convention, Regulation and Rules.

[22] Rule 10 – Procedure during a Vacancy on the Tribunal – the ICSID Convention, Regulations and Rules.

[23] See, for instance, *Vivendi I, supra* note 260; *Suez, Sociedad General de Aguas de Barcelona SA and Vivendi Universal SA* v *Argentine Republic*, ICSID Case no. ARB/03/19 and *Suez, Sociedad General de Aguas de Barcelona SA and InterAguas Servicios Integrales del Agua SA* v *Argentine Republic*, ICSID Case no. ARB/03/17,(12 May 2008) (**Suez v Argentina**); *EDF International SA, SAUR International SA and Leon Participaciones Argentinas SA* v *Argentine Republic*, ICSID Case no. ARB/03/23- (25 June 2008).

[24] See, for instance, *Amco Asia Corporation and others* v *Republic of Indonesia*, ICSID Case no. ARB/81/1,(24 June 1982) in M. Reisman et al., *International Commercial Arbitration* (New York; The Foundation Press, Inc., 1997), 624-631; *SGS Societe Generale*

2.39. Upon notification by the Secretary-General of a vacant seat in the arbitral tribunal, the proceedings are suspended or remain thus until the vacant seat is filled.

2.40. The procedure for filling vacant seats must comply with Rules 1, 4(4), 4(5) and 5, and, *mutatis mutandis*, 6(2).[26]

II.5. Arbitrators' Liability under the Commercial Arbitration Rules of the Japan Commercial Arbitration Association

2.41. Pursuant to the Commercial Arbitration Rules of the Japan Commercial Arbitration Association as amended on 1 January 2008, effective on the same date, arbitrators must be and always remain impartial and independent.[27]

2.42. If one person is approached concerning their potential appointment as an arbitrator, they must make full disclosure of any circumstances which might generate reasonable doubts concerning their impartiality and independence.

2.43. When someone is appointed as an arbitrator, they must without delay submit to the Association their written commitment to disclose any circumstances which might generate reasonable doubts concerning their impartiality and independence or to state that no such circumstances exist. The Association submits to the parties, without delay, one copy of such commitments. During the arbitration proceedings, an arbitrator must disclose to the parties and to the Association, in writing and without delay, any and all circumstances of this kind, except when they have already been notified by the arbitrator concerning such circumstances.

---

de Surveillance SA v *Islamic Republic of Pakistan,* ICSID Case no. ARB/01/13,(19 December 2002), *ICSID Reports 8* (2005): 398, *Azurix Corp.* V *Argentine Republic,* ICSID Case no. ARB/01/12, (1 September 2009).

[25] See, for instance, *Suez, Sociedad General de Aguas de Barcelona SA and Vivendi Universal SA* v *Argentine Republic,* ICSID Case no. ARB/03/19 *and Suez, Sociedad General de Aguas de Barcelona SA and InterAguas Servicios Integrales del Agua SA* v *Argentine Republic,* ICSID Case no. ARB/03/17, (22 October 2007) (*Suez* v *Argentina - Electrabel SA* v *Republic of Hungary,* ICSID Case no. ARB/07/19, (25 February 2008) (unpublished); *Saba Fakes* v *Republic of Turkey,* ICSID Case no. ARB/07/20 (14 July 2010); *Participaciones Inversiones Portuarias SARL* v *Gabonese Republic,* ICSID Case no. ARB/08/17, (12 November 2009).

[26] Rule 11 of the ICSID Convention, Regulations and Rules.

[27] Rule 28 – Impartiality and Independence of Arbitrators, Commercial Arbitration Rules of the Japan Commercial Arbitration Association.

2.44. Pursuant to these Rules, an arbitrator may be challenged when such circumstances exist which generate reasonable doubts concerning the arbitrator's impartiality or independence.[28]

2.45. One party may challenge an arbitrator appointed by that party or to whose appointment they contributed by reference or any such similar acts solely for reasons they become aware of following the appointment. One party intending to challenge an arbitrator must submit a written challenge request to the Association within two weeks following the date of receipt of the notification on the appointment of the arbitrator or from the date when it becomes aware of such circumstances as set forth at paragraph 1.

2.46. If the request set forth at the previous paragraph is performed, the Association notifies the other party and the arbitrators in this respect without delay, at the same time submitting a copy of such request. After hearing the opinions of the parties and of the arbitrators and after consultation with the Association's Committee for the Review of Challenges of Arbitrators, the Association makes a decision concerning the challenge.

2.47. The Association may remove any arbitrator who does not complete their duties, who unreasonably delays the performance of such duties or is legally or actually unable to perform them.[29]

2.48. When one arbitrator resigns or dies, the Association must immediately inform the parties and the remaining arbitrators.[30]

2.49. Unless otherwise agreed on by the parties, when the arbitrator who resigns or dies is appointed by one party or by the parties or by the remaining arbitrators, the respective parties or the remaining arbitrators appoint a substitute arbitrator within three weeks following the date when the parties or arbitrators receive notification. If the arbitrator who resigns or dies is appointed by the Association, the latter appoints a substitute arbitrator within three weeks following the date when they learn about the resignation or death. If the parties or the arbitrators do not notify the Association on the appointment of the substitute arbitrator pursuant to Rule 27 within the time limit set forth at the previous paragraph, the Association appoints such substitute arbitrator. The prior provisions apply *mutatis mutandis* to the appointment of a substitute arbitrator in case of decision by the

---

[28] Rule 29 – Challenge of Arbitrators, Commercial Arbitration Rules of the Japan Commercial Arbitration Association.

[29] Rule 30 – Removal of Arbitrator, Commercial Arbitration Rules of the Japan Commercial Arbitration Association.

[30] Rule 31 Replacement of Arbitrator, Commercial Arbitration Rules of the Japan Commercial Arbitration Association.

Association showing there are grounds for a challenge when the arbitrator is challenged pursuant to Rule 29 and in case of removal provided by the previous Rule.

III. Arbitrators' Liability under the Romanian Law

2.50. Pursuant to the former Romanian Code of Civil Procedure, arbitrators could be challenged for causes questioning their independence and impartiality. The same reasons for challenging judges were valid in the case of arbitrators.

2.51. As an element of novelty in the New Code of Civil Procedure,[31] besides the cases of incompatibility set forth in the case of judges, arbitrators can also be challenged for the enumerated reasons questioning their independence and impartiality.

2.52. Thus, Article 562 paragraph (1) of the New Code of Civil Procedure sets forth four such reasons:

a) non-compliance with the qualification requirements or other requirements concerning arbitrators, set forth in the arbitration agreement;

b) when a legal person who is an affiliate of the arbitrator or of whose management bodies the arbitrator is a member has an interest in the case;

c) when the arbitrator has work or professional relations, as applicable, or direct commercial connections with either party, with a company controlled by either party or under its joint control;

d) when the arbitrator has provided consultancy to either party, has assisted or represented either party or has testified in any of the prior phases of the dispute.

2.53. As mentioned in the previous paragraph, the cases of incompatibility as set forth by the law in the case of arbitrators are the same as in the case of judges. In the New Code of Civil Procedure, the cases of absolute incompatibility are set forth in Articles 41 and 42.

2.54. A judge is incompatible with ruling in their own judgment in the following situations:

2.55. **1.** when they have already expressed their opinion with regard to the judgment in the case they have been assigned to rule upon. Formal discussion by the parties of some issues *de facto* and *de jure* pursuant to article 14 paragraphs (4) and (5) does not make the judge incompatible;

2.56. **2.** when there are circumstances which justify concern that the judge, his/her spouse, their ascendants and descendants or their in-laws, as applicable, have an interest related to the case on the dockets;

---

[31] New Code of Civil Procedure, entered into force on 15 February 2013.

2.57.   **3.** when they are a spouse, a relation or an in-law up to the fourth degree, inclusive, with the lawyer or the representative of a party or when they are married to the sibling of the spouse of any such person;

2.58.   **4.** when the spouse or former spouse is a relative or an in-law up to the fourth degree, inclusive, of either party;

2.59.   **5.** when the judge, the spouse or their relatives up to the fourth degree, inclusive, or their in-laws, as applicable, are parties to a trial on the dockets of the court where one of the parties is a judge;

2.60.   **6.** when between the judge, his/her spouse or their relatives up to the fourth degree, inclusive, or their in-laws, as applicable, and one of the parties a criminal trial was carried out up to 5 years before they were appointed judge in the case. In the case of criminal complaints formulated by the parties during the trial, the judge becomes incompatible only if the criminal proceedings are launched against him/her;

2.61.   **7.** if the judge is a custodian or a curator of either parties;

2.62.   **8.** when the judge, their spouse, their ascendants or descendants have received gifts from or were promised gifts or other privileges by either party;

2.63.   **9.** when the judge, their spouse or one of the relatives up to the fourth degree, inclusive, or their in-laws, as applicable, are in antagonistic relations with either party, their spouse or relatives up to the fourth degree, inclusive;

2.64.   **10.** if, when vested to resolve a challenging way, their spouse, or relative up to the fourth degree, inclusive, has participated in the settlement of the same case before a different court, as a judge or a prosecutor;

2.65.   **11.** when they are a spouse or a relative up to the fourth degree, inclusive, or an in-law, as applicable, of another member of the panel of judges;

2.66.   **12.** when the spouse, a relation or an in-law up to the fourth degree, inclusive, has represented or assisted the party to the same case before a different court;

2.67.   **13.** when there are further elements giving rise to grounded doubts concerning the judge's impartiality.

2.68.   The judge or arbitrator who has ruled on an interlocutory award or decision settling the case cannot rule on the same case as part of an appeal, a second appeal or an action in annulment or revision even after submittal to a re-trial. At the same time, the person who was a witness, expert, arbitrator, prosecutor, counsel, judicial assistant, assistant to the magistrate or a mediator in the same case may not take part in the trial.

2.69.   In the same respect, the Rules of Procedure of the Chamber of Arbitration of the Bucharest Stock Exchange sets forth that the arbitrator or chair may be challenged for reasons questioning their independence or impartiality. The reasons for challenging an arbitrator were those set forth for challenging a judge.

2.70. The same is set forth by the Rules of Arbitration Procedure of the Court of International Commercial Arbitration.[32] Pursuant to Article 22 paragraph (1) of these Rules, challenge is subject to the rules in the Code of Civil Procedure and the reasons set forth in view of challenging arbitrators. The procedures are the same as those in the Code of Civil Procedure.

2.71. Considering the reasons for a challenge as specified above, the procedure to be followed where there is such a reason is, first, that the person appointed arbitrator, who is aware of the reason for their challenge, is compelled to notify the parties and the other arbitrators before accepting their duties as an arbitrator. When such reasons occur subsequent to acceptance, the arbitrator should notify the parties as soon as they learn about the reasons for a challenge.

2.72. However, following prior notice to the parties, they may express their option not to challenge in writing, in which case the person appointed arbitrator may participate in the resolution of the dispute.

2.73. As it is worded under imperative terms, inobservance of the obligation to submit a notification may trigger three major consequences. The first one may lead to the dissolution of the arbitral award for being ruled in breach of the imperative provisions of the law. The second consequence is the liability for damages from arbitrators at fault for the serious breach of their duties. The third consequence is represented by the challenge and removal of arbitrators.[33]

2.74. Pursuant to Article 563 of the New Code of Civil Procedure, the request for a challenge must be made within 10 days following the date when the party becomes aware of the arbitrator's appointment or following the occurrence of the reason for the challenge, as applicable, under the penalty of incapacity. The request for challenge is settled by the tribunal under whose jurisdiction the arbitration is carried out, by a panel for a trial who rules after summoning the parties and the challenged arbitrator, within 10 days following the notification. Judgment is not subject to any challenging method.

---

[32] Art. 22 paragraph (1) Rules of Arbitration Procedure of the Court of International Commercial Arbitration: 'challenging arbitrators, arbitral assistants and experts is subject to the provisions of the Code of Civil Procedure concerning the challenge of judges/court clerks.'

[33] VIOREL ROS, ARBITRAJ COMERCIAL INTERNAȚIONAL, București: Regia autonomă "Monitorul Oficial" 325 (2000); MIHAELA TABARCA, CODUL DE PROCEDURA CIVILA COMENTAT SI ADNOTAT CU LEGISLATIE, JURISPRUDENTA SI DOCTRINA, Editura Universul Juridic 1044 (2007).

2.75. However, both the arbitration procedure of the Court of International Commercial Arbitration and the Rules of Procedure of the Chamber of Arbitration of the Bucharest Stock Exchange provide that the request for a challenge must be settled by the arbitral tribunal in no longer than 10 days following notification. Judgment is not subject to any challenging method. The request is settled by summoning the parties and the challenged arbitrator, who is replaced by the arbitral tribunal with the appointed substitute or in their absence, by the Chair of the Chamber of Arbitration or an arbitrator appointed by the Chair. If the request for a challenge concerns the sole arbitrator, it is settled by the Chair of the Chamber of Arbitration or by an arbitrator appointed by the Chair.

2.76. Considering the provisions of Article 563 of the Code of Civil Procedure, a court of law settles the request for challenging an arbitrator unless the arbitration is organized by a permanent institution, such as the Court of International Commercial Arbitration under the Chamber of Commerce and Industry of Romania or unless its rules or arbitral agreement provide otherwise. On the other hand, a court also becomes competent when the rules of the arbitration institution are silent on this issue. An example would be when the whole arbitral tribunal is challenged and the arbitration agreement does not provide for the option for another arbitral tribunal to settle the challenge, the request then falls under the jurisdiction of the competent state court.[34]

2.77. As shown, the penalty set forth by the law consists in the impossibility of the arbitrator to resolve the dispute for which they were vested, if there is reason for challenging them.

2.78. In what concerns the arbitrators' liability, the former rules provided that arbitrators were liable for damages under the law, when:

a) after acceptance, they unjustifiably gave up their duty;

b) without any justified excuse, they failed to participate in the settlement of the dispute or failed to give the award within the deadline set forth by the arbitration agreement or by the law;

c) they did not observe the confidentiality of arbitration, by publishing or disclosing data of which they became aware as arbitrators, without the parties' consent;

d) they were in serious breach of their duties.

2.79. According to the new regulations of Article 565 of the New Code of Civil Procedure, the same are reasons for which arbitrators may become liable under the law. The only difference is that, in the case

---

[34] *Ibid.*, at 1046.

provided at paragraph (d), the wording 'they are in serious breach of' is replaced by 'they are in bad faith or negligent and gross breach of', as a result of the lawmaker's wish to be clearer about one party's ability to invoke such a case of liability.

2.80. Pursuant to Article 26 of the Rules of Arbitral Procedure of the Court of International Commercial Arbitration 'Arbitrators are liable for damages caused to the parties under the conditions of common law in the matter for the reasons set forth at article 20 letter B of these Rules'. Thus, Article 8 of the Rules of Arbitral Procedure of the Court of International Commercial Arbitration under the Chamber of Commerce and Industry of Romania provide the following:

2.81. The dispute file shall be confidential. No person besides those involved in the performance of the respective dispute shall have access to the file without the written consent of the parties.

2.82. The Court of Arbitration, the arbitral tribunal, as well as the staff of the chambers of commerce are bound to ensure confidentiality of arbitration, and they do not have the right to publish or disclose data of which they become aware as part of fulfilling their duties without the consent of the parties.

2.83. In our opinion, the assumptions under which liability for damages of arbitrators could be engaged lead to the conclusion that their liability is of a contractual nature. Upon accepting their appointment as arbitrators, they are undertaking not only to fulfill a jurisdictional function, but also to comply with the arbitration requirements and the rules of procedure. In other words, arbitrators' liability could be engaged not for the award ruled on in the dispute, but for a total or partial failure to complete their jurisdictional mission or for the commitment of other deeds thus prejudicing the parties or for one of them, in connection to the dispute referred to them.[35]

2.84. The confidentiality obligation in relation to the dispute, the debates, their content and the content of the arbitral award are also valid in the case of parties which are not only entitled to require it of the arbitrators, the lawyers, the witnesses, their counselors and opponents, but also compelled to abstain themselves from disclosing the elements of the proceedings or the data and information they become aware of as part of the proceedings. In the case of the parties involved in the dispute, the mutual confidentiality obligation is contractual, even if it is not expressly set forth in the arbitration clause.[36]

---

[35] ION DELEANU & SERGIU DELEANU, ARBITRAJUL INTERN SI INTERNATIONAL, Bucureşti: Rosetti 124 (2005).

[35] MIHAELA TABARCA, *supra* note 33, at 1048.

[36] VIOREL ROS, *supra* note 33, at 330; MIHAELA TABARCA, *supra* note 33, at 1048-1049.

2.85. Since arbitrators can be compelled to receive damages 'under the law', it means that the interested party needs to make proof of the fact that the arbitrator did commit one or several of the deeds mentioned in the text, is at fault for doing so and that such deed incurred damages to one party, thus having the deed-prejudice causality connection.

2.86. The grounds for the arbitrators' liability are deemed to be contractual as a result of non-performance or inappropriate performance by the arbitrators of mainly their obligations under the arbitration contract. Thus, the arbitrators may be compelled to pay damages unless they provide reasons for their renunciation of the duty assigned by the party, their failure to participate in the settlement of the arbitration dispute, their refusal to appoint the chair of the tribunal, etc.

2.87. Review of the arbitrator's liability for failure to perform or inappropriate performance of their mission vested in them by the parties must consider the nature of the arbitrator's mission. The jurisdictional side of the activity performed by the arbitrator prevents an exclusively contractual approach to their liability. As shown in the doctrine, the arbitration contract is placed at the confluence of the jurisdictional and the contractual elements, which means that the arbitrator's liability needs to be approached in a divided manner without neglecting the jurisdictional part of their contractual mission. This is the exact reason why the arbitrator cannot be tackled as a regular contractor.

2.88. As part of mentioning contractual non-performance or inappropriate performance of the arbitration agreement, major importance is attributed to the classification of the arbitrator's obligations into determined or outcome obligations and obligations of means or diligence, and the distinction generates major effects on the probation side. Thus, while in the former case not achieving the intended outcome is in itself a presumption of fault by the obligation debtor's arbitrator, in the latter case – the obligation of means, not achieving the outcome no longer constitutes *ipso facto* a proof of default, and the task of providing evidence is the creditor's, who needs to make proof of the fact that the arbitrator has not been diligent and prudent while attempting to achieve the intended outcome.

2.89. Pursuant to the arbitration agreement, the arbitrator has the following obligations: not to leave the arbitral tribunal without reasons to do so; to organize and take part in debates and to decide, *omnia petita*, on the obligation to provide reasons for the arbitral award. The obligations of means include the following: the confidentiality obligation, independence obligation, availability and the obligation to comply with the arbitration time limit.

2.90. In close connection with the arbitrators' liability for damages is the institution of revoking them.[37] Thus, according to Article 20 paragraph B of the Rules of Arbitration Procedure of the Court of International Commercial Arbitration:

2.91. Revoking an arbitrator is a result of their committing any of the following:

a) When after signing the Act of Mission they renounce their mission as an arbitrator/tribunal chair without solid reasons;

b) When they do not participate in the arbitration meeting without any solid reasons;

c) When they belate the settlement of the dispute without any solid reasons;

d) When they do not rule upon the dispute within the time limit provided by the provisions of these rules;

e) When they do not observe the confidential nature of the arbitration.

2.92. Considering that the reasons and causes for revoking an arbitrator tend to coincide with those set forth in the case of the arbitrators' liability for damages, we can conclude that should any of these circumstances be met, the arbitrator can lose their quality as an arbitrator in view of settling the dispute, and their liability can be subsequently triggered for prejudice caused to the parties.

IV. Conclusions

2.93. Regardless of the system of law and the regulations applicable in the matter of arbitration, the parties who resort to arbitration as an alternative to state justice need to have utter trust in the high moral conduct of arbitrators, in their good professional reputation, in their practical background and flawless behaviour during the entire arbitration proceedings.

2.94. Arbitrators' task is not an easy one, and their intense activity in view of continuous professional training, in writing articles, publications or attending conferences cover the theoretical part of this profession.

2.95. We can definitely say that, although many arbitrators are also lawyers, being an arbitrator is something else and perhaps this is why many arbitrators choose to give up their profession as lawyers, which can only support this approach of an arbitrator as a profession in itself.

---

[37] Art. 26 of the Rules of Arbitration Procedure of the Court of International Commercial Arbitration: 'arbitrators are liable for the damages caused to the parties under the requirements of the common law in the matter for the reasons set forth at art. 20 letter B of these rules'.

2.96. Furthermore, their liability during the arbitration proceedings is increasing. No arbitrator wishes to have their name associated with arbitral awards cancelled on grounds of pre-judgment, of *minus petita* or *ultra petita* or on such other grounds as the lack of ICSID jurisdiction, which would finally lead to a lower popularity as an arbitrator and lower confidence of trading companies or traders in general in resorting to arbitration.

2.97. To end on an optimistic note, arbitration has become a force and continues to be one also due to the reputation of arbitrators involved in the proceedings, as an elevated manner of solving conflicts, where the parties are granted due consideration to present their own case, and where confidentiality during the entire proceedings provide traders the opportunity to go on doing their business.

| | |

Summaries

FRA [*La responsabilité des arbitres*]

On s'est intéressé ici sur un plan strictement académique à la question de la responsabilité des arbitres et on a passé en revue les différentes modifications de la procédure. On s'est penché également sur la question de l'indépendance, de la neutralité et de l'impartialité des arbitres, tout comme sur les qualités qui leur sont demandées au cours de la procédure. Il est justement admissible de remplacer des arbitres au cours de la procédure s'ils ne remplissent pas les exigences qui ont été définies. La question de la responsabilité des arbitres est ensuite examinée en lien avec les modifications des règles et des réglementations qui s'appliquent aux procédures d'arbitrage.

Le problème de la responsabilité des arbitres est un problème qui soulève toujours beaucoup de débats et est très complexe, sans faire référence aux évolutions des réglementations se rapportant à la procédure. Cela tient entre autres à la faveur de plus en plus grande dont jouit l'arbitrage et à la confiance placée dans cette façon de résoudre les litiges envisagée comme une bonne alternative au règlement judiciaire. Vu la complexité du sujet, on a ici également comparé différentes règles de procédure et différentes modifications de ces règles, dans l'intention de présenter un point de vue clair.

CZE [*Odpovědnost rozhodců*]

Článek se zabývá otázkou odpovědnosti rozhodců z akademického hlediska a rozebírá různé právní úpravy rozhodčího řízení. Článek se rovněž zaměřuje na problematiku nezávislosti, neutrality a nestrannosti rozhodců, jako vlastností, které musí rozhodci splňovat v průběhu celého rozhodčího řízení, pro něž byli jmenováni. Nahrazení rozhodců v průběhu řízení je přípustné právě v důsledku nesplnění uvedených požadavků na rozhodce kladených. Problematika odpovědnosti rozhodců je dále pojednána též v návaznosti na změny v předpisech a pravidlech použitelných na rozhodčí řízení.

Bez ohledu na vývoj předpisů a pravidel týkajících se rozhodčího řízení je materie týkající se odpovědnosti rozhodců velmi široká a stále více komplikovaná. Souvisí to mimo jiné s rostoucí oblíbeností rozhodčího řízení a důvěrou v tento způsob řešení sporů jako alternativy k soudnímu rozhodování sporů. Vzhledem ke komplexnosti tématu a záměru autora poskytnout jasný názor, provedl autor též srovnání různých pravidel pro rozhodčí řízení a odpovídajících právních úprav.

| | |

POL *[Odpowiedzialność arbitrów]*

Artykuł omawia problematykę związaną z koncepcją odpowiedzialności arbitrów w świetle różnych regulacji postępowania arbitrażowego, np. nowego Regulaminu ICC, Regulaminu UNCITRAL, Regulaminu Amerykańskiego Stowarzyszenia Arbitrażowego, Regulaminu Japońskiego Stowarzyszenia Arbitrażu Handlowego, Regulaminu postępowania przed Izbą Arbitrażową Giełdy Papierów Wartościowych w Bukareszcie, Regulaminu postępowania arbitrażowego Międzynarodowego Sądu Arbitrażowego Międzynarodowej Izby Handlowej i Przemysłowej Rumunii, jak również z akademickiego punktu widzenia.

DEU *[Schiedsrichterliche Haftung]*

Der Beitrag setzt sich mit konzeptuellen Fragen der Haftung von Schiedsrichtern auseinander, wie sie sich aus den verschiedenen Rahmenregelungen des Schiedsverfahrens ergeben, so etwa aus den neuen ICC-Regeln, den UNCITRAL-Regeln, den Regeln der American Arbitration Association, den Regeln der Japanischen Gesellschaft für Schiedsverfahren in Handelssachen, den Prozessregeln der Schiedskammer an der Wertpapierbörse Bukarest, den Schiedsregeln des Internationalen Wirtschaftsschiedsgerichtshofs an der Industrie- und Handelskammer Rumäniens, sowie auch aus akademischer Sicht.

RUS *[Ответственность арбитров]*

В статье рассматриваются концептуальные вопросы ответственности арбитров с точки зрения различных актов, регулирующих арбитраж, например, нового Регламента ICC, Регламента ЮНСИТРАЛ, Правил Американской арбитражной ассоциации, Правил Японской ассоциации по арбитражу в коммерческих делах, Процессуальных правил Арбитражной палаты Биржи ценных бумаг в Бухаресте, Регламента арбитража Международного коммерческого арбитражного суда при Торгово-промышленной палате Румынии, а также с научной точки зрения.

ESP   [*Responsabilidad de los árbitros*]
El artículo aborda las cuestiones conceptuales de la responsabilidad de los árbitros desde la perspectiva de las diversas modificaciones del procedimiento arbitral, como las nuevas reglas de la ICC, las de CNUDMI, las normas de la American Arbitration Association, el Reglamento de Arbitraje Comercial de la Asociación Japonesa de Arbitraje, las reglas de la Cámara Arbitral de la Bolsa de Valores de Bucarest y las reglas de arbitraje de la Corte de Arbitraje Comercial Internacional adherida a la Cámara de Comercio e Industria de Rumanía. Además, observa el tema también desde el punto de vista académico.

| | |

Czech (& Central European) Yearbook of Arbitration

Alexander J. Bělohlávek

Subjective and Objective Impartiality of Arbitrators and Appointing Authorities as a Part of Procedural Public Policy (Ordre Public) in Arbitration

Key words:
arbitration | lex arbitri | objective impartiality | subjective impartiality | independence | lack of bias | arbitral tribunal | permanent arbitral institutions | appointing authority | equality of the parties | legitimate doubts | IBA standards | annulment of an arbitral award | procedural public policy (ordre public) | autonomy of the parties

Abstract | Selection and appointment of arbitrators is one of the crucial issues of arbitration. Laws and rules applicable to arbitration usually do not impose any special requirements on arbitrators, except eligibility criteria such as a minimum age and requirements of independence and impartiality. The parties may agree on the requirements for arbitrators in the arbitration agreement; an arbitration agreement exclusively results from the autonomy of the parties within the limits determined by the lex arbitri. The parties, however, may not forego the requirements of independence and impartiality. Also, an appointing authority must be fully independent of the parties. Despite the fact that this principle is not explicitly articulated in the laws and rules or any other provisions applicable to arbitration, it is a principle inherent to arbitration and is a manifestation of the principle of equality of the parties, which must be considered the procedural ordre public in arbitration. An arbitrator must always act as a person with no vested interest in the course and outcome of the dispute. The circumstances disqualifying arbitrators must be not only objective but also reasonably evident, and not merely speculative. Impartiality is a highly subjective category and, in relation to bias it might be said that bias establishes the risk of an absence of impartiality.

Univ. Professor, Dr.iur., Mgr., Dipl. Ing. oec/MB, Dr.h.c. Alexander J. Bělohlávek, Lawyer admitted and practising in Prague/CZE (Branch N.J./US), Senior Partner of the Law Offices Bělohlávek, Dept. of Law, Faculty of Economics, Ostrava, CZE, Dept. of Int. and European Law, Faculty of Law, Masaryk University, Brno, CZE (visiting), Chairman of the Commission on Arbitration ICC National Committee CZE, Arbitrator in Prague, Vienna, Kiev etc. Member of ASA, DIS, Austrian Arb. Association. The President of the WJA – the World Jurist Association, Washington D.C./USA. e-mail: office@ ablegal.cz

|||

I. Selection and Appointment of Arbitrators

I.1. Selection of Individual Arbitrators

3.01. The process of selecting individual arbitrators is undoubtedly one of the crucial issues of arbitration as it is essential for the protection and enforcement of the parties' rights in arbitration. This is despite the fact that the arbitrators are principally independent of the parties and the exercise of their duties must be impartial and unbiased. There are principally five methods of appointing arbitrators:

3.02. **First:** The arbitration agreement specifically names the individual arbitrators. This procedure is not unusual, especially in *ad hoc* arbitration. It is, however, not very useful in arbitration clauses, where the agreement on the jurisdiction of arbitrators applies to any and all potential disputes arising from a particular relationship. It is unclear in these agreements whether and if so, when and what kind of dispute are actually covered. Consequently, a dispute that ought to be resolved by the arbitrators might arise a very long time after the conclusion of the agreement. There is no guarantee that the arbitrators agreed to by the parties will not have a change of circumstances that will disqualify them from the office of arbitrator. Domestic practice, especially the case law of many countries, and fairly extensive international practice demonstrates that if the parties agree on a particular arbitrator in their arbitration agreement, i.e. a natural person identified by name or other identification data, then the clause implies that the parties wish to have their dispute resolved only by this particular arbitrator. This clause thereby becomes an essential term of the arbitration agreement. However, even an arbitrator's preliminary consent cannot replace their acceptance, which may only be done with respect to a particular dispute. Until a particular dispute arises and the agreed arbitrator accepts their duties, the parties cannot be sure that the appointment will actually be accepted. If the office of arbitrator is not accepted for whatever reason or if the arbitrator loses their capacity to discharge their office during the proceedings, then the arbitration agreement expires, and this entails expiration of one of the procedural requirements.[1] The risk could be minimized by a post-dispute arbitration clause which is concluded in connection with a particular dispute that has already arisen, usually a 'factual' dispute, although the possibility that the office will be vacated during the proceedings cannot be entirely ruled out either. However, if the parties wish to agree on

---

[1] Cf. Judgment of the Supreme Court Czech Republic, docket 33 Odo 135/2006 of 31 January 2008.

particular arbitrators, then they are free to negotiate an alternative applicable in case their original agreement cannot be realized. For instance, they may select substitute arbitrators or agree that if the originally named arbitrator refuses to accept their office or becomes ineligible for whatever reason, then the procedure of appointment or the new appointment of the *arbitral forum* will follow the general rules envisaged by laws and rules applicable to the particular arbitration. Alternatively, the parties may in this particular case agree on a third independent person, an *appointing authority*, who will select a particular arbitrator.

3.03.   An agreement of the parties on a particular arbitrator is especially common in '*ad hoc*' arbitration. However, it is also principally allowed in arbitration conducted by permanent arbitral institutions, unless the rules or statutes of these institutions exclude such agreements. However, the parties enjoy a broad margin of discretion and are also principally free to agree on a different application of the rules of permanent arbitral institutions. It would be necessary to assess in each particular case whether the rules may limit the autonomy of the parties with respect to certain issues, especially if there is any specific interest in such a limitation from the perspective of proportionality of this interest *vis-à-vis* the autonomy of the parties.

3.04.   **Second:** The parties may agree on a third independent party, an *appointing authority*, who will appoint the arbitrators instead of the parties and in consequence of their will.

3.05.   **Third:** The parties agree that the appointment of arbitrators will be executed following the procedure set forth in standardized rules.

3.06.   **Fourth:** The parties make no agreement on the arbitrators or the method of their appointment. In such case, it is automatically necessary to apply the procedure prescribed by laws and rules applicable to the particular arbitration, usually the *lex arbitri* in force in the seat of arbitration, or, in case of arbitration conducted by a permanent arbitral institution, the procedure prescribed by the rules or statutes of the permanent arbitral institution.

3.07.   **Fifth: Other methods.** Certain arbitration clauses, albeit unusual, provide for the selection of arbitrators by drawing lots. This is done either through the medium of, or at least in the presence of, a particular *appointing authority* or in the presence of a notary. The notary may also act as an *appointing authority*.[2] This procedure is not considered

---

[2]   We may ask whether the notary must be specifically identified or whether the parties may only agree on a 'notary', i.e. whether the arbitrators or any of the parties may address *any notary*. If the agreement does not give rise to any other doubts regarding its validity, then it is probably possible to accept such an agreement. This is because the office of a

impossible in practice, but it may not always be appropriate. Such determination of arbitrators may not even guarantee their full impartiality, let alone expertise. The reason is that, except for the requirement of impartiality and independence of the arbitrator with a guarantee of equal treatment for the parties in the selection of arbitrators, the Arbitration Act does not impose any limitations. Consequently, the parties' autonomy is fully respected, unless it is contrary to any mandatory legislation or overriding mandatory legal principles, especially the principles which are part of the *ordre public*.

3.08.   Naturally, it is also possible to 'combine' the above-mentioned methods, providing it does not exceed statutory limits. However, the Arbitration Act provides the parties with a relatively broad autonomy as concerns the constitution of the *arbitral forum*. This autonomy is basically limited only by the principle of impartiality and independence of the arbitrators, who are supposed to hear and resolve the dispute, and the equality of the parties which must be fully honored by the respective procedure.

I.2.   General and Special Requirements for Eligibility to Act as an Arbitrator

3.09.   Laws and rules applicable to arbitration usually do not impose any special requirements on arbitrators, except eligibility criteria, for example minimum age and requirements of independence and impartiality. Similarly, any general guideline agreed to in the arbitration agreement and not sufficiently specific, such as 'a person with sufficient knowledge in the field', can be only declarative.[3] It is certainly understandable that the parties will choose as an arbitrator a person whose professional and personal qualities they are confident about, unless they agree that the arbitrator will be selected by another, independent entity.

3.10.   The parties may, however, also agree on specific and objective criteria, which must be satisfied by the arbitrator. For instance, the parties commonly require a specific qualification; such qualification, however, must be objectively ascertainable, such as a university degree in law,

---

notary generally meets the requirements of expert skills, trustworthiness and independence, which could only be limited by the respective notary's relation to the parties or the dispute itself.

[3]   KVĚTOSLAV RŮŽIČKA, ROZHODČÍ ŘÍZENÍ PŘED ROZHODČÍM SOUDEM PŘI HOSPODÁŘSKÉ KOMOŘE ČESKÉ REPUBLIKY A AGRÁRNÍ KOMOŘE ČESKÉ REPUBLIKY [*Arbitration in the Arbitration Court at the Economic Chamber of the Czech Republic and the Agricultural Chamber of the Czech Republic*], Dobrá Voda u Pelhřimova: Aleš Čeněk 50 (2003).

etc. The parties also frequently demand that the arbitrator have specific linguistic skills. Such requirements are usually entirely legitimate and are often based on the parties' logical thinking regarding the possible subject matter of the dispute, the complexity of the dispute from the perspective of evidence, etc. These criteria, if articulated by the parties in a sufficiently specific manner, must be permitted as much as possible. However, these rules will be primarily binding upon third parties who are supposed to select the arbitrator, because it is doubtful whether these agreed rules may directly limit the choice of a particular arbitrator by one of the parties. For instance, in their arbitration agreement the parties agree on the requirement of legal qualification of the arbitrators. In a particular dispute, however, one of the parties appoints as 'their arbitrator' a person who is not a lawyer but has a degree in economics or another science. In such case, it will probably be necessary to give precedence to the autonomy of the party regarding the appointment of 'their arbitrator'. This is especially so in those cases in which the relevant 'objective' requirements imposed on the arbitrator will be agreed on in an arbitration clause, but the particular dispute, which may arise long after the arbitration agreement is concluded, will require a departure from the previously concluded agreement. However, the agreement of the parties incorporated in their arbitration agreement will be binding upon the *appointing authority*. It will also be binding upon the arbitrators chosen by the parties when they select the presiding arbitrator who is the chair of the arbitral tribunal. Naturally, it is somewhat doubtful whether the agreement of the parties will also be binding upon a court when appointing a particular arbitrator as the appointing authority.

3.11. The answer to this question ought to be positive. But it will depend on the discretion of the court whether such agreement of the parties will be assessed as a sufficiently unambiguous requirement which clearly determines the given criteria or as only a declarative guideline primarily due to the absence of sufficient clarity. The nature of the clause can often be derived from its wording, for instance '*...the arbitrator ought to especially...*' instead of '*...the arbitrator must have... degree in...*'. The conclusion that the court or appointing authority is bound by the parties' agreement follows from the fact that the power of the court to appoint the arbitrators in these cases is based not only on the law but also on the arbitration agreement. The arbitration agreement exclusively results from the autonomy of the parties within the limits determined by the *lex arbitri*, as well as by the fact that the court itself particularizes the agreement of the parties, which has not been completed in all respects or has not been fully consummated for whatever reasons.

3.12. The arbitrator should also be selected or appointed with due consideration to whether they are flexible and have enough time to deal with procedural issues as necessary. Certain permanent arbitral institutions[4] explicitly impose this requirement on their arbitrators, and some of them even expressly incorporate the requirement in their rules.[5] The arbitrators' conduct, despite their excellent professional skills, will be to no avail if the arbitrators are not able to devote maximum attention and efforts to the particular dispute. Naturally, this is very often difficult to assess. The parties involved in bigger disputes are advised to request the would-be arbitrator, before their appointment, to promise and ensure the parties that they will have enough time for a most active, i.e. effective, discharge of their office.[6]

I.3. Real and Effective Possibility to Appoint Arbitrators or Influence the Choice of an Individual Arbitrator and the Equality of the Parties in the Process

3.13. The procedure of selecting arbitrators charged with the hearing and resolution of a particular dispute must principally satisfy the criteria of impartiality, independence and especially equality of the parties. All parties to the dispute must have an equal, i.e. both legal and factual, opportunity to influence the composition of the *arbitral tribunal*, i.e. the *arbitral forum* and selection of arbitrators, which will resolve their dispute.

3.14. However, the requirement of equal opportunities for the parties to appoint arbitrators does not principally or exceptionally rule out the possibility that, depending on the circumstances of the particular case, the arbitrator will actually be determined by only one party. These

---

[4]   MARC BLESSING, THE CONDUCT OF ARBITRAL PROCEEDINGS UNDER THE RULES OF ARBITRATION INSTITUTIONS, WIPO/ASA Conference on Rules for Institutional Arbitration and Mediation, Genève 41 (1995).

[5]   This requirement has also been traditionally imposed on arbitrators by the International Arbitration and Mediation Center at the World Intellectual Property Organization (WIPO/OMPI) established in Geneva, in compliance with Article 23(a) of the Arbitration Rules and others. This requirement has also been newly incorporated in the International Chamber of Commerce (ICC) Rules (2012 edition), although the ICC Court used to apply the requirement in practice even before the new version of the ICC Rules was introduced, applicable from 1 January 2012.

[6]   GINO LÖRCHER, HEIKE LÖRCHER & TORSTEN LÖRCHER, DAS SCHIEDSVERFAHREN – NATIONAL/INTERNATIONAL – NACH DEUTSCHEM RECHT, Heidelberg: C. F. Müller Verlag 31 para. 100 (2nd ed., 2001). Currently required, for example, by the ICC International Court of Arbitration, the Vienna International Arbitral Center, etc.

situations ought to be an exception, but they are by no means unusual. This specifically applies to cases in which one of the parties, usually the respondent, fails to exercise their right to appoint the arbitrator or participate in the selection of the arbitrators despite an opportunity to do so. Usually, the party fails to appoint the arbitrator despite an ample and reasonable opportunity to do so. Obviously, the most contentious situations arise if the parties agree that each of them will appoint their arbitrator and that the two arbitrators will subsequently agree on the presiding arbitrator. This is the usual standard. Problems arise if the parties simultaneously agree that if the other party fails to avail themselves of the right to appoint an arbitrator, then the arbitrator who was already appointed by one of the parties, usually the claimant, becomes the sole arbitrator who will resolve the dispute.

3.15. This option, by no means exceptional in practice, is also possible and does not run counter to the principles governing the selection of arbitrators or constitution of the *arbitral forum*. The crucial factor is, though, whether the other party was indeed provided with a sufficient opportunity to exercise their rights in the selection of arbitrators, which can only be assessed with respect to the particular circumstances of the case. Naturally, the parties may agree on the precise procedure to be followed in these cases. After all, this is implied by the extensive autonomy also enjoyed by the parties in the selection of arbitrators. However, if the parties agree on such conditions, which would *de facto* eliminate the possibility of a party actively participating in the selection of arbitrators, then in most cases it will be necessary to conclude that the clause is invalid. This is because it conflicts with the fundamental principles of arbitration, which undoubtedly include the possibility of actively influencing the composition of the *arbitral forum*. A typical example of such an invalid clause is, for instance, an unduly short time limit stipulated for the exercise of this right.

I.4. Selection of Arbitrators by a Third Party *(Appointing Authority)* and Equality of the Parties

3.16. The possibility of selecting arbitrators other than by a direct expression of will by the parties, i.e. through the medium of another person chosen by the parties to the arbitration agreement or the dispute, is globally considered standard in arbitration. It is required, though, that the third party, the *appointing authority,* be determined either by an expression of the will of the parties or subsidiarily by law or statute, legal normative in compliance with the law or an international treaty. An international treaty that provides for such determination is the

European Convention on International Commercial Arbitration (1961). This convention identifies, within the scope and applicability of the European Convention, one person in each Member State who performs these duties unless otherwise agreed by the parties. This trend has clearly been followed by domestic law of some countries, in particular, for example, Czech *lex arbitri*,

3.17. This *third independent party* the *appointing authority* must be fully independent of the parties. Despite the fact that this principle is not explicitly articulated in laws, rules or any other provisions applicable to arbitration, it is inherent to arbitration and manifests the principle of equality of the parties, which must be considered the *procedural ordre public* in arbitration. Therefore, not only the arbitrators but also the person charged by the parties with the duty to appoint the arbitrators, the appointing authority, and, naturally, a permanent arbitral institution if the parties agreed on its jurisdiction must meet the requirements of independence, impartiality and a lack of bias. Hence, it is principally unacceptable that the agreement about a third party, which ought to select the arbitrator charged with the hearing and resolution of the dispute, should in any manner restrict, let alone entirely eliminate, the parties' right to influence the composition of the *arbitral forum*. Indeed, the right to influence the selection of the arbitrator, albeit through the medium of a third, independent person is also one of the fundamental principles of arbitration, often referred to as one of the advantages of this method of dispute resolution. The procedural autonomy of the parties is also manifested in their agreement stipulating that the arbitrators will be determined by a third entity, *appointing authority*, which will be impartial and fully independent of the parties. The assessment of the independence and impartiality of this third party authorized to select the arbitrators must be subject to the same rules which apply to the independence and impartiality of arbitrators. This would cover any type of dependence which would exclude the *appointing authority*, especially material dependence, whether direct or mediated, or any interest in the final resolution of the dispute. The absence of independence as a quality of the third party charged with the appointment or selection of arbitrators logically undermines the independence and lack of bias of the arbitrators themselves. Consequently, it constitutes a legal and factual prerequisite without which the principle of an impartial approach of the *arbitral tribunal* would not be fully implemented.

3.18. It is undoubtedly appropriate and useful if the *appointing authority* has a closer connection with arbitration, or at least with the field which the subject matter of the dispute concerns.[7] However, the laws and rules applicable to arbitration usually do not prescribe any such requirement and again fully transfer the responsibility for the method of appointment of arbitrators to the parties to the arbitration agreement, who thereby assume full responsibility for the constitution of the forum. This broad freedom of contract is guaranteed by the nature of arbitration as proceedings conducted by an entity of private law.

3.19. If the arbitrators are to be selected by a person agreed by the parties, then we can also ask if the *appointing authority* can be both a natural person and a legal person. The laws and rules applicable to arbitration do not principally stipulate any restrictions in this regard. A natural person is commonly identified by their standard identification or office. It is certainly useful if the parties agree on a person holding a particular office, such as chair of a chamber of professionals, chair of an academic, scientific, pedagogical or other institution, etc. The reason is that if the *appointing authority* is determined as an individual natural person identified by their name or any other specification, the person could easily lose their capacity to perform the office of arbitrator at their appointment, due to death, refusal to discharge the office, or ineligibility for the office for other reasons such as the person becomes dependent on the parties or the subject matter of the proceedings. In such case, the validity of the entire arbitration agreement could be jeopardized. However, the *appointing authority* may also be a collective body or an assembly which appoints the arbitrators following its own rules of procedure. Principally, however, the *appointing authority* may also be a legal person. In such case, the above-mentioned rule applicable to a *collective body* also applies to the legal person, in other words the arbitrators will be selected following the same procedure which governs the decision making and acting of the legal person. The *appointing authority* must always exhibit the same qualities of independence and impartiality which are binding upon the arbitrators. Simply speaking, it is hardly conceivable in *ad hoc* arbitration that an independent and impartial arbitrator could be selected by a person different from the parties who fails to meet the requirements of independence and impartiality.

---

[7]   KVĚTOSLAVRŮŽIČKA, *supra* note 3, at 49, who also provides, with a certain exaggeration, examples of possible but unsuitable '*appointing authorities*'.

II. Impartiality of Arbitrators and Protection of the Parties

II.1. Basic Substantive Rules for the Assessment of Lack of Bias on the Part of the Arbitrator and Correlation with the Mechanisms of Protection of the Parties

3.20. Although, in most cases, arbitrators are appointed by the parties, they do not act as a representative of that party, unlike other forms of alternative dispute resolution in which, there is no discovery procedure. Instead, an agreement between the parties is mediated. This is typical in cases of mediation, mini-trials, etc. In these other alternative dispute resolution *(ADR)* methods, the *mediator* may well express their legal opinion, but it is not usually binding on the parties, and such statements of opinion do not constitute binding decisions for the parties. In contrast, in arbitration the arbitrator must always act as a person with no 'vested interest' in the course and outcome of the dispute.[8] Instead, their connection with the party who appointed them is reflected in the fact that, on behalf of that party, they ensure compliance with procedural rules, and as such is a notional guarantor of the observance of the procedural rights of the party who appointed them.

II.2. Objective Nature of the Grounds for Bias and Challenge to an Arbitrator

3.21. The wording usually used in laws and rules applicable to arbitration regarding potential bias, is *'reasons to doubt'* in view of the arbitrator's relationship to the case cannot be construed to mean that there should be no objective basis giving rise to disqualification, . This wording, 'reasons to doubt', must be interpreted in close relation to the term *'...legitimate doubts...'*, and cannot be taken to mean anything other than *reasonable* doubts. These are doubts based on objective facts that are not just of a marginal nature. Therefore, the circumstances disqualifying arbitrators must be not only 'objective' but also 'reasonably evident,' and not 'merely speculative.' These circumstances must be assessed from the perspective of a 'neutral person' qualified as an acceptable expert to a general degree who is not involved in the proceedings. In principle, a subjective evaluation of this relationship

---

[8] Marián Šťastný, *Nestrannost rozhodce jmenovaného stranou* [*Impartiality of an Arbitrator Appointed by a Party*], (99) PRÁVNÍ ZPRAVODAJ ČESKOSLOVENSKÉHO ZAHRANIČNÍHO OBCHODU 87 (1961).

from the point of view of a person who might possibly object to the disqualification of an arbitrator is irrelevant. If the subjective perspective of a person entitled to challenge an arbitrator were to be accepted as relevant, practices aimed at frustrating the purpose of arbitration, a typically obstructive approach, would be given free rein. Therefore, there must always be a mechanism whereby a binding evaluation is carried out by an independent, neutral, third person wielding a high degree of credibility.

3.22. In areas related to the constitution of arbitral tribunals, including the conditions to be met by an arbitrator, rules on judicial proceedings, i.e. court litigation, are inapplicable. Provisions on the disqualification of a judge in civil court proceedings are even less relevant, despite the fact that certain common denominators could be found, including abstract evaluation criteria. In addition, in arbitration the constitutional principle of a *lawful judge*, which dominates civil court proceedings, gives way to the principle of the independence of the selected arbitrator. Independence, i.e. objective impartiality, should be regarded as the notional *flip side* of the principle of *lack of bias*, where independent expresses objective status, while *lack of bias* expresses the need for maximum neutrality in connection with the arbitrator's decision making on both procedural and substantive issues. Given the nature of arbitration proceedings, a prerequisite for the application of the principle of the equality of parties in arbitration, as well as the equality of parties in proceedings before a court in connection with the relevant constitutional principles, is that the proceedings are held and heard by an *unbiased* person who is not in a qualified personal relationship with the parties, their representatives or the case, and who therefore does not have an interest in the course and outcome of the proceedings.[9] In this respect, the need to assess the *lack of bias* (i.e. *objective impartiality*) from the aspect of objective criteria can be expressed as follows: any relationship to the case, the parties or their representatives is a certain indicator of possible disqualification or grounds for a challenge. To determine where there are grounds for disqualification, it is necessary to consider whether the arbitrator genuinely has an interest in the course and outcome of the proceedings or whether the risk is justified. Nor can it be suggested that the existence of a qualified connection is a rebuttable presumption of an interest in the course and outcome of the proceedings. Rather, it is an

---

[9] Cf. Pavel Vrcha, *Vyloučení soudce v civilním řízení* [*Disqualification of a Judge in Civil Proceedings*], (7) PRÁVNÍ RÁDCE 13, 13 (2004). The author also interprets the Resolution of the Supreme Court No 26 Cdo 2120/2002 of 20 December 2002 here.

indicator that should prompt a qualified evaluation of both the arbitrator and the parties as to whether there is an interest in the course and outcome of the proceedings or whether the risk of such an interest might, at least, be underestimated.

3.23. Potential bias, or the absence of objective independence (also called objective impartiality.) should always be viewed in conjunction with specific circumstances. Examples of this lack of objective impartiality or objective independence are where the appointed arbitrator is a person who is or was a member of the governing or other body of a participant in the proceedings, a bankruptcy administrator, legal representative or agent designated to represent a party, regardless of whether the subject of such an agency relationship is an issue or range of operations in any way related to the subject of the dispute in arbitration. The same applies to a person who is the legal representative or other agent of an entity – the owner of a business which has been transferred to a transferee other than a party or, conversely, whose transferee is now a party to the proceedings if the legal acts delegated to the appointed arbitrator in the past related to a business or part of a business now operated by a party.

3.24. The connection between the person appointed as an arbitrator and a party, whether directly or via a procedural counsel, must also be understood in its historical context and in the scope of activities that the appointed arbitrator could have carried out for the party in the past. This aspect is particularly important in domestic arbitration in disputes, where it should be borne in mind that many countries have just a limited community of subject matter experts. In this light, the arbitrator's independence needs to be judged according to the specific circumstances. Recent legal representation need not result in a lack of objective impartiality on the part of the arbitrator. This is especially so if, in the meantime, there has been a significant transformation in the ownership structure of a participant, accompanied by a fundamental change in the composition of the bodies of such an entity, or if only isolated or minor consultancy has been provided in the form of an opinion on a particular legal problem. Legal representation in other cases more distant in time, even if provided only once, could result in links of such closeness with the party that the arbitrator is disqualified. The disqualification of an arbitrator is evidently rarely precipitated by their association with a party if they have acted *ad hoc* for the party as an interpreter or expert, as in these cases an interpreter or expert is also required to act impartially at all times. By contrast, as with legal advisers or representatives under similar conditions activity as a tax adviser will result in incompatibility with the office of arbitrator. The disqualification of an auditor, who is also required to act impartially in the performance of their duties, is questionable. Auditors are not likely to be disqualified, for example, if they took on a one-off commission and were not in a long-standing professional and business relationship with the participant; the time factor must be taken into consideration when assessing such a relationship. Nevertheless, the prevailing view of auditors is that, at least from an ethical point of view, they should decline the office of arbitrator to be appointed by a party for whom they have worked in the past in the pursuit of their core business.

3.25. Some international standards, particularly IBA standards allow, under certain circumstances, the office of arbitrator to be accepted even if the person in question has previously provided legal advice, albeit recently, or has some form of professional association with persons providing legal advice to a party to arbitration, provided that the financial benefit from such advice, directly or indirectly, was of no *significant* material gain to the arbitrator. Even in cases where these standards are applied, the party seeking the disqualification of an arbitrator must at least claim, if not testify, that there has been such a material gain.

3.26. Such evaluation criteria can hardly be adopted in domestic practice of many countries. there are serious questions on the general applicability of the IBA standards. As with many other standards, the IBA standards are manifestly inappropriate for domestic proceedings, or even proceedings in a *civil setting*. These are standards created under the significant influence of common law, and, in particular, they are generally structured for application on a more global scale. It is no secret that these standards are heavily influenced by the actions and practices of larger global networks specializing in legal services. This is not intended to reflect in a negative manner on such corporate or professional groupings and their significance for legal practice. However, these standards are often conceived under the fact that 'thousands' of professional advisers the world over are involved in these groupings, with interrelations sometimes only latent in terms of the ability to influence the objective independence of the arbitrator. The same applies to the importance of material gain, which is often evaluated in terms of the overall turnover of these groups. These standards are unacceptable in the domestic environment, irrespective of whether a case concerns a domestic or international dispute. While under certain circumstances, these standards can play a supporting role, their direct application is, at worst, often entirely impossible and, at best, very problematic in a domestic environment. Moreover, IBA standards play a rather minor role, for example, in most countries of the Central and Eastern European *area*. In most cases, the criteria of objective independence or objective impartiality therefore need to be adapted to the specific dispute, the sphere of influence of the parties, etc. Nevertheless, the applicability of the criteria in a domestic environment of many countries can certainly hold significance for considerations such as time aspects. It is quite logical that the greater the time lag between the moment linking a certain situation between the arbitrator and the subject of the dispute, the parties or their legal representatives on the one hand and the initiation of arbitration on the other hand, the lower the risk of the arbitrator's *objective dependence* or *bias* in the course and outcome of the dispute. Since the laws and rules applicable to arbitration do not and cannot lay down any time limit, it is always necessary to adopt individual evaluation criteria. This is also confirmed by what has been stressed above, namely that the very existence of facts hinting at a link between the arbitrator and the subject of the dispute, the parties or their legal representatives is not in itself sufficient reason to disqualify an arbitrator, unless it is possible to objectively conclude that there is a high level of risk to the arbitrator's impartiality or objective independence in the process of deciding on a specific dispute. Evaluation criteria clearly include the subject and, in fact, all the circumstances of a particular dispute in which the disqualification of an arbitrator is under consideration.

3.27.   In principle, an arbitrator who has already contributed to decision making as a member of the arbitral tribunal, regardless of whether the proceedings were *ad hoc* or held before a permanent arbitral institution, in a dispute where the identity of the parties has been partly or fully disclosed is not disqualified, even if the legal or factual basis of that dispute was similar or identical to the present case.[10] It is becoming more common, particularly in international practice, for arbitrators to disclose these facts to the parties and, at the very least, to let the parties conduct their own evaluation of these facts. This is particularly the case when, due to the frequent appointment of the same arbitrator by the same party, qualified doubts may arise as to the arbitrator's interest in the outcome of the dispute for the benefit of such party in view of existing material gain for the arbitrator in the form of a fee. Essentially this case needs to be distinguished from objective circumstances forming a certain qualified link with the subject of the dispute, the parties or their legal representatives, where the objective possibility of such an interest in the outcome of the dispute might be anticipated to

---

[10]   This is entirely consistent with international practices as represented by the ICC. See, for example, Dominique Hascher, *ICC practise in relation to the appointment, confirmation, challenge and replacement of arbitrators*, 6(2) ICC BULLETIN 4, 10 (1995).

some degree. On the other hand, if an arbitrator has previously or repeatedly been appointed by the same party, although this risk is generally smaller, it is still recommended, as a matter of principle, that the arbitrator discloses this fact. This case clearly demonstrates how international views on the approach to assessing the disqualification of arbitrators are developing. Whereas just ten or fifteen years ago the possibility of an arbitrator's vested interest and thus their disqualification was rarely mentioned and the importance of this aspect was suppressed, only a relatively short time later it has become viewed, to some extent, as an international standard at least as regards the arbitrator's obligation to ensure the reasonable disclosure of such circumstances. Clearly, this is also a manifestation of the growing importance of arbitration, although the increasing interest and the growing support for this dispute resolution method nationally and internationally has not been matched, at least in terms of certain yardsticks used to assess direct correlation by the expanding group of persons acting as *frequently appointed arbitrators*.

3.28.   In contrast, an arbitrator's lack of objective independence cannot be deduced from a legal opinion which the arbitrator held in another dispute, even where the dispute arose between the same parties, the dispute had the same basis or from a legal opinion held by the arbitrator or a person nominated as arbitrator in connection with the exercise of their profession, in writings, etc. It is up to the parties, indeed, it is a responsibility required and expected of the parties, to screen the professional views maintained by a *candidate* for the office of arbitrator and, accordingly, to consider whether to appoint such a person. It would be illogical to expect a party to nominate someone who holds a different or even opposite view on fundamental legal issues associated with the subject of a dispute with the opinion the party intends to promote in the proceedings. It could even be said that significant attention is paid to the selection of the arbitrator in international arbitration practice, but unfortunately this is still less than is currently the case in the domestic environment. The extent to which an arbitrator may, for example, be contacted by the parties prior to their appointment is questionable. There is no uniform view on this matter, and no theoretical construct can provide an answer. Opinions on this issue vary significantly, depending on customary practices, particularly from a geographical and, to some extent, sectoral aspect. Professional practice and theory in many countries have yet to take up a clear stance on this issue. The establishment of a platform trying to create a standard may not be beneficial in this case. Nevertheless, the fundamental issue of whether to hold such indicative interviews with prospective arbitrators should be viewed in a positive light, provided that such contact is used solely to gauge the candidate arbitrator's opinions in a particular dispute and if such direct contact serves this purpose alone. This approach entails not only the screening of the opinion held by the person to be nominated on the subject of the dispute from a legal point of view without the need to acquaint them with the particular circumstances of the dispute in a rather highly abstract form, but it also identifies this person's flexibility and ability to devote themself to the case adequately in real time. The approach where the arbitrator is recompensed for consultation with the reimbursement of cash expenses incurred in the provision of such consultation is not contrary to the principle of impartiality either. A *candidate* may be asked to attend an interview in a place other than their seat or domicile, or even abroad. The provision of such compensation, however, must not be tied to this person's decision on whether to accept the nomination, much less to the outcome of future proceedings, or more specifically that person's decision in a particular dispute in arbitration proceedings. The same opinion on this highly sensitive issue is currently also held by the ICC International Court of Arbitration, as well as other permanent arbitral institutions and international experts in general. At the same time, the view is often voiced that contact may be necessary in specific cases to ensure that the parties have the opportunity to choose the proper arbitrator and to determine whether they are suitable and fit for office.[11] However, in the proceedings the arbitrator must avoid contact with the party or their legal representative where the purpose would be to discuss issues or procedures in connection with the proceedings. On the other hand, a situation where an arbitrator who is by profession a lawyer or tax adviser and, in entirely different working matters unrelated to the arbitration, is engaged in work for the procedural counsel of any party to arbitration proceedings in which they are an arbitrator cannot be regarded as contrary to the principle of an arbitrator's objective independence. These cases will actually be very common, provided that the professional consultant does not operate on the same corporate or similar platform as the arbitrator. In other words, this contact should not be corporate or otherwise formalized so that the professional consultant's material gains also have, directly or indirectly, but always in a legally relevant form, an impact on the arbitrator's personal sphere.

---

[11] Dominique Hascher, *supra* note 10, at 7–8, par. A.4. Likewise, Martin Hunter, *Ethics of the International Arbitrator* (53) ARBITRATION 219 (1987).

3.29. As a matter of principle, chance encounters and conversations between the arbitrator and the parties on social occasions are not a manifestation of a lack of objective independence if the arbitrator and the party or procedural counsel are in 'amicable' or close professional contact. Nevertheless, within the scope of proceedings, especially at hearings and when evidence is taken, arbitrators should avoid manifesting such relations or should reduce them to a level not exceeding normal social contact. If an arbitrator and procedural counsel belong, within a professional capacity, to a professional organization organized on a clear basis stemming from generally binding legal norms, such as a bar association, chambers of other professional consultants, other professional associations, etc., or even work at the same workplace, for example, at an educational and scientific center, in which respect the arbitrator is not usually in a position to perceive the proceedings and outcome of the dispute as an advantage or disadvantage, this is not regarded as an obstacle either. Naturally, under these circumstances, the arbitrator's conduct must guarantee objective and, in this case, subjective impartiality, they must not inform their 'colleagues', the procedural counsel of a party, of the tribunal's considerations discussed at tribunal sessions, and must not discuss the subject of the dispute or the course of the proceedings in any other way. A situation where, on the initiation of a hearing, the arbitrators do not check the identity of the procedural counsel of any of the parties who is known to them from their professional activities or other proceedings is not regarded as a lack of objective impartiality either, provided that they make reference to such professional acquaintance. This procedure is also in full compliance with such rules, according to which arbitrators are required, among other things, to conduct the proceedings without undue formalities.

II.3. Correlation between Objective and Subjective Impartiality and Bias

3.30. It should be emphasized that most laws and rules applicable to arbitration govern the *lack of bias* of an arbitrator only. The term *lack of bias* should be distinguished from *impartiality*, which is not the subject of explicit regulations, but is merely ventured as a principle. Whereas a *lack of bias* is pursued primarily by the mechanisms under the laws and rules applicable to arbitration, mechanisms for impartiality do not exist. The difference between the two concepts – *lack of bias* and *impartiality* – is significant and comprises the existence of objective facts which may form the basis for disqualification. At the same time, it is worth stressing that an approach by the arbitrator that lacks impartiality is frequently a consequence of bias. Any *bias* is based on the existence of certain objective and qualified facts due to which impartiality, to a certain degree of probability, can be envisaged without the arbitrator's approach actually being impartial. An objectively disqualified, i.e. *biased* arbitrator may not approach the hearing and adjudication of the dispute in a manner 'favouring' one of the parties in a way that is inconsistent with the results of adversary proceedings in terms of objective evaluation criteria on the merits. Nevertheless, their *bias*, i.e. qualified relationship with the case, establishes such a level of risk that they will lack impartiality, so it is necessary to disqualify that arbitrator. In contrast, the absence of impartiality may be based purely on subjective reasons on the part of the arbitrator, simply because they are unable to evaluate the case objectively. An absence of impartiality without the objective existence of reasons for *bias* is difficult to identify and is usually a matter of responsibility for each arbitrator and their professional approach. Indeed, if the arbitrator concludes that they are unable to evaluate a case objectively despite the fact that there are no circumstances which are indicative of and result in their disqualification, they must refuse the appointment, even if such a conclusion is not reached until the case is being heard. The absence of impartiality, even if it is essentially unidentifiable by means of objective evaluation criteria, based on a qualified and objectively ascertainable relationship with the merits, the parties or their legal representatives, means that eligibility to act as an arbitrator does not exist. Although impartiality is not explicitly formulated as a condition of eligibility to act as an arbitrator under the relevant laws and rules applicable to arbitration, this conclusion must be made in view of the principle that arbitration is a dispute resolution mechanism consisting in a decision making process by an impartial person independent of the parties.

3.31. The relationship between the 'lack of *bias*' and *impartiality* can be presented in the following example, which serves as a standard of sorts and is based on a specific arbitration case. In the case in question, the arbitral tribunal was duly constituted and no reasons were found to disqualify any of the arbitrators on grounds of *bias*. There was, therefore, no qualified relationship with the case, the parties or their procedural counsel, and the hearing of the dispute was initiated. Only in the course of the hearing were separate proceedings initiated before the arbitral tribunal on the basis of a separate request, which concerned another claim within the scope of the same factual and legal situation where the parties were the same but in the opposite procedural position. In this 'second case' the same arbitrators were appointed by the parties. In the constitution of the arbitral tribunal in the latter dispute, however, there was a fundamental error in procedure by which one of the arbitrators was effectively excluded from the possibility of influencing the choice of the chair of the tribunal. The reasons for the defect were not ascertained, and thus it must be assumed that this defect was independent of the arbitrators and caused by the administrative procedure. As soon as the arbitrator who was restricted in the process of selecting the chair learned of this fact, he concluded that the defect rendered him unable to consider the case objectively and in the second dispute did not accept his appointment. At the same time, however, he considered the circumstances to be of such a serious nature that he would be unable to objectively evaluate the outcome of the case in the previously commenced proceedings. Accordingly, he also resigned as arbitrator in the previously initiated arbitration. Subsequently, however, the chair of the tribunal chosen by the arbitrators in the first dispute resigned for the same reasons, because, after learning of the procedural defects, he came to the same conclusion as that member of the tribunal, i.e. that he had lost the ability to consider the case objectively. Yet, as mentioned above, circumstances constituting a basis for disqualification on grounds of bias were not established for either of the arbitrators, nor was either of them ever challenged by the parties.

3.32. Naturally, the question arises as to whether the absence of impartiality can be perceived as a reason for the annulment of an arbitral award under the laws applicable to a particular arbitration. Precisely because, in reality, the absence of impartiality renders a person unfit to act as an arbitrator, there is essentially no way of objectively assessing the impartiality of an arbitrator in cases other than if *bias* i.e. objective impartiality is also established. Impartiality is a highly subjective category. I In relation to *bias*, it might be said that *bias* establishes the risk of an absence of impartiality, and, for preventive reasons, the arbitrator is disqualified in the event of *bias*. Nevertheless, the arbitrator may side with either party in the absence of objective reasons establishing *bias* i.e. subjective impartiality. It should be noted that each evaluation in adversary proceedings contains a certain degree of subjectivity, as is the case in ordinary courts or other bodies endowed with powers to adjudicate disputes. In arbitration, however, this risk is greater than in proceedings before public authorities since, in arbitration the principle of a lawful court 'appointed' or 'designated' independently of the will of the parties is suspended, while the 'appointment' of an arbitrator is a manifestation of the free will of the parties. Therefore, more stringent criteria are placed on the arbitrator in assessing whether they are genuinely able to act impartially. The degree of *subjectivity* inherent in any evaluation in proceedings of this type exceeds the generally acceptable limit for *subjective impartiality* i.e. the absence thereof, so ultimately the evaluation rests solely with the person concerned, in other words the arbitrator.

3.33. Although, in principle, there is no mechanism to perceive the absence of subjective impartiality, the laws and rules applicable to arbitration do foresee a certain degree of protection of the parties. The absence of subjective impartiality may also, exceptionally, be manifested in such a manner that a party is deprived of the opportunity to have a case heard in arbitration. The risk of such a situation occurring is naturally much greater in cases where a sole arbitrator hears and adjudicates a case, because, presumably, tribunal decision making also incorporates 'self-regulating' mechanisms to prevent such a situation from occurring within a tribunal. Grounds for the annulment of an arbitral award under the laws applicable to arbitration cannot rely on subjective reasons, and usually it is, in fact, impossible to determine whether such action has been influenced by differences in the opinion of the tribunal and the opinion of the ordinary court which is ruling on whether to set aside the award as regards the correct procedure in the case. In principle, however, a procedural defect could be caused by the absence of subjective impartiality on the part of the *arbitral forum*. This may well be probable in some cases, but is effectively impossible to confirm objectively. Likewise, a court's conclusion on the existence of grounds to annul an arbitral award must ultimately be based on objective circumstances, and any conclusion about the absence of subjective impartiality would obviously be speculative. Grounds for the annulment of an award, however, reflect such fundamental fluctuations in correct procedure that, in most cases, these grounds and their assessment by an independent ordinary court could actually eliminate the absence of the *arbitral forum's* subjective impartiality.

III. Three-Stage Evaluation of Impartiality

3.34. The rules and laws applicable to arbitration are based on the premise of a 'three-stage evaluation' of circumstances that could give rise to doubts potentially resulting in the disqualification of the arbitrator.

3.35. The 'first stage' rests with the arbitrator, who is obliged to explore the existence of any such circumstances. If they conclude that such circumstances do exist, there are two possible scenarios. First, the arbitrator may conclude that they are disqualified, i.e. that they have an objective connection with the dispute, its subject, parties or legal representatives. In this case, they are unable to accept the appointment as they are not fit to act as an arbitrator. The assessment of disqualification is therefore terminated at this 'notional' first stage. Relevant circumstances may only emerge after the appointment or at any time during the proceedings. Theoretically, then, these circumstances may occur at any time up to the end of the proceedings. However, circumstances may arise which, in general, could be grounds for disqualification, but which the arbitrator, based on their own evaluation, does not consider to be a link so categorical or of such intensity that, in connection with the dispute in question, it could lead to disqualification. The assessment therefore proceeds to the 'notional' second stage.

3.36. The 'second stage' entails an assessment by the parties. While a subjective evaluation by the parties is not fundamentally critical, it may be significant. If all of the parties conclude that they are faced with a situation where the arbitrator is disqualified, this is undoubtedly a significant aspect that cannot be overlooked. Even if all of the parties deliver the same evaluation, the arbitrator may insist on their own evaluation, namely that their disqualification is not necessitated. Nevertheless, the arbitrator could consider resigning. This is because arbitration proceedings are typified by the fact that arbitrators are persons in whom the parties, or at least one of them, place a reasonable degree of confidence. If all of the parties believe there may be reasons to disqualify an arbitrator, this means that there are doubts as to whether conditions exist for the proceedings to meet their purpose and for the arbitrator to perform their duties properly. If the arbitrator does not enjoy the trust of any of the parties, it is doubtful, at the very least, whether they will be able to meet their duties. Moreover, if the parties unanimously express their objections or challenges regarding an arbitrator, presumably the parties will be able to reach an agreement at least on the procedure for the appointment of another arbitrator. More commonly, however, a conclusion that grounds for disqualification exist is made by only one of the parties. In this case, the arbitrator again has the option either of 'reconsidering' their own conclusion, or, considering their resignation. Such a procedure, however, cannot be enforced, and, moreover, it is impossible to rely on an objective evaluation by a party when the conclusion about disqualification is usually in respect of arbitrators appointed directly by a party made by the party which did not appoint a particular arbitrator.[12] A subjective

---

[12] In practice, there are also exceptional cases where the party which appointed the arbitrator challenges the arbitrator if newly identified circumstances come to light. There is at

evaluation, in particular by the parties to the dispute, is not fundamentally crucial. It is therefore necessary for a 'third person' to provide an independent evaluation of whether such reasons have materialized, i.e. (as mentioned above) a person enjoying general confidence and wielding a guarantee of expertise.

3.37. The 'third stage' of the evaluation of an arbitrator's disqualification is essentially entrusted to a permanent arbitral institution or to a court in *ad-hoc* arbitrations in replacement procedures or in proceedings for the annulment of an arbitral decision. A mechanism against misuse of this procedure is also provided by setting limits for challenging arbitrators at the first possible opportunity. The mechanism for assessing the reasons for the disqualification of an arbitrator is rather fragmented over various provisions of the laws and rules applicable to arbitration. In any case, the conclusion necessarily drawn from this multi-stage procedure is that a subjective evaluation of these reasons from the perspective of a party is not fundamentally crucial, and therefore aspects of objectivity and justification need to be applied.

3.38. A further control mechanism of sorts can usually also be found between the second and third stage. This is an assessment of the reasons for disqualification by the arbitral tribunal itself, provided that the challenge is not directed at a majority of the members of the arbitral tribunal. In this case, as a matter of principle, discretion is available to the autonomous arbitral tribunal, or more specifically those tribunal members that have not been challenged, to decide on whether the challenges are justified or to assess those challenges as to qualify the circumstances that could support disqualification. This procedure must essentially be used in *ad hoc* proceedings; much like the corresponding mechanisms, they usually contain standards established by the rules of permanent arbitral institutions. If a mechanism is not binding, it at least provides an opportunity for the 'other' arbitrators to express their views on the situation. Their evaluation is significant, because it provides a notional counterweight to the evaluation of the party seeking the disqualification of an arbitrator. This is because the other arbitrators are in a position to assess the situation from a perspective different from that of the party making the challenge, and presumably they enjoy the sufficient confidence of the parties. The opportunity to carry out such an evaluation, either binding to a certain degree or entirely non-binding, must be given, irrespective of the fact that laws

least one recorded and documented case in domestic practice where a party challenged the entire arbitral tribunal, including the arbitrator they had appointed. See the case heard by the District Court for Prague 5 under Judgment No 10 C 263/2010 of 20 October 2003, upheld by Judgment No 18 Co 18/2004 of 2 April 2004 of the Municipal Court in Prague.

and rules applicable to arbitration do not expressly provide for this 'intermediate stage', as it is a widely accepted standard in arbitration. Even if an opinion delivered by the other arbitrators is not binding in a particular dispute, the conclusion they reach on whether the challenged arbitrator should be disqualified could have important ramifications for further procedures. Indeed, if they conclude that a challenged arbitrator should be disqualified and the arbitrator does not confirm that disqualification as a result of that evaluation, the other unchallenged arbitrators may resign. The arbitrators should ensure at all times that the arbitration proceedings are not affected by a defect which could prompt the annulment of a future award. A conclusion by the other arbitrators that one of the members of the arbitral tribunal is to be disqualified from hearing the case establishes a reasonable risk that the future award will be affected by a defect constituting grounds for annulment. This situation, in principle, can only be resolved by the challenged arbitrator's confirmation of their disqualification or by the resignation of the arbitrators who had decided on the disqualification. Furthermore, such a move, i.e. resignation, is also possible if one of the other arbitrators alone, without the support of another member of the tribunal to form a majority opinion, concludes that the challenged arbitrator should be disqualified. This approach, moreover, is not unusual, at least in international practice. It even occasionally appears – unfortunately rather rarely – in domestic practice, especially among arbitrators with active experience of hearing international cases, where high demands are placed on an arbitrator's lack of bias.

3.39.   The reasons for the possible disqualification of an arbitrator pursuant to the particular laws and rules applicable to arbitration usually need to be interpreted as the arbitrator's specific dependence on the course and outcome of the dispute, where the arbitrator could consider a particular outcome to be to their advantage or to the advantage of a relative or entities with associated personnel and assets. This should be a substantial and, essentially, the only aspect in the final binding assessment of whether an arbitrator is to be disqualified. The importance of the criteria for *independent arbitrators* cannot be assessed other than as a factor indicative of a certain degree of probability. Should any of the parties challenge an arbitrator, it is fundamentally necessary, in all cases, for such dependence to be specified and not remain a mere theoretical construct. On the one hand, it is therefore necessary to ensure objective impartiality in the hearing and adjudication of the dispute. On the other hand, with regard to the disqualification of an arbitrator, this procedure must not provide an opportunity for a party simply to cause delays in proceedings by means of entirely or at least manifestly groundless or otherwise unsubstantiated challenges to an arbitrator based solely on assumptions about potential or even indirect dependence on the outcome of the dispute. Unfortunately, this is nothing exceptional. It is by no means unusual for a party to exploit this procedure to pave the way for arguments that it will use in proceedings seeking the annulment of the arbitral award in case it loses the dispute. It is unacceptable to admit such an approach, which would be an abuse of the law. As such, this procedure is taken to be contrary to the fundamental principles of civil adversary proceedings in general.[13]

3.40. A number of arbitration centers or permanent arbitral institutions have a practice for arbitrators, before their instatement, to prepare and sign a statement of their independence. In the statement they are also required to specify all reservations about their impartiality and circumstances that could compromise their impartiality or that the parties could consider a violation of the principle of impartiality. This procedure is regarded as standard; such a statement is usually associated with the written acceptance of the office of arbitrator. The growing importance attached to the arbitrator's own statement is also evidenced by the fact that under the 1955 ICC Rules arbitrators were not required to make such a statement, under the 1975 ICC Rules only the chair of the tribunal was required to make such a statement and in 1980 this obligation was extended to sole arbitrators. Only the 1988 ICC Rules impose the requirement of such a statement for all arbitrators.[14] Naturally, the 2012 ICC Rules pursue this practice in conjunction with now quite sophisticated procedures regarding the evaluation of arbitrators' reservations and statements. In the statement, the arbitrator makes a declaration of impartiality, expressing the arbitrator's internal relationship to the parties and the subject of the dispute, and provides a self-evaluation of the situation and any circumstances that might call their independence into question. Today, this is a general domestic and international standard. Moreover, it should be highlighted that a number of permanent international arbitral institutions in international cases require a qualified statement from arbitrators that they have sufficient capacity, especially time, to devote themselves properly to the case while meeting the parties' expectations of a flexible approach. Such statements indicate an attempt to maximize professional interest in guarantees of a high

---

[13] Dominique Hascher, *supra* note 10, at 9, para. B.3.iv.

[14] Jean-Jacques Arnaldez & Ebun Jakande, *Les amendements apportés au Règlement d'arbitrage de la CCI*, (1) REVUE ARBITRAGE 67 (1988).

standard of arbitration which is accommodating to all parties. Accordingly, some permanent arbitral institutions reserve the right of individual confirmation of a particular arbitrator to proceedings. This is the case, for example, in relation to all arbitrators in ICC Court proceedings or at the Chamber of Arbitration at the Chamber of Commerce of Milan, Italy and newly also the Vienna International Arbitral Center in its Rules effective as of 1 July 2013. A number of permanent arbitral institutions that have preserved the practice of lists of arbitrators also acknowledge the appointment of persons outside those lists, at least in relation to persons who are not entered in such lists and allow for the appointment of a sole arbitrator or for the choice of the chair of the tribunal solely from these lists of arbitrators, etc.

| | |

Summaries

FRA [*L'impartialité subjective et objective des arbitres et de leurs mandataires (appointing authority) en tant qu'élément d'ordre public dans la procédure d'arbitrage*]

Le choix et la désignation des arbitres est un problème essentiel de la procédure d'arbitrage. Les réglementations et les règles utilisées dans la procédure d'arbitrage ne fixent généralement aucune condition pour le choix des arbitres en dehors d'une aptitude comme par exemple un âge minimal et en dehors de conditions d'indépendance et d'impartialité. Les parties peuvent convenir de conditions sur le choix des arbitres dans le contrat d'arbitrage, ce contrat étant exclusivement une expression autonome des parties dans le cadre réglementaire fixé par le lex arbitri. Les parties doivent respecter les conditions d'indépendance et d'impartialité. Tout mandant des arbitres (appointing authority) doit être également indépendant. Bien que ce principe ne soit pas expressément fixé dans les règlements et les règles utilisées dans les procédures d'arbitrage, il s'agit d'un principe propre à la procédure d'arbitrage qui traduit le principe d'égalité des parties, qu'il est nécessaire de considérer comme un élément d'ordre public dans la procédure d'arbitrage. Les arbitres se comportent toujours comme n'ayant aucun intérêt dans le litige, dans son déroulement comme dans sa résolution. Cependant, les circonstances pouvant disqualifier un arbitre doivent être non seulement objectives mais aussi suffisamment flagrantes et ne peuvent être uniquement spéculatives. L'impartialité est une catégorie hautement subjective et l'on peut dire, en cas de préjudice, que le préjudice crée un risque d'absence d'impartialité.

CZE [*Subjektivní a objektivní nestrannost rozhodců a osob pověřených jmenováním rozhodců (appointing authority) jako součást procesního veřejného pořádku (ordre public) v rozhodčím řízení*]
Výběr a jmenování rozhodců je zásadní otázkou rozhodčího řízení. Předpisy a pravidla použitelná na rozhodčí řízení obvykle nestanoví zvláštní požadavky na rozhodce, s výjimkou způsobilosti jako například minimální věk a s výjimkou požadavků na nezávislost a nestrannost. Strany se mohou dohodnout na požadavcích kladených na rozhodce v rozhodčí smlouvě; rozhodčí smlouva je výlučně projevem autonomie stran v rámci omezení stanovených v lex arbitri. Strany však musí respektovat požadavky nezávislosti a nestrannosti. Na stranách nezávislá musí být rovněž třetí osoba pověřená jmenováním rozhodců (appointing authority). Ačkoliv tento princip není výslovně stanoven v předpisech a pravidlech použitelných na rozhodčí řízení, jde o princip vlastní rozhodčímu řízení a je projevem zásady rovnosti stran, kterou je nutno považovat za součást procesního veřejného pořádku v rozhodčím řízení. Rozhodci vždy jednají jako osoby, které nemají zájem na průběhu a výsledku sporu. Okolnosti diskvalifikující rozhodce však musí být nejen objektivní, nýbrž musí být přiměřeně zjevné a nesmí být pouze spekulativní. Nestrannost je vysoce subjektivní kategorie a, ve vztahu k podjatosti, lze říci, že podjatost vytváří riziko nedostatku nestrannosti.

| | |

POL [*Subiektywna i obiektywna bezstronność arbitrów i osób upoważnionych do wyznaczania arbitrów (appointing authority) jako element procesowego porządku publicznego (ordre public) w postępowaniu arbitrażowym*]
Strony mogą uzgodnić warunki dla arbitra, jednak nie mogę zrezygnować z warunku, jakim jest jego bezstronność i niezawisłość. Również osoba upoważniona do mianowania arbitrów (appointing authority) musi być niezależna i bezstronna. Bezstronność i niezawisłość arbitrów stanowi element procesowego porządku publicznego (ordre public). Należy przy tym rozróżnić bezstronność obiektywną i subiektywną, bowiem są to kategorie ściśle ze sobą powiązane.

DEU [*Subjektive und objektive Unparteilichkeit von Schiedsrichtern und von Personen, die mit der Ernennung von Schiedsrichtern betraut sind, als Bestandteil der prozessrechtlichen öffentlichen Ordnung (ordre public) im Schiedsverfahren*]
Die Parteien können vereinbaren, welche Anforderungen an den Schiedsrichter zu stellen sind – die Forderung nach dessen

Unparteilichkeit (Unbefangenheit) und Unabhängigkeit kann aber nicht abbedungen werden. Auch ein etwaiger Dritter, der mit der Ernennung des eigentlichen Schiedsrichters betraut wurde (appointing authority), muss unabhängig und unparteilich sein. Die Unparteilichkeit und Unabhängigkeit der Schiedsrichter ist integraler Bestandteil der prozessrechtlichen öffentlichen Ordnung (ordre public). Zu unterscheiden ist zwischen der objektiven und subjektiven Unparteilichkeit (wobei es sich freilich um eng verwandte Kategorien handelt).

RUS   [*Субъективная и объективная беспристрастность арбитров и лиц, ответственных за назначение арбитров (appointing authority), как составная часть процессуального публичного порядка (ordre public) в арбитраже*]

Стороны могут договориться относительно требований, предъявляемых к арбитру, однако, не могут отказаться от требования относительно их беспристрастности и независимости. Независимой и беспристрастной также должна быть третья сторона, ответственная за назначение арбитров (appointing authority). Беспристрастность и независимость арбитров является составной частью процессуального публичного порядка (ordre public). Необходимо различать объективную и субъективную беспристрастность, хотя эти категории тесно взаимосвязаны.

ESP   [*La imparcialidad subjetiva y objetiva de los árbitros y de los responsables de la designación de los árbitros (appointing authority) como parte integrante del orden público procesal (ordre public) en el procedimiento de arbitraje*]

Las partes podrán acordar requisitos aplicables al árbitro, pero no pueden renunciar al requisito de su imparcialidad e independencia. Además, debe ser independiente e imparcial también la tercera parte que es responsable de la designación de los árbitros (appointing authority). La imparcialidad e independencia de los árbitros es parte del orden público procesal (ordre public). Es ineludible distinguir entre la imparcialidad objetiva y subjetiva, incluso cuando se trata de unas categorías estrechamente interrelacionadas.

| | |

Ivaylo Dermendjiev

Does EU Law Impact an Arbitrator's Independence and Impartiality?

Key words:
Annulment procedure |
Applicable law |
Arbitration | Arbitration
award | Arbitrator |
Consumer | Enforceability |
Enforcement | EU law |
Impartiality |
Implementation |
Independence |
Interpretation | Mandatory
rules | National courts |
National law | Non-
recognition |Ordre public |
Preliminary ruling |
Principle of efficiency |
Principle of equivalence |
Principle of legal certainty |
Arbitration proceedings |
Public policy rules | Res
judicata principle |
Revocation | Submission
agreement

Abstract | The discussion stretches over the full range of arbitration matters from the autonomy of arbitration, the recognition of the arbitral award as mandatory by the parties, to the acknowledgment and enforcement of the arbitral award in one or more Member States. The article raises the question of whether the arbitral tribunal is a competent body worthy of the recognition and attention of the ECJ under article 234 TFEU. The analysis contains personal insights and opinions on the judgments in Nordsee,[1] Eco Swiss,[2] Mostaza Claro[3] and Fallimento Olimpiclub,[4] which are of fundamental significance and are building blocks on the subject. The application of the equality principle between the national criteria for annulment of an arbitral award is discussed due to the incompatibility with the mandatory legal rules of the EU or national law. Simultaneously, great attention is paid to the principles of effectiveness and legal certainty, which should be taken into consideration by arbitrators when reaching a decision. The question whether arbitral tribunals have a duty to apply EU law when the dispute is between equal parties and none of them makes reference to these legal

Ivaylo Dermendjiev is a lawyer with over 20 years of experience, founder and senior partner in the law firm *Simeonov and Dermendjiev Private Consult Ltd.* He is extremely specialized in arbitration and litigation, corporate and trade law, and administrative law and process. Ivaylo Dermendjiev is an arbitrator in CAS and LCIA, as well as in the Arbitration court of Bulgarian Chamber of

---

[1]   ECJ Judgment of 23 March 1982, C-102/81, *Nordsee Deutsche Hochseefischerei GmbH v Reederei Mond Hochseefischerei Nordstern AG & Co. KG and Reederei Friedrich Busse Hochseefischerei Nordstern AG & Co. KG* [1982] ECR I-1095.

[2]   ECJ Judgment of 1 June 1999, C-126/97, *Eco Swiss China Time Ltd v Benetton International NV* [1999] ECR I-3079.

[3]   ECJ Judgment of 26 October 2006, C-168/05, *Elisa María Mostaza Claro v Centro Móvil Milenium SL* [2006] ECR I-10421.

[4]   ECJ Judgment of 3 September 2009, Case C-2/08 *Amministrazione dell'Economia e delle Finanze and Agenzia delle Entrate v Fallimento Olimpiclub Srl* [2009] ECR I-07501.

norms is also carefully examined. The main findings lead to the conclusion that the duty imposed by the ECJ to apply provisions of EU Law and to prevent arbitration from being used to circumvent the application of public policy rules does not affect the independence and impartiality of the arbitrators. It is only necessary to recognize the EU law mandatory rules, which are the basis of the public policy, as obligatory and supranational.

Commerce and Industry. He has a Ph.D. in law. e-mail: office@ sd-legal.com

III

4.01. The answer to this question stretches over the full *scale* of arbitration matters. It begins with the autonomy of arbitration, which is perceived as a voluntary, out-of-court method of dispute resolution. The question continues through the judgment, which is reached by professionals appointed by the parties themselves, on an issue that cannot be otherwise settled. The parties agree to recognize the judgment as mandatory. It continues to the recognition and enforcement of the arbitral award in the territory of one or more Member States.

4.02. The arbitrators are chosen by the parties to resolve their dispute in the most flexible, fair and urgent way, acting on the arbitrator's discretion. The tendency, or more precisely, the *obligation,* to apply EU law, seems surprising enough in the light of the traditional approach to arbitration by both the arbitrators and the parties. The most popular discussions (in practice and in theory) concern the application of EU Law in regard to competition law rules, but in reality an arbitrator's duty to decide on the implementation of EU law principles spreads over all arbitral issues from any field. Therefore, this is currently a very delicate theme because the contemporary arbitration philosophy should find a balance between an arbitrator's autonomy (i.e. their independence and impartiality) and enforceability of the rendered arbitral awards. It is peculiar that even arbitrators outside the EU are willing to apply EU law rules. Nowadays, the role of arbitration increases with the intensity of contemporary economical and political changes and with the challenges posed by the reality of a European Union composed of different cultural, economic and legal environments. Those elements continue to play a significant role in the settlement of disputes.

4.03. Actually, the question of whether EU law should be applied by an arbitral award seems not to be disputable. The issue under discussion is how to find the balance between the parties' choice of applicable law, the arbitrator's inner conviction as to the fairness of the award and the admissibility and enforceability of the arbitral decision.

4.04. Under the rules of international law, of which EU law is also a part, contracting parties are free to choose the law to be applied in case of any dispute between them. The rules of that law bind the arbitrator's discretion in arbitration proceedings. At the same time, the parties expect to obtain a fair award, which could be recognized and enforced anywhere that the New York Convention rules are applicable. The arbitral award, which resolves the dispute between the parties in their interest but also in the interest of the EU legal environment, is grounded on the balance between these two points of the arbitration proceedings.

4.05. The benchmark of that balance is an award that answers to *public policy* requirements. Unfortunately, it is difficult to fix the content of each member state's public policy rules. Simultaneously, if the applicable law is different from the EU law, the task to establish correct criteria and rules becomes even harder. If the award is intended to be enforced outside the scope of EU law the arbitrator's public policy understanding should comply with the local requirements. But if the award would be enforced within the EU, the question of which public policy rules should be applied then arises. Should it be those of the law chosen by the contracting parties or should it be the EU law public policy rules applied *ex officio* by the arbitrator?

4.06. It looks like simple math – the correlation of the contracting applicable law to the enforceability of the award is equal to the *public policy rules,* which once considered by the arbitrator, answer both aspects of the requirement for an arbitral award. This, however, is very deceiving because the content of the *public policy* concept has as many meanings as there are contexts in which it is applied.

4.07. Generally, public policy rules get the label of 'mandatory rules' (rules allowing for no derogation). A more detailed definition within the context of international arbitration is the following:

4.08. Mandatory rules of law (lois de police in French) are defined as imperative provisions of law which must be applied to an international relationship irrespective of the law that governs that relationship; they are a matter of public policy (ordre public) and, moreover, reflect a public policy so commanding that they must be applied even if the general body of law to which they belong is not competent by application of the relevant conflicts-of-law rule.[5]

---

[5] Daniel Hochstrasser, *Choice of Law and 'Foreign' Mandatory Rules in International Arbitration,* 18 (5) J INT ARB 57, 67–68 (2001).

4.09. Obviously, public policy is recognized as a perfectly adequate tool to prevent gross violation of the basic legal principles in various fields of law – competition, consumer disputes, etc.

4.10. The contemporary understanding of the concept of public policy is not supported by the present position of the Court of European Union (former name European Court of Justice, hereby called ECJ), whose jurisprudence does not recognize the arbitrator as a competent body under art. 267 TFEU. It is expected that the arbitrator will settle a dispute by observing mandatory (either for a third party or generally, for the public interest) legislative provisions. Otherwise, it is accepted that the arbitral award might contravene relevant principles of *ordre public.* Those expectations are ungrounded because of the ECJ has a position not to accept preliminary rulings from arbitral tribunals and because the arbitrators cannot be thoroughly aware of the applicable mandatory rules. This is especially true when the governing law of the dispute pending before them is not the state law of a member state. It is true that both courts and arbitral tribunals act in the same realm, which is the 'administration of justice'. So, the position of the ECJ in *Nordsee*[6] could be confirmed. The ECJ states that arbitrators are merely private individuals and does not presume that an arbitral award may have such a direct and rapid impact on the European area that it is a necessity for the court to assist the arbitrators with the interpretation and enforcement of EU law. This view was reinstated in 1999 with the ECJ ruling *Eco Swiss* v *Benetton.*[7]

4.11. The ECJ comprehension of the nature of the arbitrator's role and powers leads to placing the burden of ensuring coherent application of EC rules on national judiciaries. This is in direct conflict with some of the main advantages of the arbitration procedure – obtaining a final award within a reasonable time frame and limiting the influence of a state's judiciary to a minimum. The existing options of posterior control in most national legislations– either at the enforcement stage or under their annulment procedure – do not substitute the advantage of the right to directly refer a question of law interpretation to the ECJ. By one side, the majority of arbitral award are not contested in court. Such awards form the arbitral jurisprudence and could be prerequisites for multiplying anti-EU law application. Certain arguments about how and why to avoid this result are discussed below.[8]

---

[6] Confirmed by judgments on cases C-125/04, *Guy Denuit and Betty Cordenier* v *Transorient – Mosaïque Voyages and Culture SA* [2005] R 2005-I-00923, art. 13.

[7] ECJ Judgment of 1 June 1999, *supra* note 2.

[8] A good example is the case *Fallimento Olimpiclub* (C-2/08), cited below.

4.12. Another argument for placing the responsibility of securing uniform application on national courts is the situation when enforcement takes place outside of the EU. Then the award could be considered enforceable but could contradict the EU public order award because in this particular case there is not a national court for the referral of any question under the article 267 TFEU procedure. At the same time, non-EU courts are not interested in keeping EU *ordre public*.

4.13. The option to control the arbitral award in the procedure of annulment could not be considered as the equivalent of the direct ECJ questioning. A good example for that is the *Eco Swiss* case.

4.14. The subject of the case and the proceedings before the preliminary ruling are well known. Benetton International and Eco Swiss concluded a licensing agreement for a period of eight years, under which Benetton granted Eco Swiss the right to manufacture watches and clocks bearing the words 'Benetton by Bulova'. The agreement restricted Eco Swiss from selling watches and clocks in Italy and Bulova could no longer do so outside Member States of the Community. The licensing agreement was subject to Netherlands law and all disputes or differences arising between the parties were to be settled by arbitration in conformity with the rules of the Netherlands Arbitration Institute.

4.15. During the arbitration proceedings neither the parties nor the arbitrators had raised the point about the applicability of Community law.

4.16. The proceedings concluded in a partial award, ordering Benetton to pay damages to Eco Swiss for breach of a licensing agreement and for the resulting damage, which they had suffered. When the parties failed to come to an agreement on the quantum of damages to be paid, the arbitrators made a final award.

4.17. Benetton applied to the respective Dutch courts of jurisdiction for annulment of the Partial Final Award and the Final Arbitral Award on the ground, *inter alia*, that those arbitral awards were contrary to public policy by virtue of the nullity of the licensing agreement under Article 85 of the Treaty. During the arbitration proceedings neither the parties nor the arbitrators had raised the point that the licensing agreement might be contrary to that provision. A number of decisions of various courts followed until the Hoge Raad referred five questions to the ECJ to which the Court gave answers in the following sense: the National Court which is hearing an application for annulment of an arbitral award should honour this application if it finds that the substance of the contested award is contrary to a rule of European law (in this case namely art. 81 EC) and if national law allows for annulment founded on failure to observe national rules of public policy.

4.18. In the response to the preliminary ruling questions, as well as in the reasoning on the *Eco Swiss* case, the leading criteria are the ones that the European legal order requires its Member States to implement in relation to the 'review' of arbitral awards: '*....in the interest of efficient arbitration proceedings that review of arbitration awards should be limited in scope and that annulment of or refusal to recognise an award should be possible only in exceptional circumstances*'.[9]

4.19. One of those criteria is the application of the *principle of equivalence*, the substance of which has already been referred to above: remedies for EC law should not be rendered impossible in practice or excessively difficult compared to those relating to similar domestic claims. In view of this specific situation (both in the *Eco Swiss* case and in more general terms concerning the Arbitration – EU Law relationship, the principle of equivalence is expressed in the commitment of the national courts to review and annul arbitral awards where there is a failure to comply with the mandatory provisions of EU law and provided that such a failure to comply with the regulations of domestic law is a ground for annulment of an arbitral award. (Paragraph 41 of C-126/97, *Eco Swiss*).

4.20. There is a natural connection between the principle of equivalence and the understanding by a court of the need for stability of arbitral awards. The principle of legal certainty, *res judicata*, is seen as a guarantee of legality and enforcement of national laws and regulations in relation to EU law.[10] In order to guarantee the stability of the law and legal relations, as well as for the sake of good administration of justice, it is necessary that court awards which have become final upon exhaustion of available remedies or after expiry of the remedial time limit should no longer be disputable.

4.21. The principle of legal certainty interacts with the principle of efficiency, which influences both the 'EU law – arbitration panel' relationship and the process of decision making in each particular case, whether it is under the jurisdiction of a national court or an arbitration body. A possible failure to apply the principle of effectiveness would lead to unlawful enforcement, which in turn would constitute a violation of the rules of public order. However, the discussion on this topic should not be overdone, insofar as any enforcement must be consistent with the

---

[9] ECJ Judgment of 1 June 1999, *supra* note 2, paragraph 35.

[10] Ibid., paragraph 46; ECJ Judgment of 30 September 2003, C-224/01, *Gerhard Köbler* v *Republik Österreich* [2003] R-I-10239, paragraph 38; ECJ Judgment (First Chamber) of 16 March 2006, C-234/04, *Rosmarie Kapferer* v *Schlank & Schick GmbH* [2006] R 2006 I-02585, art. 20; ECJ Judgment (Second Chamber) of 3 September 2009, C-2/08, *Amministrazione dell'Economia e delle Finanze and Agenzia delle entrate* v *Fallimento Olimpiclub Srl* [2009] I-07501, paragraph 22.

particularities of a case and the applicable domestic rules to it. As already mentioned several times, the ECJ's position is that it has no jurisdiction to interfere in the internal administration of justice. On the contrary, the ECJ has explicitly stated that it is the national judge, who is competent to assess the compatibility of national law with a provision of EU law.[11] The necessity to consider the specific factual environment when doing this assessment lies in the fact that the European legislator has provided a higher degree of protection for some participants in court proceedings. These are the weaker party, if we may consider any of the arguing parties as such, whose security is the responsibility of the law enforcement authority. The assessment is to be done, on the other hand, notwithstanding whether the party, in whose favour protection is provided, has requested it. The judicial authority is bound to refer to the mandatory rules of the legislature and ensure their implementation. Unlike the situation involving a weaker party in the proceedings (consumer), in situations where both parties are equal, the implementation of regulations that would support one party or the other, when not requested, would be considered as *ultra petitio* ruling. Along these lines the same reasoning has been set out in *Eco Swiss* as to why the arbitral body should not have discussed the application of Art. 81 of the Treaty (now Art. 101 TFEU) – a lack of request from either party will make the ruling of the arbitral n body *ultra petition*, which would, in itself, constitute grounds for an annulment of the award.

4.22. This justifies the necessity for the *res judicata* principle to be ignored in favour of the principle of efficiency, though such necessity may arise in exceptional circumstances, in the proceedings for annulment of the arbitration decision (C-168/05, *Mostaza Claro*) or even at the stage of issuance of the enforcement of an arbitral award (C-40/08, *Asturcom Telecomunicaciones)*.Otherwise there would be enforceable court decisions, which disposition of would allow for the misapplication of rules of EU law. This in turn would cause a multiplication of injustice, as those final decisions constitute permanent court practice, which is considered a source of law. A convincing example in support of this hypothesis is the reasoning of the ECJ in *Fallimento Olimpiclub* (C-2/08): *30. [....]*.

4.23. Accordingly, if the principle of res judicata were to be applied in that manner, the effect would be that, if ever the judicial decision that had become final were based on an interpretation of the

---

[11] Within this meaning ECJ Judgment (Fifth Chamber) of 1 April 2004, C-237/02, *Freiburger Kommunalbauten GmbH Baugesellschaft & Co. KG v Ludger Hofstetter and Ulrike Hofstetter* [2004] R 2004 I-03403, paragraph 22 and subsequent.

Community rules concerning abusive practice in the field of VAT which was at odds with Community law, those rules would continue to be misapplied for each new tax year, without it being possible to rectify the interpretation. 31. In those circumstances, it must be held that such extensive obstacles to the effective application of the Community rules on VAT cannot reasonably be regarded as justified in the interests of legal certainty and must therefore be considered to be contrary to the principle of effectiveness.

4.24.   EU law, in particular the jurisprudence of the ECJ, has an *independent* (supranational) understanding of the term 'public policy'. It includes the explicit agreement to modify an arbitration judgement by way of repeal or even, in the extreme situation, in the phase of its enforcement, solely on the basis of newly introduced grounds, such as inconsistency with EU law. On the surface this would appear to be an opportunity to defend the effectiveness of the final court decision as to its lawfulness and to prevent the implementation of judgments which are inconsistent with EU law. On the other hand, it encourages the weaker party (weak within the meaning given by European legislature) to act in bad faith, after being duly notified of the claims to it. The opinion expressed here is not intended to challenge the decision of the legislature, in which the latter assumes that the consumer is presumably more uninformed (even helpless when it comes to dealing with a monopolist) in the contracting process. But one should not overlook the fact that, once notified of the arbitration proceedings, the passiveness on behalf of the consumer causes direct harm to the other party in the arbitration which bears the expenses of the arbitration proceedings. The latter incur further costs in the revocation proceedings for annulment of the arbitral award on the grounds of an objection, which could have and should have been submitted earlier in the arbitration process. The much advocated argument in jurisprudence that the consumer is unable to afford legal assistance and should be defended is controversial. The cost of the consumer's defence in the revocation proceedings and / or enforcement stage could have been made, typically at a lower cost, in the course of the usual arbitration, rather than during a subsequent process of revocation. The lack of an objectionable preclusion on the arbitrability of the dispute, without this being explicitly provided for in the national law or in the relevant provision of EU law, creates a prerequisite for violation of procedural norms. What is more, it undermines the stability of a judgment, which then allows for annulment of the award on account of an objection, placed after the deadline set by the national legislature. It can thus be assumed that in some cases the violation of procedural rules constitutes grounds for non-recognition of the arbitral award as being contrary to public policy[12] and in other cases, a tool that is used to justify the annulment of the award. Moreover, in accordance with the principle of article 7 paragraph 5 of the Model Law, which is recognized by almost all national laws, participation in the arbitration proceedings without making an objection on the lack of the arbitration agreement (in the current hypothesis the arbitration agreement in question is null and void due to being in conflict with EU law) is to be treated as a duly concluded agreement to refer the specific dispute to arbitration (the so called *submission agreement*). Cases where a party was properly notified but did not take part in the proceedings of the arbitral tribunal are also treated as 'participation'.

4.25. The interpretation that it is at the time of the revocation proceedings and/or the phase of enforcement when it is first permissible to make an objection as to the absence of an arbitration agreement or lack of arbitrability on a dispute cannot be supported by the predominant explanation. This explanation is that inasmuch as the arbitration body may not refer its questions to the European Court of Justice, it is the earliest stage, when the dispute is referred to a national judge, and that an adequate response to the interpretation and application of the disputed legal rule may be obtained. While it is true that the ECJ does not treat arbitrators as an authority within the meaning of Art. 267 TFEU, it can not automatically be inferred that the arbitration panel would not comply with a peremptory norm of EU law. In this case the rules do not allow arbitration jurisdiction in retailer - consumer relations. The participant in good faith in the proceedings should have duly submitted an objection, so that the latter could benefit from the extraordinary means of protection provided by the legislature, such as annulment and contestation of enforcement. Otherwise there is a violation of the principles of equality between the parties and of the stability of the judicial / arbitration act.

---

[12] A textbook example in Bulgarian legal practice is the *Intracom* case [Decision No 422/18.07.1997 on the CCC No. 250/97, 5-member panel SCC] where SCC states an interpretation which is not only to be shared, but it is also to constitute a supranational conception of the nature and content of the term 'public policy': *'... finds correct the observations ... on the inclusion of the concept of 'public policy' and the respect of the principle of equality and competitiveness in the proceedings, as this is not merely a simple procedural rule, but rather a fundamental principle of civilized society which refers not only to the internal legal order of the Member exequatur state and its law enforcement agencies but also to the general principles of justice, applicable to international arbitration, which is an expression of the right to a fair trial as guaranteed by an international convention - Art. 6 item 1 of the European Convention on Human Rights.'*

4.26. Another aspect of the problem arises from the situation where the parties in the arbitration proceedings have designated the national law of a Member State as the applicable one and therefore, as EU law is an integral part of the selected law, the arbitrators are involved in the implementation of the relevant provisions of European law to the dispute – especially when there is a contradiction between national law and EU law.

4.27. One has to tread lightly in this area, particularly where the parties have pointed to an applicable national law in a period when the country was not a member of the EU but by the time the dispute has arisen that State has already become a member of the EU and its national law – subject to European law. In such situations, the parties and arbitrators alike may have difficulties in the process of defence and administration of justice. Several legitimate questions arise. Is the law at the time when the dispute arose (after the Member State's accession to the EU) the same as the law the parties have agreed to follow at the time of the conclusion of the relevant contract? Where the national law contains provisions contrary to EU regulations, such that they have no direct effect and are not transposed, how is an arbitrator, who is deprived of the powers of national courts, to interpret and enforce law by analogy? How does a legal order, which is new for the parties, relate to the voluntary act of arbitration as a judicial means of dispute settlement, which the parties have chosen to prevail under conditions that have been modified? These and other similar questions point to the need to strike an appropriate balance between the legitimacy of arbitral awards and the philosophy and legal nature of arbitration as a method of dispute resolution. Whose jurisdiction is it to find that balance then – EU, national legislation or the institutional rules of the signed arbitration clause?

4.28. As early as 2000 the ECJ, in the *Ingmar GB Ltd v Eaton Leonard Technologies Ltd.* case, stated that the applicable law chosen by the parties in the arbitration agreement cannot be used to evade the responsibilities entrusted to the participants in the particular relationship under a Regulation or other Community (now European Union law) act, especially when these rights and responsibilities are implemented on the territory of a Member State. As a consequence of this 'evasion' clause, the Court ruled that such an agreement would be invalid and in turn that defect could lead to non-enforcement of a decision, on the basis that such a clause was contrary to public policy.

4.29. It is curious to note the wording of the preliminary question and the approach of the national institution in the *Ingmar v Eaton* case regarding the balance sought between the compulsory nature of the contractual conditions (reference to applicable law) on the one hand and the compulsory provisions of EU law across the Union on the other hand. The English court asks the following question:

4.30. 'Under English law, effect will be given to the applicable law as chosen by the parties, unless there is a public policy reason, such as an overriding provision, for not so doing. In such circumstances, are the provisions of Council Directive 86/653/EEC, as implemented in the laws of the Member States, and in particular those provisions relating to the payment of compensation to agents on termination of their agreements with their principals, applicable when:

a) a principal appoints an exclusive agent in the United Kingdom and the Republic of Ireland for the sale of its products therein; and

b) in so far as sales of the products in the United Kingdom are concerned, the agent carries out its activities in the United Kingdom; and

c) the principal is a company incorporated in a non-EU State, and in particular in the State of California, USA, and situated there; and

d) the express applicable law of the contract between the parties is that of the State of California, USA?'[13]

4.31. To arrive at the above conclusion, the ECJ upholds the mandatory nature of the Directive, stating that the Directive is intended to protect freedom of establishment and the operation of undistorted competition for all commercial agents. It is along those same lines that General attorney Philippe Leger makes his statement. In light of the above, the ECJ held that it is essential for the 'Community legal order' that a principal established in a non-member country, whose commercial agent carries on his activity within the Community, cannot evade those provisions by the 'simple expedient of a choice-of-law clause'.[14]

4.32. A popular judgment that illustrates the possible adverse consequences of the failure of European arbitration law in disputes on activity conducted on the territory of the EU is the *Accentuate Ltd. v Asigra Inc. Canada*[15] case. In its judgement dated 30.10.2009, the Honourable Mr

---

[13] ECJ Judgment (Fifth Chamber) of 9 November 2000, C-381/98, *Ingmar GB Ltd* v *Eaton Leonard Technologies Inc.* [2000] I-09305, available at: http://eur-lex.europa.eu/lex/LexUriServ/LexUriServ.do?uri=CELEX:61998J0381:EN:HTML#MO (accessed on September 11, 2013).

[14] *Ibid.*

[15] *Accentuate Ltd* v *Asigra Inc* (A Company Incorporated In Canada) [2009] EWHC 2655 (QB), *a second instance proceedings in which the dispute is between a commercial agent established in a Member State and trader from outside Europe under a contract with an arbitration clause; the legal discussion pertains to the mandatory provisions or non – application of Art.s 17 to 19 of Directive 86/653/EEC.*

Justice Tugendhat of The High Court of Justice, Queen's Bench Division, referred to the interpretation adopted by the ECJ on the case *Claro* v *Centro Movil Milenium*,[16] where the national courts of the Member States maintained that arbitration decisions that are inconsistent with the mandatory provisions of EU law are to be disregarded.

4.33. The considerations set out above confirm the reasonable solicitation that the Court of the European Union should recognize arbitral tribunals as institutions entitled to request a preliminary ruling. Surely the discretion, if they need or do not need any interpretation from the ECJ, should be left to the arbitrator's competence. This approach will ensure their independence and impartiality as far as the Tribunal and its members (the arbitrators) will be not frightened if their decision is consistent with their obligation and parties' expectations. If they have any doubts they will be entitled to ask the ECJ. Such decision could compromise the speed of the arbitration process but would ensure the *irrevocable res judicata* because the arbitrator's position would be consistent with the ECJ view over the question in dispute.

4.34. For the sake of completeness, it should be mentioned that the arbitrators touch EU law even at the stage of solving security matters and other provisional issues.

4.35. The European Court of Justice assumes that the provisional (protective, security) measures eligible under the procedural law of a Member State can be pursued and consequently considered eligible under Article 31 of Regulation 44/2001[17], even when the dispute, for which collateral is sought, is within the jurisdiction of the arbitration and irrespective of whether *lex arbitri* allows for such measures. This assumption is

---

[16] ECJ Judgment of 26 October 2006, *supra* note 3, art. 35 and 39 of the Judgment: 35. […] where its *domestic rules of procedure require a national court to grant an application for annulment of an arbitration award where such an application is founded on failure to observe national rules of public policy, it must also grant such an application where it is founded on failure to comply with Community rules of this type (see, to that effect, Eco Swiss, paragraph 37). […] 39. Having regard to the foregoing, the answer to the question referred must be that the Directive must be interpreted as meaning that a national court seized of an action for annulment of an arbitration award must determine whether the arbitration agreement is void and annul that award where that agreement contains an unfair term, even though the consumer has not pleaded that invalidity in the course of the arbitration proceedings, but only in that of the action for annulment.*

[17] Council Regulation (EC) No 44/2001 of 22 December 2000 on jurisdiction and the recognition and enforcement of judgments in civil and commercial matters [2001] OJ L 12/1, art. 31: *Application may be made to the courts of a Member State for such provisional, including protective, measures as may be available under the law of that State, even if, under this Regulation, the courts of another Member State have jurisdiction as to the substance of the matter.*

evident in the Court reasoning in C-391/95, *Van Uden* v *Deco- Line.*[18] In this case the Court was asked the following:[19]

1) How far does the court before which a claim has been lodged under Article 5, point 1 of the Brussels Convention[20] have jurisdiction to decide matters such as an obligation to pay a defaulting debtor domiciled in another Contracting State a sum which, in the view of the court hearing the interim application, is very probably due to the creditor, or do additional conditions apply in relation to the jurisdiction of the court hearing the interim application, for example the condition that the relief sought from that court must take effect (or be capable of taking effect) in the Contracting State concerned?

2) Does it make any difference to the answer to the above question whether the contract between the parties contains an arbitration clause and, if so, what the place of arbitration is according to that clause?

3) ...

4) Does the possibility, provided for in the Netherlands Code of Civil Procedure, of applying for a provisionally enforceable judgment constitute a 'provisional' or 'protective' measure within the meaning of Article 24 of the Brussels Convention of September 1968?

---

[18] The dispute before the national court is between *Van Uden Maritime BV* (*Van Uden* for short), Netherlands and *Kommanditgesellschaft in Firma Deco-Line and Another* (*Deco Line* for short), Germany, in connection with the implementation of the interim (protective) measures for payments due under a contract with an arbitration clause. Due to non-payment by *Deco Line*, *Van Uden* starts arbitration proceedings before the respective arbitration court; parallel to this the latter also applied to the President of the Rechtbank (District Court), Rotterdam, for interim relief on the grounds that *Deco-Line* was not displaying the necessary diligence in the appointment of arbitrators and that non-payment of its invoices was disturbing the claimant's (*Van Uden*) cash flow. *Deco Line* objects that as a company incorporated under German law, the courts in the Netherlands had no jurisdiction over him. The Court (Rechtbank (District Court), Rotterdam) dismissed that objection on the ground that an order sought as interim relief must be regarded as a provisional measure within the meaning of Art. 24 of the Brussels Convention of 27 September 1968 on the recognition and enforcement of judgments in civil and commercial matters, which states: *Application may be made to the courts of a Contracting State for such provisional, including protective, measures as may be available under the law of that State, even if, under this Convention, the courts of another Contracting State have jurisdiction as to the substance of the matter.* The Court granted interim decision, the next court rejected the claim, it then reached the Supreme Court, the proceedings were suspended and eight preliminary questions were placed on behalf of the referring institution.

[19] Hereinafter issues that are solely relevant to this study will be referred to in unofficial translation.

[20] Brussels Convention of 27 September 1968 on Jurisdiction and the Enforcement of Judgments in Civil and Commercial Matters [1972] OJ L 299.

5) Does it make any difference to the answer to Question 4 whether substantive proceedings on the main issue are, or may become, pending and, if so, is it material that arbitration proceedings had started in the same case?

6) Does it make any difference to the answer to Question 4 that the interim relief sought is an order requiring performance of an obligation of payment, as referred to in Question 1?

4.36. It is clear from the above questions that one of the topics of interest to the national court lies in the importance of the fact that a pending dispute is referable to arbitration.

4.37. In its reasoning the ECJ has adopted the interpretation that where the parties have validly excluded the jurisdiction of the courts in a dispute arising under a contract and have referred that dispute to arbitration, there are no courts of any State that have jurisdiction as to the substance of the case for the purposes of the Convention. Therefore, a party to such a contract is not in a position to make an application for provisional or protective measures to a Member State court that would have jurisdiction under the Brussels Convention of 1968 as to the substance of the case.

4.38. However, the Court regards provisional measures as an independent method, not ancillary to arbitration proceedings but rather intended as measures of support to such proceedings. Further, the Court does not distinguish whether the main proceedings are going before a court or before arbitration. Their place in the scope of the Convention of 27 September 1968 is thus determined by the nature of the rights which they serve to protect and not by their own nature.

4.39. By the way of conclusion, it can be said that the duty imposed by the ECJ to apply the provisions of EU law and to prevent arbitration from being used to circumvent the application of public policy rules does not affect the independence and impartiality of the contemporary arbitrator. They just need to recognize the EU law mandatory rules, which are the basis of the public policy, as obligatory and supranational. The arbitrators remain 'masters of the arbitral proceedings' and their responsibility for fair and enforceable decisions still exists but the criteria for such decisions are expanded with the EU law requirement that the *ordre public* be observed. In case any arbitral award deviates from this requirement and therefore becomes unenforceable, the arbitrator turns into a mediator, who is a facilitator that assists in developing options and achieving a mutually agreed resolution, which enforceability relies on its voluntary fulfilment.

Summaries

FRA [*Le droit de l'UE a-t-il un impact sur l'indépendance et l'impartialité de l'arbitre ?*]
La discussion porte sur l'ensemble du domaine de la procédure d'arbitrage, depuis son autonomie jusqu'à la reconnaissance obligatoire des décisions d'arbitrage par les parties en passant par la reconnaissance et l'exécution des sentences arbitrales dans un ou plusieurs États membres. On se demande ici si le tribunal d'arbitrage peut être reconnu par la Cour de justice de l'Union européenne comme un organe compétent au sens de l'article 267 de la version consolidée du traité sur le fonctionnement de l'Union européenne (ex-article 234 TCE). L'analyse comprend une opinion personnelle de son auteur sur les décisions prises dans les affaires Nordsee, Eco Swiss, Mostaza Claro et Fallimento Olimpiclub, qui ont une importance capitale et marquent un jalon dans la problématique donnée. L'utilisation d'un principe d'égalité entre des critères nationaux pour invalider une sentence arbitrale est sujette à discussion, eut égard à l'absence de compatibilité avec les réglementations contraignantes de l'UE ou avec les réglementations nationales. Une grande attention a été consacrée parallèlement aux principes d'efficacité et de sécurité juridique dont les arbitres doivent tenir compte dans leur sentence. On a soigneusement étudié la question de savoir si le tribunal arbitral est tenu d'utiliser le droit de l'UE, si le litige oppose des parties égales et qu'aucune des parties ne demande qu'on s'y réfère. Les résultats de l'analyse amènent à conclure que l'obligation sous-tendue par la jurisprudence de la Cour européenne de justice / la Cour de justice de l'Union européenne, l'obligation d'appliquer le droit de l'UE et de faire obstacle à l'utilisation d'une procédure arbitrale dans les cas où seraient ainsi contournées les règles d'ordre public, ne se rapporte pas à l'indépendance et à l'impartialité des arbitres. Il est uniquement nécessaire de tenir compte des réglementations contraignantes du droit de l'UE qui constituent des éléments d'ordre public et dont l'utilisation est obligatoire et l'effet supranational.

CZE [*Má právo EU vliv na nezávislost a nestrannost rozhodce?*]
Pojednání se týká celé oblasti rozhodčího řízení, od jeho autonomie, přes obligatorní uznání rozhodčích nálezů stranami, uznání a výkon nálezů v jednom nebo více členských státech. Článek formuluje otázku, zda může být rozhodčí senát ze strany SD EU uznán jako orgán příslušný podle článku 234 SFEU. Rozbor obsažený v pojednání obsahuje osobní pohled a názor na rozhodnutí ve věcech Nordsee, Eco Swiss, Mostaza Claro a Fallimento Olimpiclub, která mají zásadní význam a

představují milníky v dané problematice. Použití principu rovnosti mezi národními kritérii pro zrušení rozhodčího nálezu je předmětem pojednání vzhledem k absenci kompatibility s kogentními předpisy EU nebo předpisy národními. Paralelně je podstatná pozornost věnována principu efektivity a právní jistoty, které musí zohlednit rozhodci při vydávání rozhodnutí. Podrobně je rozebrána otázka, zda jsou rozhodčí senáty povinny použít právo EU, je-li spor veden mezi rovnými stranami a žádná z nich se na takové normy neodvolává. Výsledky této analýzy vedou k hlavnímu závěru, že povinnost, o níž judikoval ESD / SD EU, totiž povinnost aplikovat právo EU a zabránit využití rozhodčího řízení v případech, kdy by tím měla být obcházena pravidla veřejného pořádku, se netýká nezávislosti a nestrannosti rozhodců. Je pouze nezbytné zohlednit ty kogentní předpisy práva EU, která jsou předmětem veřejného pořádku (ordre public) a jejich použití je povinné a účinek je nadnárodní.

| | |

POL   [*Czy prawo UE ma wpływ na niezawisłość i bezstronność arbitra?*]
Niniejszy artykuł zastanawia się nad kwestią, czy prawo UE wpływa na niezawisłość i bezstronność arbitrów. Znaczenie przepisów prawa unijnego analizowano w różnych sprawach arbitrażowych w odniesieniu do prawa konkurencji. W podsumowaniu analizy dokonanej w niniejszym artykule podkreślono, że bez względu na znaczenie zastosowania prawa UE prawo to nie narusza niezawisłości i bezstronności arbitrów, zaś problematyka ta pozostaje wyłącznie przedmiotem konkretnych reguł, mających zastosowanie w postępowaniu arbitrażowym.

DEU   [*Hat das EU-Recht Einfluss auf die Unabhängigkeit und Unparteilichkeit von Schiedsrichtern?*]
Der Artikel setzt sich mit der Frage auseinander, inwieweit das EU-Recht Einfluss auf die Unabhängigkeit und Unparteilichkeit (Unbefangenheit) von Schiedsrichtern hat. Untersucht wird die Bedeutung von EU-Rechtsvorschriften in verschiedenen Schiedssachen bezüglich des Wettbewerbsrechts. Dabei hebt die abschließende Analyse im Artikel hervor, dass das EU-Recht, ungeachtet der Wichtigkeit seiner Anwendung, die Unabhängigkeit und Unparteilichkeit von Schiedsrichtern nicht berührt – diese Fragen bleiben ausschließlich den konkreten auf das Schiedsverfahren anzuwendenden Regeln vorbehalten.

Czech (& Central European) Yearbook of Arbitration

RUS [*Оказывает ли право ЕС влияние на независимость и беспристрастность арбитров?*]

В статье рассматривается вопрос, влияет ли право ЕС на независимость и беспристрастность арбитров. Значение норм права ЕС было изучено в ходе рассмотрения различных арбитражных дел, касающихся закона о конкуренции. В результате анализа, проведенного в статье, был сделан вывод, что независимо от степени важности применения права ЕС, это право не влияет на независимость и беспристрастность арбитров, и данный вопрос остается исключительно предметом конкретных правил, применимых к арбитражу.

ESP [*¿Influye la legislación de la UE en la independencia e imparcialidad del árbitro?*]

El artículo investiga si es cierto que la legislación de la UE afecta la independencia e imparcialidad de los árbitros. En diversas causas de arbitraje relacionadas con la Ley de competencia fue examinada la importancia de las disposiciones de la legislación comunitaria. Finalmente, el análisis presentado en el artículo hace hincapié en que, independientemente de la importancia de la aplicación de la legislación comunitaria, ésta no afecta la independencia e imparcialidad de los árbitros, y en que esta cuestión sigue siendo el asunto exclusivo de las normas específicas y aplicables al arbitraje.

| | |

Petr Dobiáš

The Distinctive Features of Independence and Impartiality of Arbitrators in Insurance Matters

Key words:
Arbitration | Insurance |
Impartiality of Arbitrator

Abstract | We can find discussions of the independence and impartiality of arbitrators in the rules of permanent arbitration institutions. This includes both those with general jurisdiction (i.e. the Stockholm Chamber of Commerce Arbitration Institute and the American Arbitration Association) and those with special jurisdiction for resolving insurance disputes (i. e. CEFAREA, ARIAS UK, ARIAS US, ARIAS EUROPE and Lloyd's). Some arbitration courts define the impartiality and independence of an arbitrator in rules for all types of arbitration disputes (e.g. the Stockholm Chamber of Commerce Arbitration Institute), whereas others have a special standard of independence and impartiality for arbitrators in insurance disputes, which enables a focus on the specifics of insurance arbitration proceedings (e.g. ARIAS US). This gives rise to situations where the rules of an arbitration court contain different provisions on the independence and impartiality of an arbitrator. A suitable solution would be the creation of a sample standard for an arbitrator's independence at the international level (e.g. in the framework of the International Association of Insurance Law - AIDA).

JUDr. Petr Dobiáš, Ph.D. currently holds the position of Senior Lecturer at Charles University in Prague and at University of West Bohemia in Pilsen. In his research activities, he primarily focuses on international arbitration, international insurance law and European private international law (contract law, in particular, under the Rome I Regulation). Petr Dobiáš is the author of the publication *Selected Issues of the International Insurance Law in Consideration of the Resolution of Insurance Disputes in Arbitration Proceedings.* e-mail: Dobias.Petr@ seznam.cz

| | |

I. Introduction

5.01. The issue of independence and impartiality of arbitrators in resolving disputes in insurance matters is very topical. The resolution of insurance disputes before permanent arbitration courts are arising more frequently as part of international associations of insurers, as well as permanent arbitration courts with general jurisdiction. Further, the importance of independent and impartial dispute resolution by arbitrators grows with the number of insurance disputes arising between insurers and policyholders. This is particularly so because the policyholder is also classed as a consumer, and therefore enjoys additional legal protection at the level of substantive and procedural law. Finally, independence and impartiality of arbitrators in proceedings on insurance matters is crucial in any discussion of the value of the dispute. Disputes between insurers and policyholders (or beneficiaries) over high-value life insurance, or a dispute between a reinsurer and an insurer over complications during the delivery of an investment unit (e.g. the breaking of a dam under construction shortly before its completion due to flooding) would both constitute large asset value disputes. Therefore, it is crucial to continually emphasize the impartiality of arbitrators. Complications regarding an arbitrator's resignation or dismissal from office unnecessarily extend the length of a dispute in which a decision has to be taken fast and efficiently. This is particularly true if delaying could lead to additional damage (e.g. the destroyed dam has to be rapidly repaired, or built again because of the danger of additional flooding). The subject of analysis in the following article will primarily be on the rules related to the independence of an arbitrator and secondarily on the procedure for excluding an arbitrator in the arbitration rules of selected arbitration courts based in France, Sweden, United Kingdom and United States.

II. Legislation on Independence and Impartiality of Arbitrators in Arbitration Rules of the Stockholm Chamber of Commerce Arbitration Institute

One of the most renowned European arbitration courts is Stockholm Chamber of Commerce Arbitration Institute. Stockholm Chamber of Commerce Arbitration Institute was established in 1917 as the neutral centre for the resolution of the commercial disputes. A certain unusual property of the Stockholm Chamber of Commerce Arbitration Institute are the additional rules[1] (Insurance SCC Rules) that modify the

---

[1]   Insurance Arbitration Rules of the Arbitration Institute of the Stockholm Chamber of Commerce in force as of 1 January 2010 (Insurance SCC Rules).

'general'[2] and 'expedited'[3] Rules of the Arbitration Institute in disputes on insurance. The raising of such special proceedings before the Stockholm Chamber of Commerce Arbitration Institute is justified by an attempt to make the resolution of insurance disputes more efficient.

5.02. The Insurance SCC Rules do not contain special provisions concerning the independence and impartiality of an arbitrator and decisions on insurance disputes are governed by the Expedited SCC Rules. The exception is if the parties agree otherwise concerning the arbitration proceedings. In the case of insured items, there is no reason for fundamental modifications of the Expedited SCC Rules, because for this type of dispute it is important for it to be rapidly and effectively resolved. This is guaranteed by special provisions expediting the course of proceedings (e. g. Art. 19 - Conduct of the arbitration and Art. 36 – Time limit for final award).

5.03. In a similar way, the Expedited SCC Rules declare that an arbitrator has to be impartial and independent (Article 14, par. 1).[4,5] Further they

---

[2]   Arbitration Rules of the Arbitration Institute of the Stockholm Chamber of Commerce in force as of 1 January 2010 (SCC Rules).

[3]   Rules for Expedited Arbitrations of the Arbitration Institute of the Stockholm Chamber of Commerce in force as of 1 January 2010 (Expedited SCC Rules).

[4]   The criteria for excluding an arbitrator from the performance of their office due to a breach of independence and impartiality are determined by Section 8 of the Swedish Arbitration Act 1999 (SAA). What is interesting is the relatively casuistic list of circumstances, which include, inter alia, situations where the arbitrator, as an expert or in another position, formed an opinion on the dispute. This concerns situations where an arbitrator published a specialist article in which he expressed their opinion on the matter that forms the subject of the dispute. The question is whether such a regulation can be regarded as correct, when the arbitrator is to be a judge of a higher judicial instance who has expressed a qualified legal opinion that is respected in legal practice on the disputed matter. It is hard to regard such a person as biased due to the expression of a professional legal opinion that has been accepted in established case law. A decision of the Austrian Supreme Court, 6Ob235/05k, 3 November 2005, supports this argument. In the practice of international arbitration proceedings arbitrators are usually not excluded based on their professional opinion on decision-making. This is additionally so because the IBA Guidelines on Conflicts of Interest in International Arbitration dated 22 May 2004 (IBA Guidelines) place the previous general professional opinions of an arbitrator regarding a dispute on a green list and specific positions on an orange list. For a summary of decision-making practice by arbitration panels and general courts cf. Karel Daele, Challenge and Disqualification of Arbitrators in International Arbitration, Alphen aan den Rijn: Kluwer Law International 398 (2012) and Katharina Kitzberger, Die Bestellung und Ablehnung von Schiedsrichtern unter Besonderer Berücksichtigung des Schiedsräg 2006, Vienna: Universität Wien 104 (2011). Under Article 8 of the SAA an arbitrator is not independent and impartial in the event that they or a relative could suffer detriment based on the result of a dispute. This is evidently a reference to situations where an arbitrator could, when performing their office, could be motivated by a desire not to issue a ruling that could have personal unfavourable consequences.

instruct persons who are to become arbitrators on their reporting duty before appointment. After being appointed an arbitrator has to make a written statement on their impartiality and independence, which they send to the parties to the dispute (Article 14, par. 2).[6] Communicating facts that could give rise to doubts about an arbitrator's impartiality and independence is therefore a two-stage process, given a literal interpretation of the provision. Such provisions would be excessive and it would be more appropriate for the purpose of correcting grey areas to use the same diction in Article 14, par. 2, as is used in Article 16 of the VIAC Rules of Arbitration (the Vienna Rules).[7] The latter concerns the submission of a written declaration in the stage before the appointment of an arbitrator. Article 14, par. 3, of the Expedited SCC Rules logically states that the arbitrator's reporting duty lasts for the entire duration of their office.

5.04. The parties to a dispute are entitled to reject an arbitrator who is not impartial and independent by a preclusive deadline of 15 days after the moment[8] they learn of the reasons for exclusion. The other parties and arbitrators have to be familiarised with the proposal for the exclusion of an arbitrator and in practice the Stockholm Chamber of Commerce Arbitration Institute provides them with a period of two weeks to make a statement. If the other party to the dispute agrees to the proposal, the arbitrator has to resign. In the event the other party does not consent, the Chair makes a decision.[9] The rejection of an arbitrator based on a consensus comes into consideration only exceptionally, as it is fairly improbable that the party that proposed an arbitrator would agree to their exclusion. The second factor that sharply reduces the probability of exclusion of an arbitrator by both parties is that the circumstances that can establish doubts about the impartiality and independence of an

---

[5] For the sake of completeness we should refer to an article by Helena Jung, *SCC Practice: Challenges to Arbitrators SCC Board decisions 2005-2007,* (1) STOCKHOLM INTERNATIONAL ARBITRATION REVIEW 1, 2 (2008), which states that the Arbitration Institute IBA Guidelines are used as a supplement to Article 8 of the SAA.

[6] Marie Öhrström, *SCC Chapter, in* INSTITUTIONAL ARBITRATION, München: Beck ;Oxford: Hart ;Baden-Baden: Nomos 830 (Rolf A. Schütze ed., 2013).

[7] In force as of 1 July 2013.

[8] Cf. Article 14, par. 2, of the Arbitration Rules of the International Court of Arbitration of the International Chamber of Commerce in Paris (ICC Rules) in force as of 1 January 2012. They provide a thirty-day period for an objection that extends the proceedings, but enables the proper discussion of an objection and a statement by the parties and arbitrators. Also: Andreas Rainer & Christian Aschauer, *in* INSTITUTIONAL ARBITRATION, München: Beck; Oxford: Hart; Baden-Baden: Nomos 90 (Rolf A. Schütze ed., 2013).

[9] The transfer of the authorisation to make a decision on the dismissal of an arbitrator based on an agreement between the parties is enabled by Section 11 of the SAA, otherwise this power is held by the arbitrators under Section 10 of the SAA.

arbitrator usually concern one of the parties. The party to the dispute in whose favour the arbitrator would act is usually not interested in excluding them. The situation becomes more complicated if there is more than one defendant or plaintiff on one side of the dispute, because they will all have to agree to the exclusion of the arbitrator, otherwise the Chair makes the decision. A justification is not issued for a decision of the Chair.[10]

III. Independence and Impartiality of Arbitrators in Provisions on Arbitration Proceedings before the American Arbitration Association

III.1. The Varieties of Arbitration Rules for Dealing with Insurance Disputes before the American Arbitration Association

5.05. The Insurance Arbitration Rules and Mediation Procedures of 2008 (AAA Insurance Rules)[11] were created as the basic procedural legislation for insurance disputes with a value of up to and including US$100,000. The AAA Code for Commercial Disputes (AAA Rules) is used for disputes with a higher value.[12] In addition to this, the AAA has the Resolution of Intra-Industry US Reinsurance and Insurance Disputes Supplementary Procedures (RIDSP),[13] which is an annex to the AAA Code. Finally the American Arbitration Association/Joint Resolution, LLC Procedures for the Resolution of US Reinsurance Disputes (JRPRRD) were drafted in 2011.

5.06. The following interpretation will be devoted to the standard of independence and impartiality of an arbitrator in insurance matters in accordance with the AAA Insurance Rules (Articles R-11 to R-14), RIDSP (Articles R-16 to R-18) and JRPRRD (Articles 10 to 12).

---

[10] Marie Öhrström, *Decisions by the SCC Institute regarding Challenge of Arbitrators*, STOCKHOLM ARBITRATION REPORT 38 (2002), mentions that in practice arbitrators actually complete and sign a declaration before their appointment.
[11] The Insurance Rules came into force on 1 February 2008 and its schedule of charges came into force on 1 January 2010.
[12] As amended as of 1 June 2009 and its schedule of charges as amended as of 1 June 2010.
[13] RIDSP came into effect on 1 September 2005 and its schedule of charges came into effect on 1 January 2010.

III.2. The Standard of Independence and Impartiality of Arbitrator in AAA Insurance Rules

5.07. In the proceedings, a decision is made by a sole arbitrator named by the AAA,[14] who shall be an attorney independent of the parties. They shall have sufficient abilities, qualifications and knowledge of legal and business practice in the field of insurance. The arbitrator shall inform the AAA of all circumstances that could give rise to doubts about their impartiality and independence.[15] Article 11 of the AAA Insurance Rules states that the primary area for concern is the personal or financial interest of the arbitrator in the result of the dispute, or their links to the parties to the dispute and their representatives. The reporting duty of an arbitrator lasts for the entire duration of proceedings, the same as for the Arbitration Institute. The relevant definition is not surprising and corresponds to the international standard of arbitrator independence.[16] Before the start of a dispute the parties cannot contact a candidate for arbitrator in the matter of the arbitration proceedings in question.[17] With regard to the breadth of the definition in Article 11, the AAA Insurance Rules cover all the basic areas that have to be taken into consideration when assessing an arbitrator's independence.

---

[14] The AAA Rules nevertheless do not exclude the selection of an arbitrator by the parties. With regard to the fact that the parties can amend the provisions of the AAA Rules, they should have the option themselves of appointing the arbitrator.

[15] Regarding an objection of bias and non-compliance with a reporting duty cf. *Positive Software, Inc.* v *New Century Mortgage Corp.* 436 F.3d 495, 77 U.S.P.Q. 2d 1658 (5th Cir. 2006).

This is a difference in the legislation and case law in the United States of America and the Czech Republic. In accordance with Section 33 of Act No. 216/1994 Coll., the act concerning arbitration proceedings and the enforcement of arbitral awards, a court will reject an application for the cancellation of an arbitral award that is based on the arbitrator's unfitness to be an arbitrator (e.g. due to bias under Section 8). They must find that the party that claims the cancellation of the arbitral award did not claim such a reason, although it could, in arbitration proceedings before the matter itself started to be heard. In the above case from the United States of America, however, the plaintiff started to check, of its own free will, the arbitrator's past after the end of the arbitration proceedings, in which it was unsuccessful, as a part of preparations for an application for the cancellation of the arbitral award.

[16] IBA Guidelines, Part I: General Standards Regarding Impartiality, Independence and Disclosure, (1) General Principle and Article 11 of the UNCITRAL Arbitration Rules (as revised in 2010), General Assembly resolution 65/22.

[17] Two exceptions from this general rule are specified in specialist literature [Roderich C. Thümmel, *American Arbitration Association – International Arbitration Rules (IAR), in* INSTITUTIONELLE SCHIEDSGERICHTSBARKEIT, Cologne: Carl Heymans Verlag 639, 656 (R. A. Schütze ed., 2011)]: 1) Contacting an arbitrator by a party for the purpose of ascertaining their work load, independence and specialisation; 2) Negotiations with a candidate for the Chair of an arbitration panel named through co-operation between the parties.

Dealing with disputed cases is within the jurisdiction of US courts. After the circumstances giving rise to doubts about the impartiality of an arbitrator are communicated by the arbitrator himself or another person, the relevant information has to be passed to the parties and other arbitrators (understandably only if an arbitration panel is to make the decision). The AAA Insurance Rules emphasise in Article 11, par. c), that evidence documents, proposals for testimony by witnesses and opinions by parties provided before the first oral hearing do not have an influence on the impartiality and independence of an arbitrator.

5.08. The AAA decides with final validity on the exclusion of an arbitrator in the event of their claimed bias, at the proposal of the parties or an arbitrator. A weakness in the AAA Insurance Rules is that they do not stipulate a deadline for a decision by the AAA about an arbitrator's bias. Section 12 of the AAA Insurance Rules does not take into consideration the option that the parties could agree that a three-member arbitration panel could make a decision. In such an event the procedure would evidently be analogous to the provisions contained in Article 17, par. c), of the AAA Rules. These entrust the power to decide on the bias of an arbitrator to the AAA even in the case of an arbitration panel. This differentiates the aforementioned provisions from, for example, the Rules of the Arbitration Court attached to the Economic Chamber of the Czech Republic and the Agricultural Chamber of the Czech Republic.[18] These entrust the power in Article 24, par. 2, to the remaining arbitrators, unless a proposal concerns the exclusion of two or all members of an arbitration panel.

III.3. The Standard of Independence and Impartiality of an Arbitrator in RIDSP

5.09. The provisions on independence and impartiality of an arbitrator in RIDSP are almost identical to those in the AAA Insurance Arbitration Rules. However, they contain several significant differences. First of all, a dispute is usually decided by a sole arbitrator, but the parties can agree that a dispute will be decided by a three-member arbitration panel. The second significant deviation appears in Article R-17, par. a), according to which the parties can, in advance, agree in writing that an arbitrator does not have to be independent and impartial. If the parties conclude such agreement, they cannot object that there is a lack of independence or impartiality as a reason for excluding an arbitrator from hearing a dispute. The reason for enabling such an exception is the evidently specific character of a dispute in which the arbitrators can

---

[18]   In force as of 1 July 2012.

be entrepreneurs from a given industry who might have specific experience and knowledge of that industry. At the same time, it may not be possible in the industry community in question to find a completely independent expert with the necessary qualifications. Finally, the last significant difference is that under Article R-19 there is an option for the remaining members of an arbitration panel to continue hearing a dispute without the missing arbitrator and, after appointing a new arbitrator, to decide whether the production of evidence has to be repeated. The aforementioned differences correspond to the fact that the RIDSP is an annex to the AAA Rules, which contain the relevant procedure for excluding and replacing a partial arbitrator.

III.4. The Standard of Independence and Impartiality of an Arbitrator in JRPRRD

5.10. The high professional standard of an arbitrator should be guaranteed by the individual having at least 25 years of experience in insurance or re-insurance (Article 5 of JRPRRD). In contrast to the AAA Rules, JRDRRD does not allow the parties to the dispute to reach an agreement that the arbitrator does not have to be independent and impartial. This deviation is caused by the fact that usually the amount of the dispute is typically high, as can be expected in disputes on the amount of performance between an insurance company and a re-insurance company. It is therefore not possible to permit any dependence of an arbitrator on a party to a dispute. In addition, not respecting the principle of independence and impartiality of arbitrators could lead to an advantage for United States AIDA[19] Reinsurance and Insurance Arbitration Society (ARIAS US), which places great emphasis on complying with this principle when resolving re-insurance disputes as discussed later. In other matters the procedure for excluding an arbitrator does not differ from the AAA Rules.

IV. The Guarantee of Independence and Impartiality of an Arbitrator in Proceedings before CEFAREA

5.11. The French Reinsurance and Insurance Arbitration Centre (CEFAREA) was set up under auspices of the French section of AIDA in Paris on 10 January 1995. The CEFAREA principal mission is to promote mediation and arbitration as the appropriate method of resolving the

---

[19] AIDA means International Insurance Law Association which is a non-profit making international association formed in 1960 for the purpose of promoting and developing at an international level, collaboration between its members with a view increasing the study and knowledge of international and national insurance law and related matters.

disputes in insurance matters. The provisions on excluding an arbitrator under Article 11 of the CEFAREA Arbitration Rules can be regarded as fairly unusual. After notification of the existence of circumstances giving rise to doubts about the impartiality of an arbitrator, an appointment commission decides on the confirmation (or non-confirmation) of the arbitrator after consultation with the parties. An assessment of an arbitrator's bias would generally be an objective assessment of whether a certain circumstance is or is not able to give rise to doubts about independence.[20] Parties to a dispute can draw the appointment commission's attention to circumstances justifying the exclusion of an arbitrator at the moment they learn of them, but no later than fifteen days after the moment they occurred, or were ascertained. In practice, however, there could be a situation where a party learns of such circumstances more than fifteen days after the moment they occurred. In such a situation it is appropriate that impartiality objections are allowed to be made later. During the review of an objection, proceedings are suspended, which is different than the RIDSP. If an arbitrator is dismissed from their position, a new arbitrator has to be appointed, using the same procedure as the arbitrator being replaced. No justification is issued for a decision by the appointment commission and such a decision is final. An arbitrator therefore may not learn the reasons for which they were excluded from deciding a dispute. No challenge shall be admitted against a decision by the appointment commission.[21] An arbitration panel supplemented by a decision has to pass a resolution on the stage from which the proceedings will continue after the suspension.

V. Arbitration Proceedings before ARIAS UK

5.12.   The United Kingdom AIDA Insurance and Reinsurance Arbitration Society (ARIAS UK) is a non-profit society formed in 1991 at the instigation of various members of the legal profession dealing with insurance and reinsurance disputes in United Kingdom with the support of three founding members (British Insurance Brokers' Association, International Underwriting Association of London and

---

[20]   Cf. ALEXANDER J. BĚLOHLÁVEK, ARBITRATION LAW OF CZECH REPUBLIC – PRACTICE AND PROCEDURE, New York: JURIS 558 (2013).

[21]   Although Article 11 of the CEFAREA Arbitration Rules does not specify what form such a decision should have, it is possible to reach the conclusion that the parties have the option of waiving an appeal against the arbitrator in accordance with the analogically applicable Article 1522 of the French Code of Civil Procedure. This allows parties, through a special agreement, to expressly waive rights to the submission of a proposal for the cancellation of an arbitration award.

Lloyd's). The only provision in the ARIAS UK Arbitration Rules 1997[22] that deals with the question of arbitrators' impartiality is Article 9.2.1. This states that arbitrators have to act fairly and impartially, and each of the parties has to have the option of presenting its procedural opinions. Such provisions seem insufficient by comparison, as they do not contain a standard for the impartiality and independence of an arbitrator or the procedure for excluding him or her from hearing a dispute. Therefore, a party that believes an arbitrator is biased had according ARIAS UK Arbitration Rules 1997 no option but to file an application for removal with an English court in accordance with Article 24, par. 1, subpar. a), of the Arbitration Act 1996 (AA 1996), after notifying the other party to the dispute and the arbitrators. The ARIAS UK Arbitration Rules 2014[23] therefore regulate in Article 7 declaration of interest. At any time between the date when a member of the Tribunal is appointed and 14 days after the Tribunal is constituted either Party may require any member of the Tribunal to produce a declaration of interest setting out any facts or matters that may reasonably raise doubts as to impartiality of the tribunal member. Should any circumstance arise which could reasonably raise such doubts at any time prior to the issuance of an award then the relevant member of the Tribunal must make prompt declaration of such issues. Any objection must be made within 14 days of the facts and matters being made known to or coming to the attention of the objecting party. If no such objection is raised with the relevant member of the Tribunal within that 14 day period, the Party's right to object is waived and absolutely barred.

5.13. Under Article 18, par. 4, of the ARIAS UK Arbitration Rules 2014, from 'time to time' the parties may be instructed to deposit part of the expected costs of arbitration proceedings in a special account under the arbitrators' control. All interest on such amounts shall be paid to the parties and the arbitrators shall issue a final statement of account after the end of proceedings.

5.14. Finally, it is worth noting Article 18 of the ARIAS UK Arbitration Rules 2014 on the costs of proceedings. The parties to the dispute are jointly and severally under a duty to pay the arbitrators their fee, in a reasonable amount. The parties and the arbitrators should agree on the amount of the arbitrators' fee before the start of proceedings, on an hourly, daily or other basis. The arbitrators shall inform the parties, on request, of the amount of their fee and costs. The total amount of the

---

[22] In force as of 1 June 2014.
[23] In force as of 1 January 2014.

fee and costs is calculated in the final arbitration award. Such a system of remunerating arbitrators could logically lead to disputes, which are dealt with by another arbitrator appointed by the Chair of ARIAS UK at the request of a party to a dispute or its assigned arbitrator. The task of the newly appointed arbitrator is to determine the reasonable amount of the arbitrators' fee and costs. An advance on the fee, which is paid to the chairman of ARIAS UK, can be collected from a person proposing the appointment of an arbitrator for the aforementioned purpose. This method of determining the amount of costs of proceedings is a weakness in arbitration proceedings before ARIAS UK. It is because it could lead to unnecessary extra costs and the extension of arbitration proceedings in conflict with the parties' interest in foreseeing the costs of the arbitration proceedings. In addition to this, such a solution could be at the expense of the arbitrator's financial independence, as during proceedings they have to consider what amount of costs will be reasonable and answer any question of the parties during proceedings in accordance with Article 18.3 of the ARIAS UK Arbitration Rules 2014. To a certain degree, this makes an arbitrator financially dependent on the parties to a dispute. The arbitrator can only ask for a reasonable advance on the costs of proceedings in exceptional circumstances. The parties, however, can themselves deposit funds for the settlement of the costs of proceedings and charges into a special account. The voluntary payment of an advance on the costs of arbitration proceedings can hardly be expected to come from the defendant. Likewise, in the case of the plaintiff it could be motivated by an attempt to exercise an influence on the arbitrator. This shortcoming could be resolved by the creation of rules on the costs of proceedings containing a specific amount or exact method of determining the amount of the fee for arbitrators and charges for arbitration proceedings. The costs of arbitration proceedings have to be paid in full by the unsuccessful party, unless the arbitrators decide otherwise with regard to the specific circumstances of the case.

VI. Arbitration Proceedings before ARIAS US

5.15.   ARIAS US is non-profit corporation that promotes improvement of the insurance and reinsurance arbitration as the alternative method of the resolution of the international and domestic disputes, which was founded in 1994. Arbitration proceedings before ARIAS US have to deal with, on the one hand, the brief legislative provisions of the United

States of America contained in the Federal Arbitration Act, [24] and, on the other, a number of individual pieces of legislation in the various states. Therefore, ARIAS US created a set of manuals and handbooks on how to proceed in arbitration proceedings on insurance matters. To assess the guarantees of impartiality and independence of arbitrators what is primarily relevant is the *Practical Guide to Reinsurance Arbitration Procedure* of 2004 (PGR 2004) and in particular Articles 2.3, 2.4 and 3.6, and the *Guidelines for Arbitrator Conduct* (primarily guidelines I, II and IV).[25]

5.16. Arbitrators have a reporting duty to inform the parties of all circumstances that could give rise to doubts about their impartiality and ability to fairly decide a dispute. This is the case even if the arbitrator is not sure whether the circumstances could have an influence on their decisions in the specific case.[26] In order to ascertain such circumstances, ARIAS US recommends using its own questionnaire, whose content cannot include questions concerning the way an arbitrator makes decisions. Arbitrators are also placed under a duty to proceed impartially by the principles contained in the *Guidelines for Arbitrator Conduct*, which are very instructive and are supplemented by a commentary. The first principle instructs arbitrators, inter alia, to act in good faith in proceedings and not take their own interests into account. An arbitrator is under a duty to act fairly and objectively when forming their own opinions and when

---

[24]   The Federal Arbitration Act of 1925 (title 9, section 1 of the US Code, as amended as of 1 February 2010).

[25]   ARIAS US manuals and selected case law of US courts can be found at the website: http://www.arias-us.org (accessed on September 11, 2013).

[26]   The question of the impartiality of an arbitrator was examined by the District Court of Massachusetts in a ruling dated 2 June 2008 on the matter of *ALS & Associates, Inc.* v *AGM Marine Constructors, Inc.* 2008 WL 2230770 (D. Mass. 2008). In the reasoning for its decision the District Court stated that a party to the dispute had, in order to prove bias by an arbitrator, to show that a reasonable man would have to reach the conclusion on their dependence. The Supreme Court of the State of Wisconsin quite correctly found an arbitrator to be evidently biased when he was an attorney regularly representing the insurance company (*Borst* v *Allstate Insurance Company*, 717 N.W.2d 42 (Wis. 2006)] that appointed him to his position.
An arbitrator cannot be excluded from participation in two consecutive sets of arbitration proceedings between the same parties, provided the arbitrator is impartial and has not breached the duty to maintain the confidentiality of arbitration proceedings. See also *Trustmark Insurance Company* v *John Hancock Life Insurance Company*, No. 09 C 3959 (N. D. Ill. 2010); *Trustmark Insurance Company* v *Clarendon National Insurance Company and Clarendon America Insurance Company*, No. 09 C 6169 (N. D. Ill. 2010). This conclusion was confirmed in another matter (*Trustmark Insurance Co.* v *John Hancock Life Insurance Co.*, No. 09-3682 (7th Cir. 2011).

making decisions. Arbitrators may also not make decisions under external pressure, either due to fears of criticism or in their own interests. The second principle puts arbitrators under the duty to conduct proceedings fairly and only to hear matters in which they can issue correct and fair decisions. If an arbitrator is not able to conduct fair proceedings or issue a fair decision, they should withdraw. Arbitrators are therefore under a duty during proceedings to be entirely independent of the parties to the dispute that appointed them and issue a fair decision. The commentary on the second principle accentuates that after their appointment arbitrators may not enter into financial, business, family or social relations, or receive financial or personal benefits, that could influence their ability to issue a fair decision. The second principle broadly defines the group of prohibited actions that could influence impartiality and independence, including corrupt behaviour. Finally, the fourth principle places arbitrators under a duty to report all circumstances that could give rise to potential bias. Arbitrators are recommended to consider for themselves whether there is a circumstance specified above in relation to the second principle that could lead to doubts about their impartiality and independence. It is expressly requested that arbitrators consider whether they have a relationship to persons who could appear in the proceedings as witnesses. An arbitrator has to resign from their position if all the parties to the dispute so propose it. Thus, there are four conditions under which an arbitrator should withdraw from their position; first, if it is proposed by a party to the dispute; second, if the parties have agreed on a procedure to exclude an arbitrator; third, if the arbitrator finds the reason for exclusion to be well-founded and preventing them from fairly hearing and deciding the dispute; or fourth, if an agreement or legislation so provides. The recommendations for the fourth principle suffer from several shortcomings. Primarily, it is only a facultative tool that is not binding. The construction contained in the fourth principle, according to which an arbitrator should resign from their office if all the parties to the dispute propose this exclusion, is based on the idea that if parties to proceedings with opposite interests agree on the exclusion of the arbitrator, fundamental doubts can be entertained about that person's impartiality and independence. If we ignore the possibility that parties to a dispute can have various motivations for making an objection of bias, then it is not possible to accept the exclusion of an arbitrator without them learning the reasons for exclusion. An arbitrator should have, in accordance with the principle of transparency of proceedings, the option of making a statement on bias (as is the case for the Stockholm Chamber of

Commerce Arbitration Institute or the ICC International Arbitration Court[27]), or an objection should be heard by an impartial entity (e.g. ARIAS US or the ICC International Arbitration Court[28]).The fourth principle, however, leaves the exclusion of an arbitrator solely up to the parties to the dispute, and only in the case that the exclusion of an arbitrator is not proposed by all the parties. Such a vague approach by ARIAS US is striking, as the rules for assessing bias by an arbitrator are otherwise set out precisely. The PGR refers to the aforementioned principles in Articles 2.3 and 2.4, which regulate the reporting duty of arbitrators concerning circumstances that could give rise to doubts about their impartiality before an organisational meeting using a special form. In Article 2.3 there is a retreat from the requirement for the complete independence of an arbitrator, when it is shown that they cannot be controlled by or financially dependent on the parties to the dispute. It is admitted that an arbitrator could have predispositions that would not influence their fair approach to a decision. The chairman of the panel, however, must be neutral. Article 3.6 governs the reporting duty after the organisational meeting and includes the duty of commercial and personal independence of the parties to the dispute, legal representatives, arbitrators and witnesses. It can therefore be summarised that the reporting duty before the information meeting is less strict than after the information meeting. Here we have to bear in mind that the PGR are only recommendations.

5.17.   ARIAS US recommends holding an organisational meeting, covering in particular, procedural matters, a statement of the arbitrators concerning their independence and the agreement on a confidentiality clause regarding the subject of the dispute. As a part of the organisational meeting the parties are usually asked to confirm the proper establishment of the arbitration panel. The parties also undertake not to make claims against the arbitrators resulting from their decisions in the relevant proceedings.[29] The exclusion of an arbitrator's liability should result from their position, which should be similar to that of a judge in a general court when deciding a dispute. This is because eliminating an arbitrator's liability for the way he or she makes a decision is one of the conditions for that arbitrator's

---

[27]   Article 14 of the ICC Rules.

[28]   *Ibid.*

[29]   Most permanent arbitration institutions have included in their rules provisions in which an arbitration court, its employees and arbitrators do not bear any liability for actions or omissions related to arbitration proceedings. Cf. Article 40 of the ICC Rules, Article R-40, par. d), of the AAA Rules, Article 48 of the SCC Rules and Article 21 of the ARIAS UK Rules.

independence. An arbitrator cannot hear a dispute with the fear that they will be liable for damage caused by a decision in a situation where there is no uniform opinion on the issue in legal theory and case law. Despite this, it is recommended that arbitrators have the parties sign a declaration excluding arbitrators' liability[30] with regard to the various ways of dealing with the issue of an arbitrator's liability in different arbitration rules. [31] It is also a good idea to have an arbitrator preventatively insure themselves against liability for damage caused while in office.

5.18.   Rather surprisingly, ARIAS US does not have an explicit procedure in its manuals and regulations for dealing with the exclusion of an arbitrator (or a member of an arbitration panel) from the hearing of a dispute. This is because it tries to prevent such a situation coming about by setting rules for the optimum selection of a highly qualified and impartial arbitrator. Nevertheless, an arbitrator can become unfit to perform their office, e.g. for reasons of serious illness. The parties can deal with such a situation by agreeing on the procedure for the appointment of a new arbitrator in the arbitration clause in advance, or, in such a case, authorise ARIAS US to appoint one.

VII. The Independence of Arbitrators in Arbitration Proceedings Conducted in Accordance with the Rules of Lloyd's Insurance

5.19.   One of the largest world insurance and reinsurance companies, Lloyd's has also created several sets of rules and manuals for specialised insurance proceedings.[32] They concern, for example, insurance arbitration proceedings over claims and the amount of costs related to the salvage of goods when shipping by sea.[33] It is surprising that the

---

[30]   It is interesting that ARIAS US sample form no. 3.2 on holding an arbitrator harmless contains, in addition to an obligation of the parties not to file any action against an arbitrator concerning their decisions on a matter, also contains an obligation to pay all costs related to participation by arbitrators in proceedings on actions filed as a consequence of the relevant arbitration proceedings.

[31]   Cf. PŘEMYSL RABAN, *supra* note 32, at 129-135.

[32]   For example LLOYD'S PANEL OF SALVAGE ARBITRATORS' GUIDELINES FOR FIXED COST ARBITRATION PROCEDURE ON DOCUMENTS ALONE issued on 3 May 2005, last amended on 20 June 2011 (LOF – FCAP2011), or Lloyd's Standard Form of Salvage Agreement (Approved and Published by the Council of Lloyd's) PROCEDURAL RULES (pursuant to Clause I of LOF 2000) dated 5 September 1990, last amended on 1 September 2000.

[33]   A salvage operation is defined by the International Convention on Salvage dated 28 April 1989 (author: International Maritime Organization, came into force: 14 July 1996,

rules, with one exception, do not contain requirements for an arbitrator's independence. The exception is the Lloyd's Arbitration Scheme (Members and Underwriting Agents Arbitration Scheme) Byelaw, LAS[34]. This scheme is divided into two parts, which are applied depending on the value of a dispute. Part One (T1) is for disputes up to £100,000 and Part Two (T2) is for disputes exceeding this amount. The first peculiarity of the LAS is the option for the parties to the dispute to object that Lloyd's has a material interest in the result of the dispute (Article 4, of T1) and thereby exclude it from the administration of proceedings. If a single arbitrator has not been named before such an objection is made, then the arbitrator is appointed by the Chartered Institute of Arbitrators, instead of by Lloyd's. The Chartered Institute of Arbitrators takes over the function of the appointing authority, including the case when an arbitrator is excluded from hearing a dispute under Article 25 of T1. If, however, an arbitrator was named before such an objection was made, the arbitrator is entitled to decide whether Lloyd's has an interest in the dispute, and therefore can continue with the proceedings. This situation, however, should not occur, as LAS tries to prevent conflicts of interest from arising. The rules state that the member should submit the proposal for the start of proceedings informing Lloyd's whether the company could have an interest in the result of the dispute, or whether the relevant proposal includes claims made against Lloyd's. Article 3, par. 1, subpar. c), of T1 is also based on the assumption that the sole arbitrator will be proposed by the parties to the dispute and Lloyd's will only confirm that person in their office. In accordance with Article 7, par. 2, an arbitrator has to confirm that they are not linked to any of the parties to the dispute and do not have an interest in the dispute. Such a declaration corresponds to the standard contained in modern rules of permanent arbitration courts.[35] In the case of the exclusion of an arbitrator from a dispute (e.g. due to bias), Article 25, par. 1, of T1 stipulates that a new arbitrator has to be appointed by the parties from the list of arbitrators within ten days, otherwise Lloyd's will appoint an arbitrator after such a period expires. An interesting provision is the following Article 25, par. 2, of T1, which enables the parties to a dispute to propose to an administrator (i.e. Lloyd's) a hearing in the event that an arbitrator is

---

the Czech Republic is not bound by this convention) as any action or activity undertaken to assist a vessel or any other property in danger in navigable waters or in any other waters whatsoever.

[34] In force from 7 October 1992 and effective from 1993, as amended.

[35] Cf. the text of Article 16, par. 3, of the VIAC Arbitration Rules, in force as of 1 July 2013.

not proceeding quickly. The administrator may not inform the arbitrator of such a hearing. Based on this hearing a decision can be made to replace the arbitrator using the procedure in Article 25, par. 1, of T1. Such a measure should, however, be quite exceptional, as it marks interference with an arbitrator's independence. This is because the arbitrator does not learn at all that during the proceedings that a party and the administrator agreed on their replacement. Likewise, they do not have the chance to make a statement on the result of the hearing. It is possible to accept the parties' interest in a fast decision on an insurance dispute in accordance with Article 1, par. c), of the AA 1996, but the speed of the proceedings cannot have preference over properly ascertained facts of a case in accordance with Article 33, par. 1, of subpar b), of the same act. Otherwise a consequence could be excessive haste to issue an incorrect ruling.

5.20. T2, in relation to the aforementioned rules, includes a single significant deviation, which concerns the number and appointment of arbitrators. Article 3 -the proposal for start of proceedings par. 1, subpar. c), and Article 7 -the appointment of arbitrators of T2 assumes a variant where the parties agree on the appointment of a sole arbitrator, or the matter is heard by a three-member arbitration panel. Evidently, the reason for this different solution is the greater complexity of disputes concerning a value exceeding £100,000. Doubts about compliance with the principles of a fair trial and the equality of parties, however, are suggested by Article 7, par. 2, of T2. This is applied in the event the defendant does not, within ten days of notification of the action, appoint an arbitrator with residence in the EU, or does not ask the administrator to appoint one. In such a situation the arbitrator appointed by the plaintiff will decide as the sole arbitrator,[36] provided they are an English or Welsh judge (or former judge) or a lawyer with education in England entered on the list of T2 arbitrators.

5.21. If the arbitrator does not meet these requirements, the plaintiff can appoint another arbitrator who meets the requirements and also has their residence in the EU. These provisions evidently breach the equality of the parties, as they do not enable the administrator to appoint an absent member of the arbitration panel for the defendant. Furthermore, they do not require the plaintiff to ask the defendant in advance, within 7 days, to appoint an arbitrator in accordance with Article 17, par. 2, of the AA 1996. Article 18, par. 1, of the AA 1996

---

[36] Similar provisions in the event a member of an arbitration panel is not named by the defendant are contained in Article 11 of the Maritime Law Association of Australia & New Zealand Arbitration Rules, as amended as of 1 July 2007.

enables the parties to agree on a procedure in the case that one party does not appoint an arbitrator.[37] However, this cannot be done in conflict with the right to a fair decision on the dispute contained in Article 1, par. c), and the right to a hearing in accordance with Article 33, par. 1, subpar a), of the aforementioned act.[38] Nothing is changed by the fact that they are not consumer disputes in accordance with Article 89, of the AA 1996, in connection with Article 3 of the English Unfair Terms in Consumer Contracts Regulations 1999, SI 1999/2083. In addition to this, it is not clear why an arbitrator has to be an English or Welsh judge or lawyer. In the case of a judge it is possible to accept the idea that they are assumed to have the professional independence, impartiality and specialist qualifications, which could compensate for doubts about a breach of equality between the parties when the arbitrator is appointed only by the plaintiff. The stipulation of a requirement for the office of a judge or the education of a lawyer in England and Wales could entail a breach of Article 18 of the Treaty on the Functioning of the European Union.[39] The practical reason for setting such requirements is evidently a preference for persons with knowledge of the English legal system, because Lloyd's usually insists, when concluding an insurance or reinsurance contract, on the selection of English law.

---

[37] Cf. also *Minermet SpA Milan* v *Luckyfield Shipping Corpn* SA [2004] EWHC 729 (Comm) [2004] 2 Lloyd's Rep 348 (Queen's Bench Division: Coke J).

[38] This conclusion can be based on a decision of the High Court Queen's Bench Division: Technology and Construction Court on *Mylcrist Builders Ltd* v *Buck* [2008] EWHC 2172 (TCC), [2009] 2 All ER (Comm) 259 (Queen's Bench Division: Ramsey J).

[39] In the decision *Hashawani* v *Jivraj* [2011] UKSC 40, [2012] 1 All ER 629 (Supreme Court: Lord Philips P., Lord Walker, Lord Mance, Lord Clarke and Lord Dyson SCJJ), the Supreme Court of the United Kingdom reached the conclusion that an arbitration clause making the performance of the office of arbitrator conditional on the arbitrator being of Islamic religion was valid. This decision became the subject of a number of specialist discussions with regard to the ban on discrimination contained in European law (Cf. RANI MINA, UK: THE OVERSHADOWED ISSUES ARISING FROM JIVRAJ V. HASHWANI, available at: http://www.mayerbrown.com/UK--The-overshadowed-issues-arising-from-Jivraj-v-Hashwani-11-30-2012/ (accessed on 4 July 2013), OLIVER GAYNER & AUDREY AH-KAN, CASE COMMENT: NURDIN JIVRAJ V SADRUDDIN HASHWANI [2011] UKSC 40, http://ukscblog.com/case-comment-nurdin-jivraj-v-sadruddin-hashwani-2011-uksc-40 (accessed on 4 July 2013) or ELIZABETH BROOMHALL, SUPREME COURT RULING IN JIVRAJ v HASHAWANI COULD FACE ECJ CHALLENGE, available at: http://www.legalweek.com/legal-week/news/2206552/supreme-court-ruling-in-jivraj-v-hashwani-set-for-ecj-challenge (accessed on 4 July 2013). A summary of the relevant case law can be found, for example, at Halbury's Laws of England, Annual Abridgement, Lexis Nexis 514 para 893 (2011).

VIII. Conclusion

5.22. Legislation on arbitrators' independence is quite varied and non-uniform in determining the rules of arbitration courts. Arbitration courts with general jurisdiction in insurance matters apply a standard of arbitrator independence that is otherwise used in general arbitration proceeding rules (the Arbitration Institute) or is only slightly modified for resolving insurance disputes (AAA). Special permanent arbitration courts define the independence of arbitrators sometimes briefly (ARIAS UK) and at other times very precisely (ARIAS US). In the case of some insurance arbitration courts, non-standard deviations were found in the process for appointing and excluding arbitrators (ARIAS UK and ARIAS US). On the contrary, the CEFAREA arbitration rules correspond to the usual provisions on an arbitrator's independence and impartiality. Only in the case of ARIAS US do the documents for conducting arbitration proceedings have the character of recommendations. Generally speaking, in institutional insurance arbitration proceedings there is legal regulation on arbitrators' independence and impartiality that has implicit costs and extents in the rules of each arbitration court. This leads to the conclusion that it would be a good idea to create a generally accepted minimum standard of independence for arbitrators in insurance matters.

| | |

Summaries

FRA [*Particularité de l'indépendance et de l'impartialité des arbitres dans les litiges d'assurance*]

Le règlement des institutions d'arbitrage, qu'elles aient une compétence générale (Institut d'Arbitrage de la Chambre de Commerce de Stockholm ou Association Américaine d'Arbitrage) ou une compétence spéciale pour la résolution de litiges d'assurance (CEFAREA, ARIAS UK, ARIAS US, ARIAS EUROPE et Lloyd's) comprend une réglementation de l'indépendance et de l'impartialité des arbitres. Certains tribunaux arbitraux utilisent une réglementation générale de l'indépendance et l'impartialité des arbitres (comme par exemple l'Institut d'Arbitrage de la Chambre de Commerce de Stockholm), d'autres ont des normes particulières pour les litiges d'assurance qui prennent en compte la spécificité de leur arbitrage (comme par exemple l'ARIAS US). On se trouve donc dans une situation, où la réglementation de l'indépendance et de l'impartialité des arbitres diffère suivant les tribunaux arbitraux. La création d'un modèle standard pour l'indépendance des arbitres à un niveau international (par exemple dans le cadre de l'Association Internationale du Droit des Assurances AIDA) constituerait une solution appropriée.

CZE [*Charakteristické rysy nezávislosti a nestrannosti rozhodců v pojistných věcech*]
Právní úpravu nezávislosti a nestrannosti rozhodce nalezneme v řádech stálých rozhodčích institucí jak se všeobecnou jurisdikcí (Rozhodčí institut Obchodní komory ve Stockholmu a Americká arbitrážní asociace), tak i se zvláštní jurisdikcí pro řešení pojistných sporů (CEFAREA, ARIAS UK, ARIAS US, ARIAS EUROPE a Lloyd's). Některé rozhodčí soudy používají pro vymezení nestrannosti a nezávislosti rozhodce právní úpravu obsaženou v řádech pro všechny okruhy arbitrabilních sporů (např. Rozhodčí institut Obchodní komory ve Stockholmu), zatímco jiné mají zvláštní standard nezávislosti a nestrannosti rozhodce pro pojistné spory, což umožňuje reflektovat specifika pojistné arbitráže (např. ARIAS US). Vzniká tak situace, kdy se v řádech jednotlivých rozhodčích soudů nachází odlišná úprava nezávislosti a nestrannosti rozhodce. Jako vhodné řešení se jeví vytvoření vzorového standardu nezávislosti rozhodce na mezinárodní úrovni (např. v rámci mezinárodní asociace pojistitelů AIDA).

| | |

POL [*Cechy charakterystyczne bezstronności i niezawisłości arbitrów w sprawach ubezpieczeniowych*]
Niezawisłość i bezstronność arbitra została uregulowana przez szereg trybunałów arbitrażowych w sposób rozmaity i niejednorodny. Prawne uregulowanie niezawisłości i bezstronności arbitra znajduje się w regulaminach stałych organów arbitrażowych tak o właściwości ogólnej, jak i o szczególnej właściwości do rozstrzygania sporów ubezpieczeniowych. Stąd stosownym rozwiązaniem niejednorodnych regulacji mogłoby być utworzenie wzorcowego standardu niezawisłości arbitra na szczeblu międzynarodowym.

DEU [*Charakteristische Merkmale der Unabhängigkeit und Unparteilichkeit von Schiedsrichtern in Versicherungssachen*]
Die Unabhängigkeit und Unparteilichkeit von Schiedsrichtern ist in den Schiedsordnungen der Schiedsgerichte höchst vielfältig und heterogen geregelt. Regeln zur Unabhängigkeit und Unparteilichkeit von Schiedsrichtern finden wir in den Verfahrensregeln ständiger Schiedsinstitutionen sowohl mit allgemeiner Zuständigkeit als auch mit

besonderer Zuständigkeit für die Schlichtung von Versicherungsstreitigkeiten. Es erscheint geboten, die Uneinheitlichkeit der bestehenden Regelungen durch die Schaffung eines Musterstandards der schiedsrichterlichen Unabhängigkeit auf internationaler Ebene zu beheben.

RUS [*Характерные черты независимости и беспристрастности арбитров в страховых делах*]

В регламентах арбитражных судов независимость и беспристрастность арбитров определена многообразными и разнородными способами. Правовое регулирование независимости и беспристрастности арбитров можно найти в регламентах постоянных арбитражных учреждений как с общей юрисдикцией, так и со специальной юрисдикцией на разрешение страховых споров. В качестве правильного решения проблемы разнородного регулирования видится создание на международном уровне примерных стандартов независимости арбитра.

ESP [*Rasgos característicos de la independencia e imparcialidad de los árbitros en materia de seguros*]

La independencia y la imparcialidad del árbitro aparecen reguladas en los reglamentos de los tribunales de arbitraje de forma muy diversa y heterogénea. En los reglamentos de las instituciones permanentes de arbitraje, tanto de aquellas con jurisdicción general como con jurisdicción especial para resolver disputas de seguros, existe una normativa relativa a la independencia y la imparcialidad del árbitro. La creación de un estándar modelo de independencia del árbitro a escala internacional parece ser una solución adecuada para la disparidad legislativa.

| | |

Elena Zucconi Galli Fonseca |
Carlo Rasia

The Impartiality of Arbitrators in the Italian System considering the Code of Civil Procedure and Arbitration Institutional Rules[1]

Key words:
due process | contractual theory | jurisdictional theory | general liability | arbitrator's liability | tort liability | arbitrator´s misconduct | challenge of arbitrators | disclosure | review of arbitral award | impartiality | independence | public policy | institutional rules | European Human Rights Convention.

Abstract | *The impartiality of arbitrators is one of the most important principles of the arbitration system. Due to this, the Italian legislature protects it with preventive and subsequent measures. In addition to specific ethics rules and institutional arbitration rules, the main instrument is the challenge of arbitrators that may be filed in front of the state court on the grounds of lack of independence of the arbitrator. If the grounds for challenge are small their use is discouraged, although the arbitrator's liability is increased. Usually, the lack of impartiality or independence is not included in the grounds for the review of the award. The aim of the following paper is to demonstrate that the Italian legislature wants to preserve the arbitration instrument, getting it closer to the function and structure of jurisdictional proceedings.*

| | |

Elena Zucconi Galli Fonseca is a full professor of Civil Procedural Law. She teaches Civil Procedural Law and International and Domestic Arbitration Law at the Alma Mater Studiorum-University of Bologna, School of Law. She has written more than seventy books, articles and essays. Her research interests include arbitration, with particular reference to the arbitral convention, arbitration and company law, arbitral award; *res iudicata*, objective and subjective limits, connections between rights and collateral estoppel. Among her books are *La convenzione arbitrale rituale nei confronti dei terzi* (Arbitral convention and third person)

---

[1]   Sections 1, 2 and 3 were authored by Elena Zucconi Galli Fonseca while sections 4,5 and 6 were written by Carlo Rasia.

I. The Sources of the Impartiality of Arbitrators in the Italian System

6.01. The conflict between the contractual and jurisdictional natures of arbitration is particularly discussed with regard to the impartiality of arbitrators.[2] Usually an arbitrator is physiologically in a position of suspicion, opposed to a public 'natural' judge, which is named before the beginning of a lawsuit.[3] Like judges arbitrators have an effective judicial function, so they have the duty to act impartially, as a feature strictly inherent to this function. On the other hand, the contractual nature of arbitration must be seen in the power of the party to designate their own judge.

6.02. As a counterweight, it is requested that the parties assume an equal role in appointing arbitrators. It is not admitted, to use the words of Article 1034 of German arbitration law, that the arbitration agreement 'grants preponderant rights to one party, with regard to the composition of the arbitral tribunal, which place the other party at a disadvantage'.

Milan, 2006 and *Pregiudizialità e rinvio. Contributo allo studio dei limiti soggettivi dell'accertamento* (Contribute to doctrine of res judicata and third person), Bologna, 2011. She is a member of the Italian Association of Civil Procedure Law, and of the International Association of Procedural Law. She also practices civil and commercial law in Bologna. Her address is the: Università di Bologna, Scuola di giurisprudenza, via Zamboni n. 22, Bologna, Italy. e-mail: elena. zucconigallifonseca@ unibo.it.

Carlo Rasia is a researcher of Civil Procedural Law and a professor of European Procedural Law at the School of Law of the Alma Mater Studiorum-University of Bologna. His main

---

[2] The issues of arbitrators' impartiality may still be considered as one of the most controversial in the law of arbitration. Major contributions to the discussion include: Piero Bernardini, *The Role of International Arbitration*, 2 ARB. INT. 113 (2004); Gary Born, *Independence and Impartiality of Arbitrators*, INT. COMM. ARB., 1461 (2009); Emmanuel Gaillard, *Regain du sévérité dans l'appréciation de l'indépendance et l'impartialité de l'arbitre*, REVUE ARBITRAGE 1240 (2003); Chiara Giovannucci Orlandi, *Sub art. 815*, in ARBITRATO, Bologna: Zanichelli, 286 (F. Carpi ed., 2007); Chiara Giovannucci Orlandi, Ethics for International Arbitrators, UMKC LAW REVIEW 93 (1998); Edoardo F. Ricci, *Le rapport entre règles prévues par la loi et réglements des institutions arbitrales en matière de récusation des arbitres en droit italien: conflit ou conciliation?*, in L'IMPARTIALITÈ DU JUGE ET DE L'ARBITRE: ETUDE DE DROIT COMPARÉ, Bruxelles, Bruylant 263 (J. Van Compernolle & G. Tarzia eds., 2006); Laura Salvaneschi, *Sull'imparzialità dell'arbitro*, RIVISTA DI DIRITTO PROCESSUALE 409 (2004); CHIARA SPACCAPELO, L'IMPARZIALITÀ DELL'ARBITRO, Milano: Giuffrè (2012); Consolo, *Imparzialità degli arbitri. Ricusazione*, RIVISTA DELL'ARBITRATO 727 (2005); Aldo Berlinguer, *Impartiality and independence of arbitrators in International Practice*, AMER. REV. INTERN. ARB. 339 (1995).

[3] Lotario Dittrich, *L'imparzialità dell'arbitro nell'arbitrato interno ed internazionale*, RIVISTA DI DIRITTO PROCESSUALE 145 (1995).

Czech (& Central European) Yearbook of Arbitration

6.03. As in the English system, in Italy scholars say that arbitrators must be impartial, as least as far as they must be seen to be impartial.

6.04. Besides, in arbitration rules or laws, in place of impartiality it is often required that arbitrators be independent from the parties.

6.05. The difference between the two terms lies in differing views. Impartiality is a state of mind. Independence is an objectively verifiable circumstance, which can be, but not always is, an indicator of impartiality. The law can only assure independence, through the control of such circumstances. It is impossible to guarantee a state of mind, if not in an undirected way,[4] that is through the inexistence of an appearance of bias as an objective test. The European Human Rights Convention confirms that both independence and impartiality are two essential requirements for a fair trial.

6.06. Often, however, the enunciation of the principle is implicit, derived through provisions about the duty of disclosure and challenge of arbitrators.

6.07. Italian law, for example, does not mention either of the two terms. Article 815 of the Code of Civil Procedure enumerates the specific cases where an arbitrator can be challenged by the parties.

6.08. The Italian Constitution in order to adapt to the European Human Rights Convention, recently provided in Article 111, that due process of law is held before an independent[5] and impartial court.[6]

6.09. Though it is discussed, it is to be assumed that this rule is addressed to state jurisdiction. Interpreters do not however question the importance of impartiality in arbitration.[7]

research areas are focused on European Procedural Law and on National and International Arbitration. Among his works is the book *Tutela giudiziale europea e arbitrato* (European judicial protection and arbitration), Bologna, 2010. He participated in national and international research projects, as the European Commission project 'European civil procedure and e-Justice implementation within the European Union' (2010-2011). He is a member of the Italian Association of Civil Procedure Law. Since 2004 he has also practiced civil and commercial law in Bologna. His address is: Università di Bologna, Scuola di giurisprudenza, via Zamboni n. 22, Bologna, Italy. e-mail: carlo.rasia@unibo.it.

---

[4] In England, there has been a large debate on the opportunity to guarantee independence of arbitrators, in place of, or besides impartiality. For considerations about the preeminence of impartiality in *DAC* Federal 1996 Report, see BEATRICE ZUFFI, L'ARBITRATO NEL DIRITTO INGLESE, Torino: Giappichelli 224, note 61 (2008).

[5] The Italian word is 'terzo'.

[6] Article 111, paragraphs 1 and 2, of the Italian Costitution provide:'(1) Jurisdiction is implemented through due process regulated by law. (2) All court trials are conducted with adversary proceedings and the parties are entitled to equal conditions before an impartial judge in third party position. The law provides for the reasonable duration of trials'.

[7] About the applicability of due process in arbitration proceedings, see Charles

6.10. In addition to the arbitration rules of the Code of civil procedure, it is necessary to remember Article 55 of the Code of Ethics of Lawyers, amended in 2011. According to this rule, when the arbitrator is a lawyer, the arbitrator is required 'to ensure that the proceedings are conducted with impartiality and independence' and to disclose any connection or relationship they may have to the dispute and its participants, including attorneys.

6.11. Independence is guaranteed also *pro futuro*. In fact, a lawyer who has served as an arbitrator cannot have a professional relationship with one of the parties in the two years following the end of the proceedings.[8] All the guarantees are extended to associates and members of the law firm.

6.12. This ethics standard is far more restrictive than the above mentioned Article 815.

6.13. An important source in this matter is arbitration rules in institutional arbitrations. They are binding on the parties because of their contractual nature. They usually strengthen the impartiality rule with a system of tools.

II. The Preventive and Subsequent Measures to Ensure Impartiality

6.14. The measures to ensure impartiality of arbitrators can be divided into two main categories: preventive measures that can be applied before the arbitrator accepts the appointment, and subsequent measures that can bring the removal of the arbitrator, due to a lack of impartiality.[9]

Jarrosson, *L'arbitrage et la Convention européenne des droit de l'homme*, REVUE ARBITRAGE 537(1989); Claudio Consolo, *L'equo processo arbitrale nel quadro dell'art.6, par.1, della convenzione europea dei diritti dell'uomo*, RIVISTA DI DIRITTO CIVILE 469 (1994); Federico Carpi, *Profili del contraddittorio nell'arbitrato*, RIVISTA DELL'ARBITRATO 1 (2002); L'ARBITRAGE ET LA CONVENTION EUROPÉENNE DES DROITS DE L'HOMME, Bruylant: Bruxelles (2001); Carlo Rasia, *La battaglia all'arbitrato amministrato: a proposito di una recente giurisprudenza francese*, RIVISTA TRIMESTRALE DIRITTO E PROCEDURA CIVILE 733 (2003), in note to French Supreme Court, case *Société Cubic.*

The same principle is considered valid in an un-ritual arbitration ('arbitrato irrituale', ruled by Article 808 *ter*, Code of Civil Procedure) although the challenge proceedings, pursuant to Article 815 Code of Civil Procedure, is not deemed to apply, according to the case law; rather, an action of termination of the mandate to the arbitrator pursuant to Article 1726 Civil Code can be filed: see *Cass.*, 29 May 2000, n° 7045, RIVISTA DI DIRITTO PROCESSUALE 514 (2002), note CHIARA SPACCAPELO.

[8] In the Code of Ethics of the Chamber of Arbitration of Milan, the duty of independence is only provided 'during the period in which annulment of the award can be sought'.

[9] See PHILIPPE FOUCHARD, EMMANUEL GAILLARD, BERTOLD GOLDMAN, ON INTERNATIONAL ARBITRATION, The Hague: Kluwer 577 (1999); Elena Zucconi Galli

6.15. *a) Preventive measures.* These are the most preferred remedies to guarantee the effectiveness of arbitration. In fact, they guarantee *ab origine* an impartial arbitral tribunal, preventing subsequent challenges and thus saving costs and delays.[10]

1) First of all, arbitrators are asked to make a disclosure: that is to subscribe a statement of independence, declaring any circumstance that might affect their independence. In this way, parties can know in advance any grounds for challenging an arbitrator, and they have to react quickly. Therefore, the tool prevents any disputes when appealing or enforcing the award (see paragraph 5).

2) Some arbitral courts (for example, the Chamber of Arbitration of Milan) reserve the right not to appoint the arbitrator or, more frequently, not to confirm the arbitrator appointed or accepted by the party, after considering any suspicious circumstance. Of course, the power of the court must be used with wise caution, because the parties' confidence in the arbitrators is maximal when they could affect their choice. Therefore, it may be appropriate to indicate another name to be appointed as a supplement, in case the first choice should not be confirmed by the court.

3) Finally, the arbitrator may not accept the appointment[11] where there are serious doubts about their independence. It is not an 'auto-challenge',[12] simply a non-acceptance of the proposal.

6.16. *b) Subsequent measures.*

1) After the arbitrator's acceptance, there is the possibility for the parties to file a challenge before the state court, according to the conditions and modalities that will be examined in paragraph 4.

2) The possibility of challenging arbitrators does not exclude the duty of the arbitrator themselves to report, throughout the course of the arbitral proceedings, any new circumstances that might call into question their independence, a sort of later disclosure.

Fonseca, *Sub Article 7,* in REGOLAMENTO DI ARBITRATO DELLA CAMERA DI COMMERCIO INTERNAZIONALE. COMMENTARIO, Milano: Giuffrè 77, 125 (A. Briguglio & L.Salvaneschi, eds., 2005).

[10] W. LAWRENCE CRAIG, WILLIAM W. PARK, JAN PAULSSON, INTERNATIONAL CHAMBER OF COMMERCIAL ARBITRATION, New York: Dobbs Ferry, 212 (2000), who suggest using the challenge proceedings with the lowest frequency possible, according to the philosophy of 'better the devil you know than the one you do not'.

[11] According to 1 CARMINE PUNZI, DISEGNO SISTEMATICO DELL'ARBITRATO, Padova: Cedam 549 (2012), the arbitrator is not forced to waive the appointment.

[12] THOMAS CLAY, L'ARBITRE, Paris: Dalloz 345 (2001).

In this case, notwithstanding the parties, the arbitrator will properly resign, according to Article 2237 of the Italian Civil Code.[13]

Some institutions provide also that the court can replace the arbitrator in severe cases. The parties, who have agreed to this rule, will be bound by the court's decision. On the contrary, the removal of the arbitrator by the parties requires mutual consensus, according to the bilateral nature of the contract between arbitrators, on the one side, and the parties, on the other side.

3) The possibility of reviewing the award for partiality of arbitrators is subjected to restrictions, as examined in paragraph 5.It is true that it does not delay the arbitral proceedings, but, on the other hand, involves the risk of invalidating all the activities previously carried out.

III. The Disclosure in Institutional Arbitration Rules: The Case of the Chamber of Arbitration of Milan

6.17. As mentioned above, the Italian law on arbitration does not provide for disclosure. Therefore, unless the arbitrator is a lawyer, they are not bound to declare any fact that could affect their impartiality. Differently, institutional arbitration almost always provides for such a duty. The Arbitration Rules of the Chamber of Arbitration of Milan are significant in this regard.[14]

6.18. According to Article 18, the arbitrator, when giving notice of their acceptance, shall disclose any relationship not only with the parties or their counsel, but also with any other person involved in the arbitration, that is another arbitrator of the panel.[15] The arbitrator shall also declare any personal or economic interest, either direct or indirect, and more generally any bias or reservation as to the subject matter of the dispute.

---

[13] Article 2237 provides that the arbitrator can resign only when there is a 'fair reason': according to CARMINE PUNZI, *supra* note 11, at 548.The unilateral termination could not be admitted when the arbitrator knew the circumstances before the appointment: in this case, they will be exposed to a liability action.

[14] These rules entered into force on 1 January 2010. See Rinaldo Sali, *Article 18. Statement of independence and confirmation of arbitrators*, in THE CHAMBER OF ARBITRATION OF MILAN RULES: A COMMENTARY, New York: Juris Net 240 (U. Draetta & R. Luzzatto eds., 2012).

[15] Teresa Giovannini, Valeria Renna, *The Italian experience of arbitration and the arbitration rules of the chamber of arbitration of milan: a parallel view*, 14 THE VINDOBONA JOURNAL 309 (*2010*).

6.19. As the duty to disclose is limited to facts that may affect impartiality in the subject matter of the dispute, it is not always easy to evaluate. A disclosure on facts that cannot affect impartiality would nevertheless weaken the arbitrator who has accepted an appointment, with respect to the parties.

6.20. For example, it is discussed whether the arbitrator has the duty to disclose that they have already expressed their opinion on the subject matter of the dispute, such as in a law review article.[16] The International Bar Association (IBA) Guidelines on Conflicts of Interest in International Arbitration will be a useful reference.[17]

6.21. According to Article 7 of the Code of Ethics, 'all doubts as to the opportunity to disclose a fact, circumstance or relationship shall be resolved in favor of disclosure'. In fact, the arbitrator who discloses any relevant fact can nevertheless be appointed, if the institution or the parties do not object. On the contrary, an incomplete disclosure could be taken into account by itself, in the decision about the confirmation of the arbitrator, regardless of the relevance of the undisclosed facts.

6.22. Article 7 of the Code of Ethics adds an effective deterrent where facts, circumstances and relationships that should have been disclosed are subsequently discovered, the Chamber of Arbitration may deem that this fact is a ground for replacing the arbitrator during the proceedings or not confirming him in other arbitral proceedings.[18]

6.23. Looking at the cases evaluated by the Chamber of Arbitration of Milan, the relationships between arbitrators and counsel are the most frequently challenged.[19] In the relationships with the parties, particularly complicated is the case of the arbitrator appointed more than once by the same party.

---

[16] Rinaldo Sali, *supra* note 14, at 247, deems that the disclosure would be opportune, in this case. On the contrary, the previously expressed legal opinions are included in the green list, in the IBA Guidelines, only when the opinion was not focused on the case that is being arbitrated.

[17] *Ibid.*, at 263. The rules reaffirm the principle '*in dubio pro disclosure*'.

[18] See Chiara Giovannucci Orlandi, *Sub Article. 815*, in ARBITRATO, Bologna: Zanichelli, 286, 291 (F. Carpi ed., 2007).

[19] Rinaldo Sali, *supra* note 14, at 256, reports the case study. For example, the arbitrator and the counsel of one of the parties serve together as co-counsel in other proceedings; the arbitrator and the counsel of one of the parties are members of the same law firm (same branch or different branches); the arbitrator, in other proceedings, is the counsel of a party against another party whose counsel is also counsel of a party to the arbitration; the arbitrator has already been challenged in another arbitration by the counsel of one of the parties; the arbitrator is a party in another proceeding and their counterpart is represented by the same counsel who represents one of the parties to the arbitration; the arbitrator, without being associated, shares law firm premises with the counsel of one of the parties; or the arbitrator and the counsel of the appointing party share an academic or scientific relationship such as at a university collaborations or research activities.

6.24. The statement of independence is always submitted to the parties, who can, if they do not decide to file a challenge, transmit written comments. The latter might influence the decision of the Chamber of Arbitration of Milan, 'but they are not enough to determine it'.[20]

IV. The Challenge in the Italian Code of Civil Procedure and in Institutional Rules

6.25. From all remedies which can guarantee arbitrators' independence after their appointment, the instrument of the challenge has to be recorded. The challenge is considered a natural sanction of a violation of the duty of independence[21] and it has been defined by Italian interpreters as 'the salt, the soul of an arbitration procedure'.[22]

6.26. First of all, we have to underline that through the instrument of challenge the target is not to contest the arbitrator's job, it is to dispute the existence of situations that can render us doubtful regarding their third-party status.[23] Indeed, the alternative solution followed in other systems, as in common law countries, such as Article 24(6) of the *English Arbitration Act*; it is to move all disputes into the phase of appeal. Nevertheless, in these cases the state of supposed early impartiality does not matter, what simply matters is the concrete fulfillment of that state in grounds of a review.

6.27. In Italy, however, it assumes less importance. In fact not challenging the arbitrator usually prevents the possibility of raising the defect in the review phase, except in some cases we will see in paragraph 5.

6.28. In general, in an '*ad hoc*' arbitration, some systems leave to the very same arbitrators the possibility of deciding their challenge (Article 18, *Ley de arbitraje* of 2003; Article 1037, II, German *Z.p.o.*). Other systems entrust this duty to a state judge. The Italian legislature chose the second solution, giving power to a competent judge, a monocratic organ who is the president of the tribunal.

6.29. Nevertheless, due to the fact that the Italian legislature did not define the concepts of independence and impartiality of an arbitral tribunal; the cases that legitimate the removal of an arbitrator are bound to some specific relations between arbitrators and parties.

6.30. Article 815 of the Code of Civil Procedure typifies specific cases of challenges, without returning, as it used to be before the Italian arbitration reform act of 2006, to the state judge abstention grounds. In

---

[20] *Ibid.*, at 259.

[21] MARC HENRY, LE DEVOIR D'INDÉPENDANCE DE L'ARBITRE, L.G.D.J: Paris 261 (2001).

[22] SERGIO LA CHINA, L'ARBITRATO, Milano: Giuffrè, 105 (4th ed. 2011).

[23] See Chiara Giovannucci Orlandi, *supra* note 18, at 288.

paragraph 1 it established that the arbitrator has to be impartial exactly as the state judge has to be. This equation does not mean the same regulation has to be applied to both these authorities that are different in structure and appointment.[24] This conclusion brought the Italian legislature to create a list of grounds that was closer to the arbitration experience and to the features of those professionals (e.g. lawyers, accountants and consultants in general) who usually become arbitrators.[25]

6.31. The presence of a list leads us to ask ourselves whether they are specific grounds. Italian interpreters consider it an absolute list. This means it is considered a close list, without a 'safety valve', as it happens in a judiciary system.[26] This brings with it a strong degree of certainty in the relations between parties and arbitrators, reducing the risk of distortions and delaying the use of challenges.

6.32. Challenging grounds are valid for all arbitrators. It does not matter how the arbitrator is appointed, whether it is by the party, by a third party chosen by the parties, by an organization that administered arbitrations, by chosen arbitrators, by the president of the tribunal, etc.

6.33. The grounds that legitimize the challenge may be grouped into six categories listed in Article 815 of the Code of Civil Procedure. [27] Arbitrators cannot judge disputes where they have a personal interest, of their own or as a manager or administrator. This insures an arbitrator's independence from any kind of bond, be it sentimental,

---

[24] Grounds for challenge of a state judge are unsuitable to the figure of the arbitrator, being both too narrow and too rigid.

[25] Claudio Consolo, *Imparzialità degli arbitri. Ricusazione*, RIVISTA DELL'ARBITRATO 727, 729 (2005). It is provided that a challenge before the judge allows the abstention of the court in all cases where they occur 'serious reasons of convenience.'

[26] Claudio Consolo, *Ibid.*, at 728; Pier Luca Nela, *Commento all'art. 815 c.p.c.*, in 2 LE RECENTI RIFORME DEL PROCESSO CIVILE, Bologna: Zanichelli 1709 (S. Chiarloni ed., 2007).

[27] Article 815, par.1, Code of Civil Procedure provides that an arbitrator may be challenged: '1) if he or she does not have the qualifications expressly agreed by the parties; 2) if he or she or an entity, association or company of which he or she is a directors, has an interest in the case; 3) if he or she or his or her spouse is a relative up to the fourth degree or a cohabitant or a habitual table-companion of a party, one of its legal representative or counsel; 4) if he or she or his or her spouse has a pending suit against or a serious enmity to one of the parties, one of its legal representatives or counsel; 5) if he or she linked to one of the parties, to a company controlled by that party, to its controlling entity or to a company subject to common control by a subordinate labor relationship or by a continuous consulting relationship or by a relationship for the performance or remunerates activity or by other relationship of a patrimonial or associative nature which might affect his or her independence; furthermore, if he or she is a guardian or a curator of one of the parties; 6) if he or she given advice, assistance or acted as legal counsel to one of the parties in a prior phase of the same case or has testified as a fitness'.

family, friendship, enmity or work, including any other further economic or associative relation that could be influenced even just economically or emotionally. The same caution is opportunely extended to counsel and legal representatives. In the end, it is possible the challenge of the arbitrator when it is caused by lack of the qualifications settled by the parties in the arbitration clause, for example, professional specialization or qualities or the knowledge of a certain language. [28]

6.34. As anticipated, the challenge request has to be filed during a very short term, 10 days, from the arbitrator's appointment or from the knowledge of the ground. It is given to the president of the tribunal where the arbitration is settled, who decides quickly through a proceeding without formalities, after hearing the parties and the challenged arbitrator. The rationale for such a short term is clear: to avoid breaking the trust and serenity of the person who has to judge during all the arbitration proceedings. This is to avoid an arbitrator being challenged just before the decision because their position had already been filtered.

6.35. In fact, according to this, the legislature gives two subsequent remedies. [29] On one side, it sanctions all requests which '*ictu oculi*', i.e. look clearly inadmissible or clearly unfounded with the payment of a penalty to be paid to the counterpart, including the penalty of payment of the costs of the dispute. [30] On the other, the request of challenge does not automatically suspend the proceeding, except other decisions made by the arbitrators. In a case where the request is accepted, the

---

[28] Zumpano, *Sub. Article 815*, La nuova disciplina dell'arbitrato, Padova: Cedam 164 (S. Menchini ed., 2010). In these cases, the decision will be null and void for violation of the 'forms and manner of appointment of arbitrators', provided that this reason has already been raised during the arbitration (Article 829, n. 2, Code of Civil Procedure). See Cass. 8 August 1989, n° 3637, Repertorio Foro Italiano 117 (1989).

[29] Verde, Lineamenti di diritto dell'arbitrato, Torino: Giappichelli 104 (4th ed., 2013). The case law identifies as the deadline, the signing of the award, Cass., 22 June 1995, n° 7044.

[30] Paragraph 3 of Article 815 Code of Civil Procedure provides: 'In case of manifest inadmissibility or groundlessness of the application for challenge, the President [of the Tribunal] shall condemn the party having made the application to the payment, in favor of the other party, of a sum to be equitably determined but not higher than three times the compensation to which a single arbitrator is entitled based on the lawyers' tariff'.

It was asked who should be the recipient of the order for costs. Commentators (Consolo, *supra* note 25, 736) believe that in case the challenge is accepted, the defendant or the arbitrator are both punishable in accordance with the principle of causality in the individual case. Liquidation of the fee is adopted as an equitable measure, taking into account the maximum limit of three times the compensation to which a single arbitrator is entitled based on the lawyers' tariff.

consequence is the need to modify the judging council or to substitute the sole arbitrator with prorogation of the term to decide for 180 days.

6.36. Interpreters questioned if the discipline of challenge can be waived by the parties' agreement. National systems, such as Italy's, in accordance with the contractual nature of arbitration and in parallel with rules about arbitrators' nomination, usually recognize a preeminence of the parties' autonomy even in the challenge proceeding. As a consequence, it is usually recognized that state judges have a subsidiary competence in respect to the other challenge mechanisms established by the parties. So the leading thesis assumes that the parties can waive the rules established by law about challenging the arbitrators, for example making a reference to an administered arbitration regulation.[31]

6.37. The grounds for challenge in administered arbitration are not different from those established by the law, as the functioning of the challenge proceeding itself.

6.38. Indeed, usually in administered arbitration decisions about challenge are usually left to an inside body of the arbitration institution and the regulations also take care, in a full and autonomous way, of the challenge's grounds and of the procedure that has to be followed in case a party files a challenge.

6.39. Most interpreters assume the challenge proceeding raised in an arbitration institution does not imply that the parties renounce the faculty of filing a challenge to the judiciary authority under Article 815 of the Code of Civil Procedure.[32]

6.40. As a consequence, the two requests, one to the institution and the other to the judge, can be raised even at the same time, in respect of each term established by regulation and law (Article 815, par. 3, Code of Civil Procedure). It is good to underline that the institution's decision cannot be reviewed in front of the judicial authority, even if this decision is changeable – if it is a reject – by the acceptance of a parallel request to the ordinary state judge.[33]

6.41. The Italian legislature, in order to guarantee the impartiality of the arbitrator, established that in cases of administered arbitration,

---

[31] CHIARA SPACCAPELO, L'IMPARZIALITÀ DELL'ARBITRO, Milano: Giuffrè 333-334 (2009); Paolo Biavati, *Sub. art. 832*, in ARBITRATO, Bologna: Zanichelli 871 (F. Carpi ed., 2007). Sul tema, *funditus*, Laura Bergamini, *Ricusazione giudiziale e ricusazione 'amministrata' dell'arbitrato*, RIVISTA DELL'ARBITRATO 251 (2012).

[32] See, a broad summary of the doctrine and case law, in Carlo Rasia, *Sub. Article 832*, in COMMENTARIO BREVE AL CODICE DI PROCEDURA CIVILE, Padova: Cedam, 2841-2843 (7th ed., 2012). For case law, Cass., 18 May 1998 n° 4924, in RIVISTA DELL'ARBITRATO 59 (1999), note ALESSANDRO FUSILLO.

[33] See Remo Caponi, *Sub. Article 832*, in LA NUOVA DISCIPLINA DELL'ARBITRATO, Padova: Cedam, 479, 483 (S. Menchini ed., 2010).

commitment to an institution in the nature of associations or to those set up for the representation of the interests of professional categories may not appoint arbitrators in disputes where their own associates or members of the professional category are opposed to third parties. Due to this reason, rules of the Code of Civil Procedure will have to be applied.[34]

6.42. It is significant to examine the Arbitration Rules of the Chamber of Arbitration of Milan.[35]

6.43. The control of arbitrators' independence is submitted to the Chamber of Arbitration, with the intervention of its Arbitral Council, related to the challenging request and the value of the statement of independence presented by the arbitrators when they are appointed.

6.44. In the case where a statement of independence raises doubts, or if within 10 days the parties make critical observations, it is the Arbitral Council who is called to decide whether to confirm the arbitrator (Article 19 (4)).

6.45. The regulation of the Chamber of Arbitration of Milan sets forth a list of institutional incompatibilities to those who are part of the institution of the arbitral chamber or have any relation with these people (Article 16) and identifies the requirements that an arbitrator must have in independence and impartiality (Article 19).

6.46. About the challenge requests, Article 19 does not keep a detailed list of the grounds for challenge. It just refers to any suitable reason that can render us doubtful about the independence and impartiality of the arbitrators. So parties will be free to foresee additional eligibility requirements. Those eligibility criteria shall be abided by the Arbitral Council in the exercise of its powers of appointment.

6.47. The rule does not say that the decision of the Arbitral Council about the requests has to be stated in the presence of the challenged arbitrator, nor that it must state the reasons upon which it is based. If the challenge is successful, the Arbitral Council may appoint a new arbitrator. No review is allowed of the decision of the Arbitral Council.[36]

6.48. Then, it is the Secretariat of the Arbitration Chamber who values the opportunity of suspending the arbitral proceeding after the challenge request is received (Article 20 (2)).

---

[34] Elena Zucconi Galli Fonseca, *La nuova disciplina dell'arbitrato amministrato*, RIVISTA TRIMESTRALE DI DIRITTO E PROCEDURA CIVILE 1004 (2008). We think this rule can be extended for its rationale to an *ad hoc* arbitration.

[35] Claudio Consolo-Marcello Stella, *Article 19. Challenge of arbitrators*, in THE CHAMBER OF ARBITRATION OF MILAN RULES: A COMMENTARY, New York: Juris Net 267 (U. Draetta & R. Luzzatto eds., 2012).

[36] *Ibid.*, at 281.

6.49. Concluding, we can underline that arbitrator challenges have increased in the last years as the number of lawyers who accede to arbitration has increased. Also, the professional group from which arbitrators can be appointed, such as engineers and accountants, has increased. Grounds of conflict of interest also increased, in general, as all situations and relations that can involve arbitrators, parties and their lawyers did.

V. The Review of the Award and the Liability of Arbitrators

6.50. Next to the challenge, there is another remedy that allows the parties to check the requirement of the independence which arbitrators must have. This is review of the award.

6.51. In Italy, generally, not to challenge an arbitrator prevents review, because the grounds for challenge cannot be filed as the only reason to nullify the award, but they have to be absorbed in other situations. This conclusion is confirmed even by the precedents about a state judge. The *ratio legis* is to avoid the possibility of abusing the review to have the award declared null and void, like it was 'the ace in the hole' kept by the losing party who could subsequently research any kind of relation between the winning party and the arbitrators.

6.52. Some exceptions can be pointed out.[37]

   a) The review may be raised if the arbitrator has breached the principle of contradictory proceedings. The partial behavior of the arbitrator can be shown during the proceedings to affect the principle of due process, threatening the rights of defense and equality of the parties. [38] The award has to be annulled under Article 829, par. 1, n.9.

   b) If the arbitrator fraudulently breached their duty of impartiality the review may be requested. This has a double effect. It constitutes a ground for revocation of the award (Article 831) and it is source of liability in damages (see *infra*). Indeed, under this last aspect, we can say that it is possible to activate a civil liability against the arbitrator, never a tort liability, because the arbitrator, in Italy does not operate *per littera legis,* as a 'public officer'.[39]

---

[37] Chiara Spaccapelo, *supra* note 31, at 389.

[38] An award, where the arbitrator was found to be 'biased' was where the arbitrator produced documents for the party who appointed him., The award was declared null and void because he did not communicate those documents to the counterpart (Court of Appeal of Bologna, 2 July 2008, unpublished).

[39] Article 813, par. 2, Code of Civil Procedure provides: 'The arbitrators are not public officials or persons entrusted with a public service'. The arbitrators therefore do not perform a '*munus publicum.*

c) An award may be challenged when the arbitrator had an interest in the conflict. Scholars distinguish between an arbitrator's direct interest in the conflict and an indirect interest. Only in the first case, the inobservance of the duty of abstention could compare the arbitrator to a party, with the consequence of determining the nullity of the award.[40]

d) When the arbitrator decides the award even if it has been challenged already a challenge may be raised. The arbitrator who deviates from their function is an arbitrator who lacks designation, so the award is null and void under Article 829, par. 1, n. 2.

6.53. There are possible consequences for those arbitrators who violated the duty of impartiality (Article 813-*ter*).

1) The first consequence is compensation. Arbitrators shall be liable for damages caused to the parties if they have fraudulently (*dolo*) or with gross negligence (*colpa grave*) omitted or delayed acting and in other particular cases. The legislature has limited the quantification of the amount of the damages, whose amount may not exceed a sum equal to three times the agreed fee or failing an agreed determination, three times the fee established by the applicable tariff.[41]

Moreover, in case of administered arbitrations, the compensation is a further consequence of the cancellation from the list of people allowed to function as an arbitrator.

2) The second consequence is always an economic one. In cases of liability, the arbitrator loses both the fee and the reimbursement of expenses, while in case of partial nullity of the award the arbitrator is subject to reduction.

6.54. In the end, we have to say that the legislature has established that an action for liability may not be filed during the arbitral proceedings, except in case of fraud, so avoiding a liability request can be used in a twisted or deceptive way, as means to influence the arbitrators.

VI. Concluding Remarks

6.55. The impartiality of an arbitrator is a more complex phenomenon than the impartiality of a judge, because it involves more particular and

---

[40] In literature, it is disputed whether the interest of the arbitrator in the dispute involves an inability to arbitrate or constitutes a defect in the appointment or a violation of procedural public policy. V. Elena Zucconi Galli Fonseca, *Sub. Article 829 c.p.c.*, in Arbitrato, Bologna: Zanichelli 722-776 (F. Carpi ed., 2007).

[41] This limit applies only if the liability is not due to the arbitrator's fraud (Article 813-ter, par. 5).

articulated problems than those which can involve a state judge. The arbitral council is usually the result of a choice that the parties make with the purpose of solving a dispute about a specific subject, a *'juge occasionnel'*, and those parties will also be the ones who will pay the council. On the contrary, the state judge is by nature, and it is presumed, institutionally impartial. The law establishes how to choose a certain judge to decide a conflict and it is the state that pays the judge.

6.56. As a consequence it is clear how the arbitrator is related to the parties and the defenders of the parties. It is also an expression of a precise will of the parties to appoint arbitrators.

6.57. Nevertheless, impartiality and independence are requirements that can never lack in an arbitrator, because they are inborn to this judging function. Obviously, the first and essential need is to have a third party give a good decision that is free from all prejudice. In other words, it is necessary that the arbitrator remains a 'third party' from the beginning until the end of the proceeding.

6.58. This principle has to concern, with the same strictness, all arbitrators who have to decide a dispute without any distinction between arbitrators appointed by the parties or by third parties. In accordance with Article 111 of the Italian Constitution, it has to be considered that arbitrator impartiality is a public order procedural rule. This requires that impartiality is a fundamental and inalienable right and duty that, as we have seen, has specific preventive and subsequent remedies.

6.59. In particular in Italy, challenge is the true way to ensure impartiality in arbitration, together with some deontological rules and the duty of disclosure. This last is requested only by administered arbitration regulations.

6.60. The theme of the impartiality of arbitrators is developed around the challenge procedures. The Italian legislature has determined in a specific and absolute way all possible grounds for challenge and has settled on a challenge proceeding that is clearly meant to discourage as much as possible the requests of challenge. Everything comes with a heavier liability for arbitrators, and nowadays the number of arbitral liability cases exceeds those involving the state judges.

6.61. We perceive that the aim of the legislature from these rules was clearly to preserve the arbitration instrument, getting it closer to the function and to the structure of a judicial proceeding, even in its leading actors, the arbitrators.

||| |||

Czech (& Central European) Yearbook of Arbitration

Summaries

FRA [*L'impartialité des arbitres dans le système de droit italien: analyse du Code de procédure civile et des règles des institutions permanentes d'arbitrage*]

L'impartialité des arbitres est l'un des moments les plus importants de la procédure d'arbitrage. À cette fin, la protection de législateur italien avec des mesures de prévention et ultérieures. En plus des règles éthiques spécifiques et des règlements d'arbitrage administré, le principal instrument est la récusation devant les juridictions de l'Etat (le président du tribunal du siège), pour les raisons qui affectent l'indépendance de l'arbitre. Mais si d'une part, les cas de récusation sont obligatoires et leur utilisation est déconseillée, tandis la responsabilité dans la conduite des arbitres augmente. En général, il n'est pas prévu que le manque d'impartialité ou d'indépendance peut être parmi les motifs de l'appel de la sentence. Le but de ce article est de démontrer que le législateur italien a voulu ressembler la procédure d'arbitrage dans la structure et les effets de la procédure juridictionnelle, même dans ses principaux acteurs, les arbitres.

CZE [*Nestrannost rozhodců v italském právním systému: rozbor občanského soudního řádu a pravidel stálých rozhodčích institucí*]

Nestrannost rozhodců je jedním z nejdůležitějších principů rozhodčího řízení. S ohledem na tuto skutečnost chrání italské právo tuto zásadu preventivními a následnými opatřeními. Vedle zvláštních etických pravidel a pravidel stálých rozhodčích institucí je hlavním nástrojem námitka proti rozhodcům, kterou lze podat u státního soudu z důvodu absence nezávislosti rozhodce. Jiné, než významné důvody sice nemohou vést k vyloučení rozhodce, zvyšují však odpovědnost rozhodce. Absence nestrannosti a nezávislosti není důvodem pro napadnutí rozhodčího nálezu. Účelem tohoto článku je ukázat, že italské právo poskytuje podporu a ochranu rozhodčímu řízení a přibližuje ho soudnímu řízení.

| | |

POL [*Bezstronność arbitrów we włoskim systemie prawnym: analiza kodeksu postępowania cywilnego oraz reguł stałych instytucji arbitrażowych*]

Bezstronność arbitrów jest jedną z najważniejszych zasad postępowania arbitrażowego. Celem jej ochrony, w prawie włoskim podejmowane są działania prewencyjne i następcze, ze szczególnym naciskiem na wnioski o wyłączenie arbitra składane przed sądem państwowym. Artykuł pokazuje, że włoskie prawo wspiera i chroni postępowanie arbitrażowe, zbliżając je do postępowania sądowego.

Czech (& Central European) Yearbook of Arbitration

DEU   *[Unparteilichkeit der Schiedsrichter im italienischen Rechtssystem: eine Analyse der Zivilprozessordnung und der Schiedsordnungen der ständigen Schiedsgerichte]*
Die Unparteilichkeit der Schiedsrichter ist eines der wichtigsten Prinzipien des Schiedsverfahrens. Im Hinblick auf seine besondere Bedeutung genießt dieses Prinzip im italienischen Recht besonderen Schutz in Form von präventiven Maßnahmen als auch Folgemaßnahmen, mit besonderer Betonung der Möglichkeit, bei staatlichen Gerichten Einrede gegen bestimmte Schiedsrichter einzulegen. Der vorliegende Beitrag möchte zeigen, dass das italienische Recht das Schiedsverfahren fördert und schützt und dieses dem Verfahren vor allgemeinen Gerichten annähert.

RUS   *[Беспристрастность арбитров в итальянской правовой системе: анализ Гражданского процессуального кодекса и регламентов постоянных арбитражных организаций]*
Беспристрастность арбитров является одним из важнейших принципов арбитража. Учитывая данный факт, итальянское законодательство защищает вышеуказанный принцип посредством профилактических и последующих мер и уделяет особое внимание применению заявлений об отводе арбитра, направленных в государственный суд. Цель данной статьи заключается в том, чтобы показать, что итальянское законодательство оказывает поддержку и защиту арбитражу и приравнивает его к судебному процессу.

ESP   *[Imparcialidad de los árbitros en el sistema jurídico italiano: análisis de la Ley de enjuiciamiento civil y de las normas de las instituciones de arbitraje permanentes]*
La imparcialidad de los árbitros es uno de los principios más importantes del sistema del arbitraje. Por esta razón, el legislador italiano la protege con medidas preventivas y posteriores, sobre todo centrándose en el uso de la recusación que hay q presentar delante del tribunal estatal. El objetivo de este trabajo es lo de demostrar que el legislador italiano quiso acercar el procedimiento del arbitraje en su estructura y sus efectos a lo del Estado, hasta también en sus protagonistas, es decir los árbitros.

| | |

Czech (& Central European) Yearbook of Arbitration

Jan Havlíček
The Partiality of Arbitrators

Key words:
*Arbitration |
international arbitration
| bias | impartiality of
arbitrators |
independence of
arbitrators*

Abstract | *This article briefly presents the complexity of the issue of partiality in arbitration. It is a phenomenon which is complicated in national as well as international arbitration proceedings since one may not escape the impression that connections between arbitrators and legal representatives of parties are more and more obvious, and what was once considered a ground for exclusion is now common practice. Yet there are deceitful efforts of parties to arbitration to exclude arbitrators, which negatively affect the efficiency of arbitration. It is necessary to maintain cooperation between arbitrators and general jurisdiction courts.*

JUDr. Jan Havlíček
graduated from the
Faculty of Law,
Masaryk University in
Brno, and is currently
listed as a candidate for
a doctoral degree in the
Department of
International and
European Law of the
Faculty of Law, MU in
Brno. He was a
professional guarantor
for the International
Commerce Module of
the Centre for
Economic and Legal
Studies at the Faculty
of Economics and
Administration, MU.
He is an arbitrator for
domestic and
international disputes,
an attorney at law, a
member of LCIA, ICC
YAF, VIAC and of
other permanent
arbitral institutions
e-mail:
info@janhavlicek.com

| | |

I. Arbitration as a Traditional Institute for Dispute Settlement

7.01. Arbitration as an institution of settling disputes is traditional and its history dates back to the times before Christ. Scholarly literature on the subject[1] reveals that the first mentions of arbitration come from Confucian China.[2] In his book, Gary Born also mentions sources that describe dispute settlement in commercial arbitration proceedings approximately. 2,500 years B.C., specifically in ancient Egypt.[3] On the European continent, the first mentions of arbitration can be found approximately 500 B.C. as there is evidence of an established arbitration system separated from the state judiciary.[4] Also, ancient fiction mentions arbitration proceedings. Homer in *The Iliad* describes: 'two parties seeking to bring resolution to blood debt submitted their dispute to a man 'versed in law' and of their mutual choice. He presides over a tribunal of elders, which publicly heard the parties' claim and decided the dispute in a reasoned oral opinion'.[5] Sources from ancient Greece also spoke of regulation of arbitration proceedings, specifically arbitration agreement and the position of the arbitrator in a dispute settling. 'If any parties are in dispute concerning private contracts, and wish to choose any arbitrator it shall be lawful for them to choose whomsoever they wish. But when they have chosen by mutual agreement, they shall abide by his decision and shall not transfer the same charges from him to another court but the judgements of the arbitrators shall be final.'[6]

II. State Control over the Arbitration

7.02. The right to arbitration or specifically its actual existence has always been supplemented by state power. By means of legal rules, state power

---

[1] NADĚŽDA ROZEHNALOVÁ, ROZHODČÍ ŘÍZENÍ V MEZINÁRODNÍM A VNITROSTÁTNÍM OBCHODNÍM STYKU, Praha: ASPI, Wolters Kluwer 386 (2nd ed. 2008).

[2] At the time of the fading Zhou Dynasty (in power between 1027 and 256 B.C.), Confucius was born in China. Some sources state this was in 551 B.C.; others push his date of birth almost 250 years back. Therefore, when speaking of Confucian China, the timeline is not entirely accurate.

[3] 1 GARY B. BORN, INTERNATIONAL COMMERCIAL ARBITRATION, Alphen aan den Rijn: Wolters Kluwer 21 (2009).

[4] Derek Roebuck, *A Short History of Arbitration, in* HONG KONG AND CHINA ARBITRATION: CASES AND MATERIALS, Hong Kong : Butterworths xxxiii-lxv, xxxvii (Neil Kaplan, Jill Spruce & Michael J Moser eds., 1994); David W. Rivkin, *The Impact of International Arbitration on the Rule of Law*, 29(3) ARBITRATION INTERNATIONAL 327 (2013).

[5] Nicholas Hammond, *Arbitration in Ancient Greece*, 1(2) ARBITRATION INTERNATIONAL 188 (1985) (quoting Homer, The Iliad XVIII. 497-508); David W. Rivkin, *supra* note 4, at 327.

[6] GARY B. BORN, *supra* note 3, at 22-23.

sets down borders which provide a basic platform for arbitration. At the same time it provides assistance and keeps control of the process. In this context, the theoretical literature discusses control and auxiliary functions such as those assumed by the courts in the Czech Republic.[7] This is only one level of assistance and control executed by the state. The underlying premise for the existence of independent arbitration is its approbation by law. National law and state law must recognize it, and this is accomplished by means of legal regulations. The law also gives the same weight to decisions issued by courts and those issued by arbitrators. This most important feature of arbitration proceedings is based on positive law. In international situations, this phenomenon is reinforced by the New York Convention on the Recognition and Enforcement of Foreign Arbitral Awards.

III. Performance of the Function of the Arbitrator

7.03. Since the very beginning of arbitration, demands have been placed on the performance of the function of the arbitrator. In most legislation, mainly in commercial disputes, the requirements for arbitrator's qualifications have not been set. Legal regulation of arbitrator's qualifications was very limited in the Czech Republic until the amendment to Act No. 216/1994 Coll. by Act No. 19/2012 effective as of 1 April 2012, which split the Arbitration Act into two parts. One regulates issues of arbitration proceedings 'with a consumer element' and the other one without the presence of a consumer. The requirements for arbitrator's qualifications in the area of consumer disputes are high,[8] whereas there are hardly any requirements on arbitrators in disputes without the presence of a consumer.[9] It is desirable, however, that in some cases the arbitrator (or all the members of the arbitral tribunal / panel) should not be qualified in law, and this is confirmed historically and practically. What matters are the arbitrator's qualifications, for example as an expert in construction in case of a dispute concerning construction. One does not find qualification requirements on arbitrators in international arbitration proceedings.[10] Arbitrator's qualifications are

---

[7]   For example, the auxiliary function – appointment of an arbitrator or producing of evidence or the control function such as in cancelling an arbitral award.

[8]   In particular legal education or registration with the Ministry of Justice, which maintains a list for these purposes from which an arbitrator may be removed.

[9]   Unless provided otherwise by a special regulation, a citizen of the Czech Republic who is of full age, without a criminal record and legally competent may become an arbitrator.

[10]   This applies when it is not international arbitration proceedings where one party is a consumer. There we could imagine an interference of protective national regulations in the form of national law (in the Czech Republic e.g. Act No. 216/1994 Coll.) or of public

therefore one of the possible determinants of a properly executed arbitration within legal borders.

7.04. However, it is not the only one. This is because there are other requirements for the performance of the function of the arbitrator, or rather on arbitrators themselves. From a theoretical point of view, these could be divided into subjective and objective requirements. The objective categories include independence and neutrality of an arbitrator. The subjective requirements can then include the partiality of an arbitrator. Act No. 216/1994 Coll., the Arbitration Act, sets out in section 8(1) that: 'Arbitrators shall be excluded from hearing and deciding a case where there is a doubt as to their impartiality on account of their personal relationship to the case, parties to the proceedings or their representatives.'

IV. Independence and Neutrality as an Objective Category

7.05. The independence and neutrality of an arbitrator is then a general and objective category. These characteristics are regulated in section 1 of Act. No. 216/1994 Coll., the Arbitration Act, which provides: 'This Act regulates settling of property disputes by **independent and neutral arbitrators** and the enforcement of arbitral awards'[11] [emphasis by author].

7.06. The prerequisites of impartiality, neutrality and independence are in a mutual functional relationship in the sense that they are requirements for the function of arbitrator.[12] If one of these prerequisites is violated, one cannot speak of a neutral independent and impartial arbitrator. In order for an arbitrator not to be a third party and not to have concern over the method of resolving the case, it is necessary to exclude influences on the course of the proceedings in the relationship of arbitrator and parties to the proceedings.

7.07. Therefore, if we are to put the impartiality of an arbitrator in concrete terms and speak of objective facts leading to their partiality, it is a

---

order under the New York Convention on the Recognition and Enforcement of Foreign Arbitral Awards.

[11] At the same time, pursuant to section 10(1) of Act No. 216/1994 Coll., in performing the court's auxiliary functions to arbitration proceedings where one of the parties has not fulfilled its obligation and has failed to appoint an arbitrator, the arbitrator shall be appointed, on the application of the other party, by a general jurisdiction court, which shall: 'In appointing an arbitrator or a presiding arbitrator pursuant to section 9 the court shall take into account the prerequisites for his independent and impartial decision-making.'

[12] Cf. e. g. Naděžda Rozehnalová & Jan Havlíček, *Rozhodčí smlouva a rozhodci ve světle některých rozhodnutí ...aneb quo vadis...?* (3) PRÁVNÍ FÓRUM 114-119 (2010).

question of examination of a subjective relationship on the basis of objective facts or evidence, or demonstrable links to such facts. Among the components of the subjective relationship, we might include the arbitrator's inner motivations, interests and attitudes. Likewise, objective facts or links to such facts existing outside the inner feelings of the arbitrator come into play where, from the procedural point of view, it is necessary to successfully bear the burden of allegation and proof in case of proceedings to challenge the impartiality of the arbitrator.

V. The Parallel between an Arbitrator and a Judge

7.08. The parallel between an arbitrator and a judge is obvious, and therefore it is possible, in examining the partiality of arbitrator, to make use of partiality of judges in legal regulations. The issue of partiality of judges is regulated by Act No. 99/1963 Coll., the Code of Civil Procedure (sections 14 through 16b), Act No. 141/1961 Coll., the Code of Criminal Procedure (sections 30 through 31), and Act No. 150/2002 Coll., the Code of Administrative Justice (section 8). Partiality of judges consists in their objective relationship to the case, parties to the proceedings or their representatives because of which the impartiality may be reasonably doubted. A judge's relationship to a case may arise primarily from the judge's direct legal interest on the present case, such as when the judge used to be a party to the proceedings on the side of the defendant or claimant, or if the judge´s rights and concerns could be affected by a court´s decision. The relationship to a case may also be understood as a situation where a judge acquired knowledge about the case from a source other than evidence at the hearing for example a witness, which makes could make the judge's view of the facts distorted. The judge's relationship to parties to the proceedings or their representatives may be based on a family or similar relationship or, in a particular case, on a friendly or hostile relationship. Another possibility is a relationship of economic dependence.

7.09. Moreover, a judge who participated in decision-making at a lower court is excluded from decision-making of a higher court. Otherwise, the meaning and purpose of the procedure where a case is to be reviewed independently of the previous decision on the basis of a remedial measure would be frustrated. Judges who issued or heard the decision challenged by the action are excluded from hearing and deciding on an action for nullity. It is not grounds for exclusion where the question is a particular method of procedure of a judge in particular proceedings and their decision-making in other cases.

7.10. Judges shall judge their partiality throughout the proceedings themselves and where they find they should be excluded from decision-making, they shall immediately notify the president of the court, who will appoint another judge according to the work timetable. Where the facts stated by the judge as grounds for his exclusions result solely from his subjective opinion and the president of the court believes that there is no reason to doubt the judge's impartiality, the president shall refer the matter to a superior court to decide on pursuant to section 16(1) of the Code of Civil Procedure.

7.11. Any party to the proceedings may object to the judge's partiality no later than at the first hearing attended by the judge, or within 15 days of learning of the material circumstances. In addition to general requirements, the objection of partiality must meet special requirements, namely the identification of the judge whose partiality is being questioned, a listing of particular facts that constitute grounds for a doubt about that judge's impartiality, information about when the party to the proceedings learned about the reason for exclusion, and identification of evidence. The parties must be advised of their right to object to partiality in advance. A party to the proceedings may object to the judge's partiality later than stated above only where the party was not advised by the judge of the party's right to express their opinion on the judge. The objection of partiality is decided on by panel of a superior court composed of three judges. The exclusion of judges of the Supreme Court is decided on by another panel of the same court. The exclusion is decided on based on allegations and evidence stated in the petition and in the file and on the basis of the judge's statement. The decision may by rendered without to held a hearing where the court does not examine evidence to prove the grounds for the exclusion of the judge. Producing evidence is not necessary where the objection of partiality may be decided on by the court based solely on the facts listed in the file. Where the grounds for exclusion are proven, a hearing must be ordered even if the actual production of evidence would be carried out by the requested court. The reason is to allow all participants to express their opinions on the evidence produced. If a judge is excluded, another judge is appointed by the president of the respective court.

VI. Reasons for a Possible Exclusion of Arbitrator

7.12. The comments to Act No. 216/1994 Coll set out some criteria for the exclusion of an arbitrator:

7.13. However, a reason for a possible exclusion of arbitrator within the meaning of section 8 of the Arbitration Code has to be interpreted as a particular dependence of the arbitrator on the course and result of the dispute, where the arbitrator may view the result of the dispute as his advantage or an advantage of a close person or an advantage of a person in a personal or property relationship with him. Such aspect must be essential and in fact the only one in final/binding determination whether an arbitrator will be excluded or not.[13]

7.14. Pursuant to section 8(1) of the Arbitration Act, arbitrators shall be excluded from hearing and deciding a case where there is a doubt as to their impartiality on account of their personal relationship to the case, parties to the proceedings or their representatives. It follows that the arbitrator's impartiality towards any party to the proceedings or the subject-matter of the proceedings is necessary for the office of the arbitrator. In connection with section 10(1) of the Arbitration Act and due to the character of the position of arbitrator in arbitration proceedings, it may be inferred that apart from the arbitrator's partiality, their neutrality and independence must be adhered to. They must not be linked to any party to the dispute. In accordance with this provision, the effect of the exclusion occurs automatically from the very beginning. Therefore, a possible appointment of an arbitrator is ineffective. Partiality must be based on the existence of a certain objective and qualified fact. On this basis, possible neutrality may be assumed with some degree of probability, although the approach of the arbitrator need not be neutral.

7.15. Pursuant to section 8(2) of the Arbitration Act, the person who is or has been determined or appointed as arbitrator shall forthwith make a disclosure to the parties or to the court. They shall disclose all circumstances that may give rise to legitimate doubt as to their impartiality and that would exclude them as an arbitrator. Moreover, pursuant to section 8(3) of the Arbitration Act, arbitrators shall, in settling disputes arising from consumer contracts, inform the parties before the commencement of the proceedings whether they issued or participated in issuing of an arbitral award in the last 3 years or whether they are an arbitrator in a pending arbitration in a dispute where one party is a participant. This is followed by section 11 of the Arbitration Act, under which an arbitrator who has been determined or appointed shall be excluded from hearing and deciding on a case where facts appear that are listed in section 8 of the Arbitration Act and section 31(c) of the Arbitration Act. If they are listed, a court shall cancel an arbitral award issued by an incompetent – that is, *inter alia*, a partial arbitrator.

---

[13] ALEXANDER J. BĚLOHLÁVEK, ZÁKON O ROZHODČÍM ŘÍZENÍ A O VÝKONU ROZHODČÍCH NÁLEZŮ, KOMENTÁŘ, Praha: C.H.Beck 414 (2012).

7.16. In the context of various doubts about arbitration proceedings, it was objected that arbitrators become partial due to their economic dependence on a certain party to the proceedings. This objection was dealt with by the Constitutional Court in its resolution III. US 1208/10 of 30 June 2010, which stated:

7.17. If the complainant contests the overall system of selection of arbitrators from the list kept by the Association of Leasing Companies of the Czech Republic because arbitrators have, for economic reasons, a motive to make biased decisions in favour of leasing companies, doubts could arise (in general) about the impartiality of arbitrators only in the case where there are particular facts that would point to this hypothesis. Otherwise it is a mere expression of disagreement with the arbitration clause, which has been, however—as general jurisdiction courts concluded—validly negotiated. These facts, however, were not proven (nor alleged) by the complainant.

VII. The Process of Excluding an Arbitrator

7.18. First of all, partiality may be objected to during arbitration proceedings with the judge or with the arbitration senate. Institutionalized arbitration courts and their codes regulate the procedure for challenging an arbitrator during arbitration proceedings. In other words, they elaborate what is required from the party challenging the impartiality of a certain arbitrator or an arbitral tribunal member. Arbitration court authorities then decide on this petition to exclude an arbitrator from decision-making on the respective dispute.[14]

7.19. Pursuant to section 12 of the Arbitration Act, an arbitrator who has been determined or appointed and whose partiality came into light shall resign the office of arbitrator. If they fail to resign their office, parties may agree on the procedure of their exclusion. Any party may submit a petition for exclusion decided on by a general jurisdiction court. In Professor Bělohlávek's view,[15] the petition has the character of a special declaratory action pursuant to section 80(c) of the Code of Civil Procedure, with the exception of the need to prove a compelling legal interest. The court's decision replaces the resignation of the arbitrator, in that it is a replacement of expression of the arbitrator's will. The office of arbitrator terminates upon the entry into force of the decision. The range of participants follows from section 159a of the

---

[14] Section 24 of the Rules of the Arbitration Court attached to the Czech Chamber of Commerce and the Agricultural Chamber of the Czech Republic.

[15] ALEXANDER J. BĚLOHLÁVEK, *supra* note 13.

Code of Civil Procedure and it includes only parties to proceedings before arbitrators. The arbitrator, whose exclusion is in question, therefore does not have the substantive capacity to be a party to the proceedings. The position of arbitrator in these proceedings is very interesting since it cannot be even recommended that they joined as an enjoined party to the proceedings because as such they would by law have to join one of the parties.[16] Although the law further stipulates that an enjoined party acts only for itself,[17] a party to proceedings must participate on one or another side of the dispute. This will apparently lead to the fact that the counterparty will legitimately object their partiality in the arbitration proceedings.

VIII. The Challenge to the Impartiality

7.20.   The challenge to the impartiality of an arbitrator may also take place during arbitration proceedings. However, it is quite a common practice that the arbitrator is called upon by the court to express their opinion on their partiality. The discussion of judicial review of partiality during arbitration proceedings also leads to the question what to do with the arbitration proceedings while the judicial proceedings to challenge the impartiality of an arbitrator are occurring. There is a majority consensus that the arbitrator should suspend the hearing of the case until the final and conclusive termination of the proceedings to challenge their impartiality. However, the legislation of the Czech Republic does not regulate this, and therefore in fact the arbitrator may continue with the proceedings. With regard to the arbitrator's responsibility, one would not suppose that the arbitrator will continue with the hearing of the case or issue an arbitral award before the decision of the court on their partiality. On the other hand, one party may bring an action against the arbitrator's partiality which is manifestly unfounded, with no legal basis, and without the objecting party's proving its fictional claims in any way. This will be a vexatious action that seeks to delay the arbitration proceedings. In everyday reality we see examples of the transfer of assets from the debtor between the commencement and the termination of the proceedings. In this situation the debtor subsequently goes into bankruptcy for lack of assets and the creditor is not able to recover their claim once the

---

[16]   Cf. section 96(1) of Act No. 99/1963 Coll., the Civil Procedure Code: "Enjoined parties can take part in the proceedings besides the claimant and the defendant if they have legal interest in the outcome of the proceedings, except for divorce proceedings or the determination whether or not the marriage exists."

[17]   Cf. section 93(2), second sentence.

proceedings have terminated. It may be convenient to delay arbitration proceedings as part of these machinations. One may then think of abuse of rights by filing an action against partiality. If, therefore, such an action is manifestly unfounded, it is reasonable that the arbitrator continue with the arbitration proceedings with reference to section 19(2) of the Arbitration Act and terminate the proceedings by a final and conclusive award. However, the instrument of judicial protection against partiality in arbitration proceedings may not be perceived a priori negatively, with regard to abuse of this institution. It is a perfectly proper instrument for the protection of the right to a fair trial enshrined, *inter alia*, in the Constitution.

IX. Judicial Decision Making Process on Partiality[18]

7.21. In a pending arbitration **between entrepreneurs** (model case),[19] an objection of the arbitrator's partiality was raised by the defendant and the arbitrator decided in a resolution that the claimant's allegation was not substantiated. The arbitrator stated there was no partiality in the case. After the service of this resolution, the defendant filed an action before the general jurisdiction court on 25 July 2011.

7.22. to exclude the arbitrator from hearing the dispute with reference to his partiality. In the judicial proceedings to exclude the arbitrator, the defendant in the arbitration became the claimant in the proceedings before court.[20] The claimant therefore filed an action to exclude the arbitrator claiming that there were reasons to exclude the arbitrator due to his partiality since there were circumstances that gave rise to legitimate doubts about the arbitrator's impartiality.

7.23. In the action to exclude the arbitrator, the claimant substantiated the arbitrator's partiality with three allegations:
1) the executive director of the defendant and the arbitrator 'studied together' at the faculty of law, and they are therefore 'school friends',
2) they both were entrepreneurs in a similar field, which means that they closely cooperated,
3) they were both members of a closed group that organized common conference get-togethers focused on exchange of information, and

---

[18] The author of this paper has access to the files of the case described. With regard to the non-public nature of arbitration proceedings and the fact that he respects confidentiality, only an abstract is described.

[19] There were companies on the sides of the defendant as well as of the claimant.

[20] We will respect the position of claimant—in judicial proceedings (this party was the defendant in the arbitration) and the position of defendant—in judicial proceedings (this party was in the position of claimant in the arbitration).

as part of a conference they had a common lecture on the same day in the same place. The arbitrator spoke on the topic of arbitration proceedings and the executive director on the topic of receivables.

7.24. Subsequently, the arbitrator, although he was not a party to the proceedings, was asked to express his opinion on the action. The arbitrator made a comprehensive submission to the court in which he focused primarily on the claimant's allegations.

7.25. As regards the first allegation, the arbitrator provided the court with the following information. Using a publicly available information system of the university, the arbitrator found[21] that the executive director did not study law at the faculty of law of the same university, but he studied physical education at a different faculty. At the same time it was obvious beyond any doubt that the arbitrator studied in a completely different time period. However, it was found that the executive director of the claimant signed up for a rigorous examination at the same faculty where the arbitrator was studying but at a different department. The arbitrator also explained to the court that in the case of rigorous proceedings, it is an examination given on one day and there are no studies. Moreover, approximately 7,000 students study at the faculty of law and it was therefore very unlikely to have met, even accidentally, the defendant's executive director.

7.26. It was difficult to respond to the second assertion as it was rather impossible to produce evidence before the court denying the claimant's allegation. The arbitrator and the claimant's executive director did not carry out and had not carried out business activities together. However, as a negative allegation, this is difficult to prove. In this context, therefore, the arbitrator limited himself to informing the court that he did not collaborate with the defendant closely or in any other manner, and he pointed out to the court that the claimant in this respect did not successfully bear the burden of proof.

7.27. Regarding the third point, the arbitrator explained to the court that with regard to the website of the conference in which the claimant's executive director as well as the arbitrator allegedly had participated in, it is substantiated that this event never took place. This means that the arbitrator and the defendant's executive director could never have met at this event.

7.28. The court of first instance decided on these matters by issuing a resolution,[22] which it did after seven months, and decided to exclude the arbitrator citing from the reasoning of the court of first instance:

---

[21] As a graduate of the faculty, the arbitrator had free access to the database of students and graduates.

[22] Cf. Supreme Court of the Czech Republic, file No.: 29 Odo 430/2005 of 26 July 2005.

7.29. After considering all allegations raised by the parties and the arbitrator as well as the submitted documentary evidence,[23] the undersigned court reached the conclusion that there are reasons to exclude the arbitrator ... from hearing and deciding on the case in question. According to commentaries to the Arbitration Act (e.g. C. H. Beck publisher's series of laws with commentaries), merely a possibility of raising legitimate doubts about the impartiality of an arbitrator is sufficient for a decision to exclude the arbitrator when at the same time the undersigned court does not consider the fact that in the event that the arbitrator was not excluded in the current proceedings and subsequently acted and decided in the arbitration case, this would most likely be followed by a petition to annul the arbitration award issued by the incompetent arbitrator within the meaning of section 31(c) of the Arbitration Act. The question of possible incompetence of the arbitrator can therefore be closed already now before issuing an arbitration award.

7.30. The court ascertained circumstances that give rise to legitimate doubts about the impartiality, and decided as stated in verdict I hereof. The arbitrator himself firmly rejects the only petitioner's allegations that are relevant for the petition for exclusion and tries to convince the court that he has no relationship whatsoever with the executive director and the only partner of the defendant, that they have no common activities, are neither friends nor schoolmates when the arbitrator allegedly found out using (the court is reluctant to use the word abuse) the university database that the defendant's executive director graduated from a different faculty and field of studies than the arbitrator. The only thing that could be inferred from this arbitrator's allegation is that the defendant's executive director is not a lawyer. ; however, it is obvious from lists submitted by the claimant that the defendant's executive director sat a rigorous examination in ... law at the faculty of law, i.e. he is a lawyer and the arbitrator presents the court with information that could be classified at least as misleading. Similarly, if the arbitrator argues that the lecture with the claimant's executive director at the event, which however did not take place, had really not been planned as joint, it would hardly have been stated in the program that one as well as the other appear in the block between 2 pm to 5 pm. In the court's view, the planned common wellness activities of the

---

[23] This includes the claimant's extract from the Commercial Register, the arbitrator's web site, the web site of the conference, and a list of dates of rigorous examinations at the faculty of law.

participants and a get-together with exchanging information and establishing contacts during a barbecue between 6 pm and 0 am would have been precisely those activities that give rise to legitimate doubts about the arbitrator's impartiality. The arbitrator's claims are so contradictory per se that they have lead the court to believe that there are circumstances giving rise to legitimate doubts about the arbitrator's impartiality in the case in question. The court also attributes significance to the fact that the defendant operates is the area of recovery and management of receivables and the connection to the arbitrator rests at least in the fact that the defendant presented an instalment agreement (containing an arbitration agreement with the name of the arbitrator and an agreement on the fact that this particular arbitrator shall decide any dispute between the parties – author's comment) already stating the name of the arbitrator.

7.31. The defendant did not agree with this opinion of the court, faulting its reasoning, and filed an appeal against it with the regional court. The regional court decided on the parties' appeal after nine months.[24] The regional court changed the decision of the court of first instance and stated that the arbitrator should not be excluded from hearing and deciding on the case.[25] The court of appeal stated in the reasoning:

7.32. The court of appeal does not agree with the reasoning of the court of first instance. In arbitration proceedings, just like in proceedings before a court, it is possible to object the partiality of the arbitrator. This, however, as stated above, has to be justified. Objection of partiality of an arbitrator may be analogously ranked under objection of partiality of a judge. The reasons for the exclusion of a judge stated here by the law are the judge's relationship to the case, to the parties to the proceedings or their representatives, and the law bases the exclusion of a judge on the existence of a particular reason, defined by such specifically designated and determined facts that show the impartiality of the judge in the present case. The

---

[24] The claimant also appealed against the decision of the court of first instance but only to the extent of non-adjudicated costs of legal representation since he succeeded at the court of first instance. However they were not adjudicated to him by the court, except for the reimbursement of the court fee.

[25] The court of appeal also changed the decision of the court of first instance in verdict II, i.e. in deciding on the cost of the proceedings, when it stated in its verdict that it was not being decided on the costs of judicial proceedings to exclude the arbitrator. They applied the provision of section 220 of the Code of Civil Procedure citing that the costs of proceedings are also part of arbitration proceedings. They concluded that when there is a 'termination of the arbitration proceedings on the merits, the arbitrator also decides on the costs of these proceedings.'

judge's, or the arbitrator's link to the parties to the proceedings or their representatives may then be established primarily by a family or similar relationship, which can in a certain case be equated by a friendly or, on the contrary, an obviously hostile relationship, etc. The grounds for the arbitrator's partiality will be in place especially in situations where there appears not only a person close to the arbitrator pursuant to section 116 of the Civil Code, but also a close person in a wider legal meaning of the word. This is understood as a person with whom the arbitrator is in any way related, e.g. where a party to the arbitration proceedings is the arbitrator's partner from a law office or other company, or an executive of one of the parties to the dispute or a member of its supervisory body. On the contrary, grounds for partiality within the meaning of the law will not be in place in a situation where an arbitrator has collaborated with one of the parties but it was not long-term collaboration. It may therefore be stated that it is necessary to take into account all the circumstances of a particular case and not to infer partiality solely from the fact that the arbitrator and the person who is a party to the proceedings or his legal representative know each other.

7.33. In the present case, the court of appeal did not find grounds for the arbitrator's partiality. The defendant, specifically its executive director presented the court of appeal with a diploma from which it was found that the executive director graduated from ..... (faculty of law in a different state than the arbitrator did—author's comment). It follows from the above that the executive director did not study the same faculty, and they are therefore not schoolmates. Even if the executive director has sat the rigorous examination at the same faculty as the arbitrator did, this circumstance cannot constitute a ground for the arbitrator's partiality; the same applies to studies at the same school. As stated above, neither arbitrator nor the defendant's executive director are executives of the same company or its supervisory body, which could be a ground for the exclusion of the arbitrator from the present case. The fact that in ... (year) a common lecture of these persons was scheduled to take place and did not does not constitute a ground for the arbitrator's partiality either. This would have been short-term collaboration, which, moreover, did not take place. It was not found or substantiated by evidence that the two persons closely collaborate in business. The court of appeal therefore did not find any relevant grounds to exclude the arbitrator for partiality. None of the facts presented by the petitioners may be considered a fact constituting a doubt about the arbitrator's impartiality.

X. Conclusion

7.34. There is a complexity to the issue of partiality of an arbitrator in arbitration. It is a phenomenon which is complicated in national as well as international arbitration proceedings. It is clear that connections between arbitrators and legal representatives of parties are more and more obvious, and what was once considered grounds for exclusion are now common practice.[26] Yet there are deceitful efforts of parties to arbitration to exclude a certain arbitrator, which negatively affects the efficiency of arbitration. It is necessary to maintain cooperation between arbitrators and general jurisdiction courts. General jurisdiction courts must, in particular in the Czech Republic, learn to perceive commercial arbitration as a positive phenomenon provided that rules are followed. Lately courts have obviously been 'persecuting' anything related to arbitration, from auxiliary functions of courts in the exclusion of arbitrator for partiality as seen by the attitude of the court of first instance presented above to the practice during enforcement proceedings, when the conditions of the proceedings are examined by execution courts. Although these claims seem beyond one's comprehension, this is the reality in the Czech Republic. The courts' distaste for arbitration proceedings was supposed to change with the amendment 19/2012 Coll., amending the Arbitration Act, but the negative attitude of general jurisdiction courts towards arbitration proceedings may only be changed by hard and fair work of arbitrators. The principle operating here should be that of cooperation, not destruction.

7.35. Partiality, the subjective link to the case or parties which is proven by objective facts, is a problem and it has to be dealt with. It is important that an arbitrator as part of self-reflection and courts as part of judicial proceedings always correctly determine whether the existence of partiality presents sufficient relevance or whether it is an insignificant link. If we accepted the arguments of the judge of the court of first instance on education at the same university, we could in fact paralyse the Czech judiciary with such an approach. The vast majority of Czech prosecutors, attorneys, judges, executors and notaries studied at the same Czech universities teaching law, as there are currently only 4 in the Czech Republic. Such an approach would mean that everyone would be everyone's 'schoolmate', and therefore they would all be excluded for partiality. The alternative is that this is meant only in relation to arbitration proceedings and in that case this way of thinking would be discriminatory.

---

[26]   Cf. e.g. IBA Guidelines on Conflicts of Interest in International Arbitration.

7.36. Beyond the issue of partiality, I have the impression that the Czech judiciary tries to deal with the problem of 'gaps' in legislation, which may be abused by certain groups by means of shaping, or even creating law before courts. God of the gaps is a theological concept and it should not find its application in judiciary. As in the past,[27] pointing out that despite understanding of the meaning, this is not a legal way, since a legal way would be a legislative way.

7.37. The balance between the general and arbitration partiality has to be applied and it is not possible to fashionably *usurp* arbitrators at the expense of other decision-making bodies. Nevertheless, the ones who brought a negative perception into jurisprudence of general jurisdiction courts were mainly arbitrators themselves with their excesses in the past. In order to achieve correctness of arbitration proceedings, it is necessary that legal representatives of the parties properly select the arbitrator, that arbitrators decide on disputes fairly, and that the courts assess each case correctly. In addition to many other changes, this triangle of mutual respect may lead to a situation where arbitration proceedings return to their roots and will be useful for parties to disputes.

| | |

Summaries

DEU [*Voreingenommenheit des Schiedsrichters*]
Der Autor des vorliegenden Beitrags hat sich darum bemüht, in knapper Form darzulegen, wie komplex der Problemkreis der Voreingenommenheit von Schiedsrichtern im Schiedsverfahren ist. Es handelt sich in innerstaatlichen wie internationalen Schiedsverfahren um ein außerordentlich schwierig zu fassendes Phänomen, lässt sich doch der Eindruck nicht verdrängen, dass die Beziehungen zwischen Schiedsrichtern und den Rechtsvertretern der jeweiligen Schiedsparteien immer offenkundiger werden – was früher als Ausschlussgrund galt, ist heute gängige Praxis. Daneben existiert aber zugleich das Phänomen, dass die am Schiedsverfahren beteiligten Parteien aus vorgeschobenen Gründen den Ausschluss des einen oder anderen Schiedsrichters anstrengen, was sich negativ auf die Effizienz von Schiedsverfahren auswirkt. Was Not tut, ist der Erhalt der Zusammenarbeit zwischen Schiedsrichtern und der allgemeinen Gerichtsbarkeit.

---

[27] Naděžda Rozehnalová & Jan Havlíček, *supra* note 12, at 114–119.

CZE [*Podjatost rozhodce*]

Autor tohoto článku se pokusil stručně prezentovat složitosti problematiky podjatosti rozhodce v arbitráži. Jde o fenomén velice složitý ve vnitrostátním i mezinárodním rozhodčím řízení, protože nelze nenabýt dojmu, že vazby mezi rozhodci, právními zástupci stran jsou stále evidentnější, a co by dříve bylo považováno za důvod vyloučení, dnes je běžnou praxí. Přesto existuje i falešná snaha účastníků arbitráže, aby došlo k vyloučení toho či onoho rozhodce, což negativně působí na efektivitu arbitráže. Je nutno udržet kooperaci mezi rozhodci a soudy obecnými.

||||

POL [*Stronniczość arbitra*]

Autor niniejszego artykułu podjął próbę zwięzłej charakterystyki problematyki stronniczości arbitra w postępowaniu arbitrażowym. Jest to niezwykle złożony fenomen zarówno w krajowym, jak i międzynarodowym postępowaniu arbitrażowym. Powiązania pomiędzy arbitrami, zastępcami prawnymi stron są coraz wyraźniejsze, a to, co wcześniej uważano za powód do wyłączenia, dziś staje się powszechną praktyką.

FRA [*La partialité de l'arbitre*]

Il s'agit ici d'une présentation concise du problème complexe de la partialité de l'arbitre dans la procédure d'arbitrage - un phénomène extrêmement complexe aussi bien dans une procédure nationale qu'internationale, car l'on est bien obligé de constater que les liens entre les arbitres et les représentants juridiques des parties sont de plus en plus manifestes et ce qui était considéré autrefois comme motivant une récusation est aujourd'hui pratique courante.

RUS [*Пристрастность арбитра*]

Автор данной статьи попытался кратко представить сложность вопроса пристрастности арбитра в арбитражном процессе. Это очень сложное явление как во внутригосударственных, так и в международных арбитражах, так как нельзя не заметить, что связи между арбитрами и адвокатами сторон проявляются все чаще, и то, что раньше рассматривалось как серьезная причина для отвода, в настоящее время является обычной практикой.

ESP   [*Parcialidad del árbitro*]

El autor del artículo trata de presentar brevemente la complejidad de la cuestión de la parcialidad del árbitro en un procedimiento arbitral. Es un fenómeno muy complejo en el arbitraje nacional e internacional, puesto que es imposible no adquirir la impresión de que los vínculos entre los árbitros y los representantes legales de las partes involucradas son cada vez más obvios, y lo que antes habría sido considerado un motivo de exclusión, hoy en día es una práctica común.

|||

Barbara Jelonek-Jarco | Julita Zawadzka

The Influence of Violation of the Independence and Impartiality Rules on the Enforceability and Effectiveness of the Arbitral Award

Key words:
arbitrator's disqualification | arbitrator's misconduct | challenge of arbitrator | enforcement proceedings | impartiality of arbitrators | New York Convention | Polish arbitration law | public policy (ordre public) | recognition or enforcement of foreign arbitral awards

Abstract | *The rules of independence and impartiality of arbitrators are guaranteed by various mechanisms. These include the duty imposed upon an arbitrator to disclose any circumstances likely to give rise to doubts as to their impartiality or independence or the parties' right to challenge an arbitrator. A procedural error that leads to the violation of the principles of independence and impartiality of arbitrators may constitute grounds for refusal of the recognition or enforcement of an arbitral award as specified in Article V of the New York Convention (NYC). Depending on what kind of procedural error has occurred, a different ground for the refusal of the recognition or enforcement may come into question. The power of the recognition and enforcement court to refuse the recognition of an arbitral award ex officio regardless of the initiative of the parties to the proceedings is, however, crucial. If a violation of the rules of the arbitrator's independence and impartiality in the course of the arbitral proceedings turns out to be an infringement of the principles of due process of law, then not only does the refusal of the recognition of an arbitral award support the protection of the public policy of the state in which the recognition is sought, but it also contributes to the increase of trust of the parties to the arbitration as an alternative and fair method of dispute resolution.*

Dr. Barbara Jelonek-Jarco is an attorney at law and partner at the Polish law firm of KKG Kubas Kos Gaertner, coordinating the work of the real estate department. She has participated in numerous court and arbitration proceedings for institutional clients. She also focuses her practice on such fields as company law and private commercial law. Dr. Jelonek-Jarco is the author of numerous articles, commentaries, didactic publications and monographs on civil and constitutional law. Email: barbara.jelonek@kkg.pl

Dr. Julita Zawadzka is an attorney at law at the Polish law firm of KKG Kubas Kos Gaertner. She has appeared in numerous court proceedings in the scope of civil law.

| | |

I. Importance of the Rules of Independence and Impartiality of Arbitrators – General Remarks

8.01. The possibility of shaping the composition of an arbitration court by parties to the proceedings is of decisive significance for the attractive nature of arbitration in comparison to the state court system. For this very reason, it is particularly important for the parties to be certain that their dispute will be heard by impartial and independent arbitrators. The independence and impartiality of the arbitrator is one of the fundamental principles of arbitration.[1] The arbitrator, much like a state court judge, should possess these characteristics, which guarantee parties a fair trial and an award capable of being vested with the force equal to that of verdicts issued by state courts.

She also is experienced in commercial law, in which she represents companies, among others, from the construction, energy, financial, and trade sectors. Dr. Zawadzka is the author of numerous articles, commentaries, didactic publications and monographs on civil and constitutional law. Email: julita.zawadzka@kkg.pl

II. Mechanisms Guaranteeing the Issuance of an Award by Independent and Impartial Arbitrators

8.02. Both the national regulations pertaining to proceedings before arbitral tribunals and the rules of procedure of permanent courts of arbitration provide for mechanisms intended to guarantee the issuance of awards by impartial and independent arbitrators. First, it is the duty of a person proposed to be appointed as an arbitrator to disclose all and any circumstances capable of raising justifiable doubts as to their impartiality and independence. It is followed by the arbitrator's duty to immediately disclose such circumstances as of the moment of their appointment throughout the duration of the entire arbitration proceedings.[2] In turn, upon selection of the arbitrators, each of the parties has the possibility to move for the exclusion of an arbitrator if there are reasonable doubts regarding their independence or

---

[1]   Cf. ALAN REDFERN, MARTIN HUNTER, NIGEL BLACKABY, CONSTANTINE PARTASIDES, LAW AND PRACTICE OF INTERNATIONAL COMMERCIAL ARBITRATION, Sweet & Maxwell 4.75 et seq. (2008).

[2]   This duty was underlined in the UNCITRAL Model Law on International Commercial Arbitration from 1985. It is stipulated also in domestic regulations, see, *e.g.*, Article 1174 of the Polish CCP, § 1036 of the German ZPO, § 588 of the Austrian ZPO; Article 179.2 of the Swiss PIL in conjunction with Article 363 of the Swiss ZPO, Article 24.1.a) of the English Arbitration Act 1996.

impartiality.[3] If the motion is unsuccessful, a party may challenge the arbitrator before a state court. However, this does not result in staying the proceedings before the arbitral tribunal until the state court issues the decision on the motion.[4] These regulations are intended to prevent the issuance of an arbitral award with the participation of an arbitrator who does not comply with the requirements of impartiality and independence. Cases may still occur due to reasons on the part of arbitrators or both arbitrators and parties to the proceedings. Hence, it is necessary to consider whether a violation of the principle of the arbitrator's impartiality and independence may provide grounds for the refusal to recognize or enforce an award and, if so, which of the reasons for refusing the recognition (enforcement) specified in Article V of the New York Convention of 1958 (NYC)[5] might substantiate the state court's refusal. This is an issue because the grounds for non-recognition of an award specified in the NYC do not include provisions directed specifically at a lack of independence or an arbitrator's misconduct.

III. Consequences of the Violation of the Principle of the Arbitrator's Impartiality and Independence

III.1. Violation of the Disclosure Duty

8.03. The issuance of an award with the participation of an arbitrator failing to comply with the requirements of impartiality and independence may occur in cases where an arbitrator candidate fails to disclose to the parties any and all circumstances able to influence their impartiality or independence, or where the arbitrator fails to notify the parties of circumstances which emerge in the course of the proceedings. If the party does not acquire knowledge of such circumstances from other sources by the end of the proceedings, an award may be issued by a

---

[3]   In the domestic regulations, legislators as a rule grant priority to the will of the parties themselves who may determine the mode of proceedings for the exclusion of an arbitrator (see: Article 1176 § 1 of the CCP, § 1037(1) of the German ZPO, § 589(1) of the Austrian ZPO, Article 180.3 of the Swiss PIL). The above mentioned procedure applies if there is not such an agreement.

[4]   See § 1037(2)-(3) of the German ZPO, § 589(2)-(3) of the Austrian ZPO; Article 1176 § 4-6 of the CCP, similarly Article 180.3 of the Swiss PIL. See also Article 13(2)-(3) UNCITRAL Model Law on International Commercial Arbitration; Article 24.3 of the English Arbitration Act 1996, however, see also Article 20.4 of the Vienna Rules 2013.

[5]   Deliberations included in this article are based on the NYC provisions due to the fact that it is one of the most widespread legal acts in the world on recognition and enforcement of foreign arbitral awards and the statutes implementing the NYC in each state primarily reproduce the terms of the Convention.

partial arbitrator.[6] Furthermore, the party may also not be aware of the arbitrator's partiality during the recognition proceedings.

8.04. Article V(1)(d) of the NYC may constitute grounds for the refusal to recognize or enforce an arbitral award issued under such circumstances. Under this provision, the recognition of an arbitral award may be refused at the request of a party if composition of the arbitral authority or the arbitral procedure was not in accordance with the agreement of the parties, or, failing such agreement, was not in accordance with the law of the country where the arbitration took place.

8.05. If the provisions applicable to a given type of proceeding provided for a duty of an arbitrator to disclose all and any circumstances capable of causing doubts as regards their impartiality, the violation of this duty must be regarded as a violation of the provisions on arbitral procedure enacting this duty and pertaining to the court of arbitration's composition and the rules of procedure before such a court.[7] However, the Supreme Court of Poland stated in its judgment of 9 September 2010[8], that the arbitrator's failure to disclose circumstances pointing to their connections with one of the parties to the proceedings does not constitute a violation of the requirements for the arbitration court's composition or the basic principles of proceeding before such a court, stemming from a statute or specified by the parties. This is because such a violation pertains neither to the requirements related to the arbitration court's composition nor to the basic rules of procedure adopted in the court of arbitration. The Supreme Court found that the court should consider these circumstances within the framework of the award's contradiction with the public policy clause.[9]

---

[6] As regards the manner of establishing by the state court in the course of the recognition proceedings whether a given arbitrator was partial, cf. 3 GARY BORN, INTERNATIONAL COMMERCIAL ARBITRATION, Alphen aan den Rijn: Kluwer Law International 2804-2806 (2009).

[7] This is also how this matter is qualified by Andrzej W. Wiśniewski, *Niezależność i bezstronność arbitrów w świetle prawa polskiego i praktyki międzynarodowej* (*Impartiality and independence of arbitrators in light of Polish law and international practice*), *in* 2 AUREA PRAXIS AUREA THEORIA. KSIĘGA PAMIĄTKOWA KU CZCI PROFESORA TADEUSZA ERECIŃSKIEGO, Warszawa: Lexis Nexis 1966-1967 (J. Gudowski, K. Weitz eds., 2011). Similarly: TADEUSZ ERECIŃSKI, KAROL WEITZ, SĄD ARBITRAŻOWY (COURT OF ARBITRATION), Warszawa: Lexis Nexis 204 (2008); KARL-HEINZ SCHWAB, GERHARD WALTER, SCHIEDSGERICHTSBARKEIT, Munich: C.H. Beck 116 (2005). See also: Justyna Szpara, *Setting Aside an Arbitration Award*, *in* ARBITRATION IN POLAND, Warszawa: Sąd Arbitrażowy przy Krajowej Izbie Gospodarczej 118 (2011). However, a contrary conclusion must be derived from the ICCA's GUIDE TO THE INTERPRETATION OF THE 1958 NEW YORK CONVENTION. A HANDBOOK FOR JUDGES 95-98, 89 and 110 (P. Sanders ed., 2001).

[8] File ref. no I CSK 535/09, LEX no. 602748.

[9] See also OLG Stuttgart in the judgement of 6 December 2001. The position expressed in the judgement of the Supreme Court of Poland of 9 September 2010 brought a change

8.06. According to yet another view, an impartial decision by the arbitrator constitutes one of the elements of the right to a fair hearing. For this reason, the participation of a partial arbitrator in issuing an award may be regarded as a circumstance preventing the party from a chance 'to present its case'.[10] Hence, the issuance of an award by a partial arbitrator, in certain cases, may fulfill the premise set forth in Article V(1)(b) NYC.

8.07. It seems, however, that the notion of 'the composition of the arbitral authority' should also encompass the procedure for appointment of arbitrators, which extends as well to the disclosure duties imposed on the persons proposed to be appointed as arbitrators. In turn, the duties imposed on arbitrators in the course of the proceedings constitute an element of 'the arbitral procedure'. For this reason, the party whom the award is invoked against may seek the refusal of the recognition of an arbitral award due to the arbitrator's concealment of their connections with one of the parties.[11] It is also necessary to consider cases where the parties are not aware of the circumstances influencing the arbitrator's impartiality or independence in the course of proceedings for recognition and enforcement. It is not clear whether a court deciding on the recognition or enforcement of an award may allow these circumstances *sua sponte* (as the facts the court is familiar with *ex officio*), if the court acquires knowledge thereof in a manner other than as a result of an argument raised by the parties to the proceedings.

8.08. The adoption of a specific solution in the cases above depends on whether a recognition court may allow the prerequisites for the refusal of the recognition or enforcement of an arbitral award indicated in Article V(1) NYC *ex officio*. The wording of Article V(1) NYC introduces a specific rule for the distribution of the burden of proof. In the scope of the circumstances listed therein, it imposes this burden on a party to the proceedings.[12] Therefore, a court should allow the

---

of the case-law line of this court (see, *e.g.*: the judgement of the Supreme Court of 3 September 2009, file ref. no I CSK 53/09, LEX no. 527154 and the judgement of the Supreme Court of SN 3 September 1998, file ref. no I CKN 822/97, LEX no. 34448).

[10] The Judgement of the United States Court of Appeals for the Seventh District, quoted without a more specific reference in: Pieter Sanders ed., *supra* note 7, at 89.

[11] It is, however, obvious that not every disclosed connection between the arbitrator and the party will result in their recognition as a partial arbitrator; See, *e.g.*: JULIAN LEW, LOUKAS MISTELIS, STEFAN KRÖLL, COMPARATIVE INTERNATIONAL COMMERCIAL ARBITRATION, Alphen aan den Rijn: Kluwer Law International 271, 305-306 (2003).

[12] ANTON G. MAURER, THE PUBLIC POLICY EXCEPTION UNDER THE NEW YORK CONVENTION, New York: Juris 69 (2012), Patricia Nacimiento, *Article V(1)(a)*, *in* RECOGNITION AND ENFORCEMENT OF FOREIGN ARBITRAL AWARDS: A GLOBAL COMMENTARY ON THE NEW YORK CONVENTION, Alphen aan den Rijn: Kluwer Law International 210 (H. Kronke, P. Nacimiento et al. eds., 2010) and the case-law quoted therein.

grounds for the refusal of the recognition of an award indicated in Article V(1) NYC on the motion of a party whereas the court may allow *ex officio* solely the grounds for the refusal of the recognition or enforcement of an arbitral award listed in Article V(2) NYC. This, in turn, brings yet another question as to whether the court is able to qualify the violations fulfilling the grounds for the refusal of the recognition of the award listed in Article V(1) NYC as the circumstances allowed *ex officio*, listed in Article V(2) NYC, i.e. as circumstances having the result that the recognition of the award would stand in contradiction with the 'public policy of that country' (Article V(2)(b) NYC).[13]

8.09. This issue is controversial. The literature emphasizes that the public policy clause should be resorted to only in exceptional circumstances.[14] Most authors think (based mainly on the literal interpretation of Article V NYC) that until specific grounds for the refusal of the recognition or enforcement of an arbitral award apply, the public policy clause may not be applied.[15] It is emphasized that the initiative regarding the prerequisites indicated in Article V(1) NYC is left to the parties to the proceedings. Hence, if a party does not refer to these prerequisites, then, in compliance with the principle *volenti non fit iniuria*, neither should the court. Therefore, even if a state court examining the motion for the recognition or enforcement of an arbitral award notes the existence of the grounds for refusal set forth in Article V(1) NYC, it may not replace the decision of the aggrieved party and refuse the recognition upon the public policy of its country.[16]

---

[13] As regards the notion of the public policy, cf. *e.g.* Dirk Otto, Omaia Elwan, *in* RECOGNITION AND ENFORCEMENT OF FOREIGN ARBITRAL AWARDS: A GLOBAL COMMENTARY ON THE NEW YORK CONVENTION, Alphen aan den Rijn: Kluwer Law International 365 et seq. (H. Kronke, P. Nacimiento et al. (eds), 2010). Cf. also ANTON G. MAURER, *supra* note 12, at 53 et seq.

[14] Tadeusz Ereciński, *Postępowanie o stwierdzenie wykonalności zagranicznego wyroku arbitrażowego (zagadnienia wybrane)* (*Proceedings for enforcement of foreign arbitral award (selected issues)*), 5(1) ADR ARBITRAŻ I MEDIACJA 71 (2009); Mateusz Pilich, *Klauzula porządku publicznego w postępowaniu o uznanie i wykonanie zagranicznego orzeczenia arbitrażowego* (*Public policy clause in recognition and enforcement proceedings of a foreign arbitral award*), 12(1) KWARTALNIK PRAWA PRYWATNEGO 172-175 (2003), at 176.

[15] ANTON G. MAURER, *supra* note 12, at 67, 70. In Polish literature, this stance is supported by Mateusz Pilich, *supra* note 14, at 171, TADEUSZ ERECIŃSKI, KAROL WEITZ, *supra* note 7, at 401, Tadeusz Ereciński, *supra* note 14, at 70; RAFAŁ MOREK, MEDIACJA I ARBITRAŻ (ART. 183¹-183¹⁵, 1154-1217). KOMENTARZ, Warszawa: C.H. Beck 269 (2006); Karol Weitz, *Klauzula porządku publicznego jako podstawa uchylenia wyroku sądu polubownego na tle praktyki sądów*, (1) BIULETYN ARBITRAŻOWY 19 (2010).

[16] ANTON G. MAURER, *supra* note 12, at 67-71.

8.10. This position is, among others, presented in German literature. It is emphasized that if the provisions on the recognition of arbitral awards applied by the recognition court provide for specific grounds for the refusal of the recognition of an arbitral award, it is possible to find that the violation of the principle of an arbitrator's impartiality and independence is covered by this specific basis,[17] which excludes the possibility to call upon the public policy clause.[18] An example of this is Article V(1)(b) NYC, which extends to the violation of the right to present the case, a violation of the right to raise charges and rely on a procedural means of defense.

8.11. According to the opposite position, the overlapping of the grounds for the refusal of the recognition (enforcement) of the award allowed *ex officio* and on the motion is not ruled out. In truth, it depends on the gravity of the violation of the rules of procedure.[19] This view assumes that the public policy clause is useful in cases where the violation of the procedural rules included within the grounds of the refusal allowed only upon a parties' request is gross in nature. Then, the court should take the violation of these rules into consideration, even when there is no motion of a party. If a court adopts the position on the separate nature of the prerequisites listed in Article V(1) and (2) NYC, where no party files a motion, the court would be unable to refuse the recognition of an award affected with the violations set forth in Article V(1) NYC, despite the fact that the violation leads to consequences irreconcilable with the domestic public policy.[20]

---

[17] PETER SCHLOSSER, DAS RECHT DER INTERNATIONALEN PRIVATEN SCHIEDSGERICHTSBARKEIT, Tübingen: Mohr 615 (1989).

[18] *Ibid.*, at 599 and 615.

[19] JAN VAN DEN BERG, THE NEW YORK ARBITRATION CONVENTION OF 1958. TOWARDS A UNIFORM JUDICIAL INTERPRETATION, London: Kluwer Law and Taxation Publishers 62 (1981), Ulrich Haas, *in* PRACTITIONER'S HANDBOOK ON INTERNATIONAL ARBITRATION, Munich: C.H. Beck 530 (Frank-Bernd Wiegand ed., 2002), Bernard Hanotiau, Olivier Caprasse, *Public Policy, in* ENFORCEMENT OF ARBITRATION AGREEMENTS AND INTERNATIONAL ARBITRAL AWARDS. THE NEW YORK CONVENTION IN PRACTICE, London: Cameron May 799 (E. Gaillard, D. di Pietro eds., 2008). In Polish literature see: Maciej Łaszczuk, Justyna Szpara, *Postępowania postarbitrażowe*, in 8 SYSTEM PRAWA HANDLOWEGO, ARBITRAŻ HANDLOWY (8 SYSTEM OF COMMERCIAL LAW. COMMERCIAL ARBITRATION), Warszawa: C.H. Beck 612 (A. Szumański ed., 2010); Marek Neumann, *Klauzula porządku publicznego a treść wyroku sądu polubownego (Public policy clause and the content of the arbitral award)*, 2 GLOSA 2001 66-67.

[20] Marek Neumann, *supra* note 19, at 67. Cf. Andrés Jana, Angie Armer, *et al.*, *Article V(1)(b), in* RECOGNITION AND ENFORCEMENT OF FOREIGN ARBITRAL AWARDS: A GLOBAL COMMENTARY ON THE NEW YORK CONVENTION, Alphen aan den Rijn: Kluwer Law International 297-298 (H. Kronke, P. Nacimiento *et al.* eds., 2010).

8.12. It is significant to determine the relationship between the prerequisites for the refusal or the recognition of an award set forth in Article V(1) NYC and those stemming from Article V(2)(b) NYC and hence the contradiction of the recognition with the public policy of the recognizing country. This is particularly significant where, in the course of the recognition or enforcement proceedings, parties (or one of the parties) are not aware of the existence of circumstances which may substantiate the refusal of the recognition or enforcement of the award but which circumstances the adjudicating court is familiar with. It is difficult to call upon the *volenti non fit iniuria* principle if the party is not aware it is suffering an *iniuria*. It is also problematic when parties are not interested in raising the arguments listed in Article V(1) NYC such as when both parties find the award suitable to their interests and they are interested in its speedy recognition. This may be the case even if the award is burdened with the defects listed in Article V(1) NYC. Perhaps even the circumstances indicate that both the arbitration proceedings and the state court proceedings are collusive. Adopting the position which allows the court to resort to the public policy clause solely in the cases not mentioned in Article V(1) NYC means that despite the full awareness of occurrence of the circumstances listed in this provision, the court is unable to refuse the recognition of the award, thus vesting with the force of the state judgment an award, which from the point of view of its correctness, is dubious, to say the least. The view according to which the grounds of the refusal, which are allowed *ex officio* overlap with those allowed upon a motion, would permit the court to refuse the recognition of the award by calling upon the contradictory nature of the judgment with the public policy of the country where the recognition is sought. The public policy clause would constitute a type of a safety valve permitting the court to refuse the recognition of an award which is dubious from the point of view of its compliance with the law of the state where the recognition or enforcement proceedings are pending. A compromise solution is to assume that the circumstances substantiating the refusal of the recognition or enforcement of an arbitration court award allowed only upon a request (Article V(1) NYC) may be allowed *ex officio* as well, but only in exceptional cases. These would be where the violations listed in Article V(1) NYC are of such a nature that the public policy of a given country would object to vesting the award burdened with such defects with a force equal to that of judgments of this state and would object to the observance of such an award by the bodies of a given state.

8.13. Such an interpretation would mean that not every circumstance capable of substantiating the refusal of the recognition (enforcement) of an award due to the charge raised by a party on the grounds of Article V(1) NYC may also substantiate the refusal of the recognition due to the fact that the court *ex officio* assumes that the recognition (enforcement) of the award would be in contradiction with the public policy of the country in which the recognition is sought. Fundamental principles of the NYC are a pro-enforcement bias and limiting to the indispensable minimum the admissibility of revision by a state court of an award issued by a foreign court of arbitration.[21] Therefore, one must assume that the cases of violation of procedural standards falling within the category of the premises listed in Article V(1) NYC may substantiate the refusal of the recognition (enforcement) of an arbitral award *ex officio* when the violated rule of procedure is of such a type that the violation thereof would cause a threat to the public policy of the recognizing country in the event of the recognition of the award issued in such proceedings.

8.14. From this point of view, it is not important whether a party to the arbitration proceedings decides to call upon a given offense of the rules of procedure or whether it abandons this possibility since, in light of the public policy exception, it is not the interest of the party, but that of the recognizing country that is decisive in terms of the admissibility of the recognition (enforcement) of the award.[22] Hence, referring to the *volenti non fit iniuria* principle in such cases finds no grounds. Referring to the distribution of the burden of proof specified in Article V(1) NYC is also not convincing, because since the public policy exception is to serve the protection of the public policy of the country where the recognition is sought, then ensuring the protection of this policy may not be rendered dependent on the fact of whether a party to the arbitration proceedings decides to raise a specific charge and whether it is capable of proving it sufficiently. Therefore, the burden of detecting a threat to the public policy and preventing it by refusing to recognize (enforce) a foreign arbitral award rests with the state court.

8.15. Referring these comments to a violation related to the arbitral authority's composition or procedure by the arbitrator's (arbitrator candidate's) default on the disclosure duties, it is worthwhile to highlight that the requirement of impartiality and independence stems from the nature of the role fulfilled by arbitrators and, more broadly, from the nature of the function realized by the arbitral judiciary.[23] This

---

[21] See: ANTON G. MAURER, *supra* note 12, at 61-67.
[22] See, *e.g.*: Pieter Sanders ed., *supra* note 7, at 104.
[23] Anna Krysiak, Marek Wierzbowski, *Bezstronność i niezależność jako kluczowe cechy każdego arbitra* (*Independence and impartiality as key features of every arbitrator*), *in*

requirement is also decisive for the admissibility of the existence of arbitration courts as a forum for a method of dispute resolution competitive with state courts.[24] Impartiality and independence constitute the statutory premises for the admissibility to entertain the function of the arbitrator.[25] The requirement that tribunals be impartial falls within fundamental procedural principles.[26] Therefore, the lack of an arbitrator's independence and impartiality violates the right of access to the courts.[27] In this context, it is reasonable to find that the provisions guaranteeing the impartiality and independence of the arbitrator are of such importance, that their violation allows the state court to refuse the recognition of an arbitral award on the basis that recognition of such an award poses a threat to the public policy of that country.[28] Therefore, the very fact that a party did not rely upon a given violation of the disclosure duties or another violation of the duty of the arbitrator's independence and impartiality, may not be decisive for inadmissibility of allowing such a circumstance by the court *ex officio*.

KSIĘGA PAMIĄTKOWA 60-LECIA SĄDU ARBITRAŻOWEGO PRZY KRAJOWEJ IZBIE GOSPODARCZEJ W WARSZAWIE (FESTSCHRIFT: 60 YEARS ARBITRATION COURT AT POLISH CHAMBER OF COMMERCE IN WARSAW), Warszawa: Sąd Arbitrażowy przy Krajowej Izbie Gospodarczej 359 (J. Okolski, A. Całus, M. Pazdan, S. Sołtysiński, T. Wardyński, S. Włodyka eds., 2010).

[24] Michał Romanowski, *Znaczenie niezależności i bezstronności arbitra w postępowaniu arbitrażowym w świetle konstytucyjnego prawa do sądu (The meaning of impartiality and independence of an arbitrator in arbitration proceedings in light of a constitutional right to court access)*, in KSIĘGA PAMIĄTKOWA 60-LECIA SĄDU ARBITRAŻOWEGO PRZY KRAJOWEJ IZBIE GOSPODARCZEJ W WARSZAWIE (FESTSCHRIFT: 60 YEARS ARBITRATION COURT AT POLISH CHAMBER OF COMMERCE IN WARSAW), Warszawa: Sąd Arbitrażowy przy Krajowej Izbie Gospodarczej 376 (J. Okolski, A. Całus, M. Pazdan, S. Sołtysiński, T. Wardyński, S. Włodyka eds, 2010).

[25] The requirement of preservation of impartiality and independence of the arbitrator is stipulated *e.g.* by the IBA Guidelines on Conflicts of Interest in International Arbitration and by Article 12 UNCITRAL Model Law on International Commercial Arbitration. It is also stipulated in domestic regulations on arbitration proceedings (see, *e.g.*: Article 1173 et seq. of the Polish CCP, § 1036 and 1037 of the German ZPO, § 588 and 589 of the Austrian ZPO; Article 179.2 of the Swiss PIL in conjunction with Article 363 and 367 of the Swiss ZPO, Article 24.1.a) of the English Arbitration Act 1996).

[26] See: recommendation no. 1(e) of International Law Association Recommendations on the Application of Public Policy as a Ground for Refusing Recognition or Enforcement of International Arbitral Awards (Resolution 2/2002) adopted by the 70th Conference of the International Law Association held in New Delhi, India, 2-6 April 2002.

[27] Michał Romanowski, *supra* note 24, at 384.

[28] See: Maciej Zachariasiewicz, *Public policy as a ground of refusal of recognition or enforcement of the arbitral award in Poland*, 5 MIGALHAS ON INTERNATIONAL ARBITRATION 2 (2010).

III.2. Preclusion (Waiver) of the Reasons for Removal of an Arbitrator in an Action to Stop Enforcement of an Award

8.16. An award may be issued with the participation of an arbitrator who has been non-compliant with the requirements of impartiality and independence. It may also be issued where the parties had admittedly acquired the knowledge, from the arbitrator or from other sources, of the circumstances capable of influencing the arbitrator's impartiality and independence. However, before the award was issued they had not engaged in any activities capable of causing the exclusion of the arbitrator or such action had not been engaged in within the prescribed time limit. Hence, the award was issued with the participation of a partial arbitrator.

8.17. In principle, the removal of the arbitrator may take place only if a party comes forth with an appropriate demand. Therefore, a question arises whether in the case where the party is familiar with the circumstances substantiating the exclusion of an arbitrator, yet fails to file an appropriate motion or files such a motion outside of the prescribed time limit, can this issue be raised in the proceedings for the recognition (enforcement) of an arbitral award either on the parties motion or alternatively, *ex officio* by the court. It is assumed that, in principle, the failure to demand the removal of the arbitrator causes the preclusion of the reasons for removal. It is recognized as equivalent with a party's resignation from referring to these circumstances in post-arbitration proceedings.[29]

8.18. In light of the Polish provisions on arbitral proceedings, failing to raise the charge of an offense of the provisions on proceedings before the court of arbitration at the right time precludes the party who was aware of this violence from raising the charge of such an violation before the arbitration court or in the action to set aside the arbitral award. Nonetheless, commentators indicate that this preclusion does not extend to the mandatory provisions of the Code of Civil Procedure on proceedings before a court of arbitration.[30] Although this issue has not been settled anywhere, it seems also that the provisions concerning the impartiality and independence of arbitrators must be regarded as having a mandatory character.[31]

---

[29] See: JULIAN LEW, LOUKAS MISTELIS, STEFAN KRÖLL, *supra* note 11, at 308-309, 315-316; see also: GARY BORN, *supra* note 6, at 2615 and the case law quoted therein, in particular US, French, Swiss and English case law.

[30] See, in relation to the grounds of setting aside of an arbitral award, Justyna Szpara, *supra* note 7, at 118.

[31] See also: Justyna Szpara, *supra* note 7, at 118.

8.19. The Polish literature presents a view according to which the preclusion in relation to the grounds for the exclusion of an arbitrator is not effective where the arbitrator's participation in issuing the award could be found to substantiate the contradiction of this award with the fundamental principles of public policy.[32] For example, the arbitrator who was a party to the proceedings or whose rights or obligations were impacted by the outcome of the arbitration proceedings had participated in the issuance of the award. In such cases, the *nemo iudex in casua sua* principle is violated.[33] Therefore, if the arbitration proceedings are conducted according to the provisions of the Polish Code of Civil Procedure, the charge related to the lack of impartiality or independence of the arbitrator may be found not to be subject to preclusion. Thus a party's failure to raise such a charge in the course of the arbitration proceedings does not exclude the possibility of taking this procedural defect into consideration in the course of the recognition or enforcement proceedings.

8.20. The German literature adopts the stance that in the event of the issuance of an award with the participation of a partial arbitrator, the recognition or enforcement court carries out a two-step examination. First, it examines whether under the provisions on arbitration proceedings applicable in the given case, the proceedings are defective and whether under these provisions this defect may be called upon, or whether the preclusion has already occurred. If the preclusion occurred in light of the appropriate provisions on arbitration proceedings it is also effective in the recognition or enforcement proceedings before a German court. Next, however, the recognition or enforcement court must assess whether, according to the German standards, the arbitrator was sufficiently impartial and independent. The assessment is carried out from the viewpoint of the public policy exception if the specific violations do not fall under another, specific prerequisite for the refusal of the recognition (enforcement) of the arbitral award or if the provisions on the recognition of arbitral awards applied by the recognition or enforcement court provide for no special prerequisites.[34] However, the assessment of a potential violation of the German public policy by a specific violation to the provisions on arbitration

---

[32] KAROL POTRZOBOWSKI, WŁADYSŁAW ŻYWICKI, SĄDOWNICTWO POLUBOWNE. KOMENTARZ DLA POTRZEB PRAKTYKI (ARBITRAL JUDICIARY. PRACTICAL COMMENTARY), Warszawa: Wydawnictwo Prawnicze 35 (1961); RAFAŁ MOREK, *supra* note 15, at 190; TADEUSZ ERECIŃSKI, KAROL WEITZ, *supra* note 7, at 204.

[33] See: the judgement of the Supreme Court of 24 September 1999, file ref. no. I CKN 141/98, LEX no. 38857.

[34] PETER SCHLOSSER, *supra* note 17, at 615.

proceedings is not without significance where in the course of the arbitration proceedings the party had the opportunity to raise the arbitrator's impartiality and independence. If the party did have such an opportunity, then their failure to take advantage thereof should have the consequence that only exceptionally manifest violations of the principle of the arbitrator's impartiality and independence, first and foremost the violation of the principle that no-one may act as a judge in their own case, can result in the refusal of the recognition or enforcement of the award.[35]

8.21.   From a preclusion viewpoint, the above-mentioned concept of the two-step examination of the admissibility of allowing the charge of the lack of an arbitrator's impartiality and independence must be found convincing. The admissibility of raising the charge related to the violation of the rules of procedure should be examined in the light of the provisions applicable to the given arbitration proceedings. Yet, even in the case when in light of these provisions a party does not entertain such a possibility anymore, the country where the recognition is sought may not be forced to enforce or recognize such an award on its own territory if, due to this offense, the recognition of the award would contradict the public policy of that country.

III.3. Admissibility in an Enforcement Proceeding of Exclusion Charges that Were Not Allowed in the Arbitration Proceedings

8.22.   It is also worthwhile to examine those cases where the party raised the charges related to the arbitrator's impartiality and independence within the prescribed time limit, but the court of arbitration refused to exclude the arbitrator, recourse to the state court did not result in the exclusion of the arbitrator and the award was issued with the participation of the questionable arbitrator. Then a question arises whether the lack of impartiality and independence of the arbitrator whom these rulings concerned may provide the grounds for the refusal of the recognition or enforcement of the arbitral award issued in these proceedings.

8.23.   Some authors find that if the arbitrator's exclusion because of their lack of impartiality and independence raised by the party, is refused, then often this decision excludes the setting aside of the arbitral award based on the same circumstances which were not allowed in the proceedings for the arbitrator's exclusion, or such a decision at least constitutes

---

[35]   *Ibid.*, at 616. See also: the verdict of the BGH of 1 February 2001, XXIX Yearbook of Commercial Arbitration (2004), at 700-714.

convincing evidence in the proceedings for setting aside the arbitral award.[36] At times, state courts hearing motions to set aside an arbitral award refer to the fact that an earlier state court decision refusing the arbitrator's exclusion enjoys substantive validity and therefore it may not be revised in later proceedings before the state court if the charge raised in the post-arbitration proceedings is based on the same grounds as the previously dismissed motion for the arbitrator's exclusion.[37] Also, where provisions applicable to the given proceedings do not provide for the possibility of a judicial review of the arbitration court's decision refusing the arbitrator's exclusion, state courts call upon the fact that the decisions of arbitration courts are final if the appropriate provisions do not stipulate the procedure for challenging them and refuse to hear the charge of an arbitrator's partiality, heard already by the arbitration court.[38] Some state courts assume that an unsuccessful institutional challenge will not be precluded in a subsequent annulment action, for the parties may not waive the right to demand that the arbitral award be set aside due to the charge of the arbitrator's impartiality or independence.[39]

8.24. Yet another view assumes that where the exclusion is ruled on by an arbitral institution, its decision is of an administrative nature and enjoys no *res judicata* effect. *Ipso facto*, in the course of the proceedings for recognition, state courts may rule whether the challenge raised against the arbitrator and rejected by the arbitral institution constitutes a ground on which to refuse the action to enforce. However, where the challenge has been rejected by a state court, the issue of the arbitrators' independence is deemed to be finally decided and can no longer be re-examined by the courts when hearing a motion for recognition of an award, unless a defect affecting the constitution of the arbitral tribunal has since come to light.[40]

8.25. Although there are substantial arguments in favor of each of these views, yet it would seem that the state court's refusal to exclude the

---

[36] See: *e.g.* GARY BORN, *supra* note 6, at 2616.

[37] See: *e.g.* judgment of OLG Munich of 20 December 2006, 34 Sch 16/06 (available at: http://www.dis-arb.de/de/47/datenbanken/rspr/olg-münchen-az-34-sch-16-06-datum-2006-12-20-id655; accessed on: September 30, 2013).

[38] Judgment of Paris Cour d'appel of 15 May 1985, *Raffineries de pétrole d'Homs et de Banias* v. *Chambre de Commerce Internationale*, 1985 Revue de l'Arbitrage 141, regarding the procedure for the exclusion of the arbitrator based on the ICC Rules.

[39] Judgment of English Court of Appeal, AT&T Corp. v. Saudi Cable Co. [2000] 2 Lloyd's Rep. 127, 137; quoted after: GARY BORN, *supra* note 6, at 2617.

[40] FOUCHARD GAILLARD GOLDMAN ON INTERNATIONAL COMMERCIAL ARBITRATION, Alphen aan den Rijn: Kluwer Law International ¶ 1069 (E. Gaillard, J. Savage eds., 1999) and the literature and case-law quoted therein.

arbitrator should, in principle, exclude the possibility to later call upon the same circumstances in the recognition or enforcement proceedings. The dismissal of the motion for the arbitrator's exclusion should mean that the charges raised by the party against the arbitrator's impartiality and independence were analyzed by an independent state court from the viewpoint of the rules of procedure applicable in the proceedings and no violation of these rules was established. The court of the country where the recognition is sought should, however, retain the right to refuse the recognition of a foreign arbitral award in those cases where the motion for the arbitrator's exclusion was heard exclusively in the institutional challenge mode. Furthermore, such a right must also be awarded to the court of the recognizing country if this court arrives at the conclusion that, despite the previous examination of the charge of the arbitrator's partiality (be it in the institutional challenge mode or the judicial review mode), the standards of impartiality and independence of arbitrators in force in the recognizing country object to the recognition of the award issued with the participation of this arbitrator. Hence, the court of the recognizing country should retain the right to refuse the recognition of such an award if the recognition thereof would contradict that country's public policy.

III.4. Exclusion of the Arbitrator after the Rendering of the Arbitral Award

8.26. The domestic provisions on arbitration proceedings stipulate the recourse to the state court for the exclusion of an arbitrator. Simultaneously, these provisions do not assume staying of further proceedings before the arbitration court. Therefore, it is worthwhile to consider the impact which the exclusion by the state court, after the award has been issued, of the arbitrator who participated in the issuance of the arbitral award, will have on the admissibility of the recognition (enforcement) of such an award.

8.27. In the proceedings for the arbitrator's exclusion, the state court confirms (or negates) the existence of circumstances impacting the arbitrator's impartiality and independence. Hence, if the existence of such circumstances is established by virtue of the judgment issued by the state court, then it must be assumed that it is the basis for the setting aside or refusing the recognition (enforcement) of the arbitral award.[41] There are also no grounds to assume that in the event of

---

[41] See: KARL-HEINZ SCHWAB, GERHARD WALTER, *supra* note 7, at 118; TADEUSZ ERECIŃSKI, KAROL WEITZ, *supra* note 7, at 203-204; Andrzej Zieliński, *in* KODEKS

issuance of the award by the arbitration court, the proceedings for the exclusion of the arbitrator become devoid of purpose.[42] As it seems, if it was to be so, the legislators would specify in the statute that in the event a motion for the arbitrator's exclusion is filed, the arbitration proceedings are suspended or they would decide that the questionable arbitrator may continue to participate in the proceedings, but no award may be issued with such an arbitrator's participation (cf. Article 20 Vienna Rules of 2013). Possibly, another rule would be introduced providing for the discontinuation of the proceedings on the motion for the arbitrator's exclusion if the arbitral award was issued in the course of the proceedings. However, there are no such regulations since, in principle, as already indicated, it is assumed that arbitration proceedings may be pending in parallel to the proceedings for the arbitrator's exclusion. Legislators take into account the possibility that the arbitration proceedings would end sooner than the proceedings for the exclusion of the arbitrator. At the same time, it is difficult to assume that the decision on the arbitrator's exclusion issued after the arbitral award has been passed remains without any impact on the admissibility of the recognition of the award issued with this arbitrator's participation. It is so due to the fact that such a decision constitutes the confirmation that the arbitrator failed to comply with the requirements of impartiality and independence expected in light of the rules of procedure applicable in the given arbitration proceedings. Hence, a party may move for the refusal of the recognition of the award, quoting Article V(1)(b) NYC.

IV. Summary

8.28. The possibility of the refusal to recognize an arbitral award, due to a violation of the principle of impartiality and independence of arbitrators, constitutes a substantial warranty of the observance of this principle. It is the last stage at which a party may raise the charge of the lack of arbitrators' impartiality and independence. If the charge is not allowed, the arbitral award issued by a partial arbitral tribunal acquires as consequence of its recognition a force equal to that of a state court

POSTĘPOWANIA CYWILNEGO. KOMENTARZ (CODE OF CIVIL PROCEDURE. COMMENTARY), Warszawa: C.H. Beck 1672 (A. Zieliński ed., 2013).

[42] According to another opinion, at the moment of the issuance of the arbitral award, the proceedings for the exclusion of the arbitrator become devoid of purpose while in the recourse for the setting aside of the arbitral award the party may call upon the non-compliance of the composition of the arbitral tribunal with the law (see: BERNHARD BERGER, FRANZ KELLERHALS, INTERNATIONALE UND INTERNE SCHIEDSGERICHTSBARKEIT IN DER SCHWEIZ, Bern: Stampfli Verlag 294 (2006)).

judgment. For this reason, a too lenient approach of state courts hearing motions for the recognition or enforcement of arbitral awards may lead to the questioning of the arbitral awards as being issued in proceedings that do not guarantee a certain standard of due process. This may deprecate the role of arbitration as a manner of dispute resolution and may seriously impair parties' trust in arbitration since they will not have certainty that the potential violation of principles of impartiality and independence of arbitrators will result in the refusal of the recognition of the arbitral award. Therefore, in the recognition proceedings, charges based on the violation of the principles of arbitrators' impartiality and independence should be treated with special attention. It is necessary to permit *ex officio* actions of the state courts aimed at preventing the recognition of awards issued with the grave violation of these rules.

| | |

Summaries

DEU [*Einfluss des Verstoßes gegen die Regeln der Unabhängigkeit und Unparteilichkeit auf Vollstreckbarkeit und Wirkung eines Schiedsspruchs*]

Die Unabhängigkeit und Unparteilichkeit der Schiedsrichter werden durch mehrere Regelungen der Schiedsverfahrensrecht abgesichert, wie eine dem Schiedsrichter auferlegte Pflicht, alle Umstände offen zu legen, die Zweifel an seiner Unparteilichkeit oder Unabhängigkeit wecken können oder die Möglichkeit, ein Verfahren zur Ablehnung eines Schiedsrichters einzuleiten. Ein Verfahrensfehler, der zur Verstoß gegen die Grundsätze der Unabhängigkeit und Unparteilichkeit der Schiedsrichter führt, kann einen Anerkennungsversagungsgrund im Sinne von Art. V des NYC darstellen. Je nachdem, was für ein Verfahrensmangel auftritt, kann ein anderer Anerkennungsversagungsgrund in Frage kommen. Besonders wichtig sind aber die Kompetenzen des Anerkennungsgerichts, ein Anerkennungsversagungsgrund von Amts wegen zu berücksichtigen, ohne sich auf die Initiative der Parteien verlassen zu müssen. Wenn dann die Missachtung der Grundsätze der Unabhängigkeit und Unparteilichkeit des Schiedsrichters im Laufe des Schiedsverfahrens zum Verstoß gegen die Grundsätze eines fairen Gerichtsverfahrens wird, dient die Versagung der Anerkennung eines Schiedsspruchs nicht nur dem Schutz des ordre public des Anerkennungsstaates, sondern auch dem Anstieg des Vertrauens der Parteien zu der Schiedsgerichtsbarkeit als einer alternativen und fairen Konfliktlösungsmöglichkeiten.

CZE [*Vliv porušení pravidel o nezávislosti a nestrannosti na vykonatelnost a účinky rozhodčího nálezu*]

Dodržování pravidel o nezávislosti a nestrannosti rozhodců je garantováno různými mechanismy. Tyto zahrnují povinnost rozhodců informovat o jakýchkoliv okolnostech, které by mohly způsobit pochybnosti o jejich nestrannosti a nezávislosti, nebo které by mohly založit právo stran odmítnout rozhodce. Procesní pochybení vedoucí k porušení zásady nezávislosti a nestrannosti rozhodce může zakládat důvody pro odmítnutí uznání a výkonu rozhodčího nálezu uvedené v článku V Newyorské úmluvy (NYC). V závislosti na druhu procesního pochybení přicházejí v úvahu různé důvody pro odmítnutí uznání a výkonu. Je však zásadní, zda jsou soudy oprávněny odmítnout uznání a výkon rozhodčího nálezu ex officio bez ohledu na aktivní přístup stran k řízení. Zakládá-li porušení pravidel o nezávislosti a nestrannosti rozhodců v průběhu rozhodčího řízení porušení zásady spravedlivého procesu, pak právo odmítnout uznání rozhodčího nálezu podporuje nejen ochrana veřejného pořádku státu, v němž je uznání požadováno, nýbrž toto právo přispívá rovněž ve zvýšení důvěry stran v rozhodčí řízení jako alternativnímu a spravedlivému způsobu řešení sporů.

| | |

POL [*Wpływ naruszenia reguł niezależności i bezstronności na wykonalność i skuteczność wyroku sądu arbitrażowego*]

W artykule poruszono problem konsekwencji naruszenia w postępowaniu arbitrażowym zasad gwarantujących rozpoznanie sprawy przez bezstronnych i niezależnych arbitrów dla późniejszego postępowania w przedmiocie uznania (stwierdzenia wykonalności) wyroku arbitrażowego. Autorki analizują wybrane postaci naruszenia tych zasad i oceniają je z punktu widzenia podstaw odmowy uznania wyroku wymienionych w art. V ust. 1 i 2 NYC.

FRA [*L'impact de la violation des principes d'indépendance et d'impartialité sur l'exécution et l'efficacité d'une sentence d'un tribunal arbitral*]

Dans l'article, on a abordé le problème des conséquences de la violation dans l'arbitrage des principes garantissant qu'un différand sera résolu par des arbitres impartials et indépendants pour les besoins d'une procédure ultérieure de la réconnaissance (de la constatation de la force exécutoire) d'une sentence arbitrale. Les auteurs analysent des types choisis de la violation de ces principes et les évaluent de point de vue des motifs de refus de la réconnaissance d'une sentence arbitrale mentionnées dans l'art. V al. 1 et 2 de la NYC.

RUS [*Влияние нарушений правил беспристрастности и независимости на приведение в исполнение и эффективность решений арбитражных судов*]

В настоящем документе рассматривается вопрос о последствиях нарушения в арбитражном процессе принципов, гарантирующих рассмотрение дела беспристрастными и независимыми судьями в целях последующего разбирательства о признании (приведении в исполнение) арбитражного решения. Авторы анализируют выбранные примеры нарушения этих принципов и оценивают их с точки зрения оснований для отказа от признания решения, приведенных в статье V, пунктах 1 и 2 NYC.

ESP [*El impacto de la violación de las normas de la independencia e imparcialidad sobre la ejecutividad y la eficacia de la sentencia arbitral*]

En este artículo se aborda el tema de las consecuencias de la violación de las normas del procedimiento de arbitraje que garanticen el reconocimiento del caso por los árbitros imparciales e independientes para el procedimiento ulterior de reconocimiento (de declaración de ejecutividad) de la sentencia arbitral. Las autoras analizan seleccionadas formas de la violación de estas normas y las evaluan desde el punto de vista de los motivos de denegación del reconocimiento de la sentencia nombrados en el artículo V párrafos 1 y 2 de NYC.

| | |

Lukáš Klee | Daniel Nový

Construction Dispute Boards

Key words:
Adjudication | DAB |
DRB | FIDIC |
construction disputes |
alternative dispute
resolution | statutory
adjudication |
contractual adjudication.

Abstract | Legally, construction projects involve specific issues because they bring with them a large number of hazards and related risks. Each project is unique, being accompanied by variations and complications of different natures. Contracting parties usually allocate risk to the party best able to control it. However, there is sometimes uncertainty about who is to bear a particular risk and to what extent. The reason may lay in a poorly drafted contract or in ignoring its provisions. In other cases, the parties are not willing to bear the consequences of the risks allocated to them. These and many other situations often give rise to disputes. Settlement of disputes in construction requires speed, an informal approach and expertise. This is why every good contract includes a dispute resolution system. Adjudication is the most popular alternative to litigation as it is a fast and relatively cheap way of settling disputes. An impartial, third body known as a 'Dispute Board' is responsible for resolving the dispute between the parties.

| | |

Lukáš Klee – An expert on International Construction Law and FIDIC sample forms of contract, Mr. Klee currently works for a large construction company in central Europe. When away from the office, he lectures on International Construction Law at the Charles University Faculty of Law in Prague. As an extension of his teaching duties, he also trains lawyers at the Judicial Academy of the Czech Republic. Mr. Klee regularly publishes articles in the Czech Republic and abroad and is the author of three books related to International Construction Law.
e-mail: klee@email.cz

Daniel Nový – Holds law degrees from Trinity College Dublin, the University of West Bohemia and an LL.M. degree from Georgetown University Law Center. He works as a transactional lawyer for a large,

I. Dispute Boards

I.1. Introduction

9.01. A Dispute Board is a body set up to resolve disputes that have arisen within a construction project, and to do so prior to arbitration or litigation. In general, there are two kinds of Dispute Boards. First, there is the Dispute Resolution Board ('DRB') which makes recommendations. Secondly, there is the Dispute Adjudication Board ('DAB') which makes resolutions.

9.02. In practise, there are not many alternatives to Dispute Boards. Courts often lack the expertise with the exception of the countries where specialised courts are established - such as in the UK or Germany. Even when they are available they may not be used. In Poland for example, construction disputes in large infrastructure construction projects are dealt with by the High Court in Warsaw (XXV Civil Division) because the General Directorate of National Roads and Motorways ('GDDKiA') has its registered office in the Court's district. Because of a large number of disputes in Poland in recent years, a natural process of specialisation of the Court's judges has followed. Judges themselves admit that alternative dispute resolution (ADR) is a better model for hearing construction disputes. However, it is the client who selects the method of dispute resolution and it is common for public authorities in the CEE (such as GDDKiA in Poland) to consistently delete DAB and arbitration clauses from the FIDIC (International Federation of Consulting Engineers) forms in favour of domestic litigation.[1]

international public utility company in Prague, the Czech Republic. Mr. Nový is a member of the International Advisory Board of the Central European and Euroasian Law Initiative (CEELI) Institute.
e-mail: novy.daniel@gmail.com

---

[1] Jamka, M., Morek, R. (2013) Dispute Avoidance and Resolution under FIDIC Rules and Procedure: Polish Experience, presented at the seminar "Making a Success out of a Construction Project": International FIDIC Standards and Their Implementation in Ukraine. Kiev. For further reading on the topic, see DRBF (2013) Dispute Resolution Board Concept, available at: http://www.drb.org/concepts.htm (accessed on 12 September 2013); FIDIC: 2011/2012 Annual Report, available at: http://fidic.org/node/813 (accessed on 29 August 2013); FIDIC: Committees, available at: http://fidic.org/node/771 (accessed on 12 August 2013); FIDIC: International and National Lists of Adjudicators, available at: http://fidic.org/node/2555 (accessed on 12 August 2013); FIDIC: Statutes and by-laws (October 2011), available at: http://fidic.org/node/769 (accessed on 15 August 2013); FIDIC, THE FIDIC CONTRACTS GUIDE, Lausanne: FIDIC (First Edition 2000); FIDIC, FIDIC PROCUREMENT PROCEDURES GUIDE, Lausanne: FIDIC (First Edition 2011); AXEL-VOLKMAR JAEGER & GÖTZ-SEBASTIAN HÖK, FIDIC – A GUIDE FOR PRACTITIONERS, Berlin: Springer Verlag, (2010); LUKÁŠ KLEE, SMLUVNÍ PODMÍNKY FIDIC, Praha: Wolters

9.03. Construction disputes represent a large share of the arbitration market. According to the ICC, construction and engineering disputes accounted for almost 17% of the total case load in 2010.[2] Furthermore, while both litigation and arbitration are occasionally used to resolve disputes, they are costly and time-consuming.

9.04. That is why Dispute Boards are a real advantage for the construction industry. As DR. Cyril Chen noted in his writings, the statistics show that if there is an operational Dispute Board in existence on a project, close to 99% of all disputes referred to it will be successfully resolved within less than 90 days and at a cost of about 2% of the amount of the dispute.[3]

I.2. Dispute Boards: Advantages and Disadvantages

9.05. Due to the enormous volume of correspondence and occasional 'friction' between participants, it is common to see minor disputes accompany large construction projects. Therefore, a certain intermediate dispute resolution level is widely appreciated and used. It can make the interested parties sit together at a table and try to compromise and thus avoid costly arbitration or litigation proceedings. Experienced experts can provide the parties with a solution that will likely result in a required compromise. At these meetings, opinions can get vented, tensions released, and personal antagonisms extinguished in the presence of impartial, well-informed experts; a psychological phenomenon well worth mentioning. Active on these boards are experts who need not be lawyers, which is why they are more efficient. If lawyers are on the boards, they are lawyers with extensive practical backgrounds in the field of construction projects. The boards can also be made up of suitable combinations of personalities with varied experience and specialisations. One disadvantage of these boards is that they tend not to be worth the money and time invested for smaller projects.

I.3. Dispute Adjudication Board (DAB)

9.06. The DAB must decide in compliance with the dispute resolution process described in the contract. Next to this contractual adjudication, there is also statutory adjudication in some countries. This is the case in the UK, where either participant of a construction project can use

---

Kluwer (2011); ROBERT KNUTSON, FIDIC AN ANALYSIS OF INTERNATIONAL CONSTRUCTION CONTRACTS, London: Kluwer Law International (2005).

[2]   ICC International Court of Arbitration Bulletin Vol 22/Number 1-2011.

[3]   Dr. Cyril Chern, Dispute Board Federation: Cyril Chern, *The Dispute Board Federation and the Role of Dispute Boards in Construction – Benefits without Burden*, 9 REVISTA DEL CLUB ESPAÑOL DEL ARBITRAJE, Volume 5 (2010).

the opportunity to resolve a dispute in statutory adjudication, subject to a 28 day time limit. In civil law jurisdictions, decisions handed down by DABs are recommendations only and are not binding or enforceable. In common law jurisdictions, on the other hand, the decision is often final and binding if the parties do not appeal it within the contractually agreed period of time.

9.07.   If the contracting parties want to make a DAB's decision enforceable, they can modify the DAB's status to *ad hoc* arbitration. This would require that the arbitration clause be re-worded so that either the arbitration court or the *ad hoc* arbitrator/s would become the authority to examine the DAB's award or resolution, should one of the contracting parties challenge the award or resolution via a lawsuit.

I.4.   Dispute Resolution Board (DRB)

9.08.   The DRB consists of three reviewers who must be impartial, experienced and respected. Usually the employer and the contractor select one member each. The chosen member must be approved by the other party. The two appointed DRB members then choose the third member who, in turn, also needs to be approved by both parties. All members select a chair of the DRB who, again, is subject to the parties' approval. Organisation and set up of the DRB takes place before the commencement of the construction project. The DRB familiarises itself with the contractual documents, with the project procedures and with the participants themselves and closely follows the progress of the works. The members of the DRB also conduct site visits periodically. This system aims to resolve differences early on at the job level. Where formal disputes cannot be avoided, the DRB holds a hearing and issues a written recommendation. While not binding upon the parties, recommendations are, in practice, usually accepted by the parties to the dispute. By doing so, they help themselves and maintain the credibility, reputation and expertise of the DRB and its members. The contract may also provide that DRB recommendations be admissible in any potential future litigation or arbitration.[4]

II. Contractual Adjudication: The Use of DAB in FIDIC Standard Forms

9.09.   Based in Lausanne, Switzerland, the International Federation of Consulting Engineers (FIDIC) was founded in France in 1913, and has expanded by new membership all over the world. It is a non-

---

[4]   Dispute Resolution Board Concept, available at: http://www.drb.org/concepts.htm (accessed on 29 August 2013).

governmental organization recognized by the United Nations, major global banks, the European Commission, and other international institutions. The Federation was set up to support and promote the overall interests of its member associations. But the earliest days of FIDIC as a major significant organization date back to the post-WWII era. From this time, it started expanding at such a rate that it now unites the associations of more than ninety countries. The first sample Conditions of Contract for Works of Civil Engineering Construction were released in 1957, giving rise to a tradition of the 'FIDIC Red Book'. Due to the ever-advancing technological development in the construction industry the contractual conditions in their original version needed to to be revised. In 1999, the most recent and the widest used First Edition came into existence with its Red, Yellow and Silver books, as the forms commonly known.

9.10. FIDIC forms are now recognised as 'international best practise documents'. They continue to enjoy ever growing popularity, owing mainly to significant international lenders and clients who want to have foreseeable and proven 'rules of game' within their construction projects. One of the advantages of the FIDIC Forms is that (in most cases) a user is not dealing with the conditions of a contract only, but with a complete set of documents including the rules for adjudication without which successful realisation of a project would be difficult.

9.11. Dispute Boards first appeared in FIDIC Forms in 1995 at Clause 20 and are now a common part of most FIDIC forms and many other contracts. These Forms currently 'presume' three levels of dispute resolution which can be thought of as dispute resolution 'hierarchy'. Level one is resolution through the engineer (contract administrator); Level two is adjudication through a DAB. Following an unsuccessful, obligatory attempt to achieve an amicable settlement with a DAB, a dispute can end up at an arbitration senate, which is level three.[5]

---

[5] An older version of the Red Book (1957) dealt with dispute resolution in two phases. Dispute resolution was up to the engineer and their decision was deemed final and binding in relation to the employer and the contractor. Within 90 days, either of the parties could question the decision and file an arbitration suit. Barring minor modifications in arbitration clauses in the Red Book versions of 1969 (The Second Edition) and 1977 (The Third Edition), this dispute resolution concept has been retained. The above two-phase concept remained even in the Red Book of 1987 (1988), but dispute resolution had undergone substantial change. A formal obligation has been defined to refer a dispute to clause 67 to make it fully clear that such a dispute will be of a special statute (i.e. being commenced by referring it to this clause). Another formal innovation was that the period of time within which the engineer's decision could be questioned being reduced to 84 days. A fundamental change was the incorporation of amicable settlements as a compulsory item at clause 67.2 with its wording as follows: Where the notice of intention to commence arbitration as to a

9.12. The engineer will often decide, after notification and quantification a claim submitted by one of the contracting parties. The engineer's decision (as per clause 3.5) must be given within 42 days after the engineer has received a claim quantification. If unsatisfied with the engineer's decision, a party may forward the dispute to a DAB under clause 20.4. The DAB must hand down its award within 84 days.

9.13. FIDIC DBO has a new clause 20.5 that reads that if at any time the Parties so agree, they may jointly refer a matter to the DAB in writing with a request to provide assistance and/or informally discuss and attempt to resolve any disagreement that may have arisen between the Parties during the performance of the Contract. Such informal assistance may take place during any meeting, Site visit or otherwise. However, unless the Parties agree otherwise, both Parties must be present at such discussions. The Parties are not bound to act upon any advice given during such informal meetings, and the DAB shall not be bound in any future Dispute resolution process and decision by any views given during the informal assistance process, whether provided orally or in writing.[6]

9.14. In the third instance, an obligatory attempt to settle a dispute amicably can be included as a rule where there is disagreement prior to an award of the DRB. This must be made within 28 days as per clause 20.4. Amicable settlement is prescribed in clause 20.5. A particular form is not stipulated, but an expert examination or mediation will frequently be used. Arbitration is prescribed by the Arbitration Clause under 20.6 to take place before the Court of Arbitration at the International Chamber of Commerce in Paris.

---

dispute has been given in accordance with Sub-Clause 67.1, the parties shall attempt to settle such dispute amicably before the commencement of arbitration. Provided that, unless the parties otherwise agreed, arbitration may be commenced on or after the fifty-sixth day after the day on which notice of intention to commence arbitration of such dispute was given, even if no attempt at amicable settlement thereof has been made.

Therefore, a period of 56 days was newly established within which arbitration could be commenced regardless of the attempt to settle a dispute amicably. These changes, however, were not applied uniformly or in a systematic way across all FIDIC Forms.

[6] At this point, a hazard should be mentioned, appearing where the contract describes the dispute resolution obligatory instruments. In the case of *The Channel Tunnel Group* v *Balfour Beatty (1992) 56 BLR 1 Court of Appeal* the court did not grant leave for litigation to commence because 'time for arbitration had not yet come' due to the fact that the dispute had not been resolved in compliance with clause 67 (1). This was confirmed in the same case on appeal in 1993 (*BLR 22 House of Lords*) when Lord Mustill ruled: 'Those who stipulated a dispute resolution method by their mutual agreement must give significant reasons why not to use this method (...) if they had undertaken to submit their complaints to experts or, if necessary, to arbitrators, ought to take the steps like this. The fact that the plaintiffs now regard the method they selected as too slow to follow their intention is, in my opinion, groundless.'

9.15. Recently,[7] FIDIC has expressed its intention to make the failure to comply with binding but not-yet-final DAB decisions a *per se* matter that may be arbitrated pursuant to Sub-Clause 20.6.[8] In effect, the current regime of final and binding decisions would be extended to decisions that are binding only (where a Party has served a notice of dissatisfaction in accordance with Sub-Clause 20.4.).[9] Sub-Clauses 20.4 and 20.5 would not apply to such arbitration references.[10]

III. FIDIC Policy Statements to ADR

9.16. The adversarial model involving litigation or arbitration has serious limitations and drawbacks in the area of construction disputes resolution. The issues involved are usually very complex and hard attitudes of the parties involved in adversarial proceedings seldom lead to quick, effective and inexpensive resolutions. As FIDIC has noted, such a system 'delays the execution of remedial measures, increases legal costs, creates adversaries and thus wastes resources unnecessarily. It also saps the energies of the parties in dispute unnecessarily, diminishing their ability to function effectively in the future. Both outcomes are detrimental to the parties, in particular, and to society, in general.'[11] ADR models on the other hand (such as negotiation, DRB, mini-trials, adjudications, conciliation or mediation) are consensual as opposed to adversarial. While these consensual methods may not, unlike litigation or arbitration, lead to binding and final decisions, their outcome in the form of settlement agreements may be more compelling and more certain and, in any event, enforceable by courts in cases of default. For these reasons, FIDIC has asked its Member Associations to support ADR procedures.[12]

---

[7] FIDIC Guidance Memorandum to Users of the 1999 Conditions of Contract dated 1 April 2013, available at: http://fidic.org/node/1615 (accessed on 29 August 2013).

[8] *Ibid.*

[9] *Ibid.*

[10] *Ibid.* The new Sub-Clause 20.7 would read as follows:

'In the event that a Party fails to comply with any decision of the DAB, whether binding or final and binding, then the other Party may, without prejudice to any other rights it may have, refer the failure itself to arbitration under Sub-Clause 20.6 [Arbitration] for summary or other expedited relief, as may be appropriate. Sub-Clause 20.4 [Obtaining Dispute Adjudication Board's Decision] and Sub-Clause 20.5 [Amicable Settlement] shall not apply to this reference.'

[11] FIDIC: Alternative Dispute Resolution, available at: http://fidic.org/node/761 (accessed on 29 August 2013).

[12] *Ibid.*

IV. Independence and Impartiality

9.17.   The independence of adjudication can be affected by the level of funding and remuneration received by its members. Another important aspect supported by FIDIC is the establishment of a national list of independent, key experts. One of the qualification criteria for listing on the FIDIC President's *List of Approved Dispute Adjudicators*, which are assessed by FIDIC and by its Assessment Panel, is the ability of the applicant to be 'impartial [and] objective.'[13]

9.18.   Complementing the FIDIC President's *List of Approved Dispute Adjudicators*, FIDIC also supports the development of National Listings.[14] Such national lists, based upon the FIDIC guidelines, have been created in Japan and France.[15] Standards of adjudication on projects using FIDIC-based contracts are being monitored by the APA (Assessment Panel for Adjudicators).[16]

V. Statutory Adjudication

V.1.   UK Statutory Adjudication Regime

9.19.   In the UK, Section 108 of Part II of the *Housing Grants, Construction and Regeneration Act 1996* ('the Act'),[17] provides for a statutory right and prescribes procedural rules of adjudication.[18] Pursuant to the Act, 'a dispute between parties to, and arising under, a construction contract, effective as of May 1, 1998 or later, may be referred for adjudication.'[19] Disputes, in the words of the Act, encapsulate 'any difference.'[20]

9.20.   The Act prescribes what provisions a construction contract shall contain in order to avail itself of the statutory regime.[21] The contract

---

[13]   FIDIC: Adjudicators, available at: http://fidic.org/node/802 (assessed on 21 August 2013).

[14]   FIDIC: Alternative Dispute Resolution, available at: http://fidic.org/node/761 (accessed on 29 August 2013).

[15]   *Ibid.*

[16]   *Ibid.*

[17]   Available at: http://www.legislation.gov.uk/ukpga/1996/53 (accessed on 12 September 2013).

[18]   Users' Guide To Adjudication, Construction Umbrella Bodies Adjudication Task Group, April 2003 ('Users' Guide'), available at: http://www.scl.org.uk/files/CUB Users Guide May 2003.pdf (assessed on 21 August 2013), at 23-24.

[19]   Section 108(1) of the Act; *see also* Users' Guide, at 1, 4, 23. The legislation applies in the UK jurisdictions of England, Wales and Scotland In Northern Ireland, the Construction Contracts (Northern Ireland) Order 1997 provides for the same regime with regard to contracts effective as of 1 June 1999, or thereafter; Users' Guide, at 4.

[20]   Section 108(1) of the Act; *see also* Users' Guide, at 6-9.

[21]   Section 108(2) of the Act.

shall thus provide for notices of a party's intention to adjudicate, a timetable for an adjudicator's appointments and referrals, time limits within which a decision must be reached and the adjudicator's powers.[22] Relevant to our present discussion, the Act also prescribes that the parties' contract shall *'impose a duty on the adjudicator to act impartially.'*[23] The Act also requires the contract to provide that the adjudicator's decision be 'binding until the dispute is finally determined by legal proceedings, by arbitration…or by agreement.'[24] The parties may also agree upon the acceptance of the adjudicator's decision 'as finally determining the dispute.'[25]

9.21. Where the statutory requirements have not been complied with, the statutory regime of the Act will not apply and the Act itself falls back upon a default regime contained in the *Scheme for Construction Contracts (England and Wales) Regulations 1998* ('the Scheme').[26]

V.2. Conduct of the Proceedings Pursuant to the Scheme

9.22. Impartiality and independence are also required of the adjudicator in the course of adjudication proceedings conducted pursuant to the Scheme.[27] Paragraph 12(1) of the Scheme is concerned with the adjudicator's powers and imposes a duty upon the adjudicator to act impartially and in accordance with the law and the applicable contract.[28] The duty of impartiality and independence also forms part of the requirement that the adjudicator must neither *be* biased (actual bias) nor must he or she *be perceived* to be biased (apparent bias), which is an aspect of the requirement of natural justice or procedural fairness.[29] The second prong of natural justice is the duty to conduct a fair hearing.[30]

---

[22] Section 108(2)(a)-(d), (f) of the Act.

[23] Section 108(2)(e) of the Act (emphasis added).

[24] Section 108(3) of the Act.

[25] *Ibid.*

[26] Users' Guide, at 1, 6, 23; Section 108(5) of the Act ('If the contract does not comply with the requirements of subsections (1) to (4) [of Section 108 of the Act], the adjudication provisions of the Scheme for Construction Contracts apply.').

[27] Guidance for Adjudicators, Construction Umbrella Bodies Adjudication Tasks Group, July 2002 ('Adjudicators' Guide'), available at: http://www.scl.org.uk/files/GfA_0207.pdf (accessed on 21 August 2013), at 2; *see* the Scheme, available at: http://www.legislation.gov.uk/uksi/1998/649/made (accessed on 21 August 2013).

[28] Paragraph 12(a) of the Scheme. Paragraph 12(b) of the Scheme obliges the adjudicator to 'avoid incurring unnecessary expense.'

[29] Adjudicators' Guide, at 2.

[30] *Ibid.*

9.23. The test for bias is objective: whether a reasonable observer would conclude that there is a 'real possibility' of bias.[31] Personal relations with a party to the contract and the proceedings, favouring or apparent favouring or supporting one party or interest in the adjudication are examples of bias.[32]

9.24. The hearing shall be conducted fairly – that is, the parties shall have knowledge of the case and be given a reasonable opportunity to present their own case.[33] Oral hearings do not seem to be a requisite part of the adjudication process and the adjudicator has a full discretion – within the limits and constraints of the demands of procedural fairness – to decide whether or not to order an oral hearing or a meeting of the parties.[34] Lack of fairness during the adjudication process may be a ground for non-enforcement of the adjudicator's decision by court.[35]

V.3. Some Procedural Aspects of Statutory Adjudication

9.25. Under the Scheme, adjudication may be initiated by serving a written notice of adjudication to the other party.[36] The notice specifies the matters which the party seeks the adjudicator to decide.[37] An adjudicator must be appointed within seven days of the submission of the notice.[38] The adjudicator may be named in the construction contract in question; likewise, the contract may specify a panel of adjudicators or an Adjudicator Nominating Body.[39] If the contract is silent on this issue, any Adjudicator Nominating Body may be approached.[40] After an adjudicator has been appointed, a referral notice with information that the adjudicator ought to consider is sent to him or her and to the other party.[41] Generally, a decision must be rendered within 28 days of the receipt of the referral notice by the adjudicator.[42]

9.26. A party may challenge the adjudicator's jurisdiction, for instance, on the grounds of an alleged conflict of interest[43] or that the underlying

---

[31] *Ibid.*

[32] *Ibid.*

[33] *Ibid.*

[34] *Ibid.; see also* Users' Guide, at 18.

[35] Adjudicators' Guide, at 2.

[36] Users' Guide, at 10.

[37] *Ibid.*

[38] *Ibid.*, at 11-12.

[39] *Ibid.*

[40] *Ibid.*, at 11.

[41] *Ibid.*, at 12-13.

[42] *Ibid.*, at 12; *see also* Ibid., at 14 (specifying the possibilities for an extension of the time limit).

[43] Adjudicators' Guide, at 4; *see*, e.g., paragraph 4 of the Scheme.

contract is not a construction contract within the meaning of the Act.[44] Unless they are given such authority by the parties, adjudicators generally lack the power to decide upon such jurisdictional challenges; they are left to the court.[45] However, the adjudicators are advised to conduct an investigation into their jurisdiction and also in order to comply with their obligation to be, and to appear, impartial.[46]

9.27. In their decisions, adjudicators may issue an order to a party to pay money or may decide a fact or a matter of a technical nature that the parties failed to agree upon.[47] The Scheme requires that reasons for the decision be provided to the parties if and where requested.[48]

9.28. The adjudicator also decides which party pays the adjudicator's costs.[49] However, under existing law, each party is responsible for bearing their own costs and the adjudicator lacks the power to award costs orders.[50]

9.29. The party against whom the adjudicator's decision was given will either comply with the decision or the decision may be enforced in court.[51] In most cases, courts will uphold such decisions within days.[52] The exception is if a party succeeds with a jurisdictional challenge or attacks the adjudicator's decision on natural justice grounds.[53] This would mean that the adjudicator had failed to act impartially or had not provided both parties with an opportunity to present their case.[54] A party cannot appeal the adjudicator's decision but the matter may be heard *de novo*, either in court or in arbitration proceedings.[55]

VI. Conclusion

9.30. This article purported to briefly outline the system of resolution of construction disputes (disputes concerning construction contracts) by independent adjudication bodies referred to as dispute boards. We outlined several advantages of the system of using dispute boards as compared with litigation or arbitration of similar disputes. We also referred to the bases of the dispute-board-resolution system, i.e.

---

[44] *See* Section 104 of the Act (providing the definition of 'construction contracts'); Adjudicators' Guide, at 4.
[45] Adjudicators' Guide, at 4, and authorities cited therein.
[46] *Ibid.*
[47] Users' Guide, at 19.
[48] Paragraph 22 of the Scheme; *see also* the Users' Guide, at 19; the Adjudicators' Guide, at 7.
[49] Users' Guide, at 20.
[50] Adjudicator's Guide, at 10.
[51] Users' Guide, at 5.
[52] *Ibid.*
[53] *Ibid.*, at 2-3, 22.
[54] *Ibid.*
[55] *Ibid.*, at 3, 5, 23.

contracts (FIDIC) or a statutory scheme (such as the UK statutory adjudication system) and to independence and impartiality as being one of the fundamental qualification requirements placed upon members of the dispute boards.

| | |

Summaries

FRA [*Construction Dispute Boards*]

Les projets de construction sont spécifiques par le grand nombre de risques et les dangers qui les accompagnent. Chaque projet est unique et comporte des modifications et des complications de différentes sortes. Bien que les parties contractuelles se répartissent généralement les risques suivant leur capacité à les contrôler, on n'arrive pas toujours clairement à déterminer quel risque concret est supporté par quelle partie et dans quelle mesure. Cela peut être dû à un mauvais contrat ou au non-respect des dispositions contractuelles. Dans d'autres cas, les parties ne sont pas prêtes à supporter le risque important qui leur incombe. Tout cela et bien d'autres situations encore mènent souvent à des litiges, c'est pourquoi tout contrat bien fait comporte une procédure de résolution des litiges. La résolution d'un litige dans l'industrie du bâtiment exige de la rapidité, une approche informelle et des connaissances spécialisées, c'est pourquoi on utilise l'adjudication : on est le plus souvent confronté dans la pratique avec ce qu'on appelle des Comités de règlement des litiges, l'adjudication consistant un moyen rapide et relativement bon marché de règlement des différends entre les parties par un organisme impartial - un tiers.

CZE [*Construction Dispute Boards*]

Stavební projekty jsou specifické větším množstvím rizik a souvisejících nebezpečí. Každý projekt je jedinečný a zahrnuje změny a komplikace různé povahy. Přestože smluvní strany obvykle alokují rizika podle toho, která ze stran je lépe schopna je kontrolovat, ne vždy je zřejmé, kdo má konkrétní riziko nést a do jaké míry. Důvodem může být špatná smlouva anebo nedodržování smluvních ustanovení. Jindy nejsou strany ochotny nést důsledky rizik, jež jim byla alokována. Tyto a mnoho dalších situací často vedou ke sporům. Každá kvalitní smlouva proto obsahuje postup pro řešení sporů. Řešení sporů ve stavebnictví si vyžaduje rychlost, neformální přístup a odborné znalosti. Proto se využívá adjudikace. V praxi se nejčastěji setkáváme s tzv. Panely pro řešení sporů. Adjudikace je rychlým a relativně levným způsobem řešení sporů mezi stranami nestranným orgánem–třetí osobou.

POL   [*Construction Dispute Boards*]

Każda właściwie sporządzona umowa zawiera tryb rozstrzygania sporów. Rozstrzyganie sporów w budownictwie wymaga szybkości, nieformalnego podejścia i specjalistycznej wiedzy. Z tego względu stosowana jest adiudykacja. W praktyce najczęściej spotkamy się z tzw. komisjami rozjemczymi. Adiudykacja jest szybkim i stosunkowo tanim sposobem rozstrzygania sporów pomiędzy stronami przez bezstronny organ–osobę trzecią.

DEU   [*Construction Dispute Boards*]

Jeder sauber gearbeitete Vertrag gibt u. a. die Vorgehensweise im Streitfall vor. Im Bauwesen müssen Streitigkeiten rasch, informell und mit Branchenfachkenntnis gelöst werden. Von daher kommt die sog. Adjudikation zum Einsatz. In der Praxis begegnen wir zumeist sog. Streitschlichtungspanels. Die "Dispute Adjudication" ist eine rasche, relativ kostengünstige Form der Schlichtung von Streitigkeiten zwischen Parteien durch einen unabhängigen Dritten - die Schlichtungsstelle.

RUS   [*Construction Dispute Boards*]

Каждый качественный договор предусматривает процедуру разрешения споров. Для разрешения споров в области строительства требуется быстрота, неформальный подход и профессиональный опыт. Поэтому используется адъюдикация. На практике наиболее часто встречаются т. н. коллегии для разрешения споров. Адъюдикация – это быстрый и относительно недорогой способ разрешения споров между сторонами беспристрастным органом – третьими лицами.

ESP   [*Construction Dispute Boards*]

Cada contrato legal que se precie incluye un procedimiento para la resolución de disputas. Las disputa en el sector de la construcción requieren celeridad, un enfoque informal y conocimientos profesionales. Por ese motivo se emplea la adjudicación. En la práctica suelen ser cada vez más frecuentes los llamados Paneles para la solución de disputas. La adjudicación es una forma relativamente barata y rápida de resolver disputas entre las partes por una autoridad— un tercero imparcial.

|||

Salvatore Patti

Application of the Reasonableness Standard in Continental Courts and Arbitral Tribunals

Key words:
arbitration tribunal |
reasonableness | general
clauses | civil law |
common law

Abstract | *Justice pursued in front of arbitral tribunals, especially justice concerning international disputes, is characterized by few formalities, an absolute guarantee of an adversarial procedure and a great adherence to the need for a solution in a particular case. This explains the fact that arbitral awards are frequently based on the customs of international trade and their general doctrine, among others, good faith, public policy, gute Sitten etc. The "traditional" general clauses or "standards" of evaluation recently have been joined by the standard of "reasonableness", a concept which is well known in common law but traditionally absent in the legislation of the civil law legal orders. Due to the fact that frequent use of "reasonableness" does not correspond to a sufficient theoretical study, this work underlines the differences between the application of the standard of reasonableness in legal orders of common and civil law, especially by establishing correct criteria of application in arbitration proceedings.*

| | |

Prof. Salvatore Patti
has taught at the
University of Sassari,
Italy (1978-1986), the
University of Trieste,
Italy (1986-1995) as
well as the Universities
of Zurich, Switzerland
and Freiburg, Germany.
Since 1995 he has been
a full Professor of
Private Law at the
University 'La Sapienza'
in Rome, Italy. From
2005 to 2007 he taught a
course in Civil Law
focused on contracts for
work and labor at the
University "*Bocconi*" in
Milan, Italy.
He has conducted
periods of research in
Munich, London and
Stanford with
scholarships provided
by the Alexander von
Humboldt-Stiftung, the
DAAD, the British
Academy and the
American Fulbright
Commission.
Besides his activities in
his law firm with
offices in Rome, Milan
and Munich, he is
editor or co-editor of
various legal journals.
e-mail:
studiopatti@iol.it

10.01. Justice pursued in front of arbitral tribunals, especially justice concerning international disputes is characterized by few formalities, an absolute guarantee of an adversarial procedure and a great adherence to the need for a solution in a particular case.

10.02. This explains the fact that arbitral awards are frequently based on the customs of international trade and the general clauses, among others good faith, public policy, *gute Sitten*, etc. Indeed, by means of such 'blank norms', or 'valves' it is often possible to reach a solution acceptable to both parties and suited to the needs of the particular case.

10.03. In recent years, both on a national and an international level, the 'traditional' general clauses or 'standards' of evaluation have been joined by the standard of 'reasonableness'. This was well known to common law but traditionally absent in the legislation of the European codes.

10.04. The use of reasonableness as a criterion for a fair and just decision has also become common in the decisions of some constitutional courts, in the first place the Italian one, as well as in codification projects regarding European private law.

10.05. The more and more frequent use of 'reasonableness' does not correspond, however, to a sufficient theoretical study aimed at ascertaining the degree of 'innovation', compared to similar evaluation criteria, as well as the boundaries of discretion of the deciding body on the basis of such criterion and the possibilities of control of the 'correctness of the solution. The following work will address this issue by highlighting the difference of how the rule of reasonableness works in legal common law orders and continental legal orders and also by establishing correct criteria of application in arbitration proceedings.

I. The Frequent Application of Reasonableness in Decisions and Legal Doctrine

10.06. For legal professionals, the topic of reasonableness is a very relevant one. An attentive civil lawyer namely Prof. Nicolò Lipari, after having recalled that the criterion of reasonableness 'is already becoming the interpretative compass for any practical operation to be conducted, given the fact that norms that appear inherently unreasonable, namely incongruous, contradictory and unfair are declared to be contrary to the Constitution', has wondered whether the same criterion could serve to fully deny a restriction in the field of non-fulfilment (and in the field of option between contractual and ex-contractual liability) which does no longer have a reason for being.[1]

---

[1] Nicolò Lipari, *Responsabilità contrattuale ed extracontrattuale: il ruolo limitativo delle categorie concettuali*, CONTRATTI 704, 706 (2010). The considerations of the experts in

10.07. Thus, the standard of reasonableness is invoked as an instrument to find the most suitable solution as to the times and circumstances. It is a solution which is more logical and responds better to the socio-economic needs of the moment, without any excessive worries concerning the conformity of the invoked solution with the certain fact and obedience to rules of legal interpretation.

10.08. On the other hand, the law, even natural law, has to be considered to be based on reason and, therefore, it has to be 'reasonable'. But if the law is an expression of reason, one needs to ask what causes the recent attention on the topic of reasonableness, in particular regarding civil law. One can say that the actual relevance of the subject in civil law is, at least in part and indirectly, due to the evolution of the concept in constitutional law[2] and in constitutional court decisions, as well as the influence of the common law legal systems and the codification projects regarding European civil code.

10.09. It also needs to be remembered that reasonableness is present as a criterion for identifying what constitutes a norm. It is also a basis of legal decisions in some of the best writings about method in legal science, written by the famous civil lawyer, Josef Esser, in the second half of the last century. He highlighted the importance of the prior understanding in the process of identifying the law which leads to a judge's decision. Esser stated that 'The relation of the meaning with an acceptable solution according to reasonableness' needs to be obvious. Vice versa, the blind obedience to the law, as known in history, can also be understood as a complete renunciation of the reasonableness of objective arguments. It is therefore, in the same way, an 'acceptance of the authority of the law and the norm as a technical authority, incomprehensible to outsiders.'[3]

10.10. Reasonableness has been understood by German academia as 'the subjective willingness and the objective possibility of a conscious discussion with opinions and arguments that allow the formation of consent'. It is an indispensable basis of the judicial decisions, which intend to respond to society's 'horizons of expectation'.[4] The preceding

---

civil law on reasonableness began almost thirty years ago: see Giovanni Criscuoli, *Buona fede e ragionevolezza*, (1) RIV. DIR. CIV. 709 (1984). The largest work is due to STEFANO TROIANO, LA 'RAGIONEVOLEZZA' NEL DIRITTO DEI CONTRATTI, Padua: CEDAM (2005).

2   Of course, the different fields in which the 'principle of reasonableness' may apply have to be distinguished: see Livio Paladin, *Ragionevolezza (principio di), in* 1 ENC. DIR. – AGGIORNAMENTO, Milano: Giuffrè899, 901 (1997), who states that a common 'principle of reasonableness' does not exist.

3   JOSEF ESSER, *Precomprensione e scelta del metodo nel processo di individuazione del diritto*, Naples: Edizioni scientifiche italiane 22 (1983).

4   *Ibid.*, at 20.

decisions acquire, as to the theory in question, 'an argumentative weight, a significance of evidence of the reasonableness and the social adequacy of the arguments used in them'.[5] That way, the non-dogmatic method of argumentation is favoured, based on reasonableness, that is the reference to solutions being immediately evident on the basis of the "nature of things" and, at the same time, on the universally recognised inadequacy of a different solution.

II. The Normative Basis of Reasonableness

10.11. Ultimately, the standard of reasonableness is an essential component of the law, of the legal norm, of judicial decisions and of a balanced contractual agreement.

10.12. In light of such undeniable relevance, the obstinate research of the textual basis in the Italian civil code and in other laws, undertaken by some 'supporters' of the reasonableness argument, may seem a pointless exercise of a positivistic kind. The results, moreover, seem to be quite modest. For example, Article 49 of the Italian Civil Code, states that 'after the lapse of two years from the day on which the person has last been heard of, the presumptive legitimate heirs and anyone who reasonably believes he has rights in the property of the missing person dependent upon his death can petition the competent tribunal, in accordance with the preceding article, that his absence be declared'. Article 1711, paragraph 2 of the Italian Civil Code states that 'the agent may depart from the instructions received whenever circumstances unknown to the principal and such as cannot be communicated to him in time reasonably create the assumption that the principal would have given his approval'. Article 1435 of the Italian Civil Code states that 'duress must be of such a nature as to impress a reasonable person...'. According to Article 1365 of the Italian Civil Code 'when a case is mentioned in a contract in order to explain a clause, unmentioned cases to which the same clause could reasonably be extended are not presumed to be excluded'.

10.13. The last provision undoubtedly is the most relevant one. In fact, reasonableness, although from a different perspective as regards the interpretation of the contract, is referred to in the Unidroit Principles, according to which, in case the common intention of the parties cannot be determined, the contract has to be interpreted according to the meaning that 'reasonable' people, being the same kind as the parties, would give to it in the same circumstances (Article 4.1). Reason,

---

[5]   In this sense see GIUSEPPE ZACCARIA, ERMENEUTICA E GIURISPRUDENZA: SAGGIO SULLA METODOLOGIA DI JOSEF ESSER, Milan: Giuffrè 134 (1984).

therefore, guides the interpretation of the contract, while little specific meaning has to be attributed to the adverb 'reasonably,' which could be easily replaced with other terms in the abovementioned provisions. Reasonableness also found its way into the Italian Civil Code and the Italian legislation as a result of European directives and international conventions. Thus, for example, Article 1748, paragraph 3 of the Italian Civil Code, modified following the implementation of the Directive 86/653 EC, provides that the agent is entitled to receive a commission also for transactions completed after the date of the termination of the contract, as long as done within a reasonable time. Article 1783, paragraph 2, no. 3 of the Italian Civil Code, modified as a result of the 1962 Convention on the liability of hotel-keepers concerning the property of their guests, states that those things are considered brought into the hotel which the hotel-keeper takes custody of 'during a period of reasonable time prior to or following the time in which the client is accommodated'. It is also frequently used in the Consumer Code (Legislative Decree 6 September 2005 no.206): regarding the liability for damages caused by a defective product, reference is made to the conditions of normal use or those which may be 'reasonably' envisaged or to the effect of the product on other products where it can be 'reasonably' envisaged that it will be used with other products (Article 103 Consumer Code). As to the sale of consumer goods, Article 129, c) of the Consumer Code provides that consumer goods are presumed to be in conformity with the contract if they show the quality and performance which are normal in goods of the same type and which the consumer can 'reasonably' expect taking into account a number of criteria indicated by the same provision. However, the specific meaning of the term 'reasonably' shows little relevance and is perhaps even useless as the evaluation of foreseeability or legitimate expectations would not change in its absence.

10.14. Weak normative bases can also be found in other European civil codes. For example, Article 1112 of the French Civil Code defines the influence on one of the parties by making reference to the impressions of une personne raisonnable (a reasonable person). As a criterion of the evaluation of due performance, the French Civil Code uses the ancient figure of the bon père de famille (a good father), certainly a reasonable person (Article 1176).

10.15. In the German Civil Code the term does not appear. Reason, die Vernunft, which is so present in the works of philosophers, is absent in the texts of law and is rarely mentioned by jurists, although it is certainly implied in their reasoning. A criterion which, in many aspects, is equivalent to that of the good paterfamilias, that is the diligent and reasonable person, can be found in the concept of Sorgfalt (diligence). Section 276 of the German Civil Code requires the necessary Sorgfalt in legal relations and defines negligence as a violation of the necessary Sorgfalt.

10.16. In conclusion, if one considers the textual bases that can be found in the codes, the concept of reasonableness can be deemed as substantially unknown to civil law traditions of the European continent, although being fundamental for the background of legal reasoning as well as for the activity of legislators and judges, while it is quite present in the normative texts of European origin. Above all, as one can see in the following, it is present in the projects of a European civil code. An unsatisfying definition – especially because of the obvious tautology – can already be found in the principles of European contract law (PECL) prepared by the Lando Commission, according to which 'reasonableness is to be judged by what persons acting in good faith and in the same situation as the parties would consider to be reasonable' (Article 1.302). Finally, the term also appears in Articles 41 and 47 of the Charter of Fundamental Rights of the European Union.

III. The Systematic Classification of Reasonableness

10.17. In the last years, some books and various articles on the subject of civil law have been dedicated to reasonableness, classifying the concept differently. Sometimes reasonableness has been classified among general principles, general clauses, undetermined legal concepts or criteria. It is therefore appropriate to reflect on the qualification of reasonableness.

10.18. The prevalent theory classifies reasonableness among general clauses,[6] but the wording is not always rigorous as the terms of a clause or a general principle sometimes are used without any distinction. In some scholarly writings, reasonableness is identified as a judgement rule or a criterion for the evaluation of behaviour, as compliance with reason or common sense.[7] In other articles, the 'principle of reasonableness' is described as a 'rule of rationality', rooted in the way of thinking of

---

[6] See, among others Luca Nivarra, *Ragionevolezza e diritto privato*, (7) ARS INTERPRETANDI 373 (2002); 2 Claudio Scognamiglio, *L'interpretazione, in I contratti in generale,*(Enrico Gabrielli ed.), *in* TRATTATO DEI CONTRATTI, Turin 1073 (directed by Pietro Rescigno & Enrico Gabrielli, 2006); Claudio Scognamiglio, *Clausole generali e linguaggio del legislatore: lo standard della ragionevolezza nel d.p.r. 24 maggio 1988*(224) QUADRIMESTRE 65 (1992); 2 FRANCESCO GALGANO, IL CONTRATTO, Padua: CEDAM 583 (2011).

[7] In this sense, among others, Enrico del Prato, *Ragionevolezza e bilanciamento* (1) RIV. DIR. CIV. 23 (2010).

European lawyers.[8] Favor towards reasonableness has to be attributed to the debate on the 'flexible' or 'elastic' law. The subject of general clauses, on the one hand, is considered as one of the most challenging and controversial subjects of contemporary legal culture[9] and, on the other hand, one perceives that flexible law could lead to an 'undue shift from the legislative power of decision to the judiciary one'.[10] In the light of the above mentioned, reasonableness, however, has to be classified as one of the instruments that, as is the case with general conditions, allow 'the balance between the legal discipline and real happenings without the need of a continuous intervention of the legislator'.[11]

10.19. In these terms, the topic certainly is not a new one, having marked the debate on codification techniques in the last century, and moreover, accompanied the formation of the European civil code.

10.20. With regard to the past, it should be sufficient to mention the thesis that strived for a legislation made of principles, to be 'expressed in general clauses', as the only technique suited to meet the new needs.[12] This thesis could be contrasted by the oldest and shareable opinion which favours a 'mixed' system based on a rational balance of strict and elastic rules.[13]

10.21. According to the more diffused thesis in favour of a mixed system, general clauses have to be considered as 'valves' that allow to adapt the legal norm to the needs of the particular case and, with regard to the time aspect, to adapt it to the new needs.

10.22. By classifying reasonableness among general clauses, the problem of the relationship between judicial discretion and certainty of the law arises. This problem is inherently connected to the subject of 'flexible' law and therefore appears unavoidable, even if the other theses with regard to reasonableness should be approved, in the first place the one that classifies the figure to the general principles.

---

[8] MAURO BARBERIS, EUROPA DEL DIRITTO, Bologna: Il mulino 201 (2008).

[9] VITO VELLUZZI, LE CLAUSOLE GENERALI. SEMANTICA E POLITICA DEL DIRITTO, Milan: Giuffrè 9 (2010).

[10] Stefano Rodotà, *Le clausole generali nel tempo del diritto flessibile, in* LEZIONI SUL CONTRATTO, Turin: Giappichelli 97 (Andrea Orestano ed., 2009).

[11] *Ibid.*, at 103.

[12] Stefano RODOTÀ, *Ideologie e tecniche della riforma del diritto civile,*(1) RIV. DIR. COMM. 84 (1967).

[13] Justus Wilhelm Hedemann, *Über die Kunst, gute Gesetze zu machen, in* FESTSCHRIFT OTTO GIERKE ZUM SIEBZIGSTEN GEBURTSTAG, DARGEBRACHT VON SCHU☐LERN, FREUNDEN UND VEREBREN, Weimar: Bohlau Nachf. 305 (1911).

IV. Reasonableness between Principles and General Clauses

10.23. The topic of general principles has been dealt with by generations of lawyers and, obviously, cannot be all tackled in this article[14] However, some brief remarks are useful. In the vocabulary of German lawyers, various expressions,[15] have meanings that differ, although only slightly, but which seem to correspond when establishing general principles as the basis of the legal order and the instruments that integrate them.

10.24. As already stated, some authors classify reasonableness among general principles. However, the meaning and relevance of the principle of 'reasonableness' can only be determined by taking into account its origin and the function performed within different legal orders. In this regard, it is useful to juxtapose the *Rechtsprinzipien* (principles of law) of continental legal orders, which is partly a consequence of the 'weakness' of the codification with its need to overcome the limits of time and the wording of the written norm, with the principles of the Anglo-Saxon tradition.[16]

10.25. Besides, one should also question whether reasonableness must be allocated to 'universal' principles, ones of natural law, those of national legal orders, those deriving from tradition or to those formed by jurisprudence.

10.26. Finally, the function to eventually ascribe to reasonableness as a general principle and as a means to overcome lacunas should not be neglected. Apart from Article 12 of the preliminary provisions of the Italian Civil Code, conventions can be mentioned, for example the Vienna Convention on the International sale of goods, which refer to those general principles on which they themselves are based.

---

[14] See Norberto Bobbio, *Principi generali di diritto*, 13 NDI 887 (1966); Sergio Bartole, *Principi generali del diritto (dir. cost.)*, in 35 ENCICLOPEDIA DEL DIRITTO, Milan: Giuffrè 494 (1986), who considers the statement contained in Article 2043 of the Italian Civil Code (p. 497 s.) a 'principle', while the experts in civil law speak, in general, about a general clause (or norm). Guido Alpa, *Principi generali*, in TRATTATO DI DIRITTO PRIVATO , Milan (G. Iudica and P. Zatti eds., 1993).

As regards the general principles of contract law, based on norms contained in the *Uniform Commercial Code* concerning good faith and 'unconscionability', see E. ALLAN FARNSWORTH, CONTRACTS, Boston: Little, Brown 37 (1990), who underlines their vitality despite the tendencies towards specialization, and, in the Italian doctrine, FRANCESCO MACARIO, *I diritti oltre la legge. Principi e regole del nuovo diritto dei contratti*, DEM. E DIR. 191 (1997).

[15] *Grundsätze des Rechts, allgemeine Rechtsprinzipien, allgemeine Rechtsgedanken, Leitideen.*

[16] JOSEF ESSER, *supra* note 3, at 179. But as regards this point *vide infra*.

10.27. In this regard, reasonableness can be used to determine the rule that applies in a particular case in order to fill the lacuna. An unreasonable decision would definitely be in contrast with Article 12 of the preliminary provisions of the Italian Civil Code. The classification of reasonableness among the general clauses of civil law is more frequent. But is it necessary, or at least useful, to create another general clause which is not foreseen by the Italian Civil Code? On the one hand, there is a tendency to reduce the number of general clauses. It is, for instance, argued that 'good faith' in an objective way and 'correctness' express coinciding rules of conduct.[17] On the other hand, after several decades of fundamental rejection of the abuse of the law by the Italian jurisprudence, there has been a frequent application of the prohibition of abuse in fiscal matters and areas of civil law – such as the termination of a contract. These are traditionally considered to be fields of private autonomy, which detract from the discretionary evaluation of a judge. Reasonableness is indeed mentioned, in the subject of the termination of a contract, as a parameter for evaluating the behaviour of the contractors and its absence, therefore, is considered as evidence of the abuse.[18]

10.28. In any case, the standard of reasonableness requires, as was the case for general clauses,[19] an act of 'concretisation'. This from the point of view of the certainty of the law as well as from the point of view of identifying the reasons for the judgement in a specific case. The need for concretisation, which has accompanied the jurisprudential evolution of Section 242 of the German Civil Code as to good faith, with the creation of *Fallgruppen* (case groups), and even the specification of figures of a conceptual autonomy, such as the *Verwirkung* (forfeiture), determines, however, a return to specified rules and, therefore, a sort of contradiction with the concept of the

---

[17]   See, among others, C. Massimo Bianca, *La nozione di buona fede quale regola di comportamento contrattuali*,(1) RIV. DIR. CIV. 205 (1983); UMBERTO BRECCIA, DILIGENZA E BUONA FEDE NELL'ATTUAZIONE DEL RAPPORTO OBBLIGATORIO, Milan: A. Giuffrè 17 (1968); Lina Bigliazzi Geri, *Buona fede nel diritto civile*, (4) DIGESTO DISC. PRIV., SEZ. CIV. 170 (1988); Luigi Mengoni, *Autonomia privata e Costituzione*, (1) BANCA, BORSA E TITOLI DI CREDITO 85 (1997), who specifies that 'the two terms, given that they are equivalent, can unite themselves in a hendiadys'. But, in a contrary sense, Stefano Troiano, *To What Extent Can the Notion of 'Reasonableness' Help to Harmonize European Contract Law? Problems and Prospects from a Civil Law Prospective*, 17(5) EUR. REV. PRIV. LAW 778 (2009), note 112.

[18]   Italian Supreme Court, 18 September 2009, no. 20106, in *Foro it.*, 2010, I, 85 ss.

[19]   See, among others, Ralph Weber, *Einige Gedanken zur Konkretisierung von Generalklauseln durch Fallgruppen*, 192(6) ARCHIV FÜR DIE CIVILISTISCHE PRAXIS 516 (1992).

general clause. Thus the 'concretisation' of reasonableness cannot go beyond a certain limit of 'rigidity', if one does not want to run the risk of depriving an instrument of all its meaning, which is aimed at allowing, from time to time, what seems congruent, adequate and reasonable taking into account the characteristics of a particular case.

10.29. Irrespective of the problem concerning the relationship and the potential overlapping with general clauses in the Italian Civil Code and the need of a well-thought-out 'concretisation', the classification of reasonableness among general clauses gives rise to further doubt. In fact, it is considered that a general clause, as a 'reference' norm or 'blank' norm, needs to draw from values of non-state legal orders.[20]

10.30. The idea of reason and reasonableness rather seems to be inherent to the legal order. According to the most diffused theory, a delegation from the legislator to the judge to search for values beyond the boundaries of the positive legal order and to attribute values expressed in the Constitution in the field of civil law is not ascertainable, as happens with general clauses.

10.31. Besides, it should also be remembered that for a long time now a restriction on the use of reasonableness in contractual matters has been indicated by the Italian Supreme Court, according to which contractual autonomy cannot be subjected to an examination of reasonableness undertaken by the judge, as the control parameter would inevitability be outside of the agreement of the parties.[21]. In an adhesive sense, the doctrine has emphasized that in a contract which is an instrument through which parties settle their potentially conflicting interests, unitary reference values cannot be found. So, in the light of the principle of private autonomy, it is not possible to make reference to values other than the ones the contracting parties have favoured in the light of their interests, their projects and of the evaluation of the utility they have supposed to obtain[22]. Finally, where private autonomy is performed, the judgment of reasonableness concerning the content of the single contract 'is absorbed by the preliminary evaluation of the interests which that type of contract is aimed to realise' in the case of typical contracts, or by the evaluation undertaken by a judge according

---

[20] Pietro Rescigno, *Parte prima: Profili teorici e comparatistici, in* Clausole e principi generali nell'argomentazione giurisprudenziale degli anni novanta, Padova: CEDAM 30 (Luciana Cabella Pisu & Luca Nanni eds., 1998).

[21] Italian Supreme Court, 29 May 1993, no. 6031, in *Foro it.*, 1993, I, 1794 ss., 1812; Italian Supreme Court., 1 October 1993, no. 9801, *ivi*, 1994, I, 1825 ss., 1834; Italian Supreme Court., 17 May 1996, no. 4570, *ivi*, 1996, I, 1990 ss.

[22] G. Marini, *Ingiustizia dello scambio e lesione contrattuale*, Riv. crit. dir. priv. 288 (1986).

to Article 1322, paragraph 2 of the Italian Civil Code, which, however, relies on a social 'typicality'.[23]

V. Reasonableness as an Evaluation Criterion

10.32. A delegation by the legislator to the judge can be noticed in the too numerous provisions of projects of the European civil code where reasonableness or the adjective 'reasonable' appears. However, since the use of 'reasonable' regards the solution of particular cases, correspondingly resolved by national codes by means of specific norms, there is no glimpse of a reference made to values to be implemented outside of positive law. In other words, the adjective 'reasonable' could easily be replaced by the adjective 'congruent' or 'adequate' without any change of meaning. Besides, it would be difficult to sustain that a factual evaluation is not undertaken, so that reasonableness, in contrast to the by now well-established orientation in reference to the general clauses,[24] would be subtracted from the examination of the Italian Supreme Court, not constituting a question of law.

10.33. Finally, a part of legal doctrine defines reasonableness as a 'different and more concrete' criterion of evaluation, since it is closer to the circumstances of a case than the general clauses.[25]

10.34. The thesis, according to which reasonableness represents a criterion or a rule of evaluation rather than a general clause, appears to be comprehensible. However, apart from what has been mentioned with reference to the need of 'concretisation' of the standard of reasonableness, a need similar to the one which is perceived in the case of the general clauses, it can be noticed that many of the norms of European directives and international conventions, in which the terms 'reasonable' and 'reasonableness' appear in the English text, have sometimes been implemented or translated without determining any problem as to the understanding or compliance of the primary text, by using terms which are more familiar to the Italian or German jurist, by means of reference to good faith, diligence, etc. Even in cases in which the English term has been translated literally, the commentators in general have not attributed an innovative meaning to it and have

Czech (& Central European) Yearbook of Arbitration

---

[23] In this sense Luigi Mengoni, *supra* note 17, at 5.

[24] As regards this matter, see for all FEDERICO ROSELLI, IL CONTROLLO DELLA CASSAZIONE SULL'USO DELLE CLAUSOLE GENERALI, Naples: Jovene (1983).

[25] Stefano Troiano, *supra* note 17, at 749. But the 'concreteness' of the criterion does not seem to be shared by specialists of the legal language of *common law*, who define it as '*nebolous*': cfr. PETER BUTT & RICHARD CASTLE, MODERN LEGAL DRAFTING, Port Melbourne, Vict.: Cambridge University Press 63(2nd. ed. 2006).

considered 'reasonableness' and 'reasonable' as synonymous of other terms, such as congruent or adequate, or as equivalent to good faith or diligence.

10.35. Finally, given that the law has to respond to the criteria of reasonableness, the current success of the concept in the debate of jurists of the beginning of the third millennium can first be explained by the influence of the common law. It can therefore be considered an effect of the globalisation of the law. In addition, there is the frequent, indeed excessive[26] use of the term in projects of the European civil code, which, to an increasing extent, represent models of regulation for national legislators and nourish the debate of European civil lawyers.

10.36. In other words, on the one hand obviously in all continental legal experiences, one can happen to come across norms or decisions which refer to a reasonable term, delay or a commitment to undertake according to reasonableness. As already mentioned, the criterion of a paterfamilias, standard of diligence and expression of ancient wisdom refer to a reasonable person. The more or less frequent repetition of the noun or adjectives derived from 'reason' does not imply that reasonableness presents a conceptual and normative autonomy comparable to the principles and general clauses. Therefore, it can be considered more correct to speak of a criterion or rule of evaluation as regards behaviour and of a necessary basis of reasoning as regards a decision and interpretation of the law.

VI. Reasonableness in Codified Legal Orders and the Concept of Reasonableness in Legal Orders of the Common Law

10.37. At this point, however, one could question the eventual utility of reasonableness in order to harmonize Italian civil law with other European legal orders and especially with the European law in the making.

10.38. In order to address that question, it is first necessary to dwell on the meaning of 'reasonable' in the common law legal system. Anticipating the outcome of the research, it seems to me that in continental legal orders, primarily based on the concept of subjective law, the standard of reasonableness can only acquire the role of an additional parameter

---

[26] In the sense that the term 'reasonable' is 'overused' and can create uncertainty, see, among others, Benedicte Fauvarque – Cosson, *A Step Further in a Long and Incremental Process: the Feasibility Study of the Expert Group on European Contract Law, in* TOWARDS A EUROPEAN CONTRACT LAW, Munich: Sellier European Law Publishers 176 (Reiner Schulze & Jules Stuyck eds., 2011).

of evaluation to be placed side by side with the traditional ones. This role is different from the one it has in the normative system of the Anglo-Saxon countries.

10.39. It is also useful to analyse the structure and the systematic coherence of the code projects and, in particular, of the recent *Draft Common Frame of Reference* (DCFR).[27] Here 'reasonable risks' is used to represent the transplant of an organ in a body which is too different from the original one so as to not affect its functions and also the risks that are the result of compromises that demonstrate the difficulty, if not the impossibility, to achieve the consent of the editors on a specific rule.

10.40. The authors who have dealt with the issue did not highlight that the use of reasonableness in the tradition of the common law arises on a different level, as it does not limit itself in expressing a criterion of measurement or evaluation such as reasonable delay, reasonable confidence, etc., but shows a different technique of legal reasoning.

10.41. Consequently, the concept of 'reasonableness' in the common law tradition should not be compared with the rare use of the noun or of related adjectives in the civil codes applicable on the European continent, but with the way of arguing and the same structure of reasoning of the civil law jurist. In fact, while the common law jurist evaluates the case to be examined directly on the basis of the criterion of reasonableness to determine whether the action or behaviour is lawful, the civil law jurist traditionally follows the concept of subjective law, by evaluating if the act is a formally legitimate exercise of the law and if the act itself can, nevertheless, be judged as contrary to good faith or as abusive.

10.42. In this sense, the reasoning of the Anglo-Saxon jurist is described as 'flat', as opposed to the reasoning of the continental jurist, defined as 'structured'.[28] Structured legal reasoning proceeds in two phases. The first serves to identify the applicable rule, as it foresees the right. The second phase serves to qualify the act in order to eventually restrict the range and therefore the sphere of protection of the norm itself.

10.43. In other words, if the exercise of the right leads to a result considered not acceptable or 'excessive', it can be declared to be contrary to good faith, abusive or not reasonable.

10.44. The second phase of the analysis instead is not necessary for the common law jurist who directly qualifies the act according to the

---

[27] CHRISTIAN VON BAR & ERIC CLIVE, PRINCIPLES, DEFINITIONS AND MODEL RULES OF EUROPEAN PRIVATE LAW. DRAFT COMMON FRAME OF REFERENCE (DCFR), Munich: Sellier (2009).

[28] George P. Fletcher, *The Right and the Reasonable*, 98(5) HARVARD LAW REV. 949 (1989).

parameter of reasonableness. The latter, in fact, does not need to make use of a specific level of argumentation to introduce evaluation criteria which are not present in the rule and which serve to limit the legislative provision.

10.45. The concept of reasonableness at the moment of its application complements the common law, not only in matters of civil law, by allowing resolution of any case submitted to a court by means of the 'flat' reasoning that avoids the two phases of reasoning of codified legal orders. One, therefore, understands that decisions of the English courts are often based solely on the 'standard of reasonableness'.

10.46. It can be noted that the rule of continental law presents a greater precision and that the formulations in terms of absoluteness seem better suited to ensure the certainty in legal relationships. On the other hand, precision and absoluteness can be illusive, if one considers the need to make use of the abovementioned correctives and the 'vagueness' of the criteria connected to the standards such as those of 'reasonable' or 'substantial', which are used wisely by the common law jurist to solve in a direct and appropriate way the case subject to examination.

10.47. Obviously, it is not possible to even try to render a judgement on the different ways of operating the two orders. The very fact that they 'are working' shows that it is not about drafting a classification or formulating preferences. The two methods of legal analysis are expressions of different legal cultures.

10.48. Rather, one should note that the way of thinking and the type of analysis of the common law jurist, but above all the terms reasonable and reasonableness, in recent years have strongly influenced continental jurists, and that the projects of a European civil code are 'soaked' with the rule of reasonableness. In fact, there are innumerable rules that codify reasonableness, eliminating or weakening the classical absoluteness of the norms of the continental codes.

10.49. It can also be observed that the differences between the continental system and those of the common law tend to decrease due to the new meaning, which in the European directives is given to concepts and general clauses of ancient tradition, such as good faith. For example, the Italian norm that has implemented Directive 93/13/EC considers clauses to be abusive when 'despite the good faith establish a significant imbalance of the rights and obligations under the contract for the consumer' arises. Regardless of the remarks concerning the accuracy of the translation of the directive and of the formulation, in some ways going beyond the traditional reading of the clause of good faith, it has been asserted that the norm of European origin imposes a 'test of reasonableness on the content of the clause' and a 'control on reasonableness similar to the one exercised by the Constitutional Court on the law, therefore assigning to the civil judge the task of balancing the interests' of an equitable type.[29]

10.50. In a similar sense, and in the effort of identifying a specific role for reasonableness in the application of the general clauses, in the first place the one of good faith, it has been confirmed that 'evaluating the duty of good faith in the light of the standard of reasonableness would involve that the commitment imposed on the contracting parties would have to be restricted within the boundaries of the substantial sacrifice of the proper interest'.[30]

10.51. Moreover, 'translating the content of the general clauses in terms of the reasonableness' would allow it to 'shape its use in a manner more suited to the concrete characteristics', to 'objectify' their field, 'limiting the risk of pure discretional judgments by the judges'.[31]

10.52. The thesis does not seem comprehensible. First of all, the evaluation of the commitment imposed on the contracting parties within the substantial sacrifice of the proper interest is already undertaken on the basis of good faith, whereas every arbitrary evaluation of the judge has to be excluded in the correct application of the general clauses, which allow a high degree of discretion but certainly not an arbitrary judgement, and – already *per se* – offer the possibility to take into account the characteristics of the particular case.[32]

10.53. In addition, the centuries-old experience of different legal orders shows that the objective evaluation criteria and the uniformity of judgement, which would derive from reasonableness in the application of the general clauses do not depend from the expressions used but from the argumentative strictness of the decisions. Therefore, the conclusion according to which 'the notion of reasonableness does not reach the rank of a normative rule' seems to be correct. However, in our legal system the notion of reasonableness is, and remains, an empirical notion that merges into the sphere of the judge's discretion.[33]

---

[29]   In this sense Luigi Mengoni, *supra* note 17, at 16.

[30]   ANNARITA RICCI, IL CRITERIO DELLA RAGIONEVOLEZZA NEL DIRITTO PRIVATO, Padua: CEDAM 184 (2007).

[31]   *Ibid.*

[32]   C. MASSIMO BIANCA, DIRITTO CIVILE,Milan: Giuffrè 500 (3rd ed. 2000); FRANCESCO GALGANO, TRATTATO DI DIRITTO CIVILE, Padua: CEDAM 563 (2nd. ed. 2010).

[33]   Francesco D. Busnelli, *Note in tema di buona fede ed equità*, 1 RIV. DIR. CIV. 555 (2001).

VII. Reasonableness in the Projects of the European Civil Code

10.54. Given what is stated above, in my opinion and in line with the thoughts of Italian jurists, the spread of the concept has to be traced back to the circulation of the models and particularly of the projects of the European civil code, which contain innumerable references to reasonableness and the reasonable.

10.55. These projects also foresee interesting definitions, even though they are not always satisfying. For example, the already mentioned Article 1:302 of the PECL states that 'reasonableness is to be judged by what persons acting in good faith and in the same situation as the parties would consider being reasonable'. In the evaluation of 'reasonableness' one should consider, in particular, the nature and the subject of the contract, the circumstances of the case and the customs and traditions of the trades and the concerned professions.

10.56. In the DCFR of 2009, the terms 'reasonable', 'reasonableness', etc. have been used about four hundred times[34] and a definition of 'reasonable' is contained in the Annex. According to this definition, what is 'reasonable' must be determined objectively, having regard to what should be done, the circumstances of the case and all the relevant customs and practices.

10.57. There is also a significant presence of the term 'reasonable' in the Common European Sales Law (CESL). In fact, there are more than fifty utilizations in the text, which consists of 186 articles.

10.58. In the first group of provisions, the use of the term 'reasonable' does not change the normative content and the parameters of evaluation of the relevant provisions laid down in the civil codes in force, because it is used as a synonym of the traditional terms.

10.59. An example is Article II. – 7: 215 DCFR which refers to the reasonable deadline to sue for the cancellation of the contract in case of error. Also, the German Civil Code Section 121 does not provide a precise period as instead in the case of fraud or violence (Section 124), but states that avoidance must be effected 'without culpable delay (without undue delay) after the person entitled to avoid discovers the deceit'.

10.60. Instead, in another group of provisions, reasonableness represents a criterion of evaluation within the provision, which differentiates the normative content from the one of the corresponding articles of the European civil codes. In these cases a significant change in the legislative technique can be noticed. The absoluteness of the provision

---

[34] Regarding the excessive use of the concept, among others, MARTIJN WILLEM HESSELINK, CFR & SOCIAL JUSTICE, Munich: Sellier 57 (2008), who defines the concept as an 'empty formula'.

of law, possibly mitigated in exceptional circumstances by the use of an external criterion of evaluation, is replaced by an elastic provision, a formulation characterized by 'vagueness', which replaces the legislator with the judge in the formulation of the rule of the individual matter.

10.61. The change affects the structure of the project of a code, whose characteristics drift apart from those of the existing codes in the continental legal orders. It also modifies the jurist's way of reasoning, who no longer needs to rely on external criteria of evaluation to reach a different result from the one otherwise imposed by the norm. In fact, the rule of the PECL or the DCFR is not firm, but merely indicates a guideline leaving its concretisation to the interpreter.

10.62. Ultimately, the use of reasonableness in the projects of civil codes ends up with characterizing not only the drafting of the rules, making them resemble those found in legal orders not belonging to the continental tradition, but in some cases the jurist's way of arguing. Above all, it determines a shift of the regulatory power from the legislator to the judge.

10.63. It is not easy to determine whether it is a progress or a price paid, in terms of rigour and certainty, to the influence of the common law and the needs of globalization. It is important, however, to be aware of the phenomenon. In my opinion, the frequent use of reasonableness shows the awareness of the necessity to get used 'to the idea that the lawyer has to face a "mobile" law, in which the guidelines aimed to protect the fundamental rights and preserve the cornerstones of the constitutional state remain fixed'[35], but also the surrender to a real harmonization due to the lack of shared rules, with the consequence that each national judge will ascribe to reasonableness the meaning which is closer to his own understanding of the law and to the rules of his legal order, already happens in the cases of application of the principle of good faith which is foreseen, for example, in the Directive 93/13 on unfair terms in consumer contracts.

10.64. Therefore, the problem does not only consist in the need to give a new and autonomous meaning to the concept of 'reasonable', as it happens for other terms of the European private law of Anglo-Saxon origin[36], but to avoid that the future European civil code is characterized by the excessive use of vague formulas, which would confirm the doubts and perplexities of this large group of scholars, who had little trust in the process of European codification.

---

[35] GUIDO ALPA, LA CERTEZZA DEL DIRITTO DELL'ETÀ DELL'INCERTEZZA, Lezioni magistrali dell'Università Suor Orsola Benincasa, Naples, 75 (2006).

[36] Regarding this problem, see Salvatore Patti, Traduzione e interpretazione nell'Unione Europea: brevi appunti di un civilista, ARS INTERPRETANDI 309 (2003).

10.65. It should also be reiterated that in some cases the term 'reasonable' can be considered synonymous of adjectives contained in European civil codes, such as adequate, congruous and angemessen, resulting in no innovation. Finally, in other cases, mainly in the DCFR, the use of the term seems superfluous, as it is necessarily implied in the evaluation required by the norm. For this reason, the term is absent in the corresponding rules of the civil codes. Thus, for example, the legitimate expectation has to be 'reasonable', since there must be circumstances to justify the rise of an expectation of a person with common sense.

VIII. Reasonableness and Tradition

10.66. The role of reasonableness as an evaluation and decision criterion, which is placed side by side with other standards and criteria, such as the tradition, present in the jurist's analysis, is therefore confirmed. Also tradition, on the other hand, cannot contrast with reason and its authority must be verified through the criteria of reasonableness. In fact, tradition does not only impose itself by means of its own power, because it requires an ability to persuade and, therefore, reasonableness.

10.67. The jurist's way of thinking depends on what is handed down, but does not have to be limited to it, as a continuous adaptation to what is existing is necessary.

10.68. The authority of tradition – and of the meaning that the latter has assigned to principles and general clauses – does not lead to the renouncement of reason: according to the teaching of Hans Georg Gadamer,[37] also reason must be seen from a historical point of view, since anyhow it is bound to the fact. The search for a suitable solution therefore cannot disregard the data provided by tradition and not only what appears to be completely arbitrary has to be considered 'unreasonable', but also the interpretation and decision which lead to a solution unknown to the data handed out and to the characteristics of the particular case.

IX. Conclusion

The concept of reasonableness permeates the law and therefore also the private law. The use of the term has long been present in the language and decisions of the common law jurists, who pragmatically reject any legal solution that does not appear reasonable and they favour evaluation criteria based on reasonableness. Thus, for example,

---

[37] HANS-GEORG GADAMER, VERITÀ E METODO, Italian translation by G. Vattimo, Milan: Bompiani 562 (2000).

according to a well-known definition, the interpretation of the contract 'is the ascertainment of the meaning which the document would convey to a reasonable person having all the background knowledge which would reasonably have been available to the parties in the situation in which they were at the time of the contract.[38]

10.69. The focus on reasonableness finally deserves approval also by the continental jurist. However, one has to be aware that in many cases the use of the term is superfluous and that, any good jurist has never used or defended unreasonable criteria or solutions.

10.70. In the light of this last consideration it seems to me not to be comprehensible, in addition to being wrong, to try to assign specific functions to reasonableness, for example in connection with general clauses: the acting of human beings, and consequently the activity of the jurist, must always be inspired by what appears to be reasonable, thus tending to satisfy the needs of justice.

| | |

Summaries

DEU [*Die Entscheidungsfindung nach den Grundsätzen billigen Ermessens durch kontinentale Gerichte und Schiedsgerichte*]

Verfahren vor Schiedsgerichten sind vor allem in internationalen Streitigkeiten durch wenig Formalismus, eine absolute Garantie des kontradiktorischen Verfahrens und eine große Beachtung der jeweiligen Bedürfnisse einer Lösung des konkreten Falles gekennzeichnet. Dies erklärt die Tatsache, dass die Schiedssprüche häufig auf die Gebräuche des internationalen Handels und die Generalklauseln, u.a. Treu und Glauben, public policy, gute Sitten etc. Bezug nehmen. Neben den „traditionellen" Generalklauseln oder Wertungsstandards gibt es seit kurzem den „standard of reasonableness", ein Konzept, welches im Gegensatz zu dem common law in den kontinentalen Rechtsordnungen wenig bekannt ist. Da trotz des heutzutage häufigen Gebrauchs des standard of reasonableness eine ausreichende theoretische Studie fehlt, behandelt der Beitrag die Unterschiede der Anwendung des standard of reasonableness in den Rechtsordnungen des civil law als auch des common law, insbesondere durch die Bestimmung von angemessenen Kriterien zur Anwendung in Schiedsverfahren.

---

[38] The quote can be found in PETER BUTT & RICHARD CASTLE, *supra* note 25, at 67.

CZE [*Rozhodování podle zásad přiměřenosti kontinentálními soudy a rozhodčími soudy*]

Řízení před rozhodčími soudy jsou především v mezinárodních sporech charakteristické menším formalismem, absolutní garancí kontradiktornosti řízení a vysokým požadavkem na vyřešení konkrétního případu. Důvodem je skutečnost, že rozhodčí nálezy se často odvolávají na zvyklosti mezinárodního obchodu, obecné principy, m.j. principy důvěry, veřejného pořádku, dobrých mravů apod. Vedle „tradičních" základních principů a hodnotících standardů se vcelku krátkou dobu používá i „princip přiměřenosti". Jde o koncepci, která je na rozdíl od common law v kontinentálních právních řádech málo známa. I přes časté používání principu přiměřenosti však chybí podrobnější studie, která by se zabývala rozdíly mezi používáním principu přiměřenosti v právních řádech civil law, jakož i common law, obzvláště určením kritérií přiměřenosti, která by se měla používat v rozhodčím řízení.

| | |

POL [*Rozstrzyganie przez sądy kontynentalne i arbitrażowe według zasad proporcjonalności*]

Oprócz „tradycyjnych" podstawowych zasad i standardów oceny od niedawna stosowana jest również „zasada proporcjonalności". Koncepcja ta, w przeciwieństwie do common law, nie jest zbyt dobrze znana w kontynentalnych systemach prawnych. Pomimo iż zasada proporcjonalności jest dość często stosowana, nie istnieją szczegółowe opracowania dotyczące różnic pomiędzy stosowaniem jej w systemach prawnych civil law i common law, zwłaszcza jeżeli chodzi o określanie kryteriów proporcjonalności, które powinny być stosowane (również) w postępowaniu arbitrażowym.

FRA [*Les principes de proportionnalité comme motif des décisions des tribunaux continentaux et des tribunaux d'arbitrage*]

En dehors des principes généraux "traditionnels" et des standards d'évaluation, on utilise aussi globalement depuis peu le "principe de proportionnalité". C'est un concept qui est bien moins répandu dans les droits continentaux que dans la common law. Même s'il est souvent employé, il manque une étude approfondie qui se pencherait sur les différences entre son utilisation dans les systèmes de droit civil et dans ceux de droit commun, en particulier en ce qui concerne la détermination des critères d'impartialité qui devraient être utilisés (également) dans la procédure d'arbitrage.

RUS [*Принятие решений континентальными судами и арбитражами на основе принципов пропорциональности*]
Наряду с «традиционными» основными принципами и стандартами оценки с недавних пор также применяется «принцип соразмерности». Это концепция, которая, в отличие от common law, в континентальных правовых системах малоизвестна. Несмотря на частое использование принципа пропорциональности, однако, отсутствуют более подробные исследования, посвященные различиям между использованием принципа соразмерности в юрисдикциях civil law и common law, особенно путем определения критериев адекватности, которые следовало бы применять (также) в арбитраже.

ESP [*Decisiones tomadas por las cortes continentales y los tribunales de arbitraje conforme a los principios de proporcionalidad*]
Además de los principios básicos "tradicionales" y las normas de evaluación, recientemente viene aplicándose también el "principio de proporcionalidad". Se trata de un concepto que, a diferencia de la common law, es poco conocido en los sistemas jurídicos continentales. A pesar del uso frecuente del principio de proporcionalidad, sin embargo, falta un estudio más detallado que trate las diferencias entre el uso del principio de proporcionalidad en los sistemas jurídicos tanto de la civil law como de la common law, y que basándose, en particular, en los criterios de proporcionalidad, se aplicara (también) en el arbitraje.

| | |

Czech (& Central European) Yearbook of Arbitration

Harald Sippel

Double Requirement or Double Standard? A Comparison of Arbitrators' Independence and Impartiality with That of State Court Judges in Austria and Germany[1]

Key words:
IBA Guidelines |
independence |
impartiality |
international arbitration
| state court judge |
Austria | Germany

Abstract *| The double requirement of "independence and impartiality", which arbitrators have to deal with can now be found in virtually any institutional rules of procedure, applicable to arbitral proceedings, as well as in national laws governing arbitration. While it is true that the same rules do not apply around the world, the emergence of the International Bar Association Guidelines on Conflicts of Interest in International Arbitration has helped to create more unified general principles, which have in the past been applied or referred to by state courts even when not explicitly agreed upon by the parties. The two fundamental principles guiding the IBA Guidelines on Conflicts of Interest in Arbitration are, unsurprisingly, independence and impartiality.*

State court judges are also bound by principles of independence of impartiality, but not in the same way as arbitrators. As such, no state court judge is required to investigate a potential conflict of interest when "accepting/receiving" a case. On the other hand, special circumstances that might give rise to a potential conflict of interest can be waived by the parties to an

Harald Sippel works
for the Viennese law
firm Willheim Müller
where he acts as
counsel and arbitrator
in international *ad hoc*
and institutional
arbitration proceedings.
Mr. Sippel obtained a
Master in Law and PhD
in law (summa cum
laude) degree from the
University Linz
(Austria), as well as an
MBA degree from
Seoul National
University (Korea) and
a postgraduate diploma
in arbitration from
Queen Mary,
University of London
(U.K.). He is a Fellow of
the Chartered Institute
of Arbitrators.
e-mail: h.sippel@
wmlaw.at

---

[1] The author is indebted to Ms. Vera Gillessen, attorney-at-law with Lungerich Lenz Schumacher Rechtsanwälte for her assistance.

arbitration proceeding, when such conflict of interest would lead to an automatic exclusion of that judge in state court proceedings.

This paper highlights and analyses the different standards for state court judges in Austria and Germany with that of international arbitrators under the IBA Guidelines.

| | |

I. Introduction

11.01. The 18th century English philosopher and physician John Locke argued that the existence and application of established laws with the right to appeal to independent judges were essential to a civilized society. He considered societies without them to be 'in a state of nature'.[2]

11.02. Now more than a decade into the 21st century, Locke's demand for the independence of the judiciary has become the international standard[3] and is guaranteed by constitutional law[4] as well as by the European Convention on Human Rights (ECHR).[5] Art. 6(1) ECHR thus provides that '[i]n the determination of his civil rights and obligations or of any criminal charge against him, everyone is entitled to a fair and public hearing within a reasonable time by an **independent and impartial tribunal** established by law...' (emphasis added).

11.03. It is generally accepted that because of the juridical nature of the arbitration process in which the state lends its authority for the enforcement of awards, the same characteristics of a fair trial (and thus the same principles of 'independence and impartiality') must be met.[6] The double requirement of independence and impartiality[7] that

---

2   *Cf.*, JOHN LOCKE & THOMAS PRESTON PEARDON, INTRODUCTION TO THE SECOND TREATISE OF GOVERNMENT, New York: Liberal Arts Press 10 (1952).

3   That is to say in most countries at least.

4   For instance, see Constitutional Reform Act 2005, s. 3 for the UK, Art. 87(1) Federal Constitutional Law (*Bundesverfassungsgesetz*) for Austria, Art. 97(1) Basic Law (*Grundgesetz*) for Germany, Sec. 146 Constitution of 1992 (*Eesti Vabariigi põhiseadus*) for Estonia, Art. 3 Instrument of Government (*Regeringsformen*) for Sweden.

5   Also see Art. 10 Universal Declaration of Human Rights.

6   For instance, see GARY BORN, INTERNATIONAL COMMERCIAL ARBITRATION, Alphen aan den Rijn: Kluwer Law International 1616 (2009); FOUCHARD GAILLARD GOLDMAN ON INTERNATIONAL COMMERCIAL ARBITRATION, Hague: Kluwer Law International 561 (Emmanuel Gaillard & John Savage eds., 1999); NIGEL BLACKABY, CONSTANTINE PARTASIDES, ALAN REDFERN & MARTIN HUNTER, REDFERN AND HUNTER ON INTERNATIONAL ARBITRATION, Oxford; New York: Oxford University Press 199 (2009).

7   At times, also seen in its inverse form as impartiality and independence; *cf.*, Art. 5(2) LCIA Rules.

arbitrators must fulfil has therefore become the standard test to which arbitrators are subject in international arbitration and is stipulated in the UNCITRAL Rules[8] as well as in the arbitration rules of all the major arbitration organizations.[9]

11.04. The fact that this widely accepted composite standard of 'independence and impartiality'[10] has become the international norm in arbitration was even accepted by the International Court of Arbitration with the International Chamber of Commerce (ICC), the world's most important institution for international commercial arbitration. Consequently, its 2012 Rules of Arbitration amended its predecessor[11] so that arbitrators must now – by only a plain reading[12] of the 2012 Rules of Arbitration – be both, independent and impartial.[13]

11.05. At first thought, one could thus come to the conclusion that the state court judges and arbitrators are subject to the same standards as regards independence and impartiality. After all, they must both remain independent and impartial. In this paper, I will examine whether this assumption is true and highlight the differences as to the applicable standards, if any.

II. The International Standards[14] for Arbitrators concerning Independence and Impartiality

11.06. Different associations of practitioners, government representatives, and academics have developed various guidelines relevant to the conduct of arbitrators in international arbitrations. By far the most widely

---

[8]   Art. 11 UNCITRAL Rules.

[9]   For instance, Art. 11 ICC Rules of Arbitration (2012); Rule 10.1 SIAC Rules, Art. 14 SCC Rules, Art. 16 VIAC Rules.

[10]   Or, as mentioned above in FN **7**, sometimes also stipulated as 'impartiality and independence'.

[11]   *Cf.* Art. 7 ICC Rules of Arbitration (1998). This provision reads as follows: 'Every arbitrator must be and remain independent of the parties involved in the arbitration.'

[12]   This is not to say that earlier versions of the ICC International Rules of Arbitration were less stringent. If an arbitrator appointed before the 1998 ICC Rules of Arbitration was independent but nevertheless partial (or at least appeared to be so), they would typically fail to be confirmed by the Court of Arbitration following their submission of the statement of independence as required by Art. 7(2) ICC Rules of Arbitration (1998). See YVES DERAINS & ERIC A. SCHWARTZ, GUIDE TO THE ICC RULES OF ARBITRATION, The Hague: Kluwer Law International 115 (2005).

[13]   Art. 11 ICC Rules of Arbitration (2012).

[14]   The term 'standard', as used here, is by no means to imply that there is, in fact, one single international standard. For the sake of simplification, when referring to widely accepted principles and frequent usage, the author will nevertheless refer to 'standards'. Furthermore, the term was chosen as there are (national) standards for state court judges; using the same term naturally makes a comparison easier to read.

accepted and used[15] international[16] guidelines[17] in international arbitration[18] are the *IBA Guidelines on Conflicts of Interests in International Arbitration* (IBA Guidelines),[19] adopted by the International Bar Association (IBA) in May 2004. An examination of the various different international guidelines in existence would go beyond the scope of this paper. In the following only the IBA Guidelines will be discussed.

11.07. The non-binding[20] IBA Guidelines focus on the ethical obligations of arbitrators; to address this issue, the IBA Guidelines use a two-part approach. Part I provides General Standards with explanations and Part II sets forth three lists which address the practical application of the seven General Standards, categorizing various situations that an arbitrator might face according to their relative conflict of interest in colours of red, orange and green.

11.08. The first two sections[21] of the General Standards (Part I), which are the most important for this paper, provide as follows:

---

[15] For instance, see Matthias Scherer, *The IBA Guidelines on Conflicts of Interest in International Arbitration: The First Five Years 2004–2009*, 4(1) DISPUTE RESOLUTION INTERNATIONAL 5 (2010); GARY BORN, INTERNATIONAL ARBITRATION: LAW AND PRACTICE, Alphen aan den Rijn: Kluwer Law International 157 (2012); also see ibid., at 132 stating that 'institutions frequently consider [the] provisions [of the IBA Guidelines]'; KAREL DAELE, CHALLENGE AND DISQUALIFICATION OF ARBITRATORS IN INTERNATIONAL ARBITRATION, Alphen aan den Rijn: Kluwer Law International 3 (2012), who lists several of the UNCITRAL Rules and institutional rules as well as the IBA Guidelines under the subchapter 'Standard of Disclosure'.

[16] This is not to say that national standards, typically the standards applicable at the place of arbitration, will apply to an arbitration as well. However, it would go beyond the scope of this paper to shed light on national standards in different jurisdictions, which is why only reference to the IBA Guidelines is made.

[17] Here, despite the usage of the term 'standard' in this paper, the term 'guideline' was used to make clear that the IBA Guidelines are not an international standard.

[18] Other guidelines *inter alia* include *The Chartered Institute of Arbitrators Code of Professional and Ethical Conduct for Members*, the *AAA Code of Ethics in Commercial Disputes*, the *IBA Rules of Ethics for International Arbitrators*.

[19] The IBA Guidelines are available at: http://www.ibanet.org/Publications/ publications IBA guides and free materials.aspx#conflictsofinterest (accessed on October 3, 2013).

[20] Generally, the IBA Guidelines are non-binding. However, they can be agreed upon by the parties. Furthermore, courts have in the past made reference to the IBA Guidelines even when they were not agreed upon by the parties; see Matthias Scherer, *supra* note 15; also see a very recent ruling by the Austrian Supreme Court, 2 Ob 112/12b, 17 June 2013.

[21] To summarize, section 3 provides for the duties of disclosure of an arbitrator in case there are circumstances that may give rise to doubts as to the arbitrator's impartiality or independence. According to section 4, parties can (generally, but subject to some exceptions) waive objections to the arbitrator after the arbitrator has made their disclosure. Section 5 sets forth that the IBA Guidelines apply equally to tribunal chairs, sole arbitrators and party-appointed arbitrators. Section 6 further clarifies how certain terms related to relationships between arbitrators, their law firms, parties, etc. should be understood. Section 7 also puts responsibility on parties to disclose any direct or indirect

(1) General Principle

Every arbitrator shall be impartial and independent of the parties at the time of accepting an appointment to serve and shall remain so during the entire arbitration proceeding until the final award has been rendered or the proceeding has otherwise finally terminated.

(2) Conflicts of Interest

(a) An arbitrator shall decline to accept an appointment or, if the arbitration has already been commenced, refuse to continue to act as an arbitrator if he or she has any doubts as to his or her ability to be impartial or independent.

(b) The same principle applies if facts or circumstances exist, or have arisen since the appointment, that, from a reasonable third person's point of view having knowledge of the relevant facts, give rise to justifiable doubts as to the arbitrator's impartiality or independence, unless the parties have accepted the arbitrator in accordance with the requirements set out in General Standard (4).

(c) Doubts are justifiable if a reasonable and informed third party would reach the conclusion that there was a likelihood that the arbitrator may be influenced by factors other than the merits of the case as presented by the parties in reaching his or her decision.

(d) Justifiable doubts necessarily exist as to the arbitrator's impartiality or independence if there is an identity between a party and the arbitrator, if the arbitrator is a legal representative of a legal entity that is a party in the arbitration, or if the arbitrator has a significant financial or personal interest in the matter at stake.

11.09. The test for independence and impartiality is thus a two-step approach. First, the arbitrator must decide themselves whether 'he or she has any doubts as to his or her ability to be impartial or independent.'[22] Secondly, the perspective moves from that of the arbitrator to that of 'a reasonable and informed third party'.[23]

11.10. Part II of the Guidelines identifies a series of concrete conflict of interest situations arbitrators might face and categorizes them into one of four lists: the Non-Waivable Red List, the Waivable Red List, the Orange List and the Green List. As is pointed out in the Guidelines, '[t]hese lists obviously cannot contain every situation, but they provide

---

relationship between it and an arbitrator and requires the arbitrator to make enquiries to investigate any potential conflict of interest.

[22] INTERNATIONAL BAR ASSOCIATION, IBA GUIDELINES ON CONFLICTS OF INTEREST IN INTERNATIONAL ARBITRATION, London: The Association (2004), General Standard 2(a).

[23] *Ibid.*, General Standard 2(b).

guidance in many circumstances, and the Working Group has sought to make them as comprehensive as possible. In all cases, the General Standards should control.'[24]

11.11. The Red List contains a total of 18 of such situations, four of which are on the Non-Waivable Red List. These are situations which absolutely exclude the acceptance of an appointment by the arbitrator:[25]

1.1 **There is an identity between a party and the arbitrator, or the arbitrator is a legal representative of an entity that is a party in the arbitration.**

1.2. **The arbitrator is a manager, director or member of the supervisory board, or has a similar controlling influence in one of the parties.**

1.3. **The arbitrator has a significant financial interest in one of the parties or the outcome of the case.**

1.4. **The arbitrator regularly advises the appointing party or an affiliate of the appointing party, and the arbitrator or his or her firm derives a significant financial income therefrom.**

11.12. The situation is somewhat different for the Waivable Red List as it encompasses situations that are 'serious but not as severe'[26] as those on the Non-Waivable Red List. In these situations, the arbitrator, either directly or through a close family member, has previously advised the party as a client, has been involved in the case, holds a significant financial or other interest in a party, or has a close relationship with a third party liable to recourse by the losing party (or generally with a party or a counsel).[27] Situations similar to those on the Waivable Red List should be considered waivable, but only 'if and when the parties, being aware of the conflict of interest situation, nevertheless expressly state their willingness to have such a person act as arbitrator.'[28] It is

---

[24] *Ibid.*, Part II: Practical Application of the General Standards, para. 1.

[25] Again, one has to keep in mind that the IBA Guidelines are generally not binding unless agreed upon by the parties. Therefore, whether an arbitrator can accept appointment or not will depend if such agreement exists. However, even when they are not agreed upon between the parties, courts can, and have in the past, nevertheless made reference to the IBA Guidelines (*supra* note 20). It is thus recommendable not only from a moral standard, but also from a factual point of view to not accept an appointment in case there is a situation as on the 'Non-Waivable Red List'.

[26] INTERNATIONAL BAR ASSOCIATION, *supra* note 22, Part II: Practical Application of the General Standards, para. 2.

[27] For the complete list, see Ibid., Part II: Practical Application of the General Standards, 2. Waivable Red List.

[28] *Ibid.*, Part II: Practical Application of the General Standards, para. 2.

important to point out once again that express consent to the arbitrator's continuation must be made and that thus the 'silence implies consent' approach does not apply.[29]

11.13. Situations in the Orange List include an arbitrator's previous or current services for one of the parties or other involvement in the case although not directly by the arbitrator or at least not in the current dispute. The Orange List also includes situations when there is a relationship between an arbitrator and another arbitrator or counsel or between the arbitrator and a party or others involved in the arbitration as well as a view of other circumstances. An example would be where the arbitrator has a material holding in a party or its affiliate that is publicly listed.[30] As the IBA Guidelines explain, '[t]he Orange List is a non-exhaustive enumeration of specific situations which (depending on the facts of a given case) in the eyes of the parties may give rise to justifiable doubts as to the arbitrator's impartiality or independence.'[31] Opposite to the Red List, the principle of *quis tacit, consentire sentitur* applies, so that no express waiver by the parties is required.[32]

11.14. The IBA Guidelines also contain a Green List, which is a 'non-exhaustive enumeration of specific situations where no appearance of, and no actual, conflict of interest exists from the relevant objective point of view.'[33] The Green List encompasses common situations, similar to those on the Orange list (i.e. previous services for a party, current services, relationship with another arbitrator or with counsel, and relationship with a party), but in less severe circumstances.[34] To give but one example, when three years have passed since service was rendered to a party in an arbitration, this is to be considered a circumstance relating to the Green List only. Circumstances enumerated on the Green List, or those not listed on the Green List, but generally not falling into the – non exhaustive – category Orange List can, but need not be disclosed to the parties.[35]

---

[29] *Cf. ibid.*; David A. Lawson, *Impartiality and Independence of International Arbitrators – Commentary on the 2004 IBA Guidelines on Conflicts of Interest in International Arbitration*, 23(1) ASA BULLETIN 35 (2005).

[30] For the complete list, see IBA Guidelines, *supra* note 22, Part II: Practical Application of the General Standards, 3. Orange List.

[31] IBA Guidelines, *supra* note 22, Part II: Practical Application of the General Standards, para. 3; Phillip Landolt, *The IBA Guidelines on Conflicts of Interest in International Arbitration: An Overview*, 22(5) JOURNAL OF INTERNATIONAL ARBITRATION 416 (2005).

[32] *Cf.* IBA Guidelines, *supra* note 22, Part II: Practical Application of the General Standards, para. 3.

[33] *Ibid.*, para. 4.

[34] For the full list, see Ibid., Part II: Practical Application of the General Standards, 4. Green List.

[35] *Ibid.*, Part II: Practical Application of the General Standards, para. 6.

III. The Standards for State Court Judges concerning Independence and Impartiality in Austria and Germany

III.1. Austria

11.15. The independence of Austrian state court judges is guaranteed by Art. 81(1) Federal Constitutional Law[36] and Art. 6(1) ECHR (which has constitutional status in Austria).

11.16. For each individual state court judge, sec. 19 and 20 of the Law on Jurisdiction[37] provide for specific rules as to when state court judges are not to be considered independent/impartial. The Law on Jurisdiction makes a distinction between two events, namely the exclusion of judges and situations when judges may be challenged for not being independent/impartial. Sec 19 Law on Jurisdiction stipulates the two events.

'A state court judge can be challenged in civil law matters for the following reasons:
1. He is excluded by law from acting as judge in the case at hand;
2. There are sufficient grounds which cast doubts on his independence/impartiality.'

III.1.1. Exclusion by Law

11.17. Sec. 20 Law on Jurisdiction specifies the circumstances when state court judges are excluded by law:

1) In all matters in which he himself is a party, or in which his relationship to one of the parties in the proceedings is that of a co-obligee, co-obligor, or a party liable to recourse;

2) In all matters concerning his spouse or persons who are directly related to him, either by blood or by marriage, or who are or were related as fourth-degree relatives in the collateral line, or who are or were second-degree relatives by marriage in the collateral line;

3) In all matters concerning his adoptive or foster parents, his adoptive of foster children or his wards;

4) In all matters in which he was or still is appointed as attorney of record of a party;

5) In all matters in which he assisted, at a prior level of jurisdiction, in entering the contested decision.

---

[36] *Bundesverfassungsgesetz.*
[37] *Jurisdiktionsnorm.*

11.18. The above circumstances providing for exclusion are non-waivable and actions for nullification of a verdict reached by a judge who should have been excluded can be made even after final judgment.[38]

III.1.2. Sufficient Grounds Casting Doubts on a Judge's Independence/Impartiality

11.19. While sec. 20 Law on Jurisdiction is quite straightforward and leaves little doubt as to when a judge is excluded, sec. 19 is very general. However, there exist numerous decisions by courts which provide for greater clarity.

11.20. The Austrian Supreme Court ruled that most generally, a state court judge is considered not to be independent/impartial when – under objective views – there are grounds that cast doubts on a judge's independence/impartiality.[39] It is generally accepted that well-founded concern over the judge's independence/impartiality suffices[40] or that there could be appearance of bias.[41]

11.21. While this strictness might surprise, it is generally accepted that – in light of the sanctity of justice – stringent standards are to be applied.[42] Thus, in cases of doubt, a judge can be successfully challenged. However, this cannot open doors to a party which wants to rid itself of an unwanted judge; a well-balanced consideration of all circumstances will always be required.[43]

11.22. When a party challenges a judge, it is thus required to specify the grounds which cast doubt on the judge's independence/impartiality; in particular, it is insufficient to merely allege that a judge is under political pressure (without providing for specific reasons as to why there is political pressure which can cast doubts).[44]

11.23. Furthermore, it is generally not possible to challenge an entire court; instead, only individual judges, who for that reason must be named, can be challenged.[45] The only exception to that rule is the case when the same reason(s) to challenge a judge apply to every single judge of that court.[46]

---

[38] Oskar J. Ballon, *in* KOMMENTAR ZU DEN ZIVILPROZESSGESETZEN, Wien: MANZ (Hans Walter Fasching ed., 2000) , sec. 19 Law on Jurisdiction, para. 4.

[39] Austrian Supreme Court 21.04.1998, 4 Ob 117/98d.

[40] Superior Court of Vienna EFSlg 69.687 [1992].

[41] Austrian Supreme Court 13.04.1994, 7 Ob 529/94.

[42] Mayr, *in* KOMMENTAR ZUR ZPO, Wien: Springer (Walter H. Rechberger ed., 2006), sec. 19 Law on Jurisdiction, para. 4.

[43] Oskar J. Ballon, *supra* note 38, sec. 19 Law on Jurisdiction, para. 5.

[44] Austrian Supreme Court 04.12.1996, 7 Ob 2388/96v.

[45] Oskar J. Ballon, *supra* note 38, sec. 19 Law on Jurisdiction, para. 7 with further references

[46] This could be the case with small courts where all judges are well-acquainted with one another. If one of these judges were a party, it is highly unlikely that any of the other judges of that same court could be considered independent/impartial.

11.24. In previous cases, state court judges were considered to be not independent/impartial *inter alia* in the following circumstances:
— Private and personal dealings exist between the judge and a party. For instance when the judge and a party were in the same class in high school and were members of the same sports club.[47]
— Private and personal dealings exist between the judge and a party's counsel.[48]
— Private and personal dealings exist between the judge and a witness.[49]
— Non-objective and impertinent remarks were made to parties or a party's counsel;[50]
— A judge disregards procedural principles in an apparent and questionable manner. However, the judge's behaviour only results in a successful challenge if the procedural principles he disregards serve the objectivity of the procedure and concern the parties' right to be heard;[51] and
— One of the lawyers of a party's counselling law firm, who however did not act as counsel in this case, was the judge's son.[52]

11.25. In the past, Austrian courts ruled that arbitrators are <u>not</u> to be seen as dependent/partial *inter alia* in the following situations:
— The judge takes a certain legal view even if that legal view differs from the prevailing opinion on that question.[53]
— The judge expressly takes a certain legal view in 'preliminary proceedings', such as proceedings over provisional measures.[54]
— In Austria, it is the prevailing view that the same rule applies when a judge takes a certain view in an academic publication. However, the judge must be willing to objectively assess every individual case and reconsider his previous stance.[55]
— The judge renders a legally wrong verdict.[56]
— The judge exhibits a collegial relationship to a local counsel.[57]

---

[47] Regional Court for Civil Law Matters of Vienna, EFSlg 66.838 [1991].
[48] Schumacher in JBl 1990, 122.
[49] *Ibid.*, at 122.
[50] OGH-Z 1993/1263, 1264; in the case at hand, the judge noted during a break that such emotionally intense reactions could – under normal cases – only be seen when a baby had her bottle or pacifier taken away.
[51] Oskar J. Ballon, *supra* note 38, sec. 19 Law on Jurisdiction, para. 9 with further references.
[52] Austrian Supreme Court 5 Ob 93/13g, 20. 9. 2013
[53] Austrian Supreme Court 5 Ob 335/98w, 12.01.1999.
[54] Austrian Supreme Court 1 Ob 13/90, 21.05.1990.
[55] Oskar J. Ballon, *supra* note 38, sec. 19 Law on Jurisdiction, para. 10 with further references.
[56] Austrian Supreme Court 5 Ob 335/98w, 12.01.1999.
[57] Austrian Supreme Court 3 Ob 155/98k, 24.06.1998.

11.26. A judge who, in a party's view, is not independent/impartial for 'other sufficient grounds' must be challenged immediately. If the party continues with its case, in particular by making petitions, it is assumed that the party has waived their right to challenge the judge.[58]

III.2. Germany

11.27. Title 4 of the German Code of Civil Procedure (GCCP)[59] deals with disqualification and recusal of court personnel. According to sec. 41 GCCP, a judge is disqualified by law from exercising office in the following cases:

1. In all matters in which he himself is a party, or in which his relationship to one of the parties in the proceedings is that of a co-obligee, co-obligor, or a party liable to recourse;

2. In all matters concerning his spouse or former spouse;

2a. In all matters concerning his partner or former partner under a civil union;

3. In all matters concerning persons who are or were directly related to him, either by blood or by marriage, or who are or were related as third-degree relatives in the collateral line, or who are or were second-degree relatives by marriage in the collateral line;

4. In all matters in which he was appointed as attorney of record or as a person providing assistance to a party, or in which he is or was authorised to make an appearance as a legal representative of a party;

5. In all matters in which he is examined as a witness or expert;

6. In all matters in which he assisted, at a prior level of jurisdiction or in arbitration proceedings, in entering the contested decision, unless this concerns activities of a judge correspondingly delegated or requested.

7. In all matters concerning court procedures of excessive duration, if he assisted in the impugned proceedings at the level of jurisdiction, the duration of which is the basis for the claim to compensation.

8. In all matters, in which he assisted in mediation proceedings or in other proceedings of out-of-court dispute resolution.

11.28. Sec. 42 GCCP stipulates the rules of recusal of a judge from a case. According to sec. 42(1) GCCP, 'a judge may be recused from a case both in those cases in which he is disqualified by law from exercising a judicial office, and in those cases in which there is a fear of bias.' According to sec. 42(2), 'a judge will be recused for fear of bias if sound

---

[58] Oskar J. Ballon, *supra* note 38, sec. 19 Law on Jurisdiction, para. 4.
[59] Sec. 41 to 49 GCCP.

reasons justify a lack of confidence in his impartiality'. While sec. 42(3) clarifies that in all cases, both parties shall have the right to recuse a judge. Furthermore, a party loses the right to recuse a judge for fear of bias 'if that party has made an appearance before said judge at a hearing, or filed petitions, without asserting the reasons for recusal of which it is aware.'[60]

11.29. The term 'bias'[61] as used in the GCCP refers to 'partiality', which is understood to be the 'unobjective inner attitude' of a judge towards a party or the subject matter of the proceedings.[62]

11.30. The general view is that that there must be an 'objectively justified' fear of bias. It does not matter whether the judge in fact is biased or not or whether he considers himself biased. The applicable criterion, as clarified by the (German) Federal Constitutional Court is the fear of bias by a reasonable party.[63] It thus is not surprising that a strict standard is applied. As such, a motion to recuse a judge is only successful when there is certainty that reason for recusal exists. When there are doubts as to the fear of bias, the motion must be declared to be without justification and thus rejected.[64]

11.31. Under German law, the grounds for recusal are summarized in four different groups.

III.2.1. A Judge's Particular Relationship to a Party

11.32. A particular relationship that can result in bias can be of a legal nature as well as of a private nature. As to the former, this would concern (1) cases of marriage, and affinity[65] to the extent that these relationships are not already covered by sec. 41 GCCP.[66] Furthermore, a judge might be biased as a result of (2) employment or membership. As such, an earlier employment with a party can justify a motion for recusal.[67] The same applies to a judge who is a major shareholder in one of the parties. However, the opposite is true when she is the owner of only a few stocks.[68] Membership of a political party, trade union or employer association generally does not disqualify a judge; however, this might be

---

[60] Sec. 43 GCCP.
[61] The German version reads *Befangenheit*.
[62] Markus Gehrlein, *in* MÜNCHENER KOMMENTAR ZUR ZPO. München: Verlag C.H. Beck (Wolfgang Krüger & Thomas Rauscher eds., 2013), sec. 42 para. 5.
[63] BVerfG NJW 2000, 2808; 1993, 2231: *'Sicht eines vernünftigen Prozessbeteiligten'*; also see Markus Gehrlein, *supra* note 62, para. 4.
[64] Markus Gehrlein, *supra* note 62, sec. 42 para. 6 with further references.
[65] Ehe, Verwandtschaft und Schwägerschaft.
[66] As such, the judge's spouse might be called as witness.
[67] Markus Gehrlein, *supra* note 62, sec. 42 FN 28.
[68] *Ibid.*, sec. 42 para. 9 with further references.

different when the political party/organization is a party in the proceedings.[69] In the past, the mere membership of a judge in a sports club or Rotary club as well as the judge's position as a lecturer in proceedings where the university was a party were not considered to render the judge biased.[70]

11.33. Occasionally, emotional connections become grounds for recusal. Those relationships typically involve friendship and hostility, cohabitation (in the present and the past) as well as any strong emotional ties. As such, any form of personal engagement between the judge and a party typically raises fear of bias.[71] However, the applicable standard of 'relationship' must not be overly stretched: mere acquaintance alone generally does not make a judge biased, and strong hostilities between a judge and an attorney could only render the judge biased if these differences emerge against a party in legal proceedings.[72]

III.2.2. A Judge's Particular Relationship to the Subject Matter of the Case

11.34. This subgroup comprises all forms of a prior involvement besides the cases in sec. 41 4-6. However, similar facts or legal problems generally reoccur over time and naturally this alone does not disqualify a judge. However, if a judge gives legal advice on a subject matter prior to the start of the proceedings, he will typically be considered biased.[73] Problems can occur, in particular, if the judge dealt with the subject matter of the case in the past, prior to taking office. In cases where the judge acted as an attorney, public officer or expert arbitrator, a fear of bias will typically have to be substantiated although an assessment on a case by case basis must be taken.[74]

III.2.3. A Judge's Behaviour outside of the Case at Hand

11.35. A general rule applies that provoked actions can be excluded as reasons for bias when the action in question is appropriate and proportionate. Thus a party cannot force the successful challenge of a judge by means of its own actions. This even applies when the judge files a criminal complaint as a result of the party's actions.[75]

---

[69] *Ibid.*, sec. 42 para. 9 with further references.
[70] *Ibid.*, sec. 42 para. 9 with further references.
[71] *Ibid.*, sec. 42 para. 10 with further references.
[72] *Ibid.*, sec. 42 paras. 10 *et seq.* with further references.
[73] *Ibid.*, sec. 42 paras 13 *et seq.* with further references.
[74] *Ibid.*, sec. 42 para. 17 with further references.
[75] *Ibid.*, sec. 42 para. 18 with further references.

11.36. However, any inappropriate behaviour which gives reasonable suspicion to bias justifies the motion to recuse a judge. This applies, in particular, to scorching, unobjective and partial marginal notes on written submissions as well as to pejorative and unnecessarily judgemental remarks.[76]

11.37. Opinions rendered as part of legal publications generally[77] do not render a judge biased. This applies even when a judge has in the past published her opinion on a particular legal question which now is the main matter of dispute. Nevertheless, a judge must always be expected to remain open to new arguments and considerations.[78]

III.2.4. A Judge's Behaviour in Relation to the Case at Hand

11.38. As a general rule, no behaviour which is in accordance with the law and the GCCP in particular may disqualify a judge. As such, the substantial guidance of the proceedings (*materielle Prozessleitung*) and in particular a judge's duties of disclosure or information (*Aufklärungs- und Hinweispflichten*) cannot be limited by the duty of having to remain impartial.[79]

11.39. A judge's behaviour in relation to the case at hand that disqualifies him can be categorized in four different groups, (1) a lack of objectivity; (2) decisions by the judge; (3) substantial guidance of the proceedings; and (4) any other behaviour that does not fall into the first three groups.

11.40. While German judges are allowed to act lively, speak clearly and loudly and fulfil their duties diligently and even passionately,[80] this is not to be interpreted that verbal lapses, a clear lack of objectivity, or biting irony, are permitted. Interestingly, it is the general view that this applies as much to verbal and written communications as it applies to gestures and facial expressions.[81]

11.41. As such, judges have in the past been disqualified for harsh statements of displeasure such as 'That's enough! Hold your tongue! I'm the one speaking now!' or referring to a statement of facts by the attorney as 'nonsense'. This is in spite of the fact that such actions appeared understandable in the context as judges are expected to be more

---

[76] *Ibid.*, sec. 42 para. 19 with further references.

[77] Again, in particular cases – polemical and depreciating comments in particular – a judge might nevertheless be considered biased.

[78] *Ibid.*, sec. 42 para. 21 with further references.

[79] *Ibid.*, sec. 42 para. 22 with further references.

[80] Bull NJW 1956, 1669.

[81] Markus Gehrlein, *supra* note 62, sec. 42 para. 24 with further references, while nevertheless pointing out that greater weight must be given to written communications. One time slip-ups, which are excused immediately thereafter shall be permitted.

disciplined than other actors in the process.[82] Other cases of disqualification included:

— where a judge put his head on the desk and banged his forehead;[83]

— where a judge returned a written submission to the party with the comment 'I really don't care what will happen with the premises';[84] and

— where a judge made clear that he would only be led by his feelings and not by the law.[85]

11.42. The judge was not considered to be biased in the following cases:

— During in-court discussions over a settlement, the judge stated 'Then you'll be in for a shock' as one party voiced its belief to win the case.[86]

— The judge declared the overruling decision by the superior court to be wrong, while at the same time making clear that he would, of course, respect it.[87] The judge scheduled a hearing for 11 November at 11:11.[88]

11.43. Wrong decisions by a judge generally cannot disqualify that judge and only extreme cases of arbitrariness can qualify as bias. In particular, the motion to recuse the judge must not serve the purpose of validating the judge's decision.[89]

11.44. As to the substantial guidance of the proceedings, it is generally accepted that judges may advise a party to withdraw their claim, file a counterclaim, name further witnesses, etc. A judge may even assist in drafting expedient motions. However, pointing out a 'procedural trick' will generally go beyond the permitted advice of a party. Furthermore, the judge may only give his advice – and not pressure a party into any actions.[90]

11.45. Cases which do not fall into the three former groups are rather rare; they include cases of taking a judge to a restaurant or discussing the subject matter of the dispute over the phone with only one party.[91]

---

[82] *Ibid.*, sec. 42 para. 25 with further references.

[83] OLG Frankfurt FamRZ 1983, 630.

[84] LG Bayreuth NJW-RR 1986, 678.

[85] OLG Celle, AnwBl. 1984, 502.

[86] OLG Naumburg MDR 2007, 794.

[87] OLG Karlsruhe OLGZ 1984, 102, 104.

[88] OLG München NJW 200, 748 – 11:11 o'clock on 11 November is the beginning of the carnival season.

[89] Markus Gehrlein, *supra* note62, sec. 42 paras. 28 *et seq.* with further references.

[90] *Ibid.*, sec. 42 para. 33 with further references.

[91] *Ibid.*, sec. 42 paras. 35 *et seq.* with further references.

IV. The Same Double Requirement or Double Standard? The Standards in Comparison

11.46. It has been pointed out before, on several occasions that different standards apply for state court judges than for international arbitrators when it comes to independence and impartiality.[92] It should thus be no surprise that when a comparison is done between the IBA Guidelines and the standards for independence and impartiality of state court judges in Austria and Germany there are differences.

11.47. The most striking difference of course, is that the IBA guidelines unless agreed upon by the parties, are generally not binding.[93] However, this is only true at first sight as national laws as well as institutional rules most typically provide for the requirement of independence and impartiality. In determining whether an arbitrator can be challenged or not,[94] the IBA guidelines can – and have been – consulted.[95] With international arbitration gaining in importance as global trade flows increase, it can be expected that courts will in the future give even more weight to the IBA Guidelines. Therefore, the general statement that they are not binding is only true on a superficial level and should be handled with care.

11.48. Thus, one could very well say that circumstances on the Waivable Red List are the equivalent of some of the grounds in sec. 20 Law on Jurisdiction/sec. 41 GCCP as such circumstances lead to an automatic conclusion and in case of the IBA Guidelines cannot be waived.

11.49. However, the provisions regarding the exclusion by law for state court judges go beyond those for arbitrators. As such, no Austrian[96] or German[97] state court judge could sit in a case where their spouse or other close family member is a party. In contrast, close family ties to one of the parties is a circumstance under the Red List[98] and thus an

---

[92] *Cf.*, Julian D. M. Lew, Loukas A. Mistelis & Stefan Kröll, Comparative International Commercial Arbitration, The Hague: Kluwer Law International (2003), para. 11-10 with further references.

[93] *Cf.*, IBA Guidelines, *supra* note 22, Introduction, para. 6 which provides that '[t]hese Guidelines are not legal provisions and do not override any applicable national law or arbitral rules chosen by the parties. However, the Working Group hopes that these Guidelines will find general acceptance within the international arbitration community.'

[94] Or at a later stage following the issuance of the award: whether the award can be set aside or not.

[95] See *supra* note 20.

[96] Sec. 20.2 Law on Jurisdiction.

[97] Sec. 41.2; 41.2a; 41.3 GCCP.

[98] *Cf.*, item 2.3.8 Red List.

issue the parties can expressly[99] waive if they feel it will not impair the arbitrator's impartiality.[100]

11.50. The fact that express waiver must be made under such circumstances and others on the Red List[101] which would lead to automatic exclusion for Austrian and German state court judges, can certainly be seen as a safeguard for the parties. However, I personally take the view that the Non-Waivable Red List could be expanded by a few of these items. It is very hard to imagine that anyone whose spouse is a party in a dispute can remain impartial.

11.51. While the applicable standards for state court judges are thus more stringent when it comes to a judge's automatic exclusion by law, the weight of the stringent standards shifts to arbitrators when it comes to the assessment of conflicts of interest. As Landolt points out,

> In assessing whether there is a conflict of interest, the arbitrator cannot simply take refuge behind his or her own ignorance. General Standard 7 places the prospective arbitrator under a duty "to make reasonable enquiries to investigate any potential conflict of interest as well as any facts or circumstances that may cause his or her impartiality or independence to be questioned".[102,103]

11.52. This is certainly different from the role of the state judge who does not have such a duty.

11.53. As surprising as this may be at first sight, the differences as to the standards of impartiality and independence, as well as many other,[104] can be very well explained by the fact that

> Arbitrators are usually engaged in other occupations before, during and after the arbitration proceedings. They are appointed and paid for by the parties. Their special experience and reputation in a certain field is often one of the major reasons for their appointment though it may imply previous

---

[99] See *supra* note 28.

[100] However, this does not mean that an arbitrator who fails to inform about such circumstance would under normal conditions be considered biased.

[101] For instance, item 2.1.1 on the Read List reads as follows: 'The arbitrator **currently represents** or advises one of the parties or an affiliate of one of the parties.' (emphasis added) This would be seen as disqualification under sec. 20.4 Law on Jurisdiction and under sec. 41.4 GCCP.

[102] IBA Guidelines, *supra* note 22, General Standard 7.

[103] Phillip Landolt, *supra* note 31, at 414.

[104] For example, many items on the Red List and Orange List concern the prior or current involvement of an arbitrator's law firm with one of the parties/counsel. As judges by the very nature of their profession are not members of law firms, such issues could naturally never arise in state court proceedings and can, therefore, not be found in the Law on Jurisdiction or the GCCP.

contacts with the parties. In particular, party appointed arbitrators may have a loose and special relationship with the appointing party or its lawyers.[105]

V. Conclusion

11.54. The above comparison, which for lack of space unfortunately had to be limited to the above subchapter, reveals that international arbitrators have different duties regarding independence and impartiality compared to Austrian and German state court judges. However, it could also be shown that typically there are often sensible reasons for this difference, such as arbitrators being particular experts in their field. This might lead to a lighter standard regarding independence and impartiality when it comes to automatic exclusion by law. Overall, as a comparison of the IBA Guidelines and the rules for Austrian and German state court judges reveals, the applicable standards to independence and impartiality are very similar. This leaves aside cases which are characteristic for the profession of judges[106] or those of arbitrators whose main profession is that of a lawyer.[107]

11.55. It is fair to say that each of the two camps, arbitration v state courts has rules that mostly fit to its requirements. As such, it would be completely nonsensical to put the burden on a state court judge of having to investigate any potential conflict of interest for every new case they received.[108] At the same time, being too strict in a particular case where an expert arbitrator is needed might diminish one of the core strengths of arbitration. Specifically, this is the idea that the arbitrator is a person with the particular expertise involved in the dispute at hand.[109]

11.56. Eventually, it will come down to the judge/arbitrator and his/her own moral standards and sense of fairness. While challenges to independence and impartiality should not be seen as a tool to hijack the proceedings, the application of strict standards to oneself is advisable and should be honoured.

| | |

---

[105] JULIAN D. M. LEW, LOUKAS A. MISTELIS & STEFAN KRÖLL, *supra* note 92, para. 11-10.

[106] Such as involvement at a prior level of jurisdiction.

[107] Such as the arbitrator being a lawyer in the same law firm as the counsel to one of the parties.

[108] This applies in particular to judges in small towns where the judge often sees the same attorneys, but also claimants, respondents, as well as experts in court on a regular basis.

[109] For instance, see CIArb, Arbitration, available at: http://www.ciarb.org/dispute-resolution/resolving-a-dispute/arbitration (accessed on August 25, 2013), where this point is the first on the list of the advantages of arbitration.

Summaries

FRA [*Double condition ou standard redoublé ? Une comparaison de l'indépendance et de l'impartialité des arbitres avec celles des juges en Autriche et en Allemagne*]

On trouve aujourd'hui la double condition d'indépendance et d'impartialité portant sur le choix des arbitres dans le principe de toutes les règles procédurales institutionnalisées utilisées dans les procédures d'arbitrage ainsi que dans les réglementations nationales des procédures d'arbitrage. Bien que ne soient pas appliquées les mêmes règles partout à travers le monde, les standards de l'Association internationale du barreau (en anglais, International Bar Association - IBA) relatifs aux conflits d'intérêts dans une procédure d'arbitrage international ont contribué à imposer des principes généraux relativement unifiés qui sont aujourd'hui utilisés ou auxquels se réfèrent les tribunaux nationaux même dans les cas où les parties n'avaient pas expressément convenu de leur emploi. Il ne constituera donc une surprise pour personne que les deux principes de base qui irriguent tous les standards de l'IBA sur les conflits d'intérêts dans les procédures arbitrales sont précisément l'indépendance et l'impartialité.

Les juges des tribunaux nationaux sont eux aussi liés par les principes d'indépendance et d'impartialité, mais pas de la même manière que pour les arbitres. Par exemple, les juges ne sont pas tenus de s'assurer eux-mêmes de l'absence de conflit d'intérêts au moment où ils "acceptent / prennent en charge" l'affaire qui leur est échue. D'un autre côté, les mêmes circonstances qui conduisent à l'exclusion automatique d'un juge dans des procédures menées devant des tribunaux nationaux peuvent justifier dans certains cas une demande d'exclusion d'un arbitre dans une procédure d'arbitrage.

On s'intéresse ici et on passe en revue les différents standards utilisés pour les juges des tribunaux allemands et autrichiens en comparaison avec ceux utilisés pour les arbitres dans les litiges internationaux suivant les règles de l'IBA.

CZE [*Dvojí požadavek nebo duplicitní standard? Srovnání nezávislosti a nestrannosti rozhodců s nezávislostí a nestranností soudců v Rakousku a v Německu*]

Zdvojený požadavek „nezávislosti a nestrannosti", který se týká rozhodců, lze v současnosti nalézt v zásadě ve všech institucionalizovaných procesních pravidlech použitelných na rozhodčí řízení, jakož i v národních úpravách rozhodčího řízení. Ačkoliv se stejná pravidla jistě nepoužívají po celém světě, standardy Mezinárodní advokátní organizace (IBA) ohledně konfliktu zájmů v mezinárodním rozhodčím řízení pomohly vytvořit dosti sjednocené obecné principy, které se v posledních letech používají nebo na které se odvolávají státní soudy, a to i v případech, kdy jejich použití nebylo stranami výslovně sjednáno. Není překvapením, že dvěma základními principy vinoucími se standardy IBA o konfliktu zájmů v rozhodčím řízení jsou právě nezávislost a nestrannost.

Rovněž soudci státních soudů jsou vázáni principy nezávislosti a nestrannosti, nikoliv ovšem stejným způsobem, jako je tomu u rozhodců. Takto například soudci státních soudů nejsou povinni sami prověřovat případný konflikt zájmů v okamžiku, kdy „přijmou / obdrží" věc k projednání. Na druhou stranu námitku vyloučení rozhodce v rozhodčím řízení mohou odůvodňovat v některých případech stejné okolnosti, které vedou i k automatickému vyloučení soudce v řízeních před státními soudy.

Článek se zabývá a rozebírá různé standardy použitelné na soudce státních soudů v Rakousku a v Německu ve srovnání se standardy použitelnými na rozhodce v mezinárodních sporech podle pravidel IBA.

|||

POL   [**Podwójny warunek czy zdublowana norma? Porównanie niezawisłości i bezstronności arbitrów z niezawisłością i bezstronnością sędziów w Austrii i Niemczech**]
Arbitrzy, tak jak sędziowie sądów państwowych, muszą postępować zgodnie z zasadą bezstronności i niezawisłości. Chociaż są to zasady obowiązujące obie te „grupy zawodowe", istnieją tu jednak znaczne różnice co do ich treści. Niniejszy artykuł omawia i analizuje te różnice oraz podejmuje próbę ich uzasadnienia.

DEU   [**Zwei verschiedene Anforderungen oder ein Doppelstandard? Ein Vergleich der Unabhängigkeit und Unparteilichkeit von Schiedsrichtern mit der Unabhängigkeit und Unparteilichkeit von Richtern in Österreich und Deutschland**]
Schiedsrichter, so wie staatliche Richter, haben nach den Grundsätzen von Unabhängigkeit und Unvoreingenommenheit zu agieren. Wenngleich diese Prinzipien für beide „Berufsgruppen" gelten, so bestehen letztlich doch große Unterschiede in deren inhaltlicher Ausgestaltung. Dieser Aufsatz untersucht und analysiert die Unterschiede und wagt einen Erklärungsversuch dafür.

RUS [*Двойное требование или дублированный стандарт? Сравнение независимости и беспристрастности арбитров с независимостью и беспристрастностью судей в Австрии и Германии*]

Арбитры, равно как и судьи государственных судов, должны действовать в соответствии с принципами беспристрастности и независимости. Хотя эти принципы действительны в отношении обеих «профессий», существуют большие различия в их содержании. В статье рассматриваются и анализируются различия, а также делается попытка их обоснования.

ESP [*¿Un doble requisito o una norma duplicada? La comparación de la independencia e imparcialidad de los árbitros con la independencia e imparcialidad de los jueces en Austria y Alemania*]

Los árbitros, así como los jueces de los tribunales del Estado, deben actuar según los principios de imparcialidad e independencia. A pesar de que estos principios se aplican a ambos "grupos de este oficio", aún existen grandes diferencias en su contenido. El artículo aborda y analiza las diferencias y define los motivos para su justificación.

||||

Czech (& Central European) Yearbook of Arbitration

Martin Svatoš

Independence and Impartiality of Arbitrators and Mediators – The Castor and Pollux of the ADR World?

Key words:
arbitration | mediation |
impartiality of arbitrators
| impartiality of mediators
| independence of
arbitrators | independence
of mediators |
institutional rules

Abstract | *The article deals with a comparison of the independence and impartiality of arbitrators and mediators. The two ADR institutions are often assimilated, but the obligations imposed on each of the categories differ to some extent. The article opens with a theoretical definition of the terms "impartial" and "independent", while the author then focuses on a comparison of the normative rules as incorporated in selected legal systems and in the rules adopted by selected ADR institutions. The results of the research are subsequently analysed and put into context. The final part of the article examines whether the obligations are identical in both cases, or whether they differ and merely have the same title. The results of the examination are subsequently put into the context of a situation in which a single individual simultaneously acts as mediator and arbitrator in the ADR hybrid models – med-arb and arb-med.*

Dr. Martin Svatoš is a mediator and arbitrator based in Prague, Czech Republic. He has gained experience around the globe, having studied at the University of Sorbonne in Paris, at Charles University in Prague and at Cornell University. He has worked at the ICC and at the Chamber of Arbitration of Milan. He has participated in several international cases both in mediation and arbitration, especially in the central and eastern European region. He is a lecturer at the Banking Institute/College of Banking in Prague and at the Seminar of European and Comparative Law in Urbino.
e-mail: svatosmartin@forarb.com

| | |

I. Introduction

12.01. Independence and impartiality are considered to be fundamental principles of both arbitration and mediation. Though few would dispute this affirmation, there are still questions that remain to be answered. Do these principles have the same scope? Are they of the same nature or do they differ in some specific way? And finally, are they of the same importance?

12.02. Both mediation and arbitration regard neutrality as a core ethical principle.[1] This can be seen when considering the definitions of individual alternative dispute resolution (ADR) frameworks. In fact, there are plenty of definition describing arbitration and mediation with the aid of the terms impartiality or neutrality.

12.03. On the one hand, mediation is depicted as '[...] the non-binding intervention by an impartial third party who helps the disputants negotiates an agreement.'[2] On the other hand, the definition of arbitration proposed by Garry Born says that 'arbitration is a process by which parties consensually submit a dispute to a non-governmental decision-maker, selected by or for the parties, to render a binding decision resolving a dispute in accordance with neutral, adjudicatory procedures affording the parties an opportunity to be heard.'[3] Ergo, both procedures, despite being different, seem to have the same ethical grounding in impartiality.

12.04. But to what extent is this purely an illusion and to what extent is it reality? Mediation and arbitration, like the mythical Greek heroes Castor and Pollux, seem to be twin brothers. However on closer examination one can see the crucial differences.

12.05. This issue does not merely exist in the realm of theory. There are a lot of ADR professionals acting as a mediator and as an arbitrator at the same time. If asked, they are not able to distinguish the slight differences between these two positions. Such a state of affairs can lead to confusion or to much worse consequences.

12.06. Because of limited space, this article is going to study in detail neither the scope of the impartiality and the independence of an arbitrator, nor is its purpose to give an exhaustive description of independence and

---

[1]   Kai von Lewinski, *Professional Ethics in Alternative Dispute Resolution*, 15 (3) IDR 150, 150 (2004).

[2]   ARBITRATION AND MEDIATION IN INTERNATIONAL BUSINESS, Alphen aan Rijn: Kluwer Law International 176 (Christian Bühring-Uhle; Lars Kirchhof; Matthias Scherer eds., 2006).

[3]   1 GARY B. BORN, INTERNATIONAL COMMERCIAL ARBITRATION, Alphen aan Rijn: Kluwer Law International 217 (2009).

impartiality of a mediator. The aim is to focus solely on the comparison of the roles of both professions.

12.07. In order to do so, this paper will first address the confusion of the terms (II). After defining the correct terminology, it will consequently focus on a brief survey of relevant legislation and rules (III) whose results will be lastly analyzed in order to compare the impartiality and independence of arbitrators and mediators (IV).

II. Chaos in the Terminology

12.08. The use of the terms *independent, impartial* and *neutral* can be quite confusing. Scholars, as well as acts of legislation and other law provisions use them without consistency and without specified rules.

12.09. In order to unify their usage and to define their scope, I will first explore what the linguistic law theory says about these terms (II.1.) and then I will focus on how the terms are used by the leading international organizations (II.2.).

II.1. What Does the Theory Say?

12.10. The question at hand is what the distinction is between *impartial, independent* and *neutral*, since they are sometimes use as synonyms and sometimes as different terms in relevant literature.[4] I will firstly focus on the issue of *impartiality* (II.1.1.) and then I will move to the topic of independence (II.1.2).

II.1.1. Partial Neutral as an Oxymoron

12.11. According to Black's Law Dictionary, whereas the *impartial* is a synonym to *unbiased* or *disinterested*,[5] the term *independent* means three absences: Absence of control or influence of another, absence of association with another entity and absence of dependence on something or someone else.[6] Finally neutrality is a state or quality of being impartial or unbiased.[7]

---

⁴　Peter Tochtermann, Die Unabhängigkeit und Unparteilichkeit des Mediators, Tübingen: Mohr Siebeck 9-19 and conseq (2009).

⁵　Black's Law Dictionary, St. Paul: West – A Thomas Reuters business 820 (Bryan A. Garner ed., 9th ed. 2009).

⁶　*Ibid.*, at 839.

⁷　*Ibid.*, at 1140.

12.12. Hence impartiality is the neutral's real absence of preference in favour of one of the parties[8]. That is a *condition sine qua non* of real neutrality. It is a state of mind of not being interested regarding the outcome of the procedure. In other words, the presence of bias causes absence of impartiality and vice versa: the absence of bias means impartiality.

12.13. The term *neutral* describes a quality of someone who is *impartial*. Although there are different approaches explaining that the term *neutrality* is superior to the terms *independent* and *impartial* or that it describes another different quality, for purpose of this article I will use the term *neutral* as a synonym for *impartial* and *neutrality* as a synonym of *impartiality*.

II.1.2. Dependant Neutral as a Possibility

12.14. In contrast, the term *independence* has a more specific meaning. It could be presented as an absence of an economic, business, political or other relationship between the neutral person and the party. The occurrence of any relationship *may* cause dependence and consequently, absence of any such relation means independence.

12.15. *Dependence* as an opposite of *independence* does not denote the existence of bias *per se*. But it definitely means *an appearance of bias* which, according to many scholars can be a sufficient reason to prevent the prospective neutral person from becoming a mediator or an arbitrator.[9] In other words, an appearance of bias can jeopardize the ADR proceedings in some circumstances.

12.16. The relationship between impartiality and independence can be expressed as follows: There cannot be a partial neutral person, but there can be a dependant one. However, the latter will be probably acceptable for neither of the parties, nor for the majority of institutions and regulations requiring such an entity.

II.2. What Do International Instruments Say?

12.17. There are three international organizations that proposed the instruments to fight against partiality in international alternative dispute resolution. The first is the International Bar Association (IBA)

---

[8] An interesting view can be seen from a linguistic comparison of the terms in different languages for this phenomenon. In German, for instance, sometimes the term *Allparteilichkeit* is used to mean that the neutral entity is partial towards all parties. See NADJA ALEXANDER, INTERNATIONAL AND COMPARATIVE MEDIATION – LEGAL PERSPECTIVES, Alphen aan Rijn: Kluwer Law International 221 (2009).

[9] Not according to all legislation and regulation, neither according to all scholars. See below.

which created the very useful and frequently used IBA Rules on Conflict of Interest (II.2.1). The second one is the European Union with its *European Code of Conduct for Mediators* (II.2.2). The last one is the unification effort of UNCITRAL that produced the *UNCITRAL Model Law on International Commercial Arbitration* and *UNCITRAL Model Law on International Commercial Conciliation* (II.2.3.).

II.2.1. IBA Rules on Conflict of Interest

12.18. The IBA created a tool that is recognized by the majority of scholars and professionals[10] and is often used in international arbitration. However, it is to be used only in relation to arbitration and is mute regarding mediation. Therefore, it is limited in its utility for this article. Still, in order to find the proper terminology for ADR in general, it is useful.

12.19. According to the IBA Rules on Conflict of interest, 'the fundamental principle in international arbitration (is) that each arbitrator must be impartial and independent of the parties at the time he or she accepts an appointment to act as arbitrator and must remain so during the entire course of the arbitration proceedings.' Unfortunately, any further definition of the terms or some distinction between them was not proposed.[11]

II.2.2. European Code of Conduct for Mediators[12]

12.20. Whereas the previous tool was aimed only at arbitration, the European Code of Conduct for Mediators was drafted only for mediation. The European Commission issued the European Code of Conduct for Mediators as a non-binding list of the ethical duties of mediators.

12.21. The Code addresses the issue of independence and impartiality in its Article 2. The interesting approach chosen by the drafters divides *independence* and *impartiality* into two different sub-sections.

12.22. According to the Code, Independence is related to the absence of all of the following circumstances: 'any personal or business relationship [of Mediator] with one or more of the parties; any financial or other interest [of Mediator], direct or indirect, in the outcome of the

---

[10] Judith Gill, *The IBA Conflicts Guidelines – Who's Using Them and How?*, 1 (1) DRI 58, 58 (2007).

[11] Leon Trakman, *The Impartiality and Independence of Arbitrators Reconsidered*, 10 (2) INT.ALR 999 (2007).

[12] Commission (EC), 'European Code of Conduct for Mediators', 21 July 2004.

mediation; the mediator, or a member of his firm, having acted in any capacity other than mediator for one or more of the parties.'[13]

12.23. In the following sub-article, the Code addresses the problem of impartiality: 'Mediators must at all times act, and endeavour to be seen to act, with impartiality towards the parties and be committed to serve all parties equally with respect to the process of mediation.'[14]

12.24. Thus, the Code is one of the rare instruments, which explicitly explains the distinction between the two terms. Moreover, this explanation is in accord with the interpretation mentioned in Section II.1.

II.2.3. UNCITRAL Model Laws

12.25. In order to assist States in reforming and modernizing their procedural laws on international dispute resolution, the UNCITRAL drafted two model laws that take into account the particular features and needs of international commercial arbitration and mediation. Both of them touch on the problem of independence and impartiality of arbitrator and mediator.

12.26. The UNCITRAL Model Law on International Arbitration uses the phrase 'the appointment of an independent and impartial arbitrator'.[15] The UNCITRAL Model Law on International Commercial Conciliation uses almost the same terminology: 'the appointment of an independent and impartial conciliator.'[16] Unfortunately, neither of the Model Laws, nor the enclosed commentaries explains the terms in any further way.

12.27. Apart from the European Code of Conduct for Mediators, the study of relevant international tools does not help in distinguishing the terms *impartiality* and *independence*. Still, it makes clear that they are the most frequently used terms, in contrast to other terms such as neutrality.

III. Survey on Laws and Rules

12.28. After realizing what impartiality and independence are and what the approach of international organizations is to these concepts, we can now focus on the approach that individual jurisdictions have adopted

---

[13] Under such circumstances, the Code suggests the possible continuance of mediation: 'In such cases the mediator may only agree to act or continue to act if he is certain of being able to carry out the mediation in full independence in order to ensure complete impartiality and the parties explicitly consent.' Compare Ibid., at 2.1.

[14] *Ibid.*, at 2.2.

[15] United Nations Commission on International Trade Law (UNCITRAL), 'UNCITRAL Model Law on International Commercial Arbitration with amendments as adopted in 2006', Art. 11 and Art. 12, 4 December 2006.

[16] United Nations Commission on International Trade Law (UNCITRAL), 'UNCITRAL Model Law on International Commercial Conciliation, Art. 5, 19 November 2002.

towards the requirements of impartiality and independence for mediators and arbitrators (III.1.). This will be followed by a discussion of the requirements expressed by the arbitration and mediation rules of world-leading ADR institutions (III.2.).

III.1. Provisions of Selected Jurisdictions

12.29. The survey on the provisions will approach selected jurisdictions and explore their relevant provisions related to independence and impartiality of mediators and arbitrators. It will consequently examine the law of the Czech Republic, Slovakia, Germany, France and the United States.

III.1.1. The Law of the Czech Republic

12.30. An approach grounding the importance of impartiality and independence of arbitrators and mediators is well accepted by the statutory provisions of different countries. The Czech Arbitration Act[17] in its Section 1 states that 'This act regulates the decision-making of property disputes by the independent and impartial arbitrators [...]'. The placement of this declaration in the very first section of the Act highlights the importance that Czech legislators have attributed to this principle.

12.31. The recently adopted Czech Mediation Act[18], like the Arbitration Act, requires both impartiality and independence from the mediators since it states in its Section 8 entitled 'Performance of the Activity of Mediator' as follows: '(1) Mediator shall a) perform mediation personally, independently, impartially and with due diligence, (...).'

III.1.2. The Slovak Law

12.32. The Act on Arbitration Proceedings[19] Section 6a states that '[t]he one who has accepted the appointment as an arbitrator has to pledge to perform the function impartially and with due diligence [...].' The term independent is merely used in connection to an appointing authority provision.[20]

12.33. In contrast, the Slovak Mediation Act[21] Section 4 requires that

---

[17] Act No. 216/1994 Coll. on Arbitration and Enforcement of Awards.
[18] Act No. 202/2012 Coll. on Mediation.
[19] Act No. 244/2002 Coll. on Arbitration Proceedings.
[20] *Ibid.*, in Section 6.
[21] Act No. 420/2004 Coll. on Mediation.

12.34. [t]he mediator is obliged to perform his activity independently, impartially, consistently, with due professional care, instruct the parties to mediation on their rights that might be affected by mediation, and without unreasonable delay inform the parties to mediation about all facts on the basis of which he could be excluded from the execution of mediation, if, with regard to his relation to the case or to the parties to mediation, his impartiality may be questioned.

III.1.3. The German Law

12.35. Since Germany adopted the UNCITRAL Model Law on International Arbitration as its arbitration law, it is not surprising that impartiality and independence are mentioned as important qualities of arbitrators in Section 1036 of the German Code of Civil Procedure.[22]

12.36. The recently adopted German Mediation Act[23] Provision 1 paragraph 2 states that 'the Mediator is an independent and neutral person without decision making power that leads the parties throughout the mediation' Later on in Provision 3 it continues that 'The mediator shall disclose to the parties all circumstances that could jeopardize his/her independence and neutrality.' Hence German law uses the German terms *unabhängige* and *neutrale*. In this sense, the term neutral can be understood as a synonym to impartial.

III.1.4. The French Law

12.37. In France, the relevant legislation is the Civil Procedure Code[24] which regulates both arbitration and mediation. Regarding the qualities of arbitrators, the CPC requires impartiality and independence using the French terms *indépendance* and *impartialité*.

12.38. French legislators divide mediation into two different procedures: *judicial mediation* and *conventional mediation*. Whereas in the first case, *independence*[25] is mentioned as a required quality of a mediator, there is no such a demand in the second case in an analogous provision[26] intended to list the requirements of a conventional mediator. However, in Article 1530 concerning conventional mediation, the law states that the procedure is performed 'with the help

---

[22] BGBl. I S. 3202; 2006 I S. 431, Code of Civil Procedure.
[23] BGBl. I S. 1577, Act on Mediation.
[24] French New Code of Civil Procedure (CPC).
[25] *Ibid.*, in Art. 131-5.
[26] *Ibid.*, in Art. 1533.

of a third chosen by the parties accomplishing its mission with impartiality, competence and diligence.'

III.1.5. The US Law

12.39. The Federal Arbitration Act[27] does not contain a specific provision involving some similar statement. However, according to this law, an arbitral award may be set aside by a court 'where there was evident partiality or corruption in the arbitrators.'[28] This brief provision was, to date, amended by only one decision of the United States Supreme Court in the case of *Commonwealth Coatings Corp v Continental Casualty*.[29] However, this case dealt mainly with the terminology of *bias* and the *appearance of bias*.[30]

12.40. Concerning Mediation, the Uniform Law Commission prepared the Uniform Mediation Act (UMA) in 2003 which should be enacted voluntarily by the individual states of the USA.[31] Drafters emphasized the necessity of *neutrality* and *impartiality* for the credibility and integrity of the mediation process.[32]

12.41. However, the UMA contains a very specific rule completely unknown to other comparable acts. On the basis of an option, the Uniform Law Commission proposed Section 9 (g) with the following wording: 'A mediator must be impartial, unless after disclosure of the facts required in subsections (a) and (b) to be disclosed, the parties agree otherwise.' This rule is quite surprising since it enables someone who is not impartial to lawfully act as a mediator.

12.42. Furthermore, among the eleven states that have already enacted the UMA, only three decided not to opt for this provision. The remaining eight have introduced this rule in their legislatures. The states are listed in following table:

---

[27] Federal Arbitration Act (FAA), 9 U.S.C. §§ 1-14 (2009).

[28] *Ibid.*, in Section 10.

[29] *Commonwealth Coatings Corp v. Continental Casualty*, Co 393 US 145.

[30] Shivani Singhal, *Independence and Impartiality of Arbitrators*, 11(3) INT. A.L.R. 124-132 (2008).

[31] As of 2013, the UMA has been enacted in the following states: Idaho, Illinois, Iowa, Nebraska, New Jersey, Ohio, South Dakota, Utah, Vermont, Washington, and the District of Columbia. The procedure of introduction was under way in Hawaii, Massachusetts, New York in 2013. See The National Conference of Commissioners on Uniform State Law: The Uniform Mediation Act, available at: http://www.uniformlaws.org/Act.aspx?title =Mediation%20Act (accessed on 24 June 2013).

[32] The National Conference of Commissioners on Uniform State Law: The Uniform Mediation Act – Comments Uniform Mediation Act (Last Revised or Amended in 2003), 10 December 2003, p. 9, available at: http://www.uniformlaws.org/shared/docs/ mediation/uma_final_03.pdf (accessed on 24 June 2013).

States that opted for 9(g)	States that did not opt for 9(g)
District of Columbia, Idaho, Illinois, Iowa, Nebraska, Ohio, Utah, Vermont	New Jersey, South Dakota, Washington

III.2. Provisions of Selected ADR Institutions

12.43. The second part of this survey will focus on the approach chosen by the leading ADR centres that offer both arbitration and mediation services. The rules of the International Chamber of Commerce, the London Court of International Arbitration, the American Arbitration Association, the ADR Centre of the World Intellectual Property Organization, the Chamber of Arbitration of Milan (CAM), the Stockholm Chamber of Commerce and the UNCITRAL will be addressed.

III.2.1. The International Chamber of Commerce

12.44. The International Chamber of Commerce (ICC) has a well-equipped system of dispute resolution available including the International Court of Arbitration and the ADR centre.

12.45. ICC Arbitration Rules[33] state in Article 11 that '[e]very arbitrator must be and remain impartial and independent of the parties involved in the arbitration.' The ICC ADR Rules[34] dating back in 2001 use the term *neutral* instead of mediator. This is caused by the fact that the ICC ADR Rules are deemed to be used not only in relation to mediation, but also in other ADR procedures too.[35] Also, these rules count on independence[36] and impartiality[37] as fundamental qualities of a *neutral*.

III.2.2. The London Court of International Arbitration

12.46. The London Court of International Arbitration (LCIA) offers a double dispute resolution service including both arbitration and mediation. In the LCIA Arbitration rules,[38] one can read that '[a]ll arbitrators

---

[33] International Chamber of Commerce (ICC), 'ICC Rules of Arbitration', 1 January 2012.

[34] International Chamber of Commerce (ICC), 'ICC ADR Rules', 1 July 2001.

[35] Compare Ibid., in Preamble: 'The International Chamber of Commerce (the 'ICC') sets out these amicable dispute resolution rules, entitled the ICC ADR Rules (the 'Rules'), which permit the parties to agree upon whatever settlement technique they believe to be appropriate to help them settle their dispute.'

[36] Compare *Ibid.*, in Article 3 (2).

[37] Compare *Ibid.*, in Article 5 (3).

[38] London Court of International Arbitration (LCIA), ‚LCIA Arbitration Rules', 1 January 1998.

conducting an arbitration under these Rules shall be and remain at all times impartial and independent of the parties.'[39]

12.47. Similarly, according to its Mediation rules,[40] the mediator has to sign 'a declaration to the effect that there are no circumstances known to him or her likely to give rise to any justifiable doubts as to his or her impartiality or independence'.[41] Hence, this institution also requires both conditions.

III.2.3. The American Arbitration Association

12.48. The American Arbitration Association (AAA) promotes a number of rules regulating different procedures and ADR in different fields. Because of the limited space of this article and the nature of the rules already listed above, I will focus solely on the rules that concern international disputes.[42]

12.49. The AAA International Arbitration Rules state in Article 7 that '[a]rbitrators acting under these Rules shall be impartial and independent.'

12.50. In contrast, the AAA International Mediation Rules require that the mediators in an AAA Mediation procedure abide by the Model Standards of Conduct for Mediators and thus 'decline a mediation if the mediator cannot conduct it in an impartial manner, and [...] disclose, as soon as practicable, all actual and potential conflicts of interest that are reasonably known to the mediator and could reasonably be seen as raising a question about the mediator's impartiality.'

12.51. Obviously, the AAA demands that arbitrators meet both qualities, whereas in the case of mediators only impartiality is required. This is interesting especially when comparing this standard with the discussion of the Uniform Mediation Act above.

III.2.4. The WIPO Arbitration and Mediation Center

12.52. The World Intellectual Property Organization established an ADR Center called the WIPO Arbitration and Mediation Center that provides an effective system of dispute resolution including arbitration and mediation.

---

[39] *Ibid.*, in Article 5.2.

[40] London Court of International Arbitration (LCIA), ,LCIA Mediation Rules', 1 July 2012.

[41] *Ibid.*, in Article 3.1.

[42] American Arbitration Association (AAA), 'International Mediation Rules', 1 June 2009; American Arbitration Association (AAA), 'International Arbitration Rules', 1 June 2009.

12.53. The rules of this Centre are similar to those already outlined. The WIPO Arbitration Rules[43] require that '[e]ach arbitrator shall be impartial and independent' and the WIPO Mediation Rules[44] in Article 7 state that '[t]he mediator shall be neutral, impartial and independent'.

III.2.5. The Chamber of Arbitration of Milan (CAM)

12.54. The leading Italian institution of arbitrations requires the arbitrator to be and remain *independent* and *impartial*.[45] According to the newly issued rules regulating international business mediation, the mediator has to be not only *impartial* and *independent*, but also *neutral*.[46]

III.2.6. The Stockholm Chamber of Commerce (SCC)

12.55. Similarly, the Arbitration Institute of the Stockholm Chamber of Commerce included in its Arbitration rules[47] the requirement that '[e]very arbitrator must be impartial and independent.'[48]

12.56. The Mediation Rules[49] of the SCC Mediation Institute instruct the mediator to be *impartial* and *independent*. This rule is mentioned even in the very first article of said Rules, which can be read as highlighting the importance of this duty.

III.2.7. UNCITRAL

12.57. Last but not least, there is the approach chosen by UNCITRAL when drafting its Arbitration Rules and Conciliation Rules. Although UNCITRAL is not a proper ADR institution, its rules are very commonly used and thus, they should not be excluded from this short list.

12.58. The Arbitration rules utilize the terms *independent* and *impartial*.[50] Likewise, the UNCITRAL Conciliation Rules[51] state in article 7 that

---

[43] World Intellectual Property Organization, 'WIPO Arbitration Rules', 1 October 2002.

[44] World Intellectual Property Organization, 'WIPO Mediation Rules', 1 October 2002.

[45] Chamber of Arbitration of Milan, 'Arbitration Rules', 1 January 2010, Articles 18 and 19.

[46] Chamber of Arbitration of Milan, 'International Business Mediation Service', 6 December 2012, Article 4: 'Before the opening of any mediation process and in any case before meeting with the parties, the mediator signs a declaration of impartiality, independence and neutrality and undertakes to comply with to the code of ethics.'

[47] Stockholm Chamber of Commerce (SCC), 'Arbitration Rules', 1 January 2010.

[48] *Ibid.*, in Article 14.

[49] Stockholm Chamber of Commerce (SCC), 'Mediation Rules', 1 April 1999.

[50] United Nations Commission on International Trade Law (UNCITRAL), 'UNCITRAL Arbitration Rules (as revised in 2010)', Art. 6 and Art. 7, 6 December 2010.

[51] United Nations Commission on International Trade Law (UNCITRAL), 'UNCITRAL Conciliation Rules (as revised in 2010)', Art. 6 and Art. 7, 23 July 1980.

'[t]he conciliator[52] assists the parties in an independent and impartial manner in their attempt to reach an amicable settlement of their dispute.'

12.59. The following table summarizes the ADR institutions discussed and lists the terms used to describe Arbitrators and Mediators in their rules:

ADR Institution	Arbitrator	Mediator
ICC	Impartial, independent	Impartial, independent
LCIA	Impartial, independent	Impartial, independent
AAA	Impartial, independent	Impartial
WIPO	Impartial, independent	Impartial, independent, neutral
CAM	Impartial, independent	Impartial, independent, neutral
SCC	Impartial, independent	Impartial, independent
UNCITRAL	Impartial, independent	Impartial, independent

12.60. In examining this table, the tendency is obvious. *Impartiality* and *independence* are required from both mediators and arbitrators in the majority of the cases.

IV. Analysis of the Consequences

12.61. In this part of the article, I will analyse the outcomes of the brief survey conducted above. First will be addressed the scope of the demanded qualities (IV.1.) and then the practical consequences that arise, especially when these requirements come into play (IV.2.).

IV.1. Do These Requirements Have the Same Scope?

12.62. I have already shown that in most cases, impartiality and independence are required from both arbitrators and mediators. To understand their nature, it will first be necessary to discuss the consequences of the failure of respective procedures (IV.1.1.) and then provide a comparison of the content of such duties (IV.1.2.).

---

[52] The UNCITRAL Conciliation Rules work with the term of conciliator instead of mediator.

Czech (& Central European) Yearbook of Arbitration

IV.1.1. Different Sanctions, Different Duties

12.63. In the absence of impartiality and independence on an arbitrator's part, the sanctions will be different than in the absence of same qualities on mediator's part. This is because of the fundamentally different outcome of both proceedings.

12.64. In the case of arbitration, the award as a directive decision of a neutral person can be dramatically harmed by a biased arbitrator. Since the arbitrator has real power over the parties, the international[53] as well as national[54] instruments possess the tools to control and to reduce the negative consequences of such eventualities.

12.65. For instance, the most important international convention, the New York convention, admits in its article V (1) d, that the recognition and enforcement of an award may be refused when the '[t]he composition of the arbitral authority or the arbitral procedure was not in accordance with the agreement of the parties, or, failing such agreement, was not in accordance with the law of the country where the arbitration took place'.

12.66. In contrast, there is no such international instrument regarding mediation. This is obviously because of the already mentioned nature of a mediation outcome. Since the mediation agreement is consensual, the threat of a mediator influencing the results in favour of one party is less. For that reason, the resolution of such a situation would depend on the relevant State's contractual law. So at the most, such a contract could be declared null and void because of fraud. The result however will depend on the concrete situation.

IV.1.2. Same Duties, Different Scope, Same Importance

12.67. As the analysis so far has pointed out, the approach of the majority of statutory provisions is not entirely uniform. They do demand impartiality and independence from both mediator and arbitrator. However, as illustrated by the different consequences of the break of impartiality and independence, their scope is not the same.

12.68. Some authors even question the relevance of neutrality in mediation. According to Astor, the transparency and the party control are more important due to the non-binding nature of mediation.[55] Since the term *neutrality* relates to power and since there is no power of the mediator over the parties, there is no need for the impartiality and independence

---

[53] See below.

[54] Compare for instance the quoted provision of US FAA above, *supra* note 26.

[55] Hilary Astor, Mediator Neutrality: Making Sense of Theory and Practice, Legal Studies Research Paper No. 07/46, The University of Sydney – The Sydney Law School, July 2007, available at http://ssrn.com/abstract=998202 (accessed on 22 June 2013).

of the mediator.[56] In contrast, the control of the procedure is much more important, as it is the parties' consent that produces the outcome of mediation.

12.69. The reduced emphasis on impartiality and independence in mediation compared to arbitration can be further illustrated by the practice of proceedings-venue-choosing. As is the often case in international arbitration, a neutral third country is chosen as a seat of the arbitral tribunal, but this is not so common in the case in international mediation. In contrast, the parties often choose one of their respective countries or even the office of one of the parties in order to reduce the costs of mediation.[57] Such an approach would be almost unacceptable in international arbitration.

12.70. It is true that some legal rules and scholars do not put the impartiality and independence of a mediator on an equal par with the impartiality and independence of an arbitrator. In spite of that, the importance will be the same. For the transparency and smooth proceeding of mediation, the neutrality of the mediator is an essential asset. Thus, it is crucial for the mediator to be concerned about complying with it in order to perform a successful mediation.[58]

IV.2. And What if They Meet?

12.71. Difficulties can arise when one person will act in one dispute first as a mediator and subsequently as an arbitrator. This can happen if the parties choose so-called MED-ARB proceedings, i.e. the combination of mediation and arbitration (IV.2.1.), or ARB-MED proceedings, which combine both ADRs, but in an opposite way (IV.2.2.).

IV.2.1. When Mediation Comes First

12.72. In the first example, the question of impartiality pushes against the issue of effectiveness. MED-ARB is regarded as a highly effective alternative dispute resolution because it combines the advantages of mediation (i.e. the consensus of parties and non-formality) with the advantages of arbitration (i.e. certainty of outcome).

12.73. In such proceedings, the parties try to settle in mediation but in the case of failure they continue in binding arbitration. The issue raised by this ADR concerns the confusion of roles when mediation and

---

[56] Richard Delgado, *Shadowboxing: An Essay on Power*, 77 CORNELL L. REV. 813, 813-824 (1992).

[57] MICHAEL MCILWRATH & JOHN SAVAGE, INTERNATIONAL ARBITRATION AND MEDIATION – A PRACTICAL GUIDE, Alphen aan Rijn: Wolters Kluwer 207 (2010).

[58] NADJA ALEXANDER, *supra* note 8, at 222.

arbitration are performed by the very same person. In that case, the question of impartiality is at stake since the neutral entity can be privy to a lot of information especially when caucusing with the separated parties. They would never be privy to such information in common arbitration proceedings. Although criticised by some scholars,[59] there are statutory provisions that enable this double-role playing.[60]

12.74. Despite the evident effectiveness of that approach, as stated above, the duties of arbitrator and mediator are not the same, especially concerning their impartiality and independence. The danger of failure can be overcome for certain if mediation and arbitration are conducted as two distinct processes performed by two different persons.[61] Yet this approach does not solve the issue of effectiveness and cost saving, especially in cases where such issues are pertinent.[62]

IV.2.2. When Arbitration Comes First

12.75. A different issue can be seen in ARB-MED procedures. This framework is constituted as a normal arbitration except that before rendering an award, the arbitrator tries to settle the parties` dispute in mediation. As discussed above, the requirements on arbitrator's independence is higher than with a mediator.

12.76. However, this can work only in the specific case where the arbitrator that had drafted an award and had kept it from the parties tries to first settle their dispute in mediation and before revealing the award. The threat to the arbitrator's impartiality is contained in the performance of mediation, because the *job of arbitrator* would be done at the moment

---

[59] For more about the discussion on the advantages and disadvantages of MED-ARB, as well as about the distinction between the pure MED-ARB and its variants, see Mark Batson Baril & Donald Dickey, MED-ARB: The Best of Both Worlds or Just A Limited ADR Option? Available at: http://www.riverstoneresolutions.com/files/MED-ARB%20 The%20Best%20of%20Both%20Worlds%20or%20Just%20a%20Limited%20ADR%20Option 0.pdf (accessed on 22 June 2013).

[60] E.g.: Singapore International Arbitration Act, Act 23 of 1994, Chapter 143A, Article 17 (1): 'If all parties to any arbitral proceedings consent in writing and for so long as no party has withdrawn his consent in writing, an arbitrator or umpire may act as a conciliator.'

[61] ARBITRATION AND MEDIATION IN INTERNATIONAL BUSINESS, *supra* note 2, at 249.

[62] A very specific, yet interesting proposition is mentioned by Christian Bühring-Uhle & Lars Kirchhof & Matthias Scherer: 'An intermediate option exists where the tribunal is comprised of three arbitrators. Here, the separation of the tasks can be partially achieved by entrusting only certain members of the tribunal with the task of mediating a settlement. [...] The advantage is that at least one or two members of the tribunal preserve their complete impartiality by staying free of the dual role. However, those members of the tribunal who do mediate will still have to build separate compartments in their mind.' Compare Ibid., at FN 634.

of mediation although not communicated to the parties. In that very specific case, there should not be an issue regarding the arbitrator doing the job of mediator as it is in the opposite case when a mediator is serving as an arbitrator.

12.77. On the one hand, the combination of both proceedings brings complications. On the other hand, it is very effective[63] and sometimes desirable. Still, extreme attention should be constantly paid to the question of impartiality and independence.

V. Conclusion

12.78. As stated above, the quality of independence and impartiality is almost unanimously required by the national legislators and ADR institutions in both mediation and arbitration, although the scope of these terms is different and not used coherently. In arbitration, the impartiality and independence of arbitrators is not called in question. In mediation, the Scholars are not undifferentiated regarding the importance of impartiality and independence of mediators. Yet, in praxis, both these qualities are required.

| | |

Summaries

FRA *[L'indépendance et l'impartialité des arbitres et des médiateurs – Castor et Polux dans le monde des procédés alternatifs de résolution des litiges?]*

Cet article adresse la problématique de l'indépendance et l'impartialité des arbitres et médiateurs. Il commence par une recherche par rapport au sens et à la signification de mots indépendant et impartial et par l'analyse de la terminologie utilisée par les outils du droit international. L'article continue par comparaison de différentes juridictions et leurs exigences. On approche le droit tchèque, slovaque, allemand, français et le droit des États-Unis relative à l'arbitrage et à la médiation. Puis, la contribution se concentre sur les demandes des règlements des institutions de règlement alternatif des litiges. En comparent les résultats, on se consacre à l'analyse de l'importance qui est attribué aux procédures respectives. Finalement, l'article aborde la question des procédures hybrides (MED-ARB, ARB-MED) du point de vu de l'impartialité et l'indépendance du neutre.

---

[63] See *Ibid.*, at 255-259.

CZE *[Nezávislost a nestrannost rozhodců a mediátorů – Kastor a Polux ve světě alternativních způsobů řešení sporů?]*

Článek se věnuje problematice srovnání nezávislosti a nestrannosti rozhodců a mediátorů. Ačkoliv jsou tyto dvě ADR instituce často srovnávány, co se do povinností na ně kladených týče, nároky na ně jsou do jisté míry odlišné. Příspěvek se věnuje nejprve teoretickému vymezení termínů nestranný a nezávislý, aby se následně zaměřil na komparativní srovnání normativních úprav ve vybraných právních řádech a v pravidlech vybraných ADR institucí. Následně jsou výsledky tohoto průzkumu analyzovány a zasazeny do kontextu. V závěru článku je pak posouzeno, zdali se v obou případech jedná o stejné povinnosti, nebo o dvě různé mající pouze stejné označení. Výsledky tohoto zjištění jsou pak dosazeny do kontextu situace, kdy jedna osoba vykonává současně funkci mediátora a současně funkci rozhodce v tzv. hybridních modelech ADR – med-arb a arb-med.

| | |

POL *[Niezawisłość i bezstronność arbitrów i mediatorów – Kastor i Polluks w świetle alternatywnych metod rozstrzygania sporów?]*

Artykuł porównuje bezstronność i niezawisłość arbitrów i mediatorów oraz omawia wymogi zawarte w wybranych porządkach prawnych i regulaminach instytucji zajmujących się alternatywną metodą rozstrzygania sporów (ADR). Ponadto artykuł analizuje skutki naruszenia zasady bezstronności i niezawisłości przez arbitrów i mediatorów oraz omawia sytuacje, kiedy obie te funkcje, a więc arbiter i mediator, łączą się w jednej osobie.

DEU *[Unabhängigkeit und Unparteilichkeit (Unbefangenheit) von Schiedsrichtern und Mediatoren – Castor und Pollux im Reiche der alternativen Streitbeilegungsverfahren?]*

Der Beitrag vergleicht die Unparteilichkeit und Unabhängigkeit von Schiedsrichtern und Mediatoren und konzentriert sich dabei auf die von ausgewählten Rechtsordnungen gestellten Anforderungen, sowie auf die Regeln von mit alternativen Streitbeilegungsmethoden (ADR) befassten Institutionen. Der Artikel analysiert außerdem die Folgen einer Verletzung der Grundsätze der Unparteilichkeit und Unabhängigkeit von Schiedsrichtern und Mediatoren, wobei er u. a. auch Fälle ins Auge fasst, in denen die beiden Ämter des Schiedsrichters und des Mediators in Personalunion von ein und derselben Person wahrgenommen werden.

RUS   *[Независимость и беспристрастность арбитров и медиаторов - Kastor и Polux в свете альтернативных способов разрешения споров?]*

В статье сравниваются беспристрастность и независимость арбитров и медиаторов, а также она посвящена требованиям выбранных правопорядков и правил организаций, занимающихся вопросами альтернативного способа разрешения споров (ADR). Кроме того, в данной статье рассматриваются последствия нарушения принципов беспристрастности и независимости арбитров и медиаторов, а также фокусируется внимание на таких случаях, когда эти две функции, т. е. арбитра и медиатора, выполняет одно и то же лицо.

ESP   *[La independencia e imparcialidad de los árbitros y mediadores – Cástor y Pólux en el mundo de la resolución alternativa de conflictos?]*

El artículo compara la imparcialidad y la independencia de los árbitros y mediadores y se centra en los requisitos de selectos ordenamientos jurídicos, así como en las reglas de aquellas instituciones que aplican una forma alternativa de resolución de conflictos (ADR). Asimismo, el artículo analiza las consecuencias de la violación de los principios de imparcialidad e independencia por parte de los árbitros y mediadores. Se centra también en los casos en los que estas dos funciones, es decir, el árbitro y el mediador, se reúnen en una sola persona.

|||

Evangelos Vassilakakis

The Challenge of Arbitrators and the Impact on the Functioning of Arbitral Tribunals

Key words:
Arbitrator | Challenge | Greece | ICAC Rules/ICC Rules | Impartiality | Independence | International commercial arbitration | LCIA Rules | New York Convention on the Recognition and Enforcement of Foreign Arbitral Awards | public policy | UNCITRAL Model Law on International Commercial Arbitration | VIAC Rules

Abstract | *The external and internal impact of the challenge of an arbitrator are addressed. In case of a challenge, the functioning of the arbitral tribunal may become conditional upon an external factor, such as the decision of a state court, if the latter has jurisdiction to deal with the proposal on disqualification of the challenged arbitrator. This may be the case if the domestic provisions reproduce the basic solution of the UNCITRAL Model Law on International Commercial Arbitration.*

The situation is less complex for the internal functioning of the arbitral tribunal if another court or authority decides on the challenge. This is the solution adopted by important institutional arbitrations such as the ICC, ICAC, LCIA, VIAC and SCC. When the arbitral tribunal has jurisdiction to decide on the challenge, its decision may create a rift within the tribunal, in particular if the challenge has been dismissed by a not unanimous award. Irrespective of the court or authority deciding on the challenge, its dismissal may lead to a polarization between this party and the unchallenged co-arbitrators. On the other hand, the acceptance of the challenge may alienate the party who nominated the removed arbitrator.

A telling example related to the dysfunction that challenges can generate and the way to handle them can be found in an ICC arbitration and the judgment Number 11/2009 of the Greek Supreme Court related to the enforcement of the arbitral award.

Evangelos Vassilakakis – professor of Private International Law, Faculty of Law, Aristoteles University of Thessaloniki (Ph.D. Paris-Sorbonne I). Professor Vassilakakis is an attorney admitted before the Supreme Court of Greece and an arbitrator in the ICAC, VIAC, SCCI, CCIR and PAMA. He has served as a judge at the Special Supreme Court of Greece (2010-2011) in his capacity of Professor – Director of the Koufa Foundation for International Law and Human Rights. e-mail: vassilakakis@the.forthnet.gr; evasilak@hotmail.com

13.01. The system of challenging an arbitrator is aimed at the protection of the parties' fundamental right to an impartial and independent tribunal. It is a guarantee of fair and unbiased arbitral proceedings.[1] However, it implies some drawbacks for these proceedings as well as for the arbitrator whose independence or impartiality is being put into question. A challenge may result in an important delay of the arbitral proceedings, thus jeopardizing one of the main advantages of international commercial arbitration. The functioning of the arbitral tribunal may become conditional upon an external factor, such as the decision of a state court, if the latter has jurisdiction to deal with the proposal on disqualification of the challenged arbitrator. Furthermore, the internal functioning of the arbitral tribunal may be influenced by the challenge procedure, as one of the tribunal's members is stained by the allegations substantiating the challenge and damaging his/her reputation.

I. The Court or Authority which Decides on the Challenge

13.02. The challenge procedure in international arbitration is governed by the rules applicable to the arbitral proceedings at issue. It derives from a comparative survey of domestic laws on arbitration. If neither the arbitration agreement nor the arbitration rules governing the proceedings at issue contain provisions on the challenge procedure, a state court often has jurisdiction on the challenge based upon the lack of independence or the partiality of the arbitrator.[2] For instance, French law explicitly provides that, in the absence of any agreement of the parties with regard to the challenge procedure, the judge who is entitled to interfere with arbitral proceedings in case of dysfunction, the *juge d'appui*,[3] delivers a decision on the challenge (Article 1506 number 2 of the *Code de procédure civile* in conjunction with Article 1456 of the same code, to which it refers).[4] In Greek law, there is a distinction between domestic and international arbitration. As far as

---

[1]   For a complete work on challenging of arbitrators, see in particular: KAREL DAELE, CHALLENGE AND DISQUALIFICATION OF ARBITRATORS, Dordrecht/Boston/New York: Kluwer (2011).

[2]   JEAN-FRANÇOIS POUDRET/SÉBASTIEN BÉSSON, DROIT COMPARÉ DE L'ARBITRAGE INTERNATIONAL, Bruxelles: Bruylant 378(2002).

[3]   CHRISTOPHE SERAGLINI/JERÔME ORTSCHEIDT, DROIT DE L'ARBITRAGE INTERNE ET INTERNATIONAL, Paris: Montchrestien 260 (2013).

[4]   Article 1456 paragraph 3 *Code de Procédure Civile*: '*En cas de différend sur le maintien de l'arbitre, la difficulté est réglée par la personne chargée d'organiser l'arbitrage ou, à défaut, tranchée par le juge d'appui, saisi dans le mois qui suit la révélation ou la découverte du fait litigieux*'.

domestic arbitration is concerned, Article 883 paragraph 2 of the Code of Civil Procedure states that the county court of the place of the seat of the arbitration[5] has jurisdiction on the challenge. On the contrary, the arbitral tribunal decides *prima facie* on the challenge in international arbitration, pursuant to Article 13 paragraph 2 of the Law Number 2735/1999 on international commercial arbitration. This is due to the fact that this provision reproduces, as well as most provisions of this law, the United Nations Commission on International Trade Law (UNCITRAL) Model Law on International Commercial Arbitration.

13.03. The Model Law serves worldwide as a pattern for designing national legislation in the field of international commercial arbitration. Most domestic laws based upon it grant jurisdiction to the arbitral tribunal when the impartiality or independence of the arbitrator comes into question. According to Article 13 paragraph 2 of the UNCITRAL Model Law on International Commercial Arbitration, failing an agreement of the parties on the procedure for challenging an arbitrator under paragraph 1:

13.04. A party who intends to challenge an arbitrator shall (...) send a written statement of the reasons for the challenge to the arbitral tribunal. Unless the challenged arbitrator withdraws from his office and the other party agrees to the challenge, the arbitral tribunal shall decide on the challenge.

13.05. This means that the challenged arbitrator participates in the arbitral tribunal[6] as the latter is being granted jurisdiction. In the event of the arbitrator being unwilling to step down, the acceptance of the request requires at least the positive vote of the unchallenged arbitrators. The impact of the arbitral tribunal's jurisdiction on its functioning shall be examined under section III.2 of this paper. It is easy to guess that this 'primary' jurisdiction of the arbitral tribunal is not sufficient for the safeguard of the challenging party. Therefore, Article 13 paragraph 3 of the UNCITRAL Model Law states that, in the event of the challenge not being successful, the challenging party may request that a decision on the challenge submitted by it be rendered by the court or the authority specified in accordance with Article 6 by the state that has adopted the Model Law.[7]

---

[5] This place is determined by the arbitration agreement. In the absence of such a determination, the competence *ratione loci* is based upon the domicile or the residence of the challenging party. If this party has neither domicile nor residence in Greece, the courts of Athens are competent.

[6] The Commission Report: Report of the United Nations Commission on International Trade Law on the Work of Its Eighteenth Session, YB UNCITRAL XVI(1985), 3 ff., Article 13, point number 128.

[7] This decision shall not be subject to an appeal.

13.06. Consequently, the interference of state courts in the challenge procedure is not excluded when the domestic law on international commercial arbitration has been designed on the basis of Article 13 paragraph 3 of the UNCITRAL Model Law. However such interference seldom occurs in practice.[8]

13.07. In contrast, most sets of arbitration rules applicable to important institutional arbitrations in Europe prescribe that a request to challenge an arbitrator shall be dealt with in the framework of the institution in question, without any interference of state courts. Article 14 paragraph 3 of the new International Chamber of Commerce (ICC) Rules states that its International Court of Arbitration shall decide on the admissibility and, if necessary, on the merits of a challenge submitted within the framework of ICC arbitration. The London Court of International Arbitration (LCIA) Arbitration Rules,[9] the Vienna International Arbitral Centre (VIAC) Arbitration Rules,[10] the International Commercial Arbitration Court (ICAC) Arbitration Rules[11] and the Stockholm Chamber of Commerce (SCC) Arbitration Rules[12] follow the same direction.

13.08. Rules of other arbitral institutions provide for a system that has common points with the challenge procedure described in the Model Law, in as far as the arbitral tribunal is granted jurisdiction to decide on the challenge. For instance, Section 18 paragraph 2 of the German Institute of Arbitration (DIS) Rules grants jurisdiction to the arbitral tribunal, unless the parties have agreed otherwise.[13]

---

[8]   CHRISTOPHE SERAGLINI/JÉRÔME ORTSCHEIDT, *supra* note 3, at 674.

[9]   Article 11 paragraph 1 LCIA Arbitration Rules: 'In the event that the LCIA Court determines that any nominee is not suitable or independent or impartial or if an appointed arbitrator is to be replaced for any reason, the LCIA Court shall have a complete discretion to decide whether or not to follow the original nominating process.'

[10]   Article 20 paragraph 3 VIAC Arbitration Rules 2013: 'If the challenged arbitrator does not resign, the Board shall rule on the challenge. Before the Board makes a decision, the Secretary General shall request comments from the challenged arbitrator and the other party/parties. The Board may also request comments from other persons. All comments shall be communicated to the parties and the arbitrators.'

[11]   Section 18.2 ICAC Arbitration Rules: 'If the challenged arbitrator does not withdraw voluntarily or if the other party does not agree to the challenge, the decision on the release of the arbitrator from his appointment shall be made by the ICAC Presidium. The ICAC Presidium may, in its discretion, make the decision on the release of the arbitrator from his appointment for reasons referred to in subparagraph 1 of this paragraph.'

[12]   Article 14 paragraph 4 of SCC Arbitration Rules: 'If the other party agrees to the challenge, the arbitrator shall resign. In all other cases, the Board shall make the final decision on the challenge.'

[13]   Section 18.2 of the DIS Arbitration Rules: 'The challenge shall be notified and substantiated to the DIS Secretariat within two weeks of being advised of the constitution

13.09. There is also a mixed system as, for instance, the one set up by Section 18 paragraph 3 of the Rules of the Arbitration Court at the Slovak Chamber of Commerce and Industry (SCCI). This provision states that:

13.10. The dismissal of the arbitrator shall be decided by the remaining members of the tribunal. If they reach no agreement or if the objection is raised against two arbitrators, the decision shall be taken by the Presiding Board; the Presiding Board shall also decide on the rejection of the sole arbitrator.

13.11. The same solution is accepted by Article 24 paragraph 2 of the Arbitration Rules of the Arbitration Court attached to the Economic Chamber of the Czech Republic and Agricultural Chamber of the Czech Republic. Pursuant to Article 20 paragraph 2 of the Rules of Arbitration Procedure of the Court of International Commercial Arbitration attached to the Chamber of Commerce and Industry of Romania, the arbitral tribunal is competent, but the challenged arbitrator is replaced by a member of the Court College.[14] There is a similar approach in the field of investment arbitration: Article 58 of the International Centre for Settlement of Investment Disputes (ICSID) Convention grants *prima facie* jurisdiction to the unchallenged arbitrators.[15]

II. The Vulnerability of the Arbitrator

13.12. There is a distinction between impartiality and independence.[16] Independence implies a lack of connection or relationship with a particular party and is more related to facts. It is considered as an objective and fact-oriented standard imposing on the arbitrator the

---

of the arbitral tribunal pursuant to section 17 sub. 3 or of the time at which the party learns of the reason for challenge. The DIS Secretariat informs the arbitrators and the other party of the challenge and sets a reasonable time-limit for comments from the challenged arbitrator and the other party. If the challenged arbitrator does not withdraw from his office or the other party does not agree to the challenge within the time-limit fixed, the challenging party may within two weeks request the arbitral tribunal to decide on the challenge unless otherwise agreed by the parties.'

[14] Article 20 paragraph 2 of the Rules of Arbitration Procedure of the Court of International Commercial Arbitration attached to the Chamber of Commerce and Industry of Romania: 'The challenging claim shall be settled by the arbitral tribunal, in the absence of the challenged arbitrator, who will be replaced by a member of the Court College, designated by the Court of Arbitration president or prime vice-president.'

[15] Article 58 of the ICSID Convention: 'The decision on any proposal to disqualify a conciliator or arbitrator shall be taken by the other members of the Commission or Tribunal as the case may be, provided that where those members are equally divided, or in the case of a proposal to disqualify a sole conciliator or arbitrator, or a majority of the conciliators or arbitrators, the Chairman shall take that decision (....).'

[16] CHRISTOPHE SERAGLINI/JÉRÔME ORTSCHEIDT, *supra* note 3, at 658.

duty to be free from outside influence and/or pressure.[17] On the contrary, impartiality is more related to a mental element, because it is based upon a lack of predisposition. This predisposition is linked to the general background of the challenged arbitrator. It has to be noted that most sets of arbitration rules, including the new ICC Rules, make reference to both terms.[18]

13.13. Notwithstanding this distinction, any challenge constitutes a clear sign of distrust towards the arbitrator in question and may end up in an unpleasant situation. In particular, this happens when the challenging party substantiates its request by revealing personal data of the arbitrator who is, in any case, more vulnerable than the judge as far as his/her reputation is concerned.[19]

13.14. As a matter of fact, arbitrators are more exposed than judges if challenged. A judge can be challenged on the grounds that he/she may have a personal interest in the proceedings or a personal bias against a party to the case. In contrast, the arbitrator can be challenged because of his/her previous behaviour as arbitrator, in particular his/her stance in factual or legal issues similar to those of the case in question. The arbitrator can even be challenged on the basis of positions held in various occasions, including those taken in his/her academic writings. On the other hand, it should be borne in mind that the party-selected arbitrator has been often preferred on the assumption, based to a large extent upon already expressed views, that he/she may advance the arguments of the appointing party in the deliberations of the tribunal. This acquaintance creates a closeness between arbitrator and appointing party[20] and can give rise to a proposal for disqualification by the other party.

---

[17] JULIAN LEW/LOUKAS MISTELIS/STEFAN MICHAEL KRÖLL, COMPARATIVE INTERNATIONAL COMMERCIAL ARBITRATION, Dordrecht/Boston/New York: Kluwer Law International, 361(2003).

[18] Although there was no reference to impartiality in the ICC Rules, because of the lack of a satisfactory definition for this legal term, the ICC Rules 2012 refer now to impartiality and independence. Under Article 9 of the UNCITRAL Rules a proposal for disqualification is allowed if there are 'any circumstances likely to give rise to justifiable doubts as to his impartiality and independence'. Pursuant to Article 11 paragraph 1 'Every arbitrator must be and remain impartial and independent of the parties involved in the arbitration'. By virtue of Article 14, an arbitrator may be challenged for an alleged lack of impartiality or independence. According to Article 6 paragraph 4 of the Rules of the Permanent Court of Arbitration (PCA) the arbitrator must be 'independent and impartial'.

[19] This vulnerability may lead to the submission of a proposal for disqualification even if the conditions are far from being met, to the effect that the challenging party may put pressure on the challenged arbitrator who would like to appear unbiased after the dismissal of the proposal.

[20] Hilmar Raeschke-Kessler, *Die internationale Schiedsgerichtsbarkeit – ein Motor für transnationales Verfahrensrecht, in* FESTSCHRIFT FÜR PETER SCHLOSSER ZUM 70.GEBURTSTAG, Tübingen: Mohr Siebeck, 717, 722 (2005).

13.15. While the judge steps aside without having to bother as to how he/she will be replaced by another judge, a challenge may itself, even if unfounded, immediately or in the long run annihilate the arbitrator's prospect of remaining active in this capacity, in particular if he/she happens to have been challenged by the party that appointed him/her.

13.16. Furthermore, as arbitrators are a closed community, partiality issues are raised more often than in disputes pending before state courts. As a matter of fact, the persons belonging to this closed community do repeatedly switch between the two roles: they act as counsel and then as arbitrators, as well as the other way around. It is unavoidable that as counsel they take different positions from those that they may have taken as arbitrators. Although, in such an event, there is *prima facie* no lack of impartiality or independence, if the arbitrator takes a view diverging from the one he/she supported as counsel, perhaps very strongly, his/her impartiality may nevertheless suffer.[21]

13.17. It is true that the increased importance of disclosure of any circumstances that may call into question the impartiality or independence of the arbitrator[22] reduces his/her vulnerability.[23] Pursuant to Article 11 paragraph 2 of the ICC Rules, before his/her appointment or confirmation, the prospective arbitrator has to sign a 'statement of acceptance, availability, impartiality and independence'. This implies the disclosure of any facts or circumstances 'which might be of such a nature as to call into question the arbitrator's independence in the eyes of the parties[24] as well as any circumstances that could give rise to reasonable doubts as to the arbitrator's impartiality'.

---

[21] At any rate, it is difficult to agree with the judgment of the Italian *Corte di cassazione* delivered on 28 August 2004 (*Giustizia civile*, 2005, I, 3049) holding that the fact that counsel and the arbitrator shared the same law firm did not disqualify the latter, to the effect that the disqualification of the arbitrator should require additional circumstances. See also Pietro Ferrario, *Challenge to Arbitrators: Where a Counsel and an Arbitrator Share the Same Office – The Italian Perspective*, 27 JOURNAL OF INTERNATIONAL ARBITRATION 421 (2010).

[22] Ana Stanic, *Challenging Arbitrators and the Importance of Disclosure: Recent Cases and Reflections*, 16 CROATIAN ARBITRATION YEARBOOK 205 (2009).

[23] The French approach in the case *Avax v Tecnimont* is emblematical of the importance granted to disclosure (Cour d'appel de Paris, decision dated 12 February 2009, Rev. arb. 2009.186). See also Thomas Clay, *L'application perlée du règlement d'arbitrage pour la contestation des liens non révélés entre arbitre et conseil*, 2 THE PARIS JOURNAL OF INTERNATIONAL ARBITRATION 1109 (2011).

[24] As the impact is measured with regard to what appears suspicious 'in the eyes of the parties', the arbitrator is not allowed to invoke their subjective conclusion.

13.18. On the other hand, extending the scope of the duty of disclosure ('better disclose too much than too little'),[25] could lead to the opposite result, to the effect that a reasonable omission may be relied upon in view of challenging the arbitrator. It has to be added that the tendency to submit challenges leads to some of them being based upon inaccurate facts, as for instance the non-disclosure by the arbitrator of having attended a conference also attended by counsel for the party that has appointed him/her.[26]

III. The Impact on the Functioning of the Arbitral Tribunal

III.1. The External Factor: Interference of State Courts and Delay of the Proceedings

13.19. Irrespective of the court or authority having jurisdiction on the proposal of disqualification , the action may result in separate proceedings taking place within the framework of the proceedings related to the case subject to arbitration and lead to a 'trial within the trial'. In case of a challenge, the functioning of the arbitral tribunal may become conditional upon an external factor, the decision of a state court, if the latter has jurisdiction to deal with the proposal on disqualification of the challenged arbitrator.

13.20. A challenge based upon the alleged partiality or lack of independence of an arbitrator may be one of the means used by a party interested in obtaining a prolongation of the proceedings. Delaying tactics are encouraged if a state court, in most cases the *ratione materiae* competent court of the seat of the arbitration, intervenes at some stage of the challenge procedure. It can be assumed that the procedure will be time-consuming, at least in comparison to the efficient and expeditious way in which arbitral proceedings usually unfold. The award will be rendered less quickly than expected, even if the arbitral tribunal itself decides on the challenge. It has, however, to be presumed that the celerity of arbitral proceedings will be affected in the case of interference of state courts. Their interference prolongs the arbitral proceedings, in particular if the latter have to be suspended in accordance with the arbitration rules to which they are subject. Article 20 paragraph 4 of VIAC Rules offers a balanced approach to the question

---

[25] Allan Philip, *The Duties of an Arbitrator, in* THE LEADING ARBITRATORS' GUIDE TO INTERNATIONAL ARBITRATION, New York/Bern: Juris Publishing Inc./Staempfli Verlag 67, 70 (Lawrence Newmann/Richard Hill eds., 2004).

[26] The French courts rightly held that the arbitrator did not need to disclose such information (Cass., Civ. I, 4.7.2012, JCP G 2012, I, 1354, no 1, annotated by Seraglini).

as to whether the proceedings should be discontinued while the challenge is pending. This provision states that: 'The arbitral tribunal, including the challenged arbitrator, may continue the arbitration while the challenge is pending. The arbitral tribunal may not issue an award until after the Board has ruled on the challenge.' Such a solution has the advantage of reducing the delay a challenge implies.

13.21.	In the event of the arbitrator being removed, the question arises as to whether the issues already dealt with should be reconsidered. It appears as a reasonable solution to leave to the arbitral tribunal, as it is reshaped in the wake of a successful challenge, the discretionary power to opt on its own or upon motion of one of the parties in favour of reconsidering some of the issues dealt with in its previous composition.[27]

13.22.	Additional problems may arise if the arbitral tribunal is bound by the arbitration agreement to render its award within a time limit. In such an event, the delay caused by the challenge submitted by one of the parties may result in the setting aside of the final award, if the law applicable to this issue provides that this is a ground for annulling the award. It would be particularly uncomfortable for the arbitral tribunal if the extension of the time limit, within the frame of which the award is to be delivered, requires the consent of both parties and one of them, not necessarily the challenging one, refuses to agree.

13.23.	Furthermore, given the arbitrator's vulnerability, it can be very embarrassing for the challenged one if the facts which substantiate the request for disqualification are revealed before a state court. This is because the court functions without having to comply with the high standards of confidentiality that is inherent to any arbitral proceedings. The arbitrator's reputation is increasingly threatened as the contents of the request may be divulged.

13.24.	The timing of the challenge should also be taken into account. It is widely held that the disqualification must be sought promptly. Prescribing a time frame for submitting the proposal for disqualification prevents the parties from jeopardizing the arbitral proceedings at a later stage. Most arbitration rules do not prohibit a challenge being submitted after the constitution of the arbitral tribunal and before the closing of the proceedings. This is a supplementary guarantee for unbiased proceedings, as it cannot be excluded that the facts or circumstances sustaining the challenge are indeed revealed at a later stage.

---

[27]	For instance, section 18 paragraph 6 of SCCI Arbitration Rules states that 'If necessary, the tribunal or the arbitrator may, upon motions from the parties, reconsider the issues that had already been dealt with at previous hearings'.

13.25. The right to submit a challenge after the constitution of the arbitral tribunal allows a challenge to an arbitrator under the pretense that he/she lacks impartiality, but actually because he/she has already expressed in the arbitration some views that are considered as hostile by the challenging party. This may in particular be the case if the arbitral tribunal has already rendered an interim award. It is also possible that the arbitrator's impartiality is being put into question by the appointing party itself. The Swedish courts were faced with such an issue.[28] An award was set aside because the arbitrator was the managing partner of a law firm, which two days before the rendering of the final award began to represent a company in a dispute against the party that appointed as arbitrator the managing partner of the law firm.

III.2. The Internal Factor: The Rift within the Arbitral Tribunal – the Polarization between the Arbitral Tribunal and the Parties

13.26. A challenge based upon the alleged partiality or lack of independence of the arbitrator may create an unpleasant, if not hostile, climate within the tribunal itself, in particular if its members end up being involved in the 'dispute' the challenge implies. This may in particular be the case, if the arbitral tribunal decides on the challenge, as the case is with domestic laws that have adopted the UNCITRAL Model Law on International Commercial Arbitration. The most suitable solution is that an authority other than the arbitral tribunal itself decides on the disqualification of the arbitrator. This is provided for by the rules of prominent institutional arbitrations such as the ICC, LCIA, ICAC, VIAC and SCC Arbitration Rules. This solution secures, to a large extent, the celerity of arbitral proceedings and reduces the likelihood of the unchallenged arbitrators being involved in turbulences generated by the challenge procedure.

13.27. The challenging party has already shown a manifest lack of confidence in one of the members of the arbitral tribunal. The dismissal of the request may give way to a polarization between this party and the unchallenged co-arbitrators, if the latter are considered as suspiciously reluctant to admit a proposal for disqualifying another member of the tribunal. The mistrust of the challenging party is to be assumed in particular if, by virtue of domestic laws following the UNCITRAL Model Law, the challenged arbitrator has participated in the tribunal's

---

[28] Svea Court of Appeal, 27 September 2011, 2 The Paris Journal of International Arbitration 1153(2011).

decision on the challenge, instead of stepping down on his/her own. In such a case, the acceptance of the request requires, in practice, the positive vote of the unchallenged arbitrators.

13.28. The decision of the arbitrators on the challenge is likely to create a rift within the arbitral tribunal itself, in particular if the challenge has been dismissed by a not unanimous award. It cannot be taken for granted that the unsuccessfully challenged arbitrator will be untouched by the fact that one of the other arbitrators has held to his/her detriment that there was a manifest lack of the qualities required for arbitrating. Things are less complicated if the arbitrator is removed upon acceptance of the challenge. In addition, the acceptance of the challenge may alienate the party who nominated the removed arbitrator towards the reshaped arbitral tribunal.[29]

13.29. Irrespective of the court or the authority deciding on the challenge, the functioning of the tribunal may also be affected if the unsuccessfully challenged arbitrator suspects that the facts calling into question his/her qualities for arbitrating have been leaked by counsel of the challenging party. It could be assumed that there has been a leakage of the information the challenge is based upon, especially in case of a controversy as to whether the arbitrator complied with the duty incumbent upon him/her to disclose any circumstances that may affect his/her independence and impartiality.

13.30. Counsel may be knowledgeable of facts related to previous proceedings, for instance about multiple nominations of the challenged arbitrator by the same party or the same law firm,[30] as well as about the professional relationship of the challenged arbitrator with one of the attorneys taking part in the proceedings. They could consequently be held as having been instrumental in designing the disturbing proposal for disqualification.

13.31. The negative impact of a presumed leakage on the functioning of the tribunal increases, if the challenge is submitted not at the time of the tribunal's constitution, but at a later stage and is based on the behavior of the challenged arbitrator in the proceedings. In some cases, the leakage may be quite wrongly attributed to a member of the tribunal.

---

[29] This could deteriorate the position of the party who nominated the removed arbitrator towards the arbitral tribunal as the latter has been reshaped and eventually led to new challenges, this time by the other party. In such an event, the functioning of the tribunal may be seriously disturbed.

[30] See *Tidewater et al.* v *The Bolivarian Republic of Venezuela*, ICSID Case No ARB/10/5, decision of 23 December 2010 on the disqualification of the arbitrator at paragraph 59: 'The question whether multiple appointments may affect the independence is a matter of substance, not of mere mathematical calculation'.

Arbitrators should do their best to avoid being involved in the challenge procedure on the basis of what they are presumably aware of in their capacity as members of the tribunal.

13.32. In this context, a rather thorny question has arisen as to the acceptance of the *locus standi* of an arbitrator submitting a challenge against another member of the arbitral tribunal. The *locus standi* of the challenging arbitrator has been recognized in a Kuala Lampur court case.[31] However, such an approach is not acceptable, because it would displace the burden of sustaining the challenge from the party damaged by the alleged lack of independence to the arbitrators that get wind of a behavior that is far from meeting the requirements of fair and unbiased arbitral proceedings. This would entail a major disturbance for the arbitral tribunal. Its functioning would become a 'mirror' of the dispute subject to the arbitral proceedings at issue.

13.33. As a matter of fact, the arbitrator is bound not to disclose anything that the/she becomes aware of during the proceedings. The strict compliance with such a duty of non-disclosure, which is a corollary of the duty of confidentiality, but also a benchmark for the arbitrator's independence, is an efficient remedy against the suspicion that a non-permitted leakage has triggered the challenge.

IV. A Telling Example: Challenges in an ICC Arbitration and Judgment Nr. 11/2009 of the Plenary Assembly of the Greek Supreme Court

13.35. The dysfunction generated by a challenge as well as the way it can be handled is illustrated in an ICC arbitration that took place in Switzerland. It was followed by the enforcement-related judgment Nr. 11/2009 of the Plenary Assembly of the Greek Supreme Court, *Areios Pagos*.[32]

13.36. The arbitrator initially appointed by the claimant was replaced because he was no longer able to fulfil his duties, as he became his country's Minister of Justice. A new arbitrator, X, was appointed in the wake of a request submitted by the claimant. Immediately upon his nomination, X requested that the proceedings be repeated, but his request was denied by the other two arbitrators through a not unanimous partial

---

[31] *Sundra Rajoo v Mohamed Abd Majeb and Persuatan Penapis Minyak Swait (Poram)*. This case is mentioned by Niusha Bassiri, Book review of THE PRACTICE OF ARBITRATION, *Essays in Honor of Hans van Houtte*, 4 THE PARIS JOURNAL OF INTERNATIONAL ARBITRATION 542, 543 (2013).

[32] Areios Pagos (Plenary Assembly), judgment Nr. 11/2009, 50 Helliniki Dikaiossyni 981(2009).

award. Twelve days after this award was rendered, the claimant challenged the President of the Arbitral Tribunal. X considered that the Arbitral Tribunal could not deliberate until after the decision on the challenge was made and, consequently, refused to take part in the meetings of the other two arbitrators. The behaviour of X did not prevent the other tribunal members from drafting an award and sending it to X for his comments. Although in the meantime the challenge was dismissed by the Court of the International Chamber of Commerce, X insisted on the withdrawal of the draft award, invoking that it has been prepared without his participation. Instead of accepting X's request, the President of the Arbitral Tribunal prepared a final draft award and asked both arbitrators to submit their comments. Two days later, the claimant challenged both the President and the co-arbitrator appointed by the other party. The final award was issued after the second challenge was dismissed by the International Chamber of Commerce. The Swiss Federal Tribunal upheld the award. It also rejected those contentions based upon the award having being delivered although X did not participate in the deliberations of the Arbitral Tribunal, when the challenges were pending.

13.37. As the enforcement of the award was sought in Greece, the Plenary Assembly of the Greek Supreme Court in its judgment, Number 11/2009, dealt with issues related to the challenge procedure and its impact on the functioning of the arbitral tribunal. It held that the enforcement of the award would not be contrary to public policy under Article V2(b) New York Convention on the Recognition and Enforcement of Foreign Arbitral Awards. In drawing this conclusion, the Supreme Court considered that the award was rendered in accordance with the rules governing the arbitral proceedings. It was taken into account that both challenges were dismissed. Besides, the abstention of X was deemed as irrelevant with regard to the exequatur, because the claimant did not seek his replacement. In a very subtle and cautious way, the Court dissociated the behaviour of X from the procedural strategy of the party that had requested his nomination in replacement of the initially appointed arbitrator, notwithstanding the quite astonishing timing of both challenges submitted by that party. The Court confined itself to mentioning their dismissal in a not conspicuous way. In contrast, it did not refrain from sharply criticizing the behaviour of X, as it held that he obstructed the conduct of the arbitral proceedings and abstained from the tribunal's deliberations without a reasonable ground.

V. Conclusion

13.38. The challenges of arbitrators are a guarantee of fair and unbiased arbitral proceedings, but imply some drawbacks. Given the vulnerability of the arbitrator, who is affected in a stronger way than a judge by allegations against his/her impartiality or independence, even an unfounded challenge could serve as an inflammatory 'grenade' within the arbitral proceedings.

13.39. The challenge has an impact on the arbitral tribunal, the functioning of which may become conditional upon an external factor, such as the decision of a state court, if the latter has to decide on the challenge. This may entail an important delay in the finalization of the arbitral proceedings. Such a drawback is reduced if another authority decides on the challenge.

13.40. The UNCITRAL Model Law on International Commercial Arbitration and domestic laws based upon it provide that the arbitral tribunal itself decides on the impartiality and independence of its challenged member, who may step down on his/her own. In such a case, it is likely that a rift may appear within the arbitral tribunal, in particular if the request has been dismissed by a not unanimous award. Other arbitration rules state that another court or authority must decide on the challenge. In any case, the challenge procedure may lead to a polarization between the arbitral tribunal and the challenging party, if the request is dismissed, or the other party, if the arbitrator is removed.

13.41. Arbitrators should be very careful to avoid being involved in the turbulences generated by the challenge. The example of the ICC arbitration mentioned under section IV is telling, in as much as it displays the dysfunction arising out of a challenge, in particular if one of the arbitrators becomes a component of the challenging strategy.

| | |

Summaries

DEU [*Einwendungen gegen die Person von Schiedsrichtern mit Rückbindung an die Arbeitsweise von Schiedssenaten*]
Der Aufsatz setzt sich mit den externen und internen Zusammenhängen von Einwendungen gegen die Person von Schiedsrichtern auseinander. Bei einer solchen Einwendung kann die fortgesetzte Fähigkeit des Schiedssenats zu seiner berufenen Tätigkeit von äußeren Faktoren abhängig sein, wie z. B. der Entscheidung eines staatlichen (allgemeinen) Gerichts, falls die Entscheidung über den Ausschluss des Schiedsrichters in dessen Zuständigkeitsbereich fällt. Dies gilt insbesondere dort, wo die

nationalen Regelungen die grundlegende Vorgabe des UNCITRAL-Mustergesetzes über das internationale Schiedsverfahren in Handelssachen übernommen haben.

Diese Fragen sind, was die interne Arbeitsweise des Schiedsgerichts anbelangt, weniger kompliziert, solange über die Einwendung eine außenstehende Stelle entscheidet. Diese Lösung wurde von führenden ständigen Schiedsgerichten wie etwa ICC ICAC, LCIA, VIAC und SCC übernommen. Dort jedoch, wo die Kompetenz zur Entscheidung über die Einwendung beim Schiedssenat selbst liegt, kann seine Entscheidung zu einem Zerwürfnis unter den Beisitzenden führen, zumal dann, wenn die Einwendung nicht einstimmig abgewiesen wurde. Ungeachtet des Gerichts bzw. der Stelle, die über die Einwendung zu entscheiden hat, kann deren Abweisung außerdem zu einer Polarisierung der Beziehungen zwischen der einwendenden Partei und dem Schiedsrichter führen, gegen den die Einwendung gerichtet war. Wird der Einwendung hingegen entsprochen, so wird damit womöglich das Vertrauen derjenigen Partei untergraben, die den ausgeschlossenen Schiedsrichter ernannt hatte.

Als Beispiel dafür, wie die Einwendung gegen die Person eines Schiedsrichters zu Funktionsstörungen führen kann und wie derartige Situationen gelöst werden können, führt der Beitrag ein Schiedsverfahren vor dem ICC und die Entscheidung 11/2009 des Obersten Gerichtshofs Griechenlands in Sachen Vollstreckung des Schiedsspruchs an.

CZE *[Námitky proti rozhodcům a vazba na fungování rozhodčích senátů]*
Článek se zabývá vnějšími a vnitřními souvislostmi s námitkami proti rozhodcům. V případě námitky proti rozhodcům může být fungování rozhodčího senátu závislé na vnějších faktorech, jako například rozhodnutí státního (obecného) soudu, spadá-li rozhodování vyloučení rozhodce do jeho pravomoci. Tak je tomu obzvláště v případech, kdy národní úprava přebírá základní řešení Vzorového zákona UNCITRAL o mezinárodním rozhodčím řízení v obchodních věcech.
Daná problematika je méně komplikovaná v souvislosti s vnitřním fungováním rozhodčího soudu, pokud o námitce rozhoduje jiný orgán. Takové řešení převzaly významné stálé rozhodčí instituce, jako ICC, ICAC, LCIA, VIAC a SCC. Je-li však rozhodčí senát sám nadán pravomocí rozhodovat o námitce, může jeho rozhodnutí představovat důvod pro rozkol v rámci senátu, obzvláště je-li námitka zamítnuta jinak, než jednomyslným rozhodnutím. Bez ohledu na soud nebo orgán rozhodující o námitce, může její zamítnutí vést rovněž k polarizaci vztahů mezi namítající stranou a rozhodci, proti nimž námitka

nesměřovala. Na druhou stranu vyhovění námitce může narušit důvěru strany, která vyloučeného rozhodce nominovala.

Jako příklad disfunkce vyvolané námitkou proti osobě rozhodce, jakož i způsob řešení takové situace článek uvádí rozhodčí řízení u ICC a rozhodnutí řeckého Nejvyššího soudu číslo 11/2009 ve věci výkonu rozhodčího nálezu.

| | |

POL [***Wniosek o wyłącznie arbitra i jego wpływ na działanie trybunału arbitrażowego***]

Niniejszy artykuł opisuje wewnętrzny i zewnętrzny kontekst składania wniosków o wyłączenie arbitra. W przypadku wniosku o wyłączenie arbitra działanie trybunału arbitrażowego może być uzależnione od czynników zewnętrznych, na przykład decyzji sądu państwowego (powszechnego), może również dojść do znacznego przeciągania postępowania. Wniosek może mieć wpływ na wewnętrzną pracę trybunału arbitrażowego i prowadzić do rozbieżności pomiędzy arbitrem, którego dotyczy, a pozostałymi członkami trybunału. Jego efektem może być również polaryzacja pomiędzy trybunałem arbitrażowym a stroną, która zgłosiła wniosek, lub stroną, która mianowała wyłączonego arbitra.

FRA [*Les objections avancées pour récuser des arbitres et le lien avec le fonctionnement des tribunaux arbitraux*]

On se penche ici sur les liens externes et internes avec les objections avancées pour récuser les arbitres. Lorsque des objections sont avancées contre des arbitres, le fonctionnement de la chambre d'arbitrage peut être dépendant de facteurs externes, comme par exemple la décision d'une juridiction nationale (de compétence générale), et cela peut conduire à retarder de manière significative la procédure. L'objection peut également influer sur le fonctionnement externe de la chambre d'arbitrage et provoquer une scission entre l'arbitre, contre lequel l'objection est dirigée, et les autres membres du collège arbitral. Cela peut mener également à une polarisation entre le tribunal arbitral et la partie qui a déposé l'objection ou la partie qui a nommé l'arbitre récusé.

RUS [*Отводы арбитров и связь с работой арбитражных судов*]

В статье рассматриваются внешний и внутренний контекст отвода арбитров. При отводе арбитра работа арбитражного суда оказывается в зависимости от внешних факторов, например, от решения государственного суда (общей юрисдикции), причем может возникнуть значительная задержка в разбирательстве. Отвод также может повлиять на внутреннюю работу арбитражного суда и вызвать разногласия между арбитром, против которого направлено заявление об отводе, и другими членами суда. Это также может привести к противостоянию между арбитражным судом и стороной, подавшей заявление об отводе арбитра, или стороной, назначившей арбитра, в отношении которого был заявлен отвод.

ESP [*Objeciones a los árbitros y el vínculo al funcionamiento de los paneles de arbitraje*]

El artículo aborda los vínculos internos y externos con las objeciones a los árbitros. En el caso de una objeción al árbitro, el funcionamiento del panel arbitral puede depender de varios factores externos, como una resolución del tribunal nacional (general), o también pueden originarse retrasos significativos en el procedimiento. Una objeción también puede afectar el funcionamiento interno del panel arbitral y provocar una discordancia entre el árbitro, contra el cual se dirige la objeción, y el resto de miembros del panel. Asimismo, puede conducir a la polarización entre el panel arbitral y la parte que ha presentado la objeción, o la parte que ha designado el árbitro excluido.

| | |

Radka Zahradníková

Challenge Procedure in Institutional and Ad Hoc Arbitration under the New Regulations in the Revised UNCITRAL Arbitration Rules

Key words:
challenge of arbitrators |
fair trial principle |
impartiality |
independence |
UNCITRAL Rules |
appointing authority | ad
hoc arbitration |
institutional arbitration

Abstract | *The right to challenge an arbitrator is an essential part of arbitral due process. The challenge procedure depends on whether it is carried out in ad hoc arbitration or institutional arbitration. This paper explores the differences between the challenge procedures in both ad hoc and institutional arbitration. In addition, an analysis of the problems associated with the procedures is included. Finally, even if the right to challenge should be limited only to those cases in which there is a real threat to the integrity of the arbitration procedure, this right to challenge the arbitrator is often misused by the parties to delay the proceedings and postpone a negative decision of the dispute. That is why the parties have to primarily anticipate this when concluding the arbitration agreement and should regulate the situation when a party raises a challenge to an arbitrator. When they do not obey it, they have to count on the rules which govern the proceedings. In ad hoc proceedings, it can be recommended for the parties to agree on some rules for ad hoc proceedings, e.g. UNCITRAL Arbitration Rules. These are tailor-made procedural rules for ad hoc arbitration that also provide for rules of challenge procedures. The UNCITRAL Rules are examined for their ability to meet the challenges discussed in the current, non-standard system.*

JUDr. Ing. Radka Zahradníková Ph.D LL.M, graduated from the Faculty of Law, University of West Bohemia, Czech Republic and simultaneously from the Faculty of International Relations, University of Economics. In 2003, she successfully defended her Master's thesis at the University in Bayreuth, and obtained her LL.M title. In 2006, she was awarded a Ph.D title after successfully defending her dissertation on the topic of Institutional arbitration. Since 2007, she has been a judge specializing in commercial and administrative disputes and disputes with a foreign element. She is also an assistant professor at the Department of Civil Law, Faculty of Law, University of West

|||

I. Introduction

14.01. Like in court proceedings, where the parties have the right to an impartial and independent judge, parties in arbitration have the right to an impartial and independent arbitrator. The fact that the parties have entered into an arbitration agreement does not deprive them of that fundamental right which is incorporated in the fair trial principle of Art. 6 of the Human Rights Convention.[1] This concept is inherent to a developed legal society.[2] As arbitration is a form of adjudication, albeit a private one, it is important that the final outcome be the result of an impartial process in which all sides have been fully heard. 'Not only must the procedure be conducted fairly, but the parties, particularly the losing one, must also perceive it as such'.[3] As Lord Hewart, noted legal scholar said: 'It is not merely of some importance but is of fundamental importance, that justice should not only be done, but should manifestly and undoubtedly be seen to be done'.[4]

Bohemia, specializing in civil procedure and alternative dispute resolution. She is the author of at least 30 journal papers, 2 monographs, and co-author of 3 other monographs and about 15 articles in yearbooks from international conferences. She was also a member of the working group of the Ministry of Justice that amended the Czech law on arbitration and enforcement of arbitral awards. She has lectured at foreign universities, such as in Limoges, Toulouse and Thessaloniki.
e-mail: radka.zahradnik @gmail.com

14.02. Identically with court proceedings, the parties to an arbitration should be provided with an efficient tool to remove the arbitrator under certain circumstances. If one of the parties has doubts as to the impartiality and independence of the arbitrator, which could lead to a distrust of the particular arbitrator, removable should be available. This is called a 'challenge procedure'[5] or 'disqualification procedure.'[6] The English Arbitration Act of 1996 refers to 'removal of an arbitrator' if circumstances exist that give rise to justifiable doubts as to their

---

[1]   It may be applied to arbitration in light of the principles of arbitration proceedings, especially contractual autonomy, even if the case law of ECtHR indicates that the fair trial doctrine need not necessarily apply to arbitration at all. Cf. Judgment of the ECtHR in *Suovaniemi et al.* v *Finland*, No. 31737/96.

[2]   Cf. ALEXANDER J. BĚLOHLÁVEK, ARBITRATION LAW OF CZECH REPUBLIC: PRACTICE AND PROCEDURE, New York: Juris 18 (2013).

[3]   Koch Christopher, *Standards and Procedures for Disqualifying Arbitrators*, 20(4) JOURNAL OF INTERNATIONAL ARBITRATION 325-353 (2003).

[4]   Judgement *R.* v *Sussex Justices*, ex parte McCarthy [1924] 1 K.B. 256 establishing the principle that the mere appearance of bias is sufficient to overturn a judicial decision.

[5]   This term is used in AAA International Arbitration Rules (Art. 8 ff.) or ICC Rules of Arbitration (Art. 14).

[6]   This term is used in ICSID Arbitration Rules (rule 9).

impartiality.[7] The Rules of Arbitration court attached to the Chamber of Commerce of the Czech Republic and Agricultural Chamber of the Czech Republic refer to the procedure of 'excluding an arbitrator'.[8] In the official translation of the Arbitration and Dispute Resolution Act of Indonesia from 1999 the term 'recusal' is used when talking about challenging arbitrators.[9]

14.03.   Challenging an arbitrator is an important attribute of the fair trial doctrine and an essential element of the integrity of the international arbitral process. The importance attached to the independence and impartiality of the arbitrators implies that the parties cannot waive their right to challenge arbitrators in advance. Any such agreement would be contrary to public policy. [10]

14.04.   Nevertheless, it can also be used to restrain the arbitration proceedings and 'frustrate the purposes of arbitration within the framework of obstruction tactics'.[11] Moreover, challenges may also be used 'to intimidate or warn the arbitrators'.[12] The challenge procedure shifts the focus away from the subject matter of the dispute and onto the arbitrator personally, which results in delays to the arbitration proceedings. 'Whether made in good faith or simply for strategic purposes is not always easy to determine'.[13] This is the main reason why, recently, the number of challenges to arbitrators may have increased. In the past, challenges to arbitrators might have been a rare event. If a vacancy occurred, it was usually because of the death or resignation of an arbitrator. However, modern commercial arbitrations often involve vast sums of money and parties have become more inclined to engage 'specialist lawyers, who are expert in manoeuvres designed to obtain tactical advantages or at least minimise a potential disadvantage'.[14] Consequently, only a few challenges are successful,

---

[7]   English Arbitration Act 1996, ch. 23, § 24.

[8]   Section 24 Subsection 2 Rules of Arbitration Court attached to the Czech Chamber of Commerce and Agricultural Chamber of the Czech Republic.

[9]   Art. 22 Arbitration and Dispute Resolution Act of Indonesia Law No. 30 of 1999.

[10]   Cf. Decision of Bezirksgericht Affoltern am Albis of May 26 1994, Ref. No. XXIII YBCA 754 confirmed by the Court of Appeal in Zurich of July 26 1995.

[11]   ALAN REDFERN & MARTIN HUNTER, LAW AND PRACTICE OF INTERNATIONAL COMMERCIAL ARBITRATION, London: Sweet and Maxwell para 4-59 (3rd ed., 1999).

[12]   Karl H. Böckstiegel, *Practice of Various Arbitral Institutions*, (5) ICCA CONGRESS SERIES 132 (1991).

[13]   Michael W. Tupman, *Challenge and Disqualification of Arbitrators in International Commercial Arbitration*, 38(1) THE INTERNATIONAL AND COMPARATIVE LAW QUARTERLY 26 (1989).

[14]   MARTIN HUNTER & ALAN REDFERN, LAW AND PRACTICE OF INTERNATIONAL COMMERCIAL ARBITRATION, London: Sweet & Maxwell 207(4th ed., 2004).

particularly in institutional arbitration where the personality of the arbitrator is examined before being appointed.

14.05. The challenge procedure depends on whether it is carried out in *ad hoc* or institutional arbitration. Whereas *ad hoc* arbitration is arbitration conducted according to an arbitration agreement which does not refer to rules of an arbitral institution, institutional arbitration is conducted according to procedural rules rendered by the arbitral institution, such as International Chamber of Commerce (ICC), London Court of International Arbitration (LCIA) or Deutsche Institution für Schiedsgerichtsbarkeit (DIS).

14.06. If the challenge procedure is conducted within the framework of institutional arbitration, the challenge procedure will be supervised and handled by the institution according to its rules. Ultimately, it will result in a quick and efficient decision on the challenge to the arbitrator. However, if the challenge procedure is conducted in *ad hoc* arbitration, the challenge procedure is primarily subject to the agreement of the parties. If the parties do not agree on the challenge procedure, the parties are referred to the state courts according to *lex arbitri*[15] within the scope of the auxiliary functions of the court. In this case, it can be difficult to determine the competent authority to assist the arbitration. This solution might be time consuming and might lead to delays in arbitration proceedings, sometimes far beyond the limits of social efficiency. Moreover, this authority may have little or no experience in arbitration.

14.07. In addition, some *lex arbitri*, e.g. the U.S. Federal Arbitration Act, does not provide for any separate challenge procedures at the pre-award stage,[16] or if they do, their rules might not necessarily provide easy and clearly defined standards for challenging arbitrators. The Czech Arbitration Act does not define the procedure at all. It only refers a party seeking to challenge an arbitrator to lodge a motion petitioning a court to rule on the arbitrator's disqualification (Section 12 Subsection 2 of Czech Arbitration Act). It can be inferred that the court should proceed like in other contentious (adversarial) proceedings (Section 30 Czech Arbitration Act). Furthermore, it remains uncertain whether only the specific statutory provisions on arbitration should apply or should the rules on civil procedure in general also apply. This makes it unclear if the party´s challenge to an arbitrator lodged later than the first action on the merits of the case is restricted by the time limit set

---

[15] Law of the place where arbitration is to take place.
[16] In that case the parties' only option is to attack the award issued by the tribunal, where the lack of impartiality or independence is a reason for annulment or denial of enforcement.

forth in Section 15a Subsection 2 Czech Code Procedure Civil (CPC) or can that challenge be raised later.

14.08. That is why it might be worthwhile for the parties to agree to some *ad hoc* arbitration rules such as UNCITRAL Arbitration rules, which are tailor-made procedural rules for *ad hoc* arbitration. Most importantly, they also provide rules for challenge procedures (Art. 13 UNCITRAL Arbitration Rules).

II. Reasons for Challenging an Arbitrator

14.09. The reasons for challenging an arbitrator may not only be doubts about their impartiality or independence. There may also be other objective reasons for disqualifying arbitrators, which have nothing to do with their relationship with or predisposition toward the parties or the dispute. These additional possible grounds for challenging an arbitrator fall generally into four distinct categories: special qualifications, nationality, capacity and misconduct.

14.10. There may be circumstances which result in a situation where an arbitrator lacks eligibility, such as where the arbitrator does not possess the qualifications required by the arbitration agreement[17] or stipulated by the agreed upon rules.[18] This can also apply regarding the arbitrator's nationality.[19] Moreover, the arbitrator may not meet the conditions for the appointment laid down by the law. Examples of this are deprivation of legal capacity (*de jure* impossibility) or incompatibility of the function of the arbitrator with other functions[20] or if the arbitrator cannot exercise the office because of an impediment resulting in a physical or mental incapacity of conducting the proceeding (*de facto* impossibility). Another example is if the arbitrator refuses or simply fails to act and properly conduct the proceedings from other than medical reasons (default of an arbitrator/

---

[17] Pursuant to Art. 12 paragraph 2 UNCITRAL Model law an arbitrator may be challenged only if circumstances exist that give rise to justifiable doubts as to their impartiality or independence, or if the arbitrator does not possess qualifications agreed to by the parties. Mutatis mutandis, Art. 15 paragraph 1 SCC Rules or Section 18 paragraph 1 DIS Rules.

[18] According to Art. 14 paragraph 1 ICSID Convention, persons designated to serve on the Panels shall be persons of high moral character and recognized competence in the fields of law, commerce, industry or finance, who may be relied upon to exercise independent judgment.

[19] According to Rule 3 ICSID Arbitration Rules none of the arbitrators shall have the same nationality as or be a national of either party.

[20] E.g. pursuant to Section 80 par. 5 (b) Czech Act on courts and judges, No. 6/2002 Coll., a judge is not entitled to perform the function of an arbitrator or according to Canon 4 A. 4 of US Code of Conduct a judge should not act as an arbitrator.

misconduct).[21] The rules of some international arbitral institutions call the latter incapacity a 'truncated tribunal' and allow the remaining arbitrators to render an award depending on the state of arbitration even if the arbitrator was disqualified from deciding.[22] In this case, the procedure to remove the arbitrator is called 'release from appointment' instead of a challenge or disqualification procedure. Nevertheless, according to some rules of arbitration, the procedure for the challenge of an arbitrator applies.[23]

II.1. Independence v Impartiality

14.11. Challenge of arbitrators is primarily connected with their independence and impartiality. Unlike court proceedings, the nature of the arbitrator's independence and impartiality should be seen in the light of the the the arbitrator's position. Whereas cases at ordinary courts are allocated between judges by the state according to rules set prior to the determination of the judge in a particular case (the principle of 'lawful judge') and are remunerated by the state, arbitrators are chosen or nominated and remunerated by the parties even if they do not act as a representative of that party. Whereas the judge´s power derives directly from the state, the power of an arbitrator to decide a case results from a contractual relationship between the parties. Thus, the arbitrators are 'acting as agents or mandataries of the parties'.[24] It may be reflected in the fact that the arbitrators seem to stand on the side of a party who nominated them, especially because of economic dependence resulting from the arbitrator's agreed remuneration and also sometimes from deciding routine disputes always on behalf of one party.[25] Despite this fact, some jurisdictions when questioned about arbitrators refer to the rules on independence and impartiality of state

---

[21] Unreasonable delay in rendering an award can harm all the parties. Certain procedural or evidentiary rulings might be evidence of partiality.

[22] Cf. WIPO Arbitration Rules Art. 35 which refers to a failure to participate in the work of the Tribunal when talking about the truncated tribunal.

[23] UNCITRAL Arbitration Rules Art. 12 paragraph 3

[24] Cf. ADAM SAMUEL, JURISDICTIONAL PROBLEMS IN INTERNATIONAL COMMERCIAL ARBITRATION – A STUDY OF BELGIUM, DUTCH, ENGLISH, FRENCH, SWEDISH, SWISS, US AND WEST GERMAN LAW, Zurich: Schulthess Polygraphischer Verlag (1989).

[25] That is why, according to revised Czech Arbitration Act Section 8 paragraph 3 arbitrators are obliged to inform the parties prior to hearing cases resulting from consumer disputes if in the last 3 years they have rendered an award or participated in rendering an award or are arbitrating a pending case where a party was or is a party in a present case.

judges.[26] This might not always be appropriate as the arbitrator, unlike the state judge, is nominated by the party itself. Then, a question may be raised when the arbitrator crosses the fine line from being sympathetic to a party so that the party nominates them to being biased. According to Martin Hunter, well known professor of international arbitration, 'a party-appointed arbitrator should therefore combine a maximum predisposition towards the party that nominated that arbitrator with a minimum appearance of bias'.[27]

14.12.   Although the case law may show considerable similarities, the notion of independence and impartiality of arbitrators in some national laws is quite different.[28] Some national laws refer to a 'lack of bias' instead of impartiality or independence and rules on judicial proceedings do not apply (e.g. Czech law). Some national laws do not differentiate between impartiality and independence, but refer to the rules applicable to state judges (e.g. Austrian law). Some laws refer only to impartiality (e.g. English law) or only to independence (e.g. Swiss law[29]). Ultimately, some national laws distinguish between independence and impartiality (e.g. German or French law).

14.13.   Generally, impartiality (lack of bias) deals with the arbitrator's mental predisposition toward the parties, their representatives or the subject matter or controversy at hand. Independence means that an arbitrator must be free from any involvement or relationship with any of the parties[30] or their representatives or from involvement in the case itself or prior involvement in a similar case.[31] Independence can be regarded as 'the notional flip side' of the principle of lack of bias. Independence expresses an objective status, while a lack of bias expresses the need for maximum neutrality in connection with the arbitrator's decision making.[32]

---

[26]   English courts hold that arbitrators and judges must adhere to the same standard of impartiality, cf. Gillian Eastwood, *A Real Danger of Confusion? The English Law Relating to Bias in Arbitrators*, 17(3) ARB. INT'L (2001).

[27]   Christopher Koch, *Standards and Procedures for Disqualifying Arbitrators*, 20(4) JOURNAL OF INTERNATIONAL ARBITRATION 325-353 (2003).

[28]   CHRISTOPH LIEBSCHER, THE HEALTHY AWARD, The Hague: Kluwer law International 347 (2003).

[29]   It also applies to experts.

[30]   Pursuant to Art. 11 of ICC Arbitration Rules every arbitrator must be and remain impartial and independent of the parties involved in the arbitration.

[31]   The reason for disqualifying an arbitrator due to the arbitrator´s lack of impartiality does not only depend on whether the same arbitrator has expressed legal views on a similar case when hearing another case, despite the parties to the other dispute being identical and the subject of the dispute essentially being the same or the same legal relationship. Cf. Decisions of Arbitration Court attached to the Czech Chamber of Commerce and Agricultural Chamber of the Czech Republic Rsp 122/02, Rsp 148/01, Rsp 147/01.

[32]   Cf. ALEXANDER J. BĚLOHLÁVEK, *supra* note 2, at 549.

14.14. The border between independence and impartiality is sometimes very narrow and the difference is represented by the fact that independence is a verifiable 'objective' standard unlike impartiality which is a 'subjective' measure of a person's inner attitude or state of mind, which can be seen from the outside only in the behavior of the arbitrator.[33] Consequently, some statutes and case law tend to use the terms impartiality and independence interchangeably. An interesting attitude towards the differences between impartiality and independence is provided for by the International Bar Association (IBA) Rules of Ethics for International Arbitrators: 'Partiality arises where an arbitrator favors one of the parties, or where he is prejudiced in relation to the subject-matter of the dispute. Dependence arises from relationships between an arbitrator and one of the parties, or with someone closely connected with one of the parties.'[34]

14.15. It is important to say that the arbitrators need not be effectively biased (actual bias) but there might also be reasonable, legitimate[35] or justifiable[36] doubts on their lack of bias (apparent bias). Whereas actual bias is hard to prove and practically never invoked apparent bias is often argued. It is based on facts and circumstances, which would indicate that there might be grounds for bias. These circumstances need to be both objective and reasonably apparent, not just speculative.[37] Apparent or evident bias exists if the facts or circumstances are such that one may be justified in being suspicious about the impartiality of the arbitrator, so that there is a 'real danger' of bias affecting the mind of the relevant arbitrator.[38]

14.16. In summary, an impartial and independent arbitrator is such an arbitrator who always acts as a person with no interest in the course and outcome of the dispute. [39]

14.17. Moreover, most laws and rules do not distinguish between standards of behaviour expected of party-appointed arbitrators and those of sole or third arbitrators; all are equally required to be impartial and independent. [40] Nevertheless, there are some exemptions for arbitrators appointed by one party who are not subject to rules of neutrality. For

---

[33] JEAN ROBERT, L'ARBITRAGE, DROIT INTERNE, DROIT INTERNATIONAL PRIVÉ, Paris: Dalloz 135 (6th ed., 1993).

[34] Article 3 paragraph 1 (Elements of Bias) IBA Rules of Ethics.

[35] Section 8 Subsection 2 of Czech Arbitration Act.

[36] Art. 24 WIPO Arbitration Rules or Art. 11 of UNCITRAL Arbitration Rules.

[37] Cf. ALEXANDER J. BĚLOHLÁVEK, *supra* note 2, at 548.

[38] Judgement of House of Lords in *R. v Gough* [1993] AC 646.

[39] Cf. Pavel Vrcha, *Vyloučení soudce v civilním řízení (Disqualification of a judge in civil proceedings)*, (7) PRÁVNÍ RÁDCE 13-17 (2004).

[40] Michael W. Tupman, *supra* note 13, at 29.

example, pursuant to Canon X of American Arbitration Association (AAA) Code of Ethics for Arbitrators in Commercial Disputes, arbitrators may be predisposed toward the party who appointed them but in all other respects are obligated to act in good faith and with integrity and fairness.

14.18. Unlike the other members of the arbitral tribunal, challenges of a presiding arbitrator are rare, but not unknown. They are usually based upon some prior connection with one of the parties that gives rise to doubts as to the appointee´s independence. [41]

III. Challenge Procedure

14.19. When a person is approached in connection with a possible appointment as an arbitrator, they must disclose any circumstances likely to give rise to justifiable doubts as to their impartiality or independence.[42] This is a 'first stage of evaluation of circumstances' that could give rise to reasons resulting in a challenge to an arbitrator. The second stage is the possibility of parties contesting the independence and impartiality of arbitrators. In that case, the parties may agree to the challenge or that the arbitral tribunal comprised of the remaining arbitrators not affected by the challenge decides on the disqualification.[43] The last stage is entrusted generally to a court, board of the arbitral institution[44] or to an appointing authority,[45] which might assess the reasons for the disqualification of an arbitrator.[46]

14.20. Generally, the second stage of the procedure for challenge is subject to party autonomy. Agreements between the parties on such a procedure are, according to my knowledge, however, very rare in practice. Consequently, challenge procedures are either governed by applicable rules, or if no such rules have been agreed on, by the provisions in the relevant arbitration laws.

14.21. The three stages of evaluation of the circumstances that could give rise to reasons resulting in challenging arbitrators fall into the 'pre–award stage' of the arbitral process. Nevertheless, there is also a 'post–award stage' of procedural remedies for challenging an arbitrator in a particular case. The post-award remedies of the annulment of an award

---

[41]   MARTIN HUNTER & ALAN REDFERN, *supra* note 14, at 207.
[42]   Art. 11 paragraph 2 ICC Arbitration Rules.
[43]   Compare Section 24 Subsection 2 Rules of Arbitration Court attached to the Czech Chamber of Commerce and Agricultural Chamber of the Czech Republic.
[44]   *Ibid.*
[45]   Cf. Art. 13 paragraph 4 of UNCITRAL Arbitration Rules.
[46]   Cf. ALEXANDER J. BĚLOHLÁVEK, *supra* note 2, at 561-562.

or the refusal to enforce an award are available in most legal systems, on certain grounds, such as that the tribunal was improperly constituted as one of the arbitrators lacked independence. The pre-award stage is not always available in all legal systems.[47]

14.22. In institutional arbitration, a challenge to an arbitrator is made by submitting a written statement to the institution setting forth the reasons for the challenge and it must be substantiated.[48] Subsequently, the institution notifies the parties and the arbitrators of the challenge and gives them an opportunity to submit comments on the challenge. The ICC Rules even stipulate that the comments of the party are to be made available to the parties and to the arbitrators by the ICC so that there may be a second round of arbitrator and party comments.[49] If the other party agrees to the challenge, the arbitrator resigns (withdraws). Under those circumstances, the resignation is not considered an admission or acceptance of the grounds of the challenge.[50] However, having lost the confidence of both parties, the arbitrator can no longer serve their purpose.[51] In all other cases, the institution makes the final decision on the challenge.

14.23. Although the challenge procedure forms part of the arbitral proceedings, which is, by its nature, contentious, the challenge procedure is not adversarial. The fact that the challenged arbitrator and all other persons involved in the arbitration is given a chance to comment on the challenge does not make them generally stand in adversarial positions. That is why neither the arbitrator nor the challenging party appears before the institution in defense of their position.[52] Consequently, the decisions on challenges have an administrative character rather than a judicial one. According to UNCITRAL Model Law, decisions of the court are not subject to an appeal.[53]

---

[47] US Federal Arbitration Act.

[48] Art. 8 paragraph 2 AAA Rules or Art. 10 paragraph 4 LCIA Rules or Art. 25 WIPO Rules or Section 18 paragraph 2 DIS Rules.

[49] Art. 14 paragraph 3 ICC Rules.

[50] Art. 8 paragraph AAA Rules or Art. 28 WIPO Rules or Section 19 paragraph 3 DIS Rules.

[51] Unlike the Federal Arbitration Act, which does not provide for any challenge procedure conducted by state courts so that the parties are required to continue the arbitration though one party has lost confidence in the impartiality of the tribunal and it is clear that the award will be challenged. Cf. JULIAN D M LEW, LOUKAS A MISTELIS & STEFAN M KRÖLL, COMPARATIVE INTERNATIONAL COMMERCIAL ARBITRATIOR, Hague: Kluwer Law International 312 (2003).

[52] Christopher Koch, *supra* note 27, at 325-353.

[53] Cf. Art. 13 paragraph 3 UNCITRAL Model Law.

14.24. In *ad hoc* arbitration, a party wishing to challenge an arbitrator must make this known to all other parties, the arbitrator concerned and the other arbitrators. The request for disqualification should be in writing specifying the facts and circumstances on which it is based. Subsequently, if the other parties agree to the challenge, the arbitrator must withdraw from the office. If the parties do not agree to the challenge or the challenged arbitrator does not withdraw, the arbitral tribunal may decide on the challenge.[54] If the arbitral tribunal does not decide on the challenge, the party seeking the challenge requests that a court decide the challenge.[55]

14.25. In general, a party may challenge an arbitrator they appointed or in whose appointment they participated, only for reasons of which they become aware after the appointment was made.[56] Parties who appoint their arbitrator despite knowing their lack of independence or impartiality are considered to have waived any objections to the arbitrator and any personal conflict they may have in this respect.[57] Conversely, most rules of law do not restrict or even exclude the right to challenge an arbitrator appointed by the other party or a neutral appointing authority.

14.26. Nevertheless, the right to challenge an arbitrator does not exist without certain limits. Without these time limits, a party could preserve the right until the end of the arbitral proceedings to delay the proceedings or even after the award has been rendered to challenge its validity. To restrict the possibility of challenges being used for tactical and dilatory purposes most, rules and laws submit the right to challenge an arbitrator to certain time limits.

14.27. The challenge must generally be exercised within a very short period after being notified by the other party of the arbitrator's appointment or after the facts giving rise to the challenge become known. This period is usually 15 days following gaining knowledge of the concerned facts[58] or two weeks[59] and rarely exceeds the 30 days provided under ICC Rules.[60] Some rules stipulate that the challenge must be made not later than by the beginning of the first oral hearing. If the challenge is

---

[54] Art. 13 paragraph 3 UNCITRAL Model Law.

[55] Section 12 Subsection 2 of Czech ArbAct.

[56] Art. 12 paragraph 2 UNCITRAl Model Law or Art. 10 paragraph 3 LCIA Rules or Section 18 paragraph 1 DIS Rules.

[57] JULIAN D M LEW, LOUKAS A MISTELIS & STEFAN M KRÖLL, *supra* note 51, at 304.

[58] Art. 8 paragraph 1 AAA Rules; Art. 10 paragraph 4 LCIA Rules; Art. 15 paragraph 2 SCC Rules.

[59] Section 18 paragraph 2 DIS Rules.

[60] Art. 14 paragraph 2 ICC Rules.

made later it must be taken into account only if there were reasons deserving special attention not raising it timely.[61] Ultimately, there are a few rules which do not define a certain time limit but state that a proposal for disqualification must be made promptly but in any case before the closing of the procedure.[62]

14.28. Generally, failure by a party to challenge an arbitrator within the stipulated time period constitutes a waiver of the right to make the challenge.[63] In general, there is no right to challenge an award on the basis of a lack of independence or impartiality of an arbitrator where those facts were known to the parties before the award was rendered. Accordingly, the court must dismiss a motion to annul an arbitral award which is based on the grounds for disqualification of an arbitrator if the party requesting the annulment failed to raise the corresponding objection in the arbitral proceedings before the party´s first act in the merits of the case, despite having an opportunity to do so (Section 33 Czech Arbitration Act).[64] There are some exceptions to this rule. According to revised Section 33 of the Czech Arbitration Act, it does not apply to disputes arising from consumer contracts.

14.29. In institutional arbitration, the body who decides the challenge is, as a rule, the institution itself, whatever the designation of it might be. Accordingly, it might be an administrator,[65] court,[66] center[67] or board. [68] There are a few rules inspired by the UNCITRAL Model law which do not attribute the decision on the challenge to the institution but to the arbitral tribunal like in *ad hoc* arbitration.[69] Some experts (e.g. Koch) argue that this solution is problematical, because the tribunal becomes a judge in its own cause, which is hardly

---

[61] Section 24 paragraph 1 Rules of Arbitration court attached to the Czech Chamber of Commerce and Agricultural Chamber of the Czech Republic.

[62] Rule 9 paragraph 1 ICSID Arbitration Rules.

[63] Art. 15 paragraph 2 SCC Rules.

[64] Similarly, the Supreme Court of Canada stated in the case of Ghirardosi v Minister of Highways (BC) in 1996:'... an award will not be set aside if the circumstances alleged to disqualify an arbitrator were known to both parties before the arbitration commenced and they proceeded without objection.'

[65] The International Centre for Dispute Resolution pursuant Art. 1 paragraph 3 AAA Rules.

[66] LCIA Court pursuant to Art. 10 paragraph 4 LCIA Rules or ICC Court pursuant to Art. 14 paragraph 3 ICC Rules.

[67] Pursuant to Art. 29 WIPO Rules.

[68] Board of the Court pursuant to Section 24 paragraph 2 Rules of Arbitration court attached to the Czech Chamber of Commerce and Agricultural Chamber of the Czech Republic or Board of the Institute pursuant to Art. 15 paragraph 4 SCC Rules.

[69] Pursuant to DIS Rules or Rule 9 paragraph 4 ISCID Rules.

14.30. compatible with the notion that a judge should not sit in their own cause (*nemo iudex in causa sua*). In the case of a three-member tribunal, all three arbitrators take part in the decision, if it is a sole arbitrator that person decides alone. The International Centre for Settlement of Investment Disputes (ICSID) Rules introduce a certain compromise inspired by UNCITRAL Model Law, which is compatible with the principle of *nemo iudex in causa sua*. Accordingly, only if the challenge is directed at one (or at a minority) of the arbitrators, will it be decided by the majority of all other arbitrators in the absence of the arbitrator concerned. In all other cases, if the challenge relates to a sole arbitrator or to the majority of an arbitral tribunal, will it be decided by the Chairman of the ICSID Administrative Council. ICSID has avoided the unfortunate solution of the Model Law, by leaving the decision on the challenge with the arbitral tribunal for as long as it is consistent with the notion of justice being seen to be done.[70]

14.31. In *ad hoc* arbitration, which is not conducted under rules like those of UNCITRAL, the parties will have to refer a challenge to the national courts in accordance with *lex arbitri* of the place of arbitration. If the *lex arbitri* is based on the UNCITRAL Model Law, then there will be a two-step process.[71] First, the arbitral tribunal, in its full composition, decides the challenge. Like under DIS Rules, the challenged arbitrator participates in the decision-making process and, if they are a sole arbitrator, they decide themselves.

14.32. If this procedure is not successful, the challenging party may, usually within thirty days, apply to the state courts to decide the challenge. Nevertheless, this possibility should be *ultima ratio* and an agreement regarding the challenge procedure is preferred. Pursuant to Czech case law, this procedure is of an adversarial nature.[72] Active legitimacy is shown by the party bringing the action and passive legitimacy is attributed to the dispute's other party so that the result of the proceedings is binding for all the parties (Section 159a CzechCPC). The party making the challenge bears the burden of proof. The arbitrator concerned is not a party or participant of the court proceedings. The judgment of the court should provide the reasoning of the particular decision and it replaces the voluntary resignation of the arbitrator.[73]

---

[70] Christopher Koch, *supra* note 27, at 325-353.

[71] Art. 13 paragraph 2 and 3 UNCITRAL Model Law.

[72] Judgment of the District Court of Prague 5 of 20 October 2003, ref. No. 10 C 263/2003 (confirmed by judgment of Municipal Court in Prague of 2 April 2004, ref. No. 18 Co 18/2004).

[73] ALEXANDER J. BĚLOHLÁVEK, ACT ON ARBITRAL PROCEEDINGS AND ON ENFORCEMENT OF ARBITRAL AWARDS. COMMENTARY, Praha: C. H. BECK 94 (1st. ed., 2004).

14.33. As mentioned above, referring challenge procedures to state courts may lead to delays in the arbitration proceedings. This danger is only partially alleviated by the provision that the arbitration may proceed while the challenge is pending before the state courts.[74]

14.34. Differences exist when it comes to the form of the decision concerning the challenge to the arbitrator. Most institutional rules do not stipulate anything to this effect and it will be left to the discretion of the institution to decide whether and in what length it wishes to give reasons for its decision. Nevertheless, ICC rules stipulate that no reasons for the decision accepting or rejecting a challenge should be communicated.[75] The ICC's refusal to communicate the reasons for its decisions on challenges has been criticized as lacking transparency.[76] By not communicating the reasons for its decisions, the ICC seeks not only to protect the finality[77] of those decisions, but also hopes to spare arbitrators from the embarrassment which might be caused by a decision concerning their independence.[78]

14.35. Ultimately, once decided within the arbitral regime, the matter should be final and not subject to judicial review.

III.1 Challenge Procedure under Revised UNCITRAL Arbitration Rules

14.36. Also under UNCITRAL Arbitration Rules, when a person is approached in connection with their possible appointment as an arbitrator, they must disclose any circumstances likely to give rise to justifiable doubts as to their impartiality or independence (Art. 11 UNCITRAL Arbitration Rules). Even from the time the arbitrator has been appointed and throughout the arbitral proceedings, the arbitrator must, without delay, disclose any such circumstances to the parties and the other arbitrators unless they have already been informed of these circumstances.

14.37. Also, the parties have the right to challenge the arbitrator if they become aware of circumstances that give rise to justifiable doubts as to the arbitrator's impartiality or independence (Art. 12 UNCITRAL Arbitration Rules). The party who has appointed the particular arbitrator may challenge them only for reasons they become aware of after the appointment has been made. Consequently, a party who

---

[74] Christopher Koch, *supra* note 27, at 325-353.
[75] Article 11 paragraph 4 of the ICC Rules.
[76] Michael W. Tupman, *supra* note 13, at 26.
[77] Cf. Art. 11 paragraph 4 ICC Rules.
[78] Christopher Koch, *supra* note 27, at 325-353.

appoints their arbitrator despite knowing their lack of independence or impartiality is considered to have waived any objections to the arbitrator.

14.38. Because the UNCITRAL Rules were developed for *ad hoc* arbitration, they can not rely on an internal authority to deal with a challenge procedure. To shield the arbitration from the intervention of national courts, the UNCITRAL Rules created a mechanism for designating an 'appointing authority'.[79]

14.39. A party that intends to challenge an arbitrator must first send notice of its challenge within 15 days after it has been notified of the appointment of the challenged arbitrator, or within 15 days after the circumstances giving rise to justifiable doubts as to the arbitrator´s impartiality or independence became known to that party (Art. 13 UNCITRAL Arbitration Rules). The notice of challenge must state the reasons for the challenge. Thereafter, the notice of challenge must be communicated to all other parties the arbitrator who is challenged and the other arbitrators.

14.40. When an arbitrator has been challenged by a party, all parties may agree to the challenge. The arbitrator may also, after the challenge, withdraw from their office. In neither case does this imply acceptance of the validity of the grounds for the challenge. If, within 15 days from the date of the notice of challenge, all parties do not agree to the challenge or the challenged arbitrator does not withdraw, the party making the challenge may elect to pursue it. In that case, within 30 days from the date of the notice of challenge, they must seek a decision on the challenge by the appointing authority. The appointing authority may be chosen by the parties. A failure to do so will then designate the Secretary-General of the Permanent Court of Arbitration (PCA), pursuant to Art. 6 paragraph 2 UNCITRAL Arbitration Rules. That appointing authority will ultimately decide on the challenge.

14.41. The procedure to challenge an arbitrator regarding their independence or impartiality applies also in the event that an arbitrator fails to act (misconduct) or in the event of the *de jure* or *de facto* impossibility of performing their functions.

14.42. Appointing authorities offer further guidance as to the determination of independence and impartiality. They include such terms such as 'justifiable doubts' standard referred to in Art. 11 and ff. UNCITRAL Arbitration Rules. In a relatively recent decision in a North American Free Trade Agreement (NAFTA) dispute, Gallo v. Canada (2009), the ICSID Deputy Secretary-General, acting as the appointing authority in

---

[79] *Ibid.*, at 325-353.

the case, stated that 'under the UNCITRAL Arbitration Rules doubts are justifiable [...] if they give rise to an apprehension of bias that is, to the objective observer, reasonable'.[80] That decision and others also indicate that non-binding authorities such as the IBA Guidelines that describe and proscribe certain problematic relationships can provide guidance to determine whether doubts are objectively reasonable.[81] Appointing authorities applying the UNCITRAL Rules have noted that disqualification may be warranted for 'prudential' concerns in order to help ensure the arbitration's perceived legitimacy.[82]

IV. Conclusion

14.43. The right to challenge an arbitrator is an essential part of arbitral due process. Especially, a right to an independent and impartial arbitrator is a fundamental right incorporated in the fair trial principle of Art. 6 of the Human Rights Convention. Even if the right to challenge should be limited only to those cases in which there is a real threat to the integrity of the arbitration procedure, this right to challenge the arbitrator is often misused by the parties to delay the proceedings and postpone a negative decision of the dispute. That is why the parties have to primarily anticipate this when concluding the arbitration agreement and should regulate the situation when a party raises a challenge to an arbitrator

14.44. When they do not obey it, they have to count on the rules which govern the proceedings. Primarily, the challenge procedure depends on whether it is carried out in *ad hoc* arbitration or institutional arbitration. Whereas *ad hoc* arbitration is arbitration conducted exclusively according to an arbitration agreement, which does not refer to rules of an arbitral institution, institutional arbitration is conducted according to procedural rules rendered by the arbitral institution, e.g. ICC, LCIA or DIS.

14.45. If the challenge procedure is conducted within the framework of institutional arbitration, the challenge procedure will be supervised and handled by the institution according to its rules. Ultimately, it will probably result in a quick and efficient decision on the challenge to the arbitrator. However, if the challenge procedure is conducted in *ad hoc* arbitration, the challenge procedure is primarily subject to an

---

[80] Nathalie Bernasconi-Osterwalder, Lise Johnson, Fiona Marshall, *Arbitrator Independence and Impartiality: Examining the dual role of arbitrator and counsel*, IV ANNUAL FORUM FOR DEVELOPING COUNTRY INVESTMENT NEGOTIATORS BACKGROUND PAPERS NEW DELHI, 27-29 October 2010, at 9.

[81] *ICS v Argentina* (2009), para. 2.

[82] Nathalie Bernasconi-Osterwalder, Lise Johnson, Fiona Marshall, *supra* note 80, at 9.

agreement of the parties. If the parties do not agree on the challenge procedure, the parties are referred to the state courts according to *lex arbitri* within the scope of the court's auxiliary functions. In this case it can be difficult to determine the competent authority to assist the arbitration. This solution might be time consuming and lead to delays in arbitration proceedings, sometimes far beyond the limits of social efficiency. Moreover, this authority may have little or no experience with arbitration.

14.46. That is why it might be worthwhile to agree on some *ad hoc* arbitration rules, such as the UNCITRAL Arbitration rules, which are tailor-made procedural rules for *ad hoc* arbitration that also provide rules for challenge procedures (Art. 13 UNCITRAL Arbitration Rules). Because the UNCITRAL Rules were developed for *ad hoc* arbitration, they do not rely on an internal authority to deal with a challenge procedure. To shield the arbitration from the intervention of national courts, the UNCITRAL Rules created a mechanism for designating an appointing authority. The appointing authority may be chosen by the parties. If there is a failure to do so, the appointing authority is designated by the Secretary-General of the PCA pursuant to Art. 6 paragraph 2 UNCITRAL Arbitration Rules. That appointing authority will ultimately decide the challenge.

|||

Summaries

FRA [*La récusation d'un arbitre dans une procédure d'arbitrage institutionnel et dans une procédure d'arbitrage ad hoc en particulier à la lumière de la nouvelle réglementation de la CNUDCI*]

Le droit à récuser un arbitre est un élément fondamental du droit à un procès équitable. La récusation d'un arbitre diffère dans une procédure d'arbitrage institutionnel et dans une procédure d'arbitrage ad hoc. On s'intéresse ici à ces différences dans la récusation entre l'arbitrage institutionnel et l'arbitrage ad hoc. On analyse également ici les problèmes liés à la récusation. Il n'est pas secondaire que les parties abusent bien souvent de leurs droits à récuser un arbitre pour prolonger la procédure et différer la résolution du litige au détriment d'une des parties, alors que le droit de récusation devrait être limité exclusivement aux cas dans lesquels la menace d'une violation de l'intégrité de la procédure d'arbitrage est réelle. Les parties devraient donc anticiper cette situation au moment de conclure le contrat d'arbitrage en prévoyant des règles lorsqu'une des parties récuse un arbitre. Si les parties ne procèdent pas de cette manière, elles doivent alors se fier aux règles contraignant la procédure. Dans les arbitrages ad hoc, on peut recommander aux parties d'adopter certaines règles, par exemple les Règles d'arbitrage applicables à des arbitrages ad hoc de la CNUDCI. Ce sont des règles de procédure mises au point spécialement pour les arbitrages ad hoc qui codifient en particulier la récusation des arbitres. On a également examiné ici la capacité des Règles d'arbitrage de la CNUDCI à faire obstacle aux problèmes ci-dessus mentionnés.

CZE [**Vyloučení rozhodce v institucionálním rozhodčím řízení a rozhodčím řízení ad hoc s důrazem na novou úpravu v novelizovaném UNCITRAL řádu**]
Právo na vyloučení rozhodce je nezbytnou součástí práva na spravedlivý proces. Vyloučení rozhodce závisí na tom, zda je prováděno v rozhodčím řízení ad hoc nebo institucionálním rozhodčím řízení. Tento článek se zabývá rozdíly mezi řízením o vyloučení rozhodce v ad hoc nebo institucionálním rozhodčím řízení. Navíc analyzuje problémy spojené s tímto řízením. V neposlední řadě, i přesto, že by právo na vyloučení rozhodce mělo být omezeno pouze na případy, kde je skutečná hrozba narušení integrity rozhodčího řízení, je právo na vyloučení rozhodce často zneužíváno stranami k prodlužování řízení a oddálení případného negativního rozhodnutí sporu pro některou z nich. Proto by to strany měly primárně předvídat v době uzavírání rozhodčí smlouvy a měly by upravit situaci, kdy jedna strana vznese námitku vyloučení rozhodce. Pokud tak však strany neučiní, musí se spolehnout na pravidla upravující řízení. V ad hoc rozhodčím řízení lze doporučit stranám dohodnout se na některých pravidlech pro ad hoc rozhodčí řízení, např. UNCITRAL Arbitration Rules. Ty jsou procesními pravidly šitými na míru ad hoc rozhodčímu řízení a upravují také pravidla pro vyloučení rozhodce. V článku jsou analyzovány UNCITRAL Arbitration Rules také z hlediska jejich schopnosti čelit problémům zmiňovaným shora.

| | |

POL [**Wykluczenie arbitra w instytucjonalnym postępowaniu arbitrażowym i postępowaniu arbitrażowym ad hoc, ze szczególnym uwzględnieniem nowych regulacji w znowelizowanym regulaminie UNCITRAL**]
Wykluczenie arbitra zależy od tego, czy dokonuje się go w postępowaniu arbitrażowym ad hoc, czy też w instytucjonalnym postępowaniu arbitrażowym. Jeżeli arbiter jest wykluczany w ramach postępowania instytucjonalnego, dokonuje tego instytucja arbitrażowa na własnych

zasadach. Jeżeli jednak arbiter jest wykluczany w postępowaniu arbitrażowym ad hoc, jego wykluczenie stanowi przede wszystkim przedmiot porozumienia stron. Jeżeli strony nie dojdą do porozumienia, muszą odwołać się do sądu powszechnego zgodnie z lex arbitri, co stanowi przejaw funkcji pomocniczej sądów w postępowaniu arbitrażowym.

DEU [*Der Ausschluss von Schiedsrichtern im institutionellen Schiedsverfahren und im Ad-hoc-Schiedsverfahren, unter Betonung der Neuregelung in der überarbeiteten UNCITRAL-Ordnung*]

Beim Ausschluss von Schiedsrichtern kommt es darauf an, ob dieser im Rahmen eines Ad-hoc-Schiedsverfahrens oder eines institutionellen Schiedsverfahrens ausgeschlossen wird. Im letzteren Fall wird der Ausschluss von der Schiedsinstitution gemäß deren eigenen Regeln vorgenommen. Bei einem Ausschluss eines Schiedsrichters im Ad-hoc-Schiedsverfahren ist der Ausschluss aber primär Sache der Vereinbarung zwischen den Parteien. Falls diese zu keinem Konsens gelangen, werden sie gemäß lex arbitri an die allgemeinen Gerichte verwiesen, die hier in einer Helferrolle innerhalb des Schiedsverfahrens fungieren.

RUS [*Отвод арбитра в институциональном арбитражном разбирательстве и арбитражном разбирательстве ad hoc с учетом поправок, внесенных в Правила ЮНСИТРАЛ*]

Отвод арбитра зависит от того, если это происходит в институциональном арбитражном разбирательстве или в арбитражном разбирательстве ad hoc. В первом случае отвод арбитра осуществляется арбитражным учреждением в соответствии с его правилами. Во втором случае отвод арбитра является в первую очередь предметом договоренности сторон. Не будет ли по данному вопросу между сторонами заключено соглашение, его решение находится в компетенции суда общей юрисдикции на основании lex arbitri в рамках вспомогательной функции судов в арбитражном разбирательстве.

ESP [*Exclusión de un árbitro en un procedimiento de arbitraje institucional y en un procedimiento de arbitraje ad hoc con hincapié en la nueva revisión del Reglamento de la CNUDMI*]

La exclusión de un árbitro depende de si se realiza en un procedimiento de arbitraje ad hoc o en un procedimiento de arbitraje institucional. Si la exclusión del árbitro se realiza en el marco de un procedimiento institucional, la lleva a cabo la institución de arbitraje con arreglo a su normativa. Si, por el contrario, la exclusión del árbitro se realiza en un procedimiento de arbitraje ad hoc, la exclusión del árbitro es principalmente objeto de acuerdo entre las partes. Si las partes no alcanzaran un acuerdo, deberán ir a un tribunal ordinario según la lex arbitri y con arreglo a las funciones auxiliares desempeñadas por los tribunales en un procedimiento de arbitraje.

| | |

Case Law

I. Case Law of Czech Courts on Independence and Impartiality of Arbitrators and on Appointment of Arbitrators

Alexander J. Bělohlávek

Abbreviations

ArbAct [CZE]	Act [Czech Republic] No. 216/1994 Coll., on Arbitration and Enforcement of Arbitral Awards, as subsequently amended.[1]
CC [CZE]	Act [Czech Republic] No. 40/1964 Coll., as subsequently amended, Civil Code.[2]
CCP [CZE]	Act [Czech Republic] No. 99/1963 Coll., as subsequently amended, Code of Civil Procedure.
CZE	Czech Republic
ESP	Spain
NYConv	Convention on the Recognition and Enforcement of Foreign Arbitral Awards, the New York Convention.[3]

1. Judgment of the Regional Court in Olomouc (in the statement of grounds) No 22 Cm 18/2001-90 of 30 May 2001 (upheld by the Resolution of the High Court in Olomouc of 10 October 2001)[4]

Key words:
independence | impartiality | entities other than a permanent arbitral institution | lists of arbitrators | entry in the list of arbitrators

15.01. A challenge raised on account of doubts about the independent and impartial decision making of an arbitrator registered in the list of arbitrators maintained by a private entity other than a permanent arbitral institution[5] is legally meaningless if no other good reason is given

---

[1] See also the 'Amendment to the ArbAct'.

[2] Replaced with a new Code. The New Civil Code replaced the CC [CZE] with effect from 1 January 2014.

[3] See the Minister of Foreign Affairs Decree No. 74/1959 Coll. [CZE], available online in English at: http://www.uncitral.org/uncitral/en/uncitral_texts/arbitration/NYConvention.html.

[4] M. Doubrava, *Rozhodčí řízení – jmenování rozhodce* (Arbitration – Appointment of an Arbitrator), 3(8) JURISPRUDENCE 32–34 (2001).

[5] See the commentary on Sections 7 and 13 of the ArbAct [CZE].

as to why the person in question should not be appointed as arbitrator. Likewise, the mere inclusion of an arbitrator chosen by the claimant and the inclusion of the claimant's legal representative in the same list of arbitrators in which lawyers from across the Czech Republic are registered is not a reason to doubt their impartial decision making.

2. Judgment of the Constitutional Court of the Czech Republic No II. ÚS 105/01 of 3 July 2001[6]

Key words:

requirements for judges | independence | impartiality | person participating in proceedings | the relationship of economic dependence

15.02. (1) A judge, as a representative of public authority,[7] may be (and often is) a target of unjustified criticism in the media; at the same time, however, a higher degree of tolerance and perspective than for individual citizens should be anticipated and demanded. It should also be taken into account that the principle of independent, impartial and fair decision making is essential for the functioning of the judiciary, and judges have a legal, constitutional, and moral duty to observe this principle.

15.03. (2) A judge may be disqualified from hearing and adjudicating on a case only when it is evident that the judge's relationship to the case, the parties, or their representatives is of such a nature and intensity that, notwithstanding his statutory obligations, he will have neither the ability nor the capacity to decide independently and impartially. These are clearly cases where the judge is also on the side of a party or witness or where his rights could be prejudiced in the proceedings; this equally applies if the judge has family, friendly, or manifestly hostile relations or a relationship of economic dependence with the parties to the proceedings.

[Author's Note]

15.04. This decision was included in the review of case law simply for comparison, as it solely affects judges as public-law persons. The personality characteristics that a judge should have are considerably influenced in arbitration by the autonomy of the parties; the right to choose (designate/appoint) a particular arbitrator or to participate (while taking into account the principle of equality and the full exercise of

---

[6] Sbírka rozhodnutí (ústavní) (Collection of Rulings (Constitutional)), Orac (now LexisNexis CZ), 2004, No 52.

[7] Arbitrators and arbitral tribunals are bodies, but not bodies of public authority. The view held by the ConCourt in its case law should therefore be considered only to the relevant degree, taking into account the specifics of arbitration, the constitution of the forum empowered and entitled to hear and adjudicate on a case in arbitration, etc.

rights) in the designation/appointment thereof is one of the fundamental principles of arbitration. It could be inferred that the principle of independent, impartial, and fair decision making has essentially the same basis and the same character in arbitration as in judicial proceedings. This particularly holds true following the change in the constitutional concept behind the classification of arbitration as adopted by the Constitutional Court of the Czech Republic in 2011. The conclusions in question can certainly also be applied to arbitration from the perspective of the unacceptability of combining the status of an arbitrator with any other person participating in the proceedings, as well as issues of "economic dependence". Nevertheless, considerable caution should be exercised in terms of personal ties between arbitrators and, in particular, procedural counsels, because arbitrators actively practice in a relatively closed community of people who are involved in this area, so "personal acquaintance" is the very least that should be expected.

3. Resolution of the Supreme Court of the Czech Republic No 32 Cdo 2282/2008 of 31 July 2008[8]

Key words:
designation of an arbitrator | method of designation of an arbitrator

15.05. (1) Adjudication of a dispute in arbitration is not a violation of Article 36(1) of the Charter of Basic Rights and Freedoms[9] provided that the

---

[8] Preceded by the following rulings: (i) Resolution of the Regional Court in Brno No 25 Cm 101/2007-24 of 11 October 2007; (ii) Resolution of the High Court in Olomouc No 7 Cmo 452/07-40 of 23 January 2008. The Supreme Court agreed with the conclusions reached by previous courts; the appeal on a point of law was partly dismissed (the decision on the merits) and partly rejected (the decision on costs). The arbitration clause was included in the "General Terms and Conditions of the Financial Leasing of Tangible Assets". The text was as follows (as quoted in the statement of grounds of the Supreme Court's order): "The lessor and the lessee agree that property disputes arising in connection with the lease contract shall be resolved according to applicable Czech law by an arbitrator selected by the claimant from the list of arbitrators maintained by the Association of Leasing Companies of the Czech Republic." See also: *IA. Přehled rozhodnutí Nejvyššího soudu ČR neschválených v roce 2010 do sbírky soudních rozhodnutí a stanovisek* (*Overview of Decisions Rendered by the Supreme Court of the Czech Republic in 2010 Not Selected for Publication in the Collection of Court Rulings and Opinions*), 17(2) SOUDNÍ ROZHLEDY 41, 44 (2011). Note from the cited annotation: The decision was not accepted for publication in the Collection, but was discussed together with the Resolution of the High Court in Prague No 12 Cmo 496/2008 of 28 May 2009, which maintained the opposite view. Also quoted, for example, in: Jan Kocina, *Rozhodčí doložky sjednané ve prospěch „soukromých rozhodčích soudů"* (*Arbitration Clauses Agreed for the Benefit of 'Private Arbitration Courts'*), (7-8) BULLETIN ADVOKACIE 48–49 (2011).

parties have the opportunity to influence which arbitrator (or a group of arbitrators) will be adjudicating on their rights and obligations in accordance with a valid arbitration agreement as defined in Section 2 of the ArbAct [CZE].[10] In this respect, the relatively broad requirements imposed by Sections 4 and 8 of the ArbAct [CZE][11] on the person of an

---

[9]   Charter of Rights and Freedoms of the Czech Republic – Resolution of the Presidium of the Czech National Council No. 2/1993 Coll. of 16 December 1992 on the promulgation of the Charter of Fundamental Rights and Freedoms as a part of the constitutional order of the Czech Republic, as amended by the Constitutional Act of the Czech Republic No. 162/1998 Coll.

[10]   Section 2 ArbAct [CZE] reads in unofficial translation: (1) The parties are free to agree that their property disputes, except disputes arising from the enforcement of decisions and except incidental disputes, which would otherwise fall within the jurisdiction of the courts or which are subject to arbitration under special laws, shall be decided by one or more arbitrators or by a permanent arbitral institution (arbitration agreement). (2) The arbitration agreement will be valid if the law allows the parties to resolve the subject matter of their dispute by settlement.[1)][1) Section 99 of the CCP [CZE].] (3) The arbitration agreement may apply to: (a) an individual dispute which has already arisen (post-dispute arbitration agreement), or (b) all disputes which would arise in the future under a defined legal relationship or under a defined category of legal relationships (arbitration clause). (4) Unless the arbitration agreement stipulates otherwise, it governs both the rights directly arising from the legal relationships and the issue of the legal validity of these legal relationships, as well as any rights associated with the aforementioned rights. (5) The arbitration agreement is also binding upon the legal successors to the parties, unless explicitly excluded by the parties in their agreement.

[11]   Section 4 ArbAct [CZE] reads in unofficial translation: (1) Any citizen of the Czech Republic who is of legal age, has a clean criminal record and has legal capacity can act as an arbitrator unless a special law[1)] stipulates otherwise. (2) A foreigner may act as an arbitrator if he or she meets the condition of majority, clean criminal record and legal capacity; the requirement of legal capacity shall be governed by the person's lex patriae. It shall suffice, however, if he or she has legal capacity under the laws of the Czech Republic. (3) In order to meet the requirement of a clean criminal record under subsections (1) and (2), the person must have no previous final and conclusive conviction for a criminal offense unless the person's criminal record is expunged and the person is deemed never to have been convicted. (4) An arbitrator designated by an arbitration clause to resolve disputes arising from consumer contracts must be registered in the list of arbitrators administered by the Ministry of Justice ("Ministry"). [Author´s note: an amendment to the Section 4 ArbAct [CZE] expected.]

Section 8 ArbAct [CZE] reads in unofficial translation: (1) An arbitrator shall be disqualified from hearing and adjudicating on a case where, in view of his relationship to the case, the participants, or their representatives, there are reasons to doubt lack of bias on his part. (2) A person who is to be or has been nominated or appointed as an arbitrator shall notify the parties or the institution without delay of any and all circumstances which could give rise to legitimate doubts regarding the lack of bias on his part and for which he would be disqualified as an arbitrator. (3) When adjudicating on disputes arising from consumer contracts, an arbitrator shall inform the parties before the hearing of whether he has rendered or contributed to the rendering of an arbitral award in the past three years, or whether he is an arbitrator in arbitration pending in respect of a dispute to which any of

arbitrator and on the determination of the number and persons of the arbitrators (or the method to determine the number and persons of the arbitrators) within the meaning of Section 7 of the ArbAct [CZE] are intended to aid the parties.

15.06. **(2)** Arbitration pursuant to the ArbAct [CZE] allows the parties to exclude certain disputes from the jurisdiction of courts and to subject them to special proceedings in which such disputes will be resolved by private persons – one or more arbitrators, or a permanent arbitral institution. In order to attain this objective, the parties are endowed with contractual freedom which allows them to define the types of disputes they will submit to the jurisdiction of arbitrators and agree whether the dispute will be resolved by one or more arbitrators or a permanent arbitral tribunal (Section 2(1) of the ArbAct [CZE]).[12]

15.07. **(3)** The Arbitration Act does not stipulate that if the parties did not agree on the jurisdiction of a permanent arbitral institution, then they must name a [particular] arbitrator. The parties may (but do not have to) agree on the names of particular arbitrators. The disadvantage of such an arbitration clause is that the period from the conclusion of the clause to the moment a dispute arises may be quite long, and it is not possible to rule out the possibility that the appointed arbitrator may become ineligible for (may be disqualified from executing) the office of arbitrator. This is the reason for the mechanism pursuant to Section 7(1) of the ArbAct [CZE][13] (as in the present case), which determines the method of selecting a particular arbitrator for the resolution of future disputes. Whether the parties decide to have their potential disputes resolved by an arbitrator(s) registered in a list administered by permanent arbitral institutions or other private-law entities, it is up to the parties' agreement.

15.08. **(4)** The parties may agree in their arbitration agreement on the number of arbitrators and their identity or determine the method of their appointment. However, if the parties fail to agree on the number and identity of the arbitrators, then it is necessary to apply the rule incorporated in Section 7(2) of the ArbAct [CZE],[14] according to which each of the parties appoints one arbitrator and these two arbitrators elect the presiding arbitrator.

---

the participants has been or is a party. The time limit under the preceding sentence shall be calculated from the date of termination of arbitration covered by the obligation to provide information until the date of commencement of the arbitration in which the arbitrator is bound by the obligation to provide information.

[12] Provision cited above.
[13] Provision cited above.
[14] Provision cited above.

15.09. (5) If the parties agreed that disputes arising from the lease agreement would be resolved by an arbitrator chosen by the claimant from a list of arbitrators administered by the Czech Association of Leasing Companies and not by an arbitral tribunal within the meaning of Section 13 of the ArbAct [CZE],[15] then it is not possible to accept the claimant's objection that the "mechanism whereby the arbitrator(s) will be chosen [...] must be agreed explicitly and unambiguously", providing that the mechanism must be created by a permanent arbitral institution established by law pursuant to Section 13(1) of the ArbAct [CZE]. [16] Whereas private entities other than permanent arbitral institutions established pursuant to Section 13(1) ArAct[17] of the ArbAct [CZE] are also entitled to administer a list of arbitrators and to issue rules for the parties to the arbitration which are binding upon the arbitrators, the parties have agreed that the arbitrator, who will resolve their potential disputes arising from their lease agreement, will be chosen from a list administered by the Czech Association of Leasing Companies, instead of a list administered by a permanent arbitral institution.[18]

---

[15] Section 13 ArbAct [CZE] reads in unofficial translation: (1) Permanent arbitral institutions may only be established by another law or only if another law expressly allows their establishment. (2) Permanent arbitral institutions can issue their own statutes and rules which must be published in the Business Journal[3)]; these statutes and rules may determine the method of appointment and the number of arbitrators and may stipulate that the arbitrators shall be selected from a list administered by the permanent arbitral institution. The statutes and rules may also determine how the arbitrators shall conduct the proceedings and render their decisions, as well as resolve other issues connected with the activities of the permanent arbitral institution and the arbitrators, including rules regulating the costs of proceedings and fees for the arbitrators. (3) If the parties agreed on the jurisdiction of a particular permanent arbitral institution and failed to agree otherwise in the arbitration agreement, they shall be deemed to have submitted to the regulations specified in subsection (2), as applicable on the day of commencement of the proceedings in the permanent arbitral institution. (4) No entity may carry out its activities using a name which evokes a misleading impression that the entity is a permanent arbitral institution under this law unless a different law or regulation or an international agreement integrated in the legal system authorizes the entity to use the name.

[16] Provision cited above.

[17] Provision cited above.

[18] In connection with this legal opinion of the SC (the *ratio decidendi* quoted above), it is necessary to mention the correction made by the SC in its later case law (although mainly targeted at disputes arising from contracts concluded with consumers). Consequently, the author points out that the opinion (expressed in this particular paragraph) was, in a certain regard, somewhat superseded by subsequent case law. In this connection, see the note attached to the specification of this decision after the courts accepted Resolution of the HC in Prague, Case No. 12 Cmo 496/2008 of 28 May 2009 (also published in the Reports).

4. Resolution of the High Court in Prague, Case No. 12 Cmo 496/2008 of 28 May 2009

Key words:

agreement on arbitrator | permanent arbitral institution | method of selecting (identifying) arbitrator | rules on procedure | "ad hoc" arbitration

15.10. (1) In their arbitration agreement, the parties must agree on (an) *ad hoc* arbitrator(s) or on a permanent arbitral institution established under the law (Section 2(1) of the ArbAct [CZE]).[19] An *ad hoc* arbitrator, or arbitrators should there be more than one, must always be (a) natural person(s)[20] and be identified directly in the arbitration agreement, or the arbitration agreement can define the method of appointment and the number of arbitrators.[21]

15.11. (2) The determination of the method of appointment of the arbitrator must be interpreted only as a determination of such method of appointment which does not depend exclusively on the will of only one party, as the principle is articulated in Section 269(3) of the Commercial Code of the Czech Republic.

15.12. (3) As opposed to arbitrators appointed *ad hoc*, permanent arbitral institutions may issue their own rules (statutes and rules) which may set forth the process of appointment and determine the number of arbitrators (the arbitrators can be selected from a list), as well as stipulate the manner whereby the arbitrators shall case manage the proceedings and the costs of arbitration payable by the parties. These rules (statutes and rules) must be published in the *Business Journal*, and the arbitrators' decisions are rendered pursuant to the above-mentioned rules of the permanent arbitral institution, as applicable on the day the request for arbitration (statement of claim) is filed with the arbitral institution. Unless the parties agree otherwise, the permanent arbitral institution shall follow said rules.

15.13. (4) A permanent arbitral institution follows its own rules (statutes and rules) published in the *Business Journal*, unless the parties agree otherwise.

15.14. (5) If an entity other than a permanent arbitral institution established under a special law,[22] as anticipated under Section 13 of the ArbAct

---

[19] Provision cited above.

[20] Section 4 of the ArbAct [CZE].

[21] Section 7(1) of the ArbAct [CZE].

[22] This phrase used in the resolution of the High Court in Prague [CZE] is closer to the wording of the ArbAct [CZE] (Section 13(1) of the ArbAct [CZE]), after the Amendment to the ArbAct [CZE] rather than before the Amendment.

[CZE],[23] carries out activities which, according to the ArbAct [CZE], are reserved for permanent arbitral institutions, the entity clearly intends to evade the law and the entity's conduct is contra legem.

15.15. (6) An entity other than a permanent arbitral institution (Section 13 of the ArbAct [CZE])[24] is not entitled to issue its own statutes and rules which would govern the case management of the proceedings and set forth provisions, binding on the parties and applicable unless the parties agree otherwise, which provide for the costs of proceedings and the remuneration of the arbitrators.

15.16. (7) The fact that arbitration principally involves (oral) hearings (Section 19(3) of the ArbAct [CZE])[25] is, from the procedural perspective, a very important requirement. If the proceedings are to be conducted on the basis of written submissions (although the arbitrators have the possibility to summon the parties to an oral hearing, if necessary), such procedure must be explicitly agreed in the arbitration agreement. Only proceedings before a permanent arbitral institution allow that such procedure be agreed by a mere reference to the statutes (rules) of this permanent arbitral institution.

[Factual and legal findings and the trial court's decision]

15.17. The trial court issued a special payment order for bills of exchange / promissory notes.[26] The respondent lodged his objections, especially challenging the jurisdiction of the court. The respondent invoked an arbitration clause contained in the parties' contract (contract on the reservation of real property and the provision of assistance in the

---

[23] Provision cited above.

[24] Provision cited above.

[25] Section 19 ArbAct [CZE] reads in unofficial translation: (1) The parties may agree on the procedure to be followed by the arbitrators in conducting the proceedings. Matters regarding the proceedings may be resolved by the presiding arbitrator if he has been authorized to do so by the parties or by all arbitrators. (2) In the absence of an agreement pursuant to paragraph (1) or in the absence of a determination of the procedure pursuant to paragraph (4), the arbitrators shall conduct the proceedings as they see fit. They shall conduct the arbitral proceedings in such a manner that the facts of the case necessary for the resolution of the dispute are ascertained without any unnecessary formalities and while giving all parties equal opportunity to plead their case. (3) Unless the parties agree otherwise, the arbitral proceedings shall be oral. In all cases, proceedings shall be conducted to the exclusion of the public. (4) The parties may also determine the procedure to be followed in the rules on arbitration, provided that the rules are annexed to the arbitration agreement. This provision shall not prejudice the application of rules adopted by a permanent arbitral institution.

[26] Payment order for bills of exchange / promissory notes issued by the Regional Court in Hradec Králové, Case No. 52 Cm 159/2008-9 of 10 September 2008.

purchase of real property[27]). The court found the arbitration clause valid, cancelled its own payment order, and terminated the proceedings.[28] The arbitration clause stipulated that *"[a]ny and all potential disputes which arise from or in connection with this contract (including potential disputes over the validity of this contract or the arbitration clause) shall be resolved by a sole arbitrator, in compliance with the [ArbAct]. The parties have agreed that the arbitral proceedings shall be conducted pursuant to the Arbitration Rules issued by [XY s. r. o.][29] and that the arbitrator shall be selected by the claimant from a list of arbitrators administered by [XY s. r. o.], with its registered office [in xxx, Company ID No. yyy]"*.[30]

[Appeal and decision of the court of appeals]

15.18.   (•) The claimant appealed against the resolution terminating the proceedings; the claimant argued that a bill of exchange (promissory note) belonged to the category of abstract securities (negotiable instruments) and, as such, contained no arbitration clause. The claimant (appellant) argued that the trial court had erroneously inferred that an arbitration clause incorporated in a contract also covered the relationship established by the bill of exchange.

15.19.   (•) The court of appeals set aside the resolution terminating the proceedings. However, the court focused on the issue of validity of the arbitration clause (arbitration agreement) as a preliminary question. The court discovered that the entity (legal person / *XY s.r.o.*), which the arbitration agreement referred to, was not a permanent arbitral institution. The court of appeals therefore proceeded to the issue of whether the parties had agreed in their arbitration clause that their dispute was to be resolved by (an) arbitrator(s) appointed *ad hoc*. Only a positive answer to this question would preserve the validity of the arbitration agreement; the court maintained that the parties must either agree on an *ad hoc* arbitrator or on the jurisdiction of a permanent arbitral institution.

15.20.   (•) The court highlighted that the parties had not agreed on any particular arbitrator but had authorized the party who would file the request for arbitration (statement of claim) with *[XY s.r.o.]*[31] to choose a

---

[27]   The contract was entered into on 7 April 2008.

[28]   Decision of the Regional Court in Hradec Králové, Pardubice Office, Case No. 36 Cm 197/2008-16 of 10 October 2008.

[29]   Made anonymous by the author. The case concerned a corporation which was not a permanent arbitral institution pursuant to Section 13 of the ArbAct [CZE].

[30]   Made anonymous by the author.

[31]   Abbreviation 's.r.o.' means 'a Limited Liability Company'.

single arbitrator from a list of arbitrators administered by said company. However, the possibility to maintain a list of arbitrators is reserved exclusively for permanent arbitral institutions, not for an entity which does not belong to that category. It is also necessary to point out that the determination of the method of appointment of arbitrator must be interpreted only as a determination of such method of appointment which does not depend exclusively on the will of one party only, as the principle is articulated in Section 269(3) of the Commercial Code Czech Republic.[32]

15.21. (▪) The court therefore concluded that in the present case the parties had neither agreed on the jurisdiction of a permanent arbitral institution nor on an *ad hoc* arbitrator. The court also held that, considering the conduct and the rules adopted by [*XY s.r.o.*], the entity assumed the powers ("copied" the activities) of a permanent arbitral institution whereby the entity evaded Section 13 of the ArbAct [CZE].[33] Consequently, if the arbitration agreement lacks any direct identification of an *ad hoc* arbitrator or a specific description of the method of his or her appointment and merely refers, as concerns the selection of the arbitrator and determination of the rules of arbitration, to a legal entity other than a permanent arbitral institution established under the law, and refers to statutes and rules adopted by that corporation which provide for the appointment and selection of arbitrators, as well as the case management of arbitration and the rules governing the costs of proceedings, then the arbitration agreement is invalid pursuant to Section 39 of the CC [CZE], for evading the law. The arbitration agreement in the present case was therefore invalid, and it was not necessary to examine whether the invalid arbitration agreement also covered disputes relating to the contested bill of exchange or not. Due to the fact that the arbitration agreement was invalid, the court was obliged to hear the respective property dispute pursuant to Section 106(1) of the Code on Civil Procedure Czech Republic.

---

[32] The author believes that a reference to Section 7 of the ArbAct [CZE] is more suitable.
[33] Provision cited above.

5. Resolution of the Supreme Court of the Czech Republic, Case No. 23 Cdo 4967/2007 of 23 September 2009[34]

Key words:
entertaining a dispute before the body of a professional association

15.22. (1) If the parties conclude a work agreement in which they agree that any potential disputes arising from the agreement shall be resolved by a particular body (Professional Tribunal of the Czech Chamber of Architects) before the parties file their claims with a court, then failure to adhere to this agreement does not affect the jurisdiction of courts to hear and resolve the case (Section 7 of the CCP [CZE]).[35]

15.23. (2) Such an agreement is not an arbitration clause which would exclude the jurisdiction of courts. (Section 106 of the CCP [CZE]).

6. Resolution of the Supreme Court of the Czech Republic, Case No. 23 Cdo 1175/2008 of 28 January 2009[36]

Key words:
sole arbitrator | arbitrator challenge | agreement on the identity of the sole arbitrator | appointment of the sole arbitrator by a third party | annulment of arbitral award | unauthorized arbitrator

15.24. (1) If the appointment of the sole arbitrator (here by the Chairman of the AC pursuant to Section 21(4) of the Domestic Rules) is contingent on a condition that the parties fail to agree on the sole arbitrator, then

---

[34] The jurisdiction of the conciliation and arbitration commissions of sports associations can be considered a similar issue. Concerning this topic, see for instance the Resolution of the Supreme Court of the Czech Republic, Case No. 28 Cdo 2916/2006 and the Decision of the RC in Hradec Králové, Case No. 23 Co 148/2011 of 30 March 2011.

[35] Adopted from Jan Hušek. *Z rozhodovací praxe – Soudy České republiky: III. Pravomoc soudu – sjednání předchozího řešení sporu před stavovským soudem České komory architektů (Case Law – Courts of the Czech Republic: III. Jurisdiction of Courts – Agreement on a Preceding Resolution of the Dispute by the Professional Court of the Czech Chamber of Architects)*, 18(11) OBCHODNÍ PRÁVO 27, 27 (2009).

[36] The preceding stages of the litigation also involved the following decisions:
▶ Judgment of the District Court for Prague 1, Case No. 24 C 184/2005-56 of 14 February 2007: The first-instance court ordered enforcement of the arbitral award. This judgment dismissed the motion to annul the arbitral award rendered in arbitration at the Arbitration Court attached to the Economic Chamber of the Czech Republic and Agrarian Chamber of the Czech Republic under Case Docket Rsp 170/04 of 4 May 2005;
▶ Resolution of the Municipal Court in Prague, Case No. 20 Co 313/2007-69 of 8 November 2007: The court upheld the decision of the first-instance court.

it is necessary to examine whether the parties had attempted to conclude such agreement. If the claimant refused to conclude the agreement on the sole arbitrator in the arbitral proceedings, then it is necessary to examine the claimant's refusal. In proceedings for annulment of an arbitral award pursuant to Section 31(c) of the ArbAct [CZE],[37] as a question of fact the court examines whether one of the parties refused to agree on the arbitrator. It shall not suffice if the claimant (claimant in the arbitral proceedings, i.e. respondent in the proceedings for annulment of arbitral award), merely resigns on the agreement regarding the sole arbitrator by commencing proceedings with an arbitral tribunal.[38]

15.25. **(2)** When considering the fulfillment of the requirements under Section 33 of the ArbAct[39] [CZE] for a motion to annul an arbitral award pursuant to Section 31(c) of the ArbAct [CZE], it is necessary to examine the actual contents of the challenge made in the arbitral proceedings. If the respondent (in the arbitral proceedings) challenged the jurisdiction of the arbitral tribunal, but the objection also included

---

[37] Section 31 ArbAct [CZE] reads in unofficial translation: At the request of any party the court annuls the arbitral award if: (a) It was made in a case which cannot be submitted to arbitration (cannot be the subject of a valid arbitration agreement); (b) The arbitration agreement is invalid for other reasons, the agreement was cancelled, or it does not apply to the agreed case; (c) The arbitrator(s) who took part in the proceedings was/were not authorized to make decisions in the case, whether under the arbitration agreement or otherwise, or lacked the capacity to act as arbitrator(s); (d) The arbitral award was not adopted by the majority of the arbitrators; (e) A party was denied the opportunity to plead his or her case in the arbitral proceedings; (f) The arbitral award orders a party to provide performance which was not requested by the creditor or to provide performance which is impossible or illegal under domestic law; (g) The arbitrator or the permanent arbitral institution resolved a dispute arising from a consumer contract contrary to consumer protection laws, clearly in violation of good morals, or contrary to public policy; (h) An arbitration agreement relating to disputes arising from consumer contracts lacks the information required under Section 3(5) or such information is intentionally or to a non-negligible extent incomplete, inaccurate, or false; or (i) It transpires that there are reasons which would otherwise justify the reopening of civil proceedings in court[4] [4] Section 228(1)(a) and (b) of the CCP [CZE].].

[38] In his request for arbitration (statement of claim) whereby the arbitration was commenced pursuant to Section 14 of the ArbAct [CZE], the claimant stated as follows (cit. from the reasons for the Supreme Court of the Czech Republic decision): *"Considering the fact that the claimant does not expect to agree with the respondent on any particular arbitrator, the claimant hereby notifies the above-mentioned Court that the claimant agrees with the arbitrator who will be appointed by the Chairman of the Arbitration Court."*

[39] Section 33 ArbAct reads in unofficial translation: The court shall dismiss a motion to annul an arbitral award which is based on the grounds specified in Section 31(b) or (c) if the party requesting the annulment failed to raise the corresponding objection in the arbitral proceedings before the party's first act in the merits of the case, despite having an opportunity to do so. This does not apply to disputes arising from consumer contracts.

a refusal of the sole arbitrator, then the respondent has satisfied the requirements for demanding annulment of the arbitral award pursuant to Section 31(c) of the ArbAct [CZE].[40]

7. Resolution of the Constitutional Court of the Czech Republic No III. ÚS 1208/2010 of 3 June 2010

Key words:
economic dependence of the arbitrator | tendentious decision making | burden of pleading and proving the facts

15.26. (1) Where the claimant challenges the overall system for the selection of arbitrators from the list maintained on the grounds that the arbitrators, for economic reasons, make tendentious decisions, doubts about the lack of bias of arbitrators could generally arise only if there were specific facts to suggest this hypothesis.

15.27. (2) Otherwise, this would merely constitute disagreement with the arbitration clause.

15.28. (3) The parties are required to confirm and prove any tendentious decision making by the arbitrators.

8. Judgment of the District Court for Prague 5 No 10 C 263/2003 of 20 October 2003 (upheld by the Judgment of the Municipal Court in Prague No 18 Co 18/2004 of 2 April 2004)

Key words:
nature of court proceedings on the disqualification of an arbitrator | parties to court proceedings | status of arbitrators in court proceedings pursuant to Section 12(2) of the ArbAct [CZE]

15.29. Claimant X, who had the procedural status of the respondent in *ad hoc* arbitration, filed an application with the court, within the meaning of the second sentence of Section 12(2) of the ArbAct [CZE],[41] which was directed against all arbitrators in the tribunal which had been constituted in the meantime. The claimant identified all members of the tribunal, i.e. all the arbitrators, as the respondent in these court proceedings. The application was rejected as the respondents (the respondents/arbitrators) lacked standing to defend themselves in court.

---

[40] In this connection, the court of appeals held that the requirements of Section 33 of the ArbAct [CZE] were not fulfilled.
[41] Provision cited above.

According to the statement of grounds drawn up by the first-instance court, it is necessary to take into account Section 12(2) of the ArbAct [CZE][42] and Section 159a(1) of the CCP [CZE] Czech Republic, under which, unless otherwise provided by law, the operative part of a final judgment is binding only on the parties. It follows from Section 12(2) of the ArbAct [CZE][43] in conjunction with Section 159a(1) of the CCP [CZE] Czech Republic that the other participant in the arbitration must be a party to court proceedings as the respondent, otherwise the court's decision would not be binding on that participant and therefore would be of no relevance to the arbitration. The group of participants in court proceedings must be the same as the group of participants in arbitration. As an arbitrator is not classified as a participant in arbitration, he lacks standing to defend himself in court in such a dispute. In these proceedings, the group of participants is determined by Section 90 of the CCP; therefore, the definition of the group of participants in court proceedings is up to the claimant, i.e. the group of participants is not determined by law as laid down in Section 94 of the CCP.

9. Resolution of the SC No 29 Odo 430/2005 of 26 July 2005:[44]

Key words:
nature of the court's decision | relationship to court proceedings on the merits

15.30. Although the decision on whether the arbitrators are disqualified from hearing the case (Section 12(2) of the Act)[45] ends the court proceedings,

---

[42] Section 12 ArbAct [CZE] reads in unofficial translation: (1) A designated or appointed arbitrator with respect to whom the circumstances stipulated in Section 11 have transpired shall resign from the office of arbitrator. (2) If an arbitrator fails to resign, the parties may agree on procedure for the disqualification of that arbitrator. Any of the parties may lodge a motion petitioning a court to rule on the disqualification.

[43] Provision cited above.

[44] Soubor civilních rozhodnutí a stanovisek Nejvyššího soudu (*Collection of Civil Decisions and Opinions of the Supreme Court*), Prague: C. H. Beck, 2008, case law Reference RNs C3819, 2007, Installment Number CD_3. See also Pavel Vrcha, *Malá poznámka k charakteru řízení o jmenování rozhodce podle zákona o rozhodčím řízení (A Small Note on the Nature of Procedure for the Appointment of an Arbitrator under the Arbitration Act)*, (7) SOUDNÍ ROZHLEDY 248 (2006), though the author of the cited paper primarily offers a clearly much needed opinion on the proceedings under Section 9 of the ArbAct [CZE] in response to the Resolution of the Regional Court in Brno, Zlín Branch, No 60 Cdo 125/2005 (cited in the commentary on Section 9 of the ArbAct [CZE]) and in response to the observations made on this last-cited piece of case law by the author M. Králík in: (1) SOUDNÍ ROZHLEDY 2006.

[45] Provision cited above.

this is only a procedural decision. This decision cannot be applied to any questions raised in the arbitration proceedings on the merits.

10. Resolution of the Constitutional Court of the Czech Republic, Case No. IV. ÚS 189/10 of 10 May 2010

15.31. (1) (a) The state of recognition is allowed to review the arbitral award from the perspective of compliance of its effects with the fundamental principles of the state's law [public policy exception pursuant to Article V(2)(b) of the NYConv].

15.32. (1) (b) Due to the absence of any uniform and internationally recognized definition of public policy, the term must be interpreted [in each individual case] consistently with jurisprudence and practice in the particular country of recognition and enforcement. Generally, a conflict with public policy would occur if the enforceability of the arbitral award were contrary to the fundamental principles of the constitutional and legal order, the social order, and public policy as such, and the breach would concern an interest which must be insisted on, unequivocally and in every respect.

15.33. (1) (c) A conflict with public policy arises in those cases where the fundamental rights of the party to the proceedings were breached in the proceedings in which the respective decision of the foreign court was rendered.[46] Insistence on the protection of the individual's fundamental rights undoubtedly belongs to such essential principles of Czech law.[47]

15.34. (1) (d) The concept of public policy ought to be interpreted in a relatively restrictive manner; mere differences in the procedural laws of a foreign arbitral tribunal and the state of recognition do not establish a conflict with public policy.[48]

---

[46] The author is of the opinion that the Constitutional Court of the Czech Republic adjudicated correctly, i.e. that Article V(2)(b) of the NYConv mainly covers procedural public policy, i.e. the issue of whether overriding fundamental procedural standards were observed in the proceedings.

[47] The Constitutional Court invoked the Judgment of the Constitutional Court of the Czech Republic, Case No. I. ÚS 709/05, published in: 41 Sb.n.u. (*Reports of Judgments and Resolutions*), at 143.

[48] The Constitutional Court held that, if the court of the state of origin proceeded in compliance with procedural laws, a conflict with public policy is only possible in the most exceptional cases. The Constitutional Court of the Czech Republic invoked: Viktor Vaške, *Uznání a výkon cizích rozhodnutí v České republice* (*Recognition and Enforcement of Foreign Decisions in the Czech Republic*), Prague: C. H. Beck 44 (2007). In this connection,

15.35. **(2) (a)** Therefore, an argument stating that other parties to the proceedings were represented by more legal counsels, and consequently incurred higher costs of proceedings, focuses only on the issue of interpretation. Application of the words "reasonable" or "adequate" regarding the costs of proceedings, as such, cannot establish a conflict with constitutional law.

15.36. **(2) (b)** If the applicant argues that the costs which the applicant incurred in the part of the proceedings in which the forum ruled on the disqualification of an arbitrator for being biased were unreasonable, then such objection cannot be found justified. It is certainly in the interest of all parties to the proceedings, including the applicant, to make sure that the proceedings and the decision in the merits do not suffer from any defect which would undermine their correctness and equitableness. It is only natural that the costs are paid by the party who did not have standing in the merits and did not succeed in the proceedings.

15.37. **(3)** An objection criticizing the delivery of an arbitral award by a messenger service, not by the holder of a postal license or in any other manner provided for in the CCP, is formalistic and groundless. The main point is that the arbitral award entered the sphere of the applicant, or his or her legal counsel, in compliance with the [UNCITRAL Rules].

15.38. **(4)** An objection that the arbitral award is not stamped with a confirmation of legal force and effect and the confirmation of enforceability is incongruous. The reason is that the [NYConv], which prevails over statutes, namely Section 39 [of the ArbAct [CZE]], does not prescribe any such requirement (cf. Article IV [of the NYConv]). It is sufficient if the arbitral award is final and binding upon the parties and the parties undertake to perform under the award without delay (cf. Article 32(2) of the UNCITRAL Model Rules).[49]

15.39. **(5)** It is in the interests of all participants in the proceedings for the proceedings and decision on the merits to be free of any defect casting doubt on the correctness and fairness thereof. Proceedings on the disqualification of an arbitrator are therefore proceedings [a stage of proceedings] conducted in the interests of all parties.

[From the factual and legal findings]

15.40. The case concerned enforcement of an LCIA arbitral award. The claims under the award were subject to execution which was ordered pursuant

---

the ConCourt again confirmed that the public policy exception under Article V(2)(b) of the NYConv should rather be interpreted as a procedural public policy exception.

[49] The author has applied the uniform terminology chosen for this book. The original of the Constitutional Court judgment refers to „Rozhodčí řád UNCITRAL" ('UNCITRAL Arbitration Rules').

to Section 44(2) of the Code of Enforcement [*Execution*] Procedure Czech Republic. The court upheld the decision. The applicant argued that the arbitral award was neither final nor enforceable, because it lacked reasons, was not stamped with a confirmation of legal force and effect and a confirmation of enforceability, and the delivery by a messenger service cannot be deemed proper delivery under the CCP [CZE] Czech Republic. The applicant also argued that the award was contrary to public policy due to an excessively high amount of the costs of proceedings to be paid by the applicant and due to the fact that the award practically lacked any reasons. All of the above-said constitutes breach of the right to a fair trial, i.e. conflicts with public policy. In this regard, the applicant also considered it unacceptable that the applicant should share the costs of the proceedings for disqualification of arbitrator whom the applicant did not challenge; moreover, this stage of the proceedings did not concern the merits. The Constitutional Court of the Czech Republic dismissed the constitutional complaint as manifestly unsubstantiated.

11. Resolution of the Supreme Court of the Czech Republic, Case No. 31 Cdo 1945/2010 of 11 May 2011[50]

Key words:
arbitration clause which impairs the position of the "weaker" contracting party | permanent arbitral institutions versus "ad hoc" arbitrators

---

[50] Available at the website of the SC [last access 12 January 2011]. Also published in Sbírka soudních rozhodnutí [Court Reports], 2011, Ref. No. 121. Also cited in: Miloš Tomsa, *K problematice právní úpravy rozhodčího řízení* (*Regarding Laws on* Arbitration), 3(9) OBCHODNĚPRÁVNÍ REVUE 267, 269 (2011). For an annotation, see also: Zbyšek Kordač, *K neplatnosti určení rozhodce ad hoc: Rozsudek Nejvyššího soudu ze dne 11. 5. 2011, sp. zn. 31 Cdo 1945/2010* (*Regarding the Invalidity of Appointment of Ad Hoc Arbitrators: Judgment of the Supreme Court of 11 May 2011, Case No. 31 Cdo 1945/2010*), (4) BULLETIN ADVOKACIE 41 (2012). This decision is also referred to in certain later rulings, for instance in the Resolution of the Supreme Court of the Czech Republic [CZE], Case No. 30 Cdo 4415/2010 of 27 July 2011, etc. It is also necessary to highlight the Judgment of the RC in Brno, Case No. 44 Co 246/2010 of 27 September 2011, which refused the retroactive application of case law if the parties negotiated their arbitration agreement in good faith. The judgment of the Regional Court in Brno [CZE] in: M. Kulhánek, *Krajský soud v Brně: Nepřípustnost retroaktivního využití judikatury (konkrétně k usnesení velkého senátu NS ČR ze dne 11. 5. 2011, sp. zn. 31 Cdo 1945/2010)* (*Regional Court in Brno: Prohibited Retroactive Application of Case Law (Specifically Regarding the Resolution of the Grand Panel of the SC CR of 11 May 2011, Case No. 31 Cdo 1945/2010)),* 20(3) PRÁVNÍ ROZHLEDY 112 (2012), and also annotated in this commentary (Sections 2, 3, 7, 13, and 50 of the ArbAct [CZE]).

15.41. **(1)** The principle of party autonomy[51] must not be (mis)used to negate [the consequences consisting in the invalidity of] arbitration clauses which violate the law and which clearly indicate an intention to harm the "weaker" contracting party (a party to the contractual relationship).[52] A democratic country honoring the principle of the rule of law must not give up on the protection of the rights and legitimate interests which could be jeopardized in alternative proceedings conducted instead of litigation.

15.42. **(2)** If the arbitration agreement lacks any direct identification of an *ad hoc* arbitrator, or a specific description of the method of his or her appointment, and refers to *"Rules on Arbitration"* issued by a legal entity (corporation) other than a permanent arbitral institution established under the law, the arbitration agreement is invalid pursuant to Section 39 of the CC [CZE].[53]

15.43. **(3)** Section 2(1) of the ArbAct [CZE][54] indicates that an arbitration agreement (or a clause incorporated in the main contract, as the case may be) must include the parties' agreement on either (an) *"ad hoc"* arbitrator(s) or a permanent arbitral institution established under the law. **(4)** The *ad hoc* arbitrator must always be a natural person (Section 4 of the ArbAct [CZE]).[55]

15.44. **(5)** The *ad hoc* arbitrator(s) must be identified [by his, her, or their name(s)], or the arbitration agreement (arbitration clause) may define, in compliance with Section 7(1) of the ArbAct [CZE], [56] the method of appointment and the number of arbitrators.

---

[51]   The Supreme Court of the Czech Republic refers to the importance of autonomy pursuant to the legal opinions of the Constitutional Court of the Czech Republic; these constitutional opinions are also quoted elsewhere in this book, and they undoubtedly still apply. However, the Supreme Court of the Czech Republic also invokes the doctrine adjudicated by the Constitutional Court of the Czech Republic, i.e. that the arbitrator (arbitral tribunal) does not find the law but creates (or determines, clarifies, i.e. settles) an obligation (relationship) on behalf of the parties and that the arbitrator's (arbitral tribunal's) powers are not delegated by the sovereign power of the state but originate from the private power of the parties themselves to determine their destiny; however, this conclusion already seems to be superseded, as confirmed by the Judgment of the Constitutional Court of the Czech Republic, Case No. I ÚS 3227/07 of 8 March 2011, which represents revolutionary progress from the contractual concept to the jurisdictional basis of arbitration.

[52]   The SC held that this was the case here.

[53]   This *ratio decidendi* was adopted from the database of the Supreme Court of the Czech Republic (in the section regarding the decision published at the court's website).

[54]   Provision cited above.

[55]   Provision cited above.

[56]   Provision cited above.

15.45. **(6)** As opposed to arbitrators appointed *ad hoc*, [only] permanent arbitral institutions may issue their own rules (statutes and rules) which may set forth the process of appointment and determine the number of arbitrators (the arbitrators can be selected from a list), as well as stipulate the manner whereby the arbitrators shall case manage the proceedings and the costs of arbitration payable by the parties. Such rules must be published in the *Business Journal*. **(7)** If an entity other than a permanent arbitral institution established under a special law (Section 13 of the ArbAct [CZE]) carries out activities which, according to the ArbAct [CZE], are reserved for permanent arbitral institutions, logic dictates that this entity clearly and intentionally violates the law.[57]

15.46. **(8)** Proceedings before a permanent arbitral institution also allow that the parties agree to depart from the rules adopted by the permanent arbitral institution. Unless the parties agree otherwise, the arbitrator(s) shall follow the rules adopted by the permanent arbitral institution, as applicable on the day the request for arbitration (statement of claim) is filed with the arbitral institution.

[From the factual and legal findings and the decisions of the trial court and the court of appeals]

15.47. **(♦)** The parties entered into a real property purchase contract (real property transfer contract); the contract contained an arbitration clause. The arbitration clause stipulated that *"[a]ny and all disputes which arise or could arise between the parties, or any other claims, shall be resolved in arbitration before a sole arbitrator, in compliance with the* [ArbAct [CZE]], *pursuant to the Rules on Arbitration and the Tariff adopted by* [XY, s.r.o.];[58] *the valid version of these documents is available at the website of the above-mentioned association of*

---

[57] See also Jiří Spáčil, *Nejvyšší soud České republiky: Neplatnost rozhodčí smlouvy, která neobsahuje přímé určení rozhodce „ad hoc". Neplatnost rozhodčí smlouvy, kterou si účastníci smluvili, že rozhodce vybere žalující strana ze seznamu vedeného soukromou osobou* (*Supreme Court of the Czech Republic: Invalidity of the Arbitration Agreement Which Lacks Direct Identification of the 'Ad Hoc' Arbitrator. Invalidity of the Arbitration Agreement in Which the Parties Had Agreed that the Arbitrator Shall be Selected by the Claimant from a List Administered by a Private Person*), 3(12) OBCHODNĚPRÁVNÍ REVUE 361–363 (2011). *J. Spáčil* annotates the conclusion as follows: *"The parties to the agreement may not validly agree that the disputes arising from their agreement will be decided by an arbitrator selected by the complainant from a list of arbitrators administered by a private entity other than a permanent arbitral institution established pursuant to Section 13 of the ArbAct [CZE] and that the arbitral proceedings will follow the rules adopted by such a private entity."*

[58] Anonymized by the author. The decision mentions a specific entity.

arbitrators".[59] The important aspect was that [XY, s.r.o.] was not an entity which could be classified as a permanent arbitral institution pursuant to Section 13 of the ArbAct [CZE].[60]

15.48. (•) The subject matter of the dispute was the determination of the (ownership) title to real property; the claimant argued that the purchase contract was invalid. The District Court in Frýdek Místek [Czech Republic], as the trial court, terminated the proceedings initiated by the petition for the determination of (ownership) title to the particular real property[61] filed with said court; the reason for the termination was a timely jurisdictional challenge. The Regional Court in Ostrava, as the court of appeals, upheld the trial court's decision.[62] An arbitration clause covers not only the rights arising from legal relationships established directly by the contract, but also the issue of the legal validity of these relationships as well as the rights associated therewith. If the arbitration agreement is included in a real property purchase contract (real property transfer contract), the arbitration clause also covers disputes over the determination of (ownership) title to the real property.

[Cassation appeal]

15.49. (•) In her appeal, the claimant argued, *inter alia*, that the courts had erroneously interpreted the first sentence of Section 7(1) of the ArbAct [CZE].[63] The claimant emphasized that the parties had only agreed on the number of arbitrators (a sole arbitrator) without identifying any particular arbitrator. If we applied the second part of the sentence in Section 7(1) of the ArbAct [CZE][64] to the present case, then – considering the relevant arbitration clause – we could conclude that the method of determining the number of arbitrators and identifying the individual arbitrators stipulated in said provision was not agreed by the parties either. The signing of the purchase contract containing the arbitration clause did not imply that the claimant got acquainted with the "Rules on Arbitration and the Tariff of [XY, s.r.o.]" to which the

---

[59]   The arbitration agreement is not available. Adopted from the interpretation articulated in the reasons for the resolution of the Supreme Court of the Czech Republic [CZE], in the part summarizing the contents of the claimant's cassation appeal; the text is *reconstructed* from information regarding various parts of this arbitration clause.

[60]   Provision cited above.

[61]   Resolution of the District Court in Frýdek-Místek, Case No. 15 C 238/2008-18 of 2 February 2009.

[62]   Resolution of the Regional Court in Ostrava, Case No. 57 Co 150/2009-51 of 15 February 2010.

[63]   Provision cited above.

[64]   Provision cited above.

arbitration clause refers. The claimant therefore argued that the arbitration clause violated Section 2(1) of the ArbAct [CZE][65] and Section 7(1) of the ArbAct [CZE][66] and was an invalid juridical act. The claimant also argued that, if her petition on the merits pleaded invalidity of the purchase contract, it entailed a plea of invalidity of the arbitration clause contained therein.

15.50. (▪) The claimant also argued that in criminal proceedings conducted before the same court[67] a connection had transpired between the legal counsel for the respondent and [XY., s.r.o.] in other similar cases, which unacceptably violates the principle of impartiality of any eventual arbitral proceedings. The claimant argued that her conclusion regarding the invalidity of the purchase contract itself was supported by the acts of a particular natural person [M. T.] for which the person was convicted;[68] the person was simultaneously being prosecuted for another part of the committed act relating to the subject matter of the purchase contract. The claimant also emphasized that she could not abide by the *Rules on Arbitration and the Tariff* issued by an entity which was not authorized to do so, because it was not a permanent arbitral institution. The respondent therefore challenged the legal conclusions of the court of appeals as concerns the validity of the arbitration agreement.

[The decision of the cassation court and the cassation court's arguments]

15.51. (▪) The three-member Panel No. 30 of the Supreme Court of the Czech Republic, which was called upon to hear and decide the cassation appeal according to the court's schedule, arrived at a legal opinion which departs from the preceding decisions.[69] The Supreme Court [SC] concluded that the decision of the court of appeals was not correct.

---

[65] Provision cited above.

[66] Provision cited above.

[67] District Court in Frýdek-Místek, Case No. 1 T 97/2008; the current status of the proceedings was not specified.

[68] Judgment of the District Court in Frýdek-Místek [CZE], Case No. 80 T 127/2009 of 3 February 2010. No information on whether the judgment is final.

[69] Judgment of the Supreme Court of the Czech Republic, Case No. 32 Cdo 2312/2007 of 21 January 2009. In said decision, the cassation court adopted, *inter alia*, a legal opinion according to which "[i]f the court of appeals in the given case held that the terms of the arbitration agreement had been validly contracted by reference to the rules specified therein (Rules of Arbitration Procedure adopted by Společnost pro rozhodčí řízení a.s.), such a provision appears, to say the least, as a vague and ambiguous provision, in that the rules were made for ad hoc arbitral proceedings and were not incorporated in the arbitration agreement and, as opposed to statutes issued by permanent arbitral institutions (Section*

15.52. (▪) The Supreme Court of the Czech Republic analyzed the issue of whether the arbitration clause in the present case required that the resolution of the eventual dispute between the parties be entrusted to (an) *ad hoc* arbitrator(s); the Supreme Court highlighted that both the trial court and the court of appeals in the present case had actually answered the question in the affirmative (despite no detailed analysis of said issue).

15.53. (▪) At the same time, the Supreme Court emphasized that we could not dismiss the fact that the selection of the respective arbitrator was subjected to the regime of [XY., s.r.o.] which, however, had never been authorized to issue statutes and rules that would, *inter alia*, regulate the way in which the arbitrator(s) case manage(s) the arbitral proceedings or determine the method of appointment of arbitrator(s), etc. [XY., s.r.o.] is a corporation; the line of business of that corporation in the decisive period was specified as follows: consultancy services for arbitrators in arbitration, services provided by organizational and economic consultants relating to the services for arbitrators and arbitration, and agency services for arbitrators and arbitration.

15.54. (▪) The Supreme Court of the Czech Republic classified such a situation, i.e. when entities other than permanent arbitral institutions issue their own rules which also provide for the method of appointment of arbitrators, as a manifest imposition of conditions which raise reasonable doubts as to the perspective of independent and impartial dispute resolution. The court also held that we could not postulate that the parties had perhaps agreed on having their eventual dispute resolved by an *ad hoc* arbitrator. This was because no such arbitrator

---

13(2) of the 1963 ArbAct [CZE]), these rules were not published in the Business Journal."
The opinion voiced in said decision also corresponds to the Resolution of the High Court in Prague, Case No. 12 Cmo 496/2008 of 28 May 2009, annotated elsewhere in this book.
However, this decision was preceded by another decision, namely Resolution of the SC, Case No. 32 Cdo 2282/2008 of 31 July 2008, which reads as follows (cit.): *"The parties to the agreement may validly agree that the disputes arising from their agreement will be decided by an arbitrator selected by the complainant from a list of arbitrators administered by a private entity other than a permanent arbitral institution established pursuant to Section 13 [of the ArbAct [CZE]] and that the arbitral proceedings will follow the rules adopted by such a private entity."*
See also: IA. *Přehled rozhodnutí Nejvyššího soudu ČR neschválených v roce 2010 do Sbírky soudních rozhodnutí a stanovisek* (*An Overview of Decisions Rendered by the Supreme Court of the Czech Republic in 2010 Which Were Not Selected for Publication in the Reports of Judgments and Opinions*), 17(2) SOUDNÍ ROZHLEDY 41, 44 (2011); Jan Kocina, Rozhodčí doložky sjednané ve prospěch „soukromých rozhodčích soudů". [Title in translation: Arbitration Clauses Which Vest Jurisdiction in "Private Arbitration Courts"]. Bulletin advokacie, 2011, Nos. 7–8, pp. 48–49; Tomáš Sokol, *K aktuálním problémům rozhodčího řízení* (*Regarding Current Problems in* Arbitration), 19(9) PRÁVNÍ RÁDCE 4, 9 (2011).

was identified in the arbitration agreement, or rather the arbitration agreement contained no clear terms, compliant with the law, which would provide for the method of selecting the respective arbitrator; the aforementioned reference (and a very general reference at that) to the rules adopted by [XY, s.r.o.] cannot be accepted as an alternative (substitute) method of appointing the *ad hoc* arbitrator due to the reasons specified above. The Supreme Court of the Czech Republic held that the respective arbitration clause had been a clear attempt to impair the position of the weaker contracting party. This is the first case in which such an opinion was explicitly voiced, at the general level, with respect to arbitration agreements, i.e. not only in connection with contracts concluded by consumers. Although we do not know any details regarding the terms of the main contract concluded in the present case, it might prove difficult to infer that the contract was a typical, so-called consumer contract. Consequently, the Supreme Court based its conclusions not on the special protection afforded to consumers but on general legal principles [civil-law principles], which constitute a principle superior to the special protection of consumers (though not endowed with higher *force*).

15.55.   (▪) The trial court's decision and the appellate court's decision were both vacated, and the case was remanded to the trial court for a new hearing.

12. Judgment of the Regional Court in Brno, Case No. 44 Co 246/2010 of 27 September 2011[70]

Key words:
unacceptable retroactive application of case law | good faith of the parties to an arbitration agreement

15.56.   (1) The conclusions of the Grand Panel of the Supreme Court of the Czech Republic of 11 May 2011, Case No. 31 Cdo 1945/2010, regarding the invalidity of arbitration clauses referring to rules issued by an entity other than a permanent arbitral institution must be accepted in courts, because their purpose is to unify the fragmented case law; from the

---

[70]   The author does not have at his disposal the original (full) text of the decision. Consequently, the author fully adopted the *rationes decidendi* from: Martin Kulhánek, *Krajský soud v Brně: Nepřípustnost retroaktivního využití judikatury (konkrétně k usnesení velkého senátu NS ČR ze dne 11. 5. 2011, sp. zn. 31 Cdo 1945/2010). (Regional Court in Brno: Prohibited Retroactive Application of Case Law (Specifically Regarding the Resolution of the Grand Panel of the Supreme Court of the Czech Republic of 11 May 2011, Case No. 31 Cdo 1945/2010)),* 20(3) Právní rozhledy 112 (2012).

perspective of these conclusions, the arbitration clause negotiated on 26 April 2007 must be held invalid.

15.57. (2) However, the case exhibits certain circumstances which have led the court of appeals to believe that the application of these conclusions is contrary to Section 3(1) of the CC [CZE]. It turned out that both parties had accepted the arbitration clause, had not had doubts about the clause being possible and permitted, and had performed juridical acts on the basis thereof, at the time when applicable case law considered such a clause valid. The first landmark decision challenging the possibility to select an arbitrator by reference to the rules of arbitration issued by an entity other than a permanent arbitral institution was the Decision of the High Court in Prague [Czech Republic] of 28 May 2009, Case No. 12 Cmo 496/2008; an older resolution of the Supreme Court of the Czech Republic, Case No. 32 Cdo 2282/2008 of 31 July 2008, had arrived at completely contradictory conclusions.

15.58. (3) Consequently, the court of appeals identified with the respondent's objection regarding the unacceptable retroactive application of case law (contrary to *bonos mores*) to the assessment of acts of the parties which were, at the time they were performed, based on the parties' joint will and conviction about the validity of the arbitration clause.

13. Resolution of the Constitutional Court of the Czech Republic, Case No. II. ÚS 3057/10 of 5 October 2011[71]

Key words:
agreement on case management of the proceedings | rules on procedure | permanent arbitral institutions | "ad hoc" arbitration | independence | impartiality | invalidity of the arbitration clause

15.59. (1) The Constitutional Court of the Czech Republic has repeatedly accentuated the principle of freedom of contract, also in relation to arbitration clauses. The mere incorporation of arbitration clauses in the

---

[71] The decision is available at the website of the ConCourt. The litigation involved the following decisions:

▶ Resolution of the District Court for Prague 2, Case No. 18 C 218/2009-59 of 29 October 2010;

▶ Resolution of the Municipal Court in Prague, Case No. 58 Co 332/2010 of 16 July 2010.

For a detailed annotation including an analysis of the factual and legal findings and comments on this decision, see: ALEXANDER J. BĚLOHLÁVEK, OCHRANA SPOTŘEBITELŮ V ROZHODČÍM ŘÍZENÍ (*Protection of Consumers in Arbitration*), Prague: C. H. Beck marg. 386 (2012).

laws and regulations is not considered a restriction of access to court, i.e. no violation of Article 36(1) of the Charter of Basic Rights. However, it is desirable that the waiver of the right to have the dispute reviewed by a court be permissible, unambiguous, and made out of one's own free will. [72] This requirement entails the obligation of the court to examine the arbitration clause, in each particular case, from the perspective of reasonability of the clause (Directive),[73] taking into account the unequal position of the consumer as a party to the arbitration agreement.

15.60.   (2) Autonomy of will and freedom of individual conduct are primarily based on Section 2(1) of the ArbAct [CZE]. [74]

15.61.   (3) The method of entering into and the wording of arbitration agreements (or arbitration clauses, as the case may be) must be subject to a special approach if incorporated in consumer contracts regulated under Section 52 et seq. of the CC [CZE]. These provisions are based on the Directive, which was adopted with the aim of enhancing the protection of consumers against unfair contractual terms. Article 3(1) and Article 6(1) of the Directive[75] indicate that a national court is authorized to examine an arbitration clause incorporated in a contract concluded between a consumer and a trader (professional) in light of the Directive, even if the consumer himself or herself did not plead unfairness of the clause.[76]

---

[72]   The Constitutional Court invokes the Judgment of the European Court of Human Rights, Application No. 1643/06 of 28 October 2010 (*Suda v Czech Republic*), in which the ECtHR examined the right to a fair trial pursuant to Article 6(1) of the European Convention of Human Rights. *Suda v Czech Republic* concerned a Czech citizen living in the Czech Republic (the complainant/applicant). He was a minority shareholder in a joint stock company. His shares were redeemed by the majority shareholder in compliance with the provisions of the Commercial Code, which anticipated the possibility that the compensation for the shares would in such cases be reviewed by an arbitral tribunal instead of a court. The applicant argued that his fundamental right to a fair trial had been violated in these cases, because he was bound by an arbitration clause which he himself had not negotiated. Cf. also Christa Roodt, *Conflicts of Procedure Between Courts and Arbitral Tribunals with Particular Reference to the Right of Access to Court*, 19 AFRICAN JOURNAL OF INTERNATIONAL AND COMPARATIVE LAW 236 (2011).

[73]   Council Directive 93/13/EC of 5 April 1993 on unfair terms in consumer contracts. *Official Journal EC L* 95 of 21 April 1993, at 29–34. CELEX: 31993L0013.

[74]   Provision cited above.

[75]   *Supra* note 73, at 29–34.

[76]   For a comparison, cf. also the decision of the Madrid Appeals Court [ESP], Case No. 28079370102010100498 of 12 November 2010 (*Juan Pedro v. Metrovacesa S. A.*), regarding the principle of good faith which protects both the consumer and the professional. In this case, the Spanish court reached (*inter alia*) the following conclusions: (i) The principle of good faith prevents the consumer, who had initiated the arbitration by referring to the arbitration clause incorporated in a consumer contract, from pleading invalidity of the

15.62. **(4)** Article 3(1) of the Directive[77] in conjunction with paragraph 1(q) of the Annex to the Directive stipulate that arbitration clauses can also be considered unfair terms in consumer contracts.

15.63. **(5)** Section 56 of the CC [CZE] stipulates that consumer contracts must not contain terms causing a significant imbalance in the parties' rights and obligations. Terms which (i) were not individually negotiated or which (ii) simultaneously cause a significant imbalance in the parties' rights and obligations are invalid.

15.64. **(6)** The court examines all circumstances of the case. Despite the fact that arbitration clauses are not explicitly listed in the indicative list of potentially unfair terms in consumer contracts as specified in the CC [CZE],[78] the court may conclude that a particular arbitration clause must be classified as unfair.

15.65. **(7)** If the arbitration clause is incorporated in a consumer contract, then the wording of the clause must be subject to a more rigorous assessment. The same applies to the criteria regarding the arbitrators who might be called upon to resolve potential future disputes between the contracting parties – the method of their appointment must be subject to a particularly rigorous test. Considering the nature of consumer contracts, it is necessary to lay special emphasis on the rule that both parties must have equal rights in selecting their arbitrators.

15.66. **(8)** In the case of an arbitration clause [in a consumer contract] which is, contrary to the law, clearly aimed at causing detriment to the "weaker" contracting party, the principle of party autonomy must not

---

arbitration clause in subsequent proceedings for annulment of the arbitral award. (ii) The consumer's defense of invalidity of the arbitration agreement should be rejected, since he had only objected to the validity of the arbitration agreement during the proceedings for annulment of the arbitral award, despite the fact that the consumer had already had the opportunity to raise such defense during the arbitral proceedings. (iii) A party who knows that a non-mandatory provision of the *lex arbitri* was violated and fails to object within the established time limit, or, in the absence of a set time limit, as soon as practicable, will be deemed to have waived his or her right to object. This also applies to the possibility of pleading invalidity of the arbitration agreement. The Madrid Appeals Court invoked Article 6 of the Arbitration Act [ESP] (approximate translation, cit:) Article 6. *"Tacit waiver of the right to plead invalidity. Where a party, aware of the non-compliance with any non-binding provision of this Act or any requirement of the arbitration agreement, does not state his objection within the period provided or, in the absence of such a period, as soon as possible shall be deemed to have waived the right to raise the corresponding defense under this Act."* Annotation: *Mandilla-Serrano, F.* In: 11(4) ITA ARBITRATION (2011), edition of 20 April 2011. See also ALEXANDER J. BĚLOHLÁVEK, *supra* note 71, at marg. 488 et seq. and elsewhere in the book.

[77] *Supra* note 73, at 29–34.

[78] Section 56(2) of the Civil Code of the Czech Republic, as amended. We ought to mention that the NCC expressly broadens this non-exhaustive list to include arbitration clauses.

be (mis)used to negate the protection of that party. A democratic country honoring the principle of the rule of law must not give up on the protection of the rights and legitimate interests which could be jeopardized in alternative proceedings conducted instead of litigation.[79]

15.67. **(9)** Assessment of the validity of an arbitration clause must take into account the importance of arbitration as a dispute resolution method, including the appointment of the arbitrator, i.e. the person who the parties choose because they have confidence in him or her. The principle of selecting one's arbitrator is not fulfilled by a mere reference to a list of arbitrators.

15.68. **(10)** Section 2(1) of the ArbAct [CZE][80] provides that an arbitration agreement (or an [arbitration] clause incorporated in the main contract, as the case may be) must include the parties' agreement on either (an) *ad hoc* arbitrator(s) or a permanent arbitral institution established under the law.[81] The *ad hoc* arbitrator, always a natural person (Section 4 of the ArbAct [CZE]),[82] can be identified *(by his, her, or their name(s), should there be more than one arbitrator, directly in the arbitration agreement)*, or the arbitration agreement (clause) can define the method of appointment and the number of arbitrators – Section 7(1) of the ArbAct [CZE]. [83]

15.69. **(11)** Section 19 of the ArbAct [CZE][84] provides that the parties may agree on how the arbitrators shall case manage the proceedings and, in the absence of such agreement, the arbitrators shall conduct the proceedings in any manner they shall see appropriate (the proceedings are oral unless the parties agree otherwise). As opposed to arbitrators appointed *ad hoc*, permanent arbitral institutions may issue their own rules (statutes and rules) which may set forth the process of appointment and determine the number of arbitrators (the arbitrators can be selected from a list), as well as stipulate the manner whereby the

---

[79]   In this case, the Constitutional Court agreed with the opinion expressed in the decision of the Grand Panel of the Civil Law Division and the Commercial Law Division of the Supreme Code of the Czech Republic, Case No. 31 Cdo 1945/2010 of 11 May 2011.

[80]   Provision cited above.

[81]   The Amendment to the ArbAct [CZE] effective as of 1 April 2012 modified the Section 13 of the ArbAct [CZE] by amending subsection (1) of Section 13 of the ArbAct [CZE] and inserting a new subsection (4) in Section 13 of the ArbAct [CZE]. Compared to the previous version of the provisions, i.e. before the Amendment to the ArbAct [CZE], subsections (2) and (3) of Section 13 of the ArbAct [CZE] continue to apply unamended.

[82]   The Amendment to the ArbAct [CZE] effective as of 1 April 2012 modified Section 4 of the ArbAct [CZE], with respect to consumer arbitration, and amends Section 4 of the ArbAct [CZE] in its entirety.

[83]   Provision cited above.

[84]   Provision cited above.

arbitrators shall case manage the proceedings and the costs of arbitration payable by the parties. Such rules must be published in the *Business Journal*.[85] Decisions are[86] rendered pursuant to the above-mentioned rules issued by the permanent arbitral institution, as applicable on the day the request for arbitration is filed with the arbitral institution.

15.70. **(12)** If an entity other than a permanent arbitral institution under the ArbAct [CZE] carries out activities which, according to the ArbAct [CZE], are reserved for permanent arbitral institutions, then logic dictates that this entity clearly and intentionally violates the law. It is a manifest attempt to impose conditions which raise reasonable and justified doubts regarding the perspective of an independent and impartial dispute resolution.

15.71. **(13)** If the arbitration agreement lacks any direct identification of an *ad hoc* arbitrator or a specific description of the method of his or her appointment, but only refers to a selection made by a "tribunal/court", i.e. a legal entity (corporation) other than a permanent arbitral institution established under the law, then the arbitration agreement is invalid.

15.72. **(14)** The arbitration clause is also likely to be classified as invalid if the clause refers to a legal entity whose company name contains the words *"arbitral court/institution/tribunal"* despite the fact that it is not a *permanent arbitral institution* pursuant to Section 13 of the ArbAct [CZE],[87] because such a reference can be considered a fraudulent term misleading the consumer as a deceitful company name.

15.73. **(15)** The parties may also agree to depart from the rules issued and published by the permanent arbitral institution; in the absence of such agreement, however, the permanent arbitral institution follows the rules.

15.74. **(16)** The court examines all circumstances of the case. Despite the fact that arbitration clauses are not explicitly listed in the indicative list of potentially unfair terms in consumer contracts as specified in the CC

---

[85] See Section 13(2) of the ArbAct [CZE]. Regarding the conditions for the establishment of a "permanent arbitral institutions", see Section 13(1) of the ArbAct [CZE].

[86] Although the Constitutional Court of the Czech Republic in its resolution speaks of "decision-making subject to the respective rules", the author believes that the Constitutional Court of the Czech Republic means the entire procedure which the final decision only brings to an end. It is a somewhat inaccurate statement incorporated in the reasons for the resolution adopted by the Constitutional Court of the Czech Republic; in the author's opinion, though, it will not cause any problems with the interpretation of the ruling.

[87] Provision cited above.

[CZE],[88] the court may conclude that a particular arbitration clause must be classified as unfair.

15.75. **(17)** If the arbitration clause is incorporated in a consumer contract, then the wording of the clause must be subject to a more rigorous assessment. The same applies to the criteria regarding the arbitrators who might be called upon to resolve potential future disputes between the contracting parties – the method of their appointment must be subject to a particularly rigorous test. Considering the nature of consumer contracts, it is necessary to lay special emphasis on the rule that both parties must have equal rights in selecting their arbitrators.[89]

| | |

---

[88] Section 56(2) of the CC [CZE], as amended. We ought to mention that the New CC [CZE] (in force as of 1 January 2014) expressly broadens this non-exhaustive list to include arbitration clauses.

[89] For a detailed annotation, including an analysis of the factual and legal findings and comments on this decision, see: ALEXANDER J. BĚLOHLÁVEK, *supra* note 71, AT marg. 386 et seq.

II. The Supreme Court Judgments and Decisions of Appellate Courts: Poland

Maciej Durbas, associate, KKG Kubas Kos Gaertner – Adwokaci,
e-mail: maciej.durbas@kkg.pl

Kuba Gąsiorowski, associate, KKG Kubas Kos Gaertner – Adwokaci,
e-mail: kuba.gasiorowski@kkg.pl

Kamil Zawicki, attorney at law, partner, KKG Kubas Kos Gaertner-Adwokaci (ed.)
e-mail: kamil.zawicki@kkg.pl

Abbreviations

kick. [POL]	Kodeks cywilny z dnia 23 kwietnia 1964 r. [Civil Code] published in: Dziennik Ustaw [Journal of Laws] 1964, No. 15, item 93, as amended;
k.p.c. [POL]	Kodeks postępowania cywilnego z dnia 17 listopada 1964 r. [Code of Civil Procedure of November, 17 1964], published in: Dziennik Ustaw [Journal of Laws] 1964, No. 43, item 296, as amended;
New York Convention	New York Convention on the Recognition and Enforcement of Foreign Arbitral Awards of June, 10 1958 [Konwencja o uznawaniu i wykonywaniu zagranicznych orzeczeń arbitrażowych, sporządzona w Nowym Jorku dnia 10 czerwca 1958 r.], published in: Dziennik Ustaw [Journal of Laws] 1962, No. 9, item 41;[1]
Poland – China Agreement	Umowa między Polską Rzecząpospolitą Ludową a Chińską Republiką Ludową o pomocy prawnej w sprawach cywilnych i karnych z 5 czerwca 1987 [*Agreement between Poland and China on cooperation in civil and criminal cases of June, 5 1987*], published in: Dziennik Ustaw [*Journal of Laws*] 1988, No. 9, item 65, as amended;
PIL [POL]	k.s.h. [POL] Kodeks spółek handlowych z dnia 15 września 2000 r. [*Code of commercial companies of*

---

[1] Poland signed the New York Convention on the Recognition and Enforcement of Foreign Arbitral Awards on June, 10 1958; it was ratified by Poland on October, 3 1961 and entered into force in Poland on January, 1 1962. The text of the New York Convention was published in Polish in the Journal of Laws 1962, No. 9, item 41.

September, 15 2000], published in: Dziennik Ustaw *[Journal of Laws]* 2000, No. 94, item 1037, as amended; Prawo prywatne miedzynarodowe z dnia 12 listopada 1965 r. *[Private International law of November, 12 1965]*, published in: Dziennik Ustaw *[Journal of Laws]* 1965, No. 46, item 290, as amended;

u.z.n.k. [POL]   Ustawa z dnia 16 kwietnia 1993 r. o zwalczaniu nieuczciwej konkurencji *[Act of 4 April 1993 on Combating of Unfair Competition]*, published in: Dziennik Ustaw *[Journal of Laws]* 1993, No. 47, item 211, as amended;

1. Party Cannot Invoke New Grounds for Setting Aside the Award after the Lapse of the Time Period for Filing the Recourse (Supreme Court (*Sąd Najwyższy*) Civil Chamber Decision, Case No. V CSK 222/12 of March, 27 2013)[2]

Key words:
arbitration award | annulment of the award | domestic arbitration | judicial review | polish arbitration law | public policy | review of arbitral award | state courts

States Involved:

[POL] - [Poland];

Laws Taken into Account in This Ruling:
➢   Kodeks postępowania cywilnego z dnia 17 listopada 1964 r. *[Code of Civil Procedure of November, 17 1964]* [k.p.c.] [POL], published in: Dziennik Ustaw *[Journal of Laws]* 1964, No. 43, item 296, as amended; Articles: 1206 § 1 point 1; Article 1206 § 2 point 2;[3] Article 1208 § 1 and 2;[4]

---

[2]   Full text of this Decision available in Polish on the website of the Supreme Court at: http://www.sn.pl/sites/orzecznictwo/Orzeczenia2/V%20CSK%20222-12-1.pdf.

[3]   Article 1206 k.p.c. [POL] (unofficial translation): § 1. A party may by petition demand that an arbitral award be set aside if: 1) there was no arbitration agreement, or the arbitration agreement is invalid, ineffective or no longer in force under the provisions of applicable law; 2) the party was not given proper notice of the appointment of an arbitrator or the proceeding before the arbitral tribunal or was otherwise deprived of the ability to defend its rights before the arbitral tribunal; 3) the arbitral award deals with a dispute not covered by the arbitration agreement or exceeds the scope of the arbitration agreement; however, if the decision on matters covered by the arbitration agreement is separable from the decision on matters not covered by the arbitration agreement or

16.01. Party cannot invoke new grounds for setting aside the award after the lapse of the time period for filing the recourse. The state court deciding on the recourse cannot take into account *ex officio* grounds set forward in art. 1206 § 1 point 1 k.p.c. that were not raised in the recourse.

16.02. Finding that a contract is binding even when it does not contain its necessary elements would be contrary to the basic principles of public policy of the Republic of Poland.

[Description of Facts and Legal Issues]

16.03. On June 26, 2007, two Polish companies, P and I entered into a framework agreement aimed at creating an environment for concluding options contracts on the financial market. On July 11, 2008 the parties entered into an additional agreement securing I's claims against P.

16.04. According to the framework agreement, option contracts were concluded during a telephone conversation and later on I sent to P a confirmation in writing, which P had to send back to I. The lack or resending was treated as a tacit acceptance. P was obligated to pay a premium in case of buying put options and I was obligated to pay one in case of call options. Each party gained certain right (put or call option) according to conditions set forward by the party to ensure the reciprocity of the transaction. The remuneration was meant to be equal and subject to set off. In any other case, a party was obligated to pay the difference.

16.05. From August 1, 2007 to October 3, 2008 parties entered into a number of transactions according to the abovementioned conditions. Twelve of

---

exceeding the scope thereof, then the award may be set aside only with regard to the matters not covered by the arbitration agreement or exceeding the scope thereof; exceeding the scope of the arbitration agreement cannot constitute grounds for vacating an award if a party who participated in the proceeding failed to assert a plea against hearing the claims exceeding the scope of the arbitration agreement; 4) the requirements with regard to the composition of the arbitral tribunal or fundamental rules of procedure before such tribunal, arising under statute or specified by the parties, were not observed; 5) the award was obtained by means of an offence or the award was issued on the basis of a forged or altered document; or 6) a legally final court judgment was issued in the same matter between the same parties. § 2. An arbitral award shall also be set aside if the court finds that: 1) in accordance with statute the dispute cannot be resolved by an arbitral tribunal, or 2) the arbitral award is contrary to fundamental principles of the legal order of the Republic of Poland (public order clause).

⁴ Article 1208 k.p.c. [POL] (unofficial translation): § 1 A recourse for setting aside an arbitral award should be filed within three months from the date when the award was received or if the party motioned for supplementation, correction or interpretation of the award – within three months from the date when the arbitral tribunal delivered its decision on this motion. § 2 If the recourse for setting aside an arbitral award is based on reasons stated art. 1206 § 1 point 5 or 6, the time period for filing the recourse starts on the date when the party gained knowledge of these reasons. The party cannot file the recourse after five years from receiving the arbitral award.

them concluded before July 16, 2007 brought PLN 200.000 of income to P. Remaining, amounting to PLN 18.231.734,96 had not been settled.

16.06. According to § 48 of the framework agreement, all the disputes arising out of the framework agreement were submitted to arbitration under auspices of the Court of Arbitration at the Polish Bank Union, according to its rules.

16.07. P initiated arbitration for establishing that abovementioned transactions for PLN 18.231.734,96 were void. The court dismissed the claim and awarded I's counterclaim for payment of these sums.

16.08. P filed a recourse to set aside the award. On May 10, 2011, the Regional Court dismissed the recourse against the award. The court found that the award did not violate art. 1206 § 1 point 1 in conjunction with art. 1161 § 2, art. 1206 § 1 point 2 and 4 and art. 1206 § 2 point 2 k.p.c. The arbitration agreement did not violate the principle of equality of the parties and was fully effective, P had the full possibility to defend its rights, there was also no violation of the tribunal's rules and the award was not contrary to the basic principles of the public policy.

16.09. The Appellate Court shared this assessment of the case and dismissed P's appeal. The Court found that the arbitral tribunal did not violate the principle of equality of the parties. P had a chance to appoint an arbitrator from outside of the list prepared by the Court of Arbitration at the Polish Bank Union. The Court also found that the arbitral award did not violate the basic principles of public policy of Republic of Poland. This is because the arbitral tribunal correctly dismissed P's allegation that the framework agreement was void due to the fact that it did not specify the necessary features of the contract (*essentialia negotii*). Furthermore, P did not prove that it suffered damage and its amount.

16.10. P filed a cassation to the Supreme Court repeating its argumentation.

[Decision of the Supreme Court]

16.11. The Supreme Court dismissed the cassation. First of all, the Court underlined that Polish Code of civil procedure consists of rules of different nature. The rules on the admissibility of the recourse against the award and those specifying the formal prerequisites thereof and the conduct of proceedings are of strictly procedural nature. However, the rules on the grounds for a recourse against the award – creating a basis for court's substantive decision – constitute an equivalent to substantive law.

16.12. The Court reminded as well that it is bound by the grounds invoked by the party filing the recourse. However, it can assess *sua sponte* grounds referred in art. 1206 § 1 point 1 k.p.c. (inarbitrability) and art. 1206 § 1 point 2 (public policy). A party can obviously rely on these two grounds as well.

16.13. However, the Supreme Court underlined, relying on its previous decisions, that as far as the remaining grounds are concerned, a party cannot invoke new ones after the lapse of the time to file the recourse. Consequently, in the case at hand the Supreme Court could not assess the ground specified in art. 1206 § 1 point 1 k.p.c. (validity and effectiveness of the arbitral agreement) as P raised it outside of the time limit described above.

16.14. The Court agreed with P that if a contract does not specify the necessary features of the contract (*essentialia negotii*) and an arbitral tribunal bases its decision thereon, such an award is contrary to public policy of the Republic of Poland. However, in the case at hand such a situation did not occur. The Appellate Court correctly found that the framework agreement was precise enough.

16.15. Furthermore, the Court found that awarding damages to I was not contrary to principles of social coexistence. The Appellate Court correctly found that P was aware of the risk stemming from option contracts. It also did not question previous transactions which brought it profit.

2. The Court Rules on the Recognition or Enforcement of the Award on a Public Hearing Both When It Grants and Dismisses the Motion (Supreme Court (*Sąd Najwyższy*) Civil Chamber Decision, Case No. I CSK 186/12 of January, 23 2013)[5]

Key words:
arbitration award | enforcement proceedings | judicial review | new york convention | official translation | polish arbitration law | recognition and enforcement of foreign arbitral awards | review of arbitral award | right to be heard | state courts

States Involved:

[POL] - [Poland];

[GER] – [Germany]

---

5 Full text of this Decision available in Polish on the website of the Supreme Court at: http://www.sn.pl/Sites/orzecznictwo/Orzeczenia2/I%20CSK%20186-12-1.pdf.

Laws Taken into Account in This Ruling:

➤ Kodeks postępowania cywilnego z dnia 17 listopada 1964 r. [*Code of Civil Procedure of November, 17 1964*] [k.p.c.] [POL], published in: Dziennik Ustaw [*Journal of Laws*] 1964, No. 43, item 296, as amended; Article; 148;[6] Article 379 point 5;[7] Article 1213,[8] Article 1215 § 1;[9]

➤ New York Convention on the Recognition and Enforcement of Foreign Arbitral Awards of June, 10 1958 [*Konwencja o uznawaniu i wykonywaniu zagranicznych orzeczeń arbitrażowych, sporządzona w Nowym Jorku dnia 10 czerwca 1958 r.*], [New York Convention], published in: Dziennik Ustaw [*Journal of Laws*] 1962, No. 9, item 41;[10] Article II;[11] Article IV.[12]

---

[6] Article 148 k.p.c. [POL] (unofficial translation): § 1 If there is no provision to the contrary, the hearings are open and the court examines the case on a public hearing. § 2 The court can delegate the case to a public hearing and set a trial also when the case is to be decided on a closed hearing.

[7] Article 379 k.p.c. [POL] (unofficial translation): There is a mistrial when (...) 5) a party was deprived of the right to present its case.

[8] Article 1213 k.p.c. [POL] (unofficial translation): The court rules on the recognition or nonrecognition of the award upon a motion of a party. A party is obligated to append the motion with an original version of the award or a settlement or a copy thereof certified by the court of arbitration along with an original version of the arbitration agreement or an official copy thereof. If the arbitral award or a settlement concluded before the court of arbitration are not made in Polish, a party is obligated to append the motion with a certified translation thereof.

[9] Article 1215 k.p.c. [POL] (unofficial translation): § 1 The court rules on the recognition or enforcement of the award or a settlement concluded before a court of arbitration on a public hearing.

[10] Poland signed the New York Convention on the Recognition and Enforcement of Foreign Arbitral Awards on June, 10 1958; it was ratified by Poland on October, 3 1961 and entered into force in Poland on January, 1 1962. The text of the New York Convention was published in Polish in the Journal of Laws 1962, No. 9, item 41.

[11] Article II of the New York Convention:

1. Each Contracting State shall recognize an agreement in writing under which the parties undertake to submit to arbitration all or any differences which have arisen or which may arise between them in respect of a defined legal relationship, whether contractual or not, concerning a subject matter capable of settlement by arbitration.

2. The term "agreement in writing" shall include an arbitral clause in a contract or an arbitration agreement, signed by the parties or contained in an exchange of letters or telegrams.

3. The court of a Contracting State, when seized of an action in a matter in respect of which the parties have made an agreement within the meaning of this article, shall, at the request of one of the parties, refer the parties to arbitration, unless it finds that the said agreement is null and void, inoperative or incapable of being performed.

[12] Article IV of the New York Convention: 1. To obtain the recognition and enforcement mentioned in the preceding article, the party applying for recognition and enforcement shall, at the time of the application, supply:

(a) The duly authenticated original award or a duly certified copy thereof;

16.16. The phrase "the court rules on the recognition or enforcement of the award on a public hearing" refers not to the a type of the decision of the court but a type of case the court is deciding. Consequently, the court shall decide on the motion on a public hearing irrespectively of the type of the decision it is going to issue (both granting and dismissing the motion). If the court rules on a closed hearing instead of a public one, a party is deprived of its right to present the case, which leads to mistrial (art. 379 point 5 k.p.c.).

16.17. Consequently, the proceedings for the recognition of a foreign arbitral award should be conducted on the basis of the New York Convention with the supplementary application of k.p.c. As a result, the form requirements have to be taken from the New York Convention and not from art. 1162 k.p.c.

16.18. The lack of documents required by art. 1213 k.p.c. is a formal flaw of the motion, which can be cured by a party.

[Description of Facts and Legal Issues]

16.19. G (Germany) entered into an agreement with S.K. conducting business under the name A.-P. (Poland) for the sale of grain. The contract was concluded by a broker, according to the customs of grain market. The contract contained an arbitration clause submitting all disputes arising thereof or relating thereto to a London arbitration under Grain and Feed Trade Association (GAFTA).

16.20. G initiated arbitration proceedings claiming that S.K. breached the contract. Tribunal in an award of July 14, 2008 awarded EUR 285.450 to G. Subsequently, G sought to enforce the award in Poland and filed an appropriate motion, appending it with a copy of the award certified by GAFTA General Director along with a sworn translation into Polish and the copies of the contract prepared by the brokers along with a sworn translation. G invoked English law as the proper law to assess the effectiveness of the arbitration agreement.

16.21. Regional Court in its decision of December 14, 2011 dismissed the motion 6on the grounds that G did not append the motion with an original or an official copy of the award.

16.22. G filed a complaint however it was dismissed by the Appellate Court in a decision of November 10, 2011. The Appellate Court indicated that

---

(b) The original agreement referred to in article II or a duly certified copy thereof.

2. If the said award or agreement is not made in an official language of the country in which the award is relied upon, the party applying for recognition and enforcement of the award shall produce a translation of these documents into such language. The translation shall be certified by an official or sworn translator or by a diplomatic or consular agent.

the copy of the award was not appended with a stamp or a signature. Notarial copy thereof did not relate to the content of the award but to the GAFTA General Director's statement of compliance of the copy with the original. The Court found that failure to append the motion with a certified copy as required by art. 1213 k.p.c. is not a defect of form of the motion, but a circumstance justifying dismissal of the motion on the grounds of not proving prerequisites for recognizing or enforcing the award.

16.23. Furthermore, the Appellate Court found that under art. 1215 § 1 k.p.c. only recognizing the award requires conducting a public hearing. Dismissing the motion does not require such a hearing. Consequently the fact that the Regional Court dismissed the motion in camera does not constitute a violation of the said provision of k.p.c. Moreover, as G did not append the motion with necessary documents, conducting an open hearing would not change G's situation.

16.24. G filed a cassation to the Supreme Court repeating its argumentation. In particular it underlined that it did submit "an original version of the award or a settlement or a copy thereof certified by the court of arbitration along with an original version of the arbitration agreement or an official copy thereof" within the meaning of art. 1213 k.p.c. It also raised that the decision of the Appellate Court violated art. IV(1)(a) of the New York Convention by wrong interpretation the notion of "the duly authenticated original award or a dully certified copy thereof" and consequential wrong finding that G did not submit the award in the required form. G attacked the decision also on the grounds of art. IV(1)(b) in connection with art. II(1) and (2) of the New York Convention by wrong interpretation of this provision and in consequential wrong finding that G did not submit "an agreement" in the required form.

[Decision of the Supreme Court]

16.25. The Supreme Court allowed the cassation and remitted the case to the Appellate Court. The Court agreed with G's position that a court needs to decide on the motion for recognition or enforcement of an arbitral award on a public hearing, irrespectively whether it allows or dismisses the motion. Article 1215 § 1 k.p.c. confirms the principle stipulated in art. 148 § 1 k.p.c. that the court examines the case during a hearing. Any exception to this rule must stem directly from a provision of law and in any case shall be interpreted narrowly. The phrase "the court rules on the recognition or enforcement of the award" refers not the a type of the decision of the court but a type of case the court is deciding. Furthermore, the Supreme Court reminded that the similar position had also been presented in its decision of June 24, 2009, file ref. no I CSK 538/08 and of July 4, 2008, I CZ 139/07.

16.26. If the court rules on a closed hearing instead of a public one, a party is deprived of its right to present the case, which leads to mistrial (art. 379 point 5 k.p.c.). The Appellate Court should have noticed the mistral and take it into account *ex officio*. As it did not, its decision had to be set aside.

16.27. The Supreme Court instructed the Appellate Court as well to take into account the provisions of the New York Convention, which take precedence over k.p.c., as decided by the Supreme Court in the decision of January 18, 2007, file ref. no I CSK 330/06. The Supreme Court in this decision underlined that the New York Convention specifies so called substantive prerequisites for recognizing an award (primarily in art. IV and V). Consequently, the proceedings for the recognition of a foreign arbitral award should be conducted on the basis of the New York Convention with the supplementary application of k.p.c. As a result, the form requirements have to be assessed on the basis of the New York Convention and not on the basis of art. 1162 k.p.c. According to art. II(2) of the New York Convention the term "agreement in writing" shall include an arbitral clause in a contract or an arbitration agreement, signed by the parties or contained in an exchange of letters or telegrams.

16.28. This provision has to be interpreted liberally and also other means of concluding an arbitration agreement are possible. As to the issue of carrying the arbitral award, it should be asses on the basis of law of the state where the award was rendered. The Supreme Court disagreed as well with the opinion of the Appellate Court on the qualification of the documents required to recognize or enforce an award. The Supreme Court reminded that it already ruled in the decision of the November 3, 2004, file ref. no III CK 510/03 that lack of documents required by art. 1213 k.p.c. is a formal flaw of the motion, which can be cured by a party.

16.29. As an additional issue, the Supreme Court found that the arbitral award in the case at hand did not specify the name of defendant (a person), but only specified the name of its business. The law applicable to the arbitral award decides on these issues, as underlined in the decision of the Supreme Court of July 17, 2007, file ref. no III CZP 55/07.

3. Arbitration Agreement Signed by a Polish Partnership Not According to Its Rules of Representation Is Not Binding for This Partnership (Appellate Court of Katowice (*Sąd Apelacyjny w Katowicach*) 1ˢᵗ Civil Division Decision, Case No. I ACz 279/13 of May, 17 2013)[13]

Key words:
arbitration award | arbitration clause | conflict of law | conflict-of-law | enforcement proceedings | judicial review | new york convention | recognition and enforcement of foreign arbitral awards | state courts

States Involved:

[POL] - [Poland];

[CHI] – [China];

Laws Taken into Account in This Ruling:

➢ Umowa między Polską Rzecząpospolitą Ludową a Chińską Republiką Ludową o pomocy prawnej w sprawach cywilnych i karnych z 5 czerwca 1987 [*Agreement between Poland and China on cooperation in civil and criminal cases of June, 5 1987*] [Poland-China Agreement] [POL]; published in: Dziennik Ustaw [*Journal of Laws*] 1988, No. 9, item 65, as amended; Article 16(1)(d);[14] Article 21;[15]

➢ Kodeks spółek handlowych z dnia 15 września 2000 r. [*Code of commercial companies of September, 15 2000*] [k.s.h.] [POL]; published in: Dziennik Ustaw [*Journal of Laws*] 2000, No. 94, item 1037, as amended; Article 29;[16]

---

[13] Full text of this Decision available in Polish on the website of the Polish Ministry of Justice at: http://orzeczenia.ms.gov.pl/content/$N/151500000000503 I ACz 000279 2013 Uz 2013-05-17 001.

[14] Article 16(1)(d) Poland-China Convention [POL] (unofficial translation): 1. On the conditions set forwad by this Agreement, the Contracting Parties shall recognize and allow to enforce on its territory the following judgments rendered on the territory of the Contracting Party after this agreement enters into force: (...) d) arbitral awards.

[15] Article 21 Poland-China Convention [POL] (unofficial translation): The Contracting Parties shall recognize and enforce arbitral awards rendered on the territory of the Contracting Party under the Convention on the Recognition and Enforcement of Foreign Arbitral Awards done at New York on 10 June 1958.

[16] Article 29 k.s.h. [POL] (unofficial translation): § 1. Each partner shall have the right to represent the partnership. § 2. The right of the partner to represent the partnership shall include all acts in court and out of court. § 3. The right of representation may not be limited with effect towards third parties.

> Prawo prywatne miedzynarodowe z dnia 12 listopada 1965 r. [*Private International law of November, 12 1965*] [PIL] [POL]; published in: Dziennik Ustaw [*Journal of Laws*] 1965, No. 46, item 290, as amended; Article 9 § 2;[17]

> New York Convention on the Recognition and Enforcement of Foreign Arbitral Awards of June, 10 1958 [*Konwencja o uznawaniu i wykonywaniu zagranicznych orzeczeń arbitrażowych, sporządzona w Nowym Jorku dnia 10 czerwca 1958 r.*], [New York Convention], published in: Dziennik Ustaw [*Journal of Laws*] 1962, No. 9, item 41;[18] Article II;[19] Article IV;[20] Article V(1)(a).[21]

16.30. If a rules of representation of a Polish partnership stipulate for a joint representation of the partnership by at least two partners acting together, the arbitration agreement signed by only one partner is not binding.

---

[17] Article 9 PIL [POL] (unofficial translation): § 2 The legal capacity of a legal entity is assessed on the basis of the law of its seat.

[18] Poland signed the New York Convention on the Recognition and Enforcement of Foreign Arbitral Awards on June, 10 1958; it was ratified by Poland on October, 3 1961 and entered into force in Poland on January, 1 1962. The text of the New York Convention was published in Polish in the Journal of Laws 1962, No. 9, item 41.

[19] Article II of the New York Convention:

1. Each Contracting State shall recognize an agreement in writing under which the parties undertake to submit to arbitration all or any differences which have arisen or which may arise between them in respect of a defined legal relationship, whether contractual or not, concerning a subject matter capable of settlement by arbitration.

2. The term "agreement in writing" shall include an arbitral clause in a contract or an arbitration agreement, signed by the parties or contained in an exchange of letters or telegrams.

3. The court of a Contracting State, when seized of an action in a matter in respect of which the parties have made an agreement within the meaning of this article, shall, at the request of one of the parties, refer the parties to arbitration, unless it finds that the said agreement is null and void, inoperative or incapable of being performed.

[20] Article IV of the New York Convention: 1. To obtain the recognition and enforcement mentioned in the preceding article, the party applying for recognition and enforcement shall, at the time of the application, supply:

(a) The duly authenticated original award or a duly certified copy thereof;

(b) The original agreement referred to in article II or a duly certified copy thereof.

2. If the said award or agreement is not made in an official language of the country in which the award is relied upon, the party applying for recognition and enforcement of the award shall produce a translation of these documents into such language. The translation shall be certified by an official or sworn translator or by a diplomatic or consular agent.

[21] Article V of the New York Convention: 1. Recognition and enforcement of the award may be refused, at the request of the party against whom it is invoked, only if that party furnishes to the competent authority where the recognition and enforcement is sought, proof that: (a) The parties to the agreement referred to in article II were, under the law applicable to them, under some incapacity, or the said agreement is not valid under the law to which the parties have subjected it or, failing any indication thereon, under the law of the country where the award was made; (...).

16.31. Arbitration agreement can be either an arbitration clause, or a submission agreement, concluded after the dispute emerges.

[**Description of Facts and Legal Issues**]

16.32. A and B concluded a contract of sale on December, 27 2007. By this contract A appointed B as its agent in terms of the brand X and temporarily empowered B to sell two models of its product. B obligated itself to actively conduct sales of these two models and make its best efforts to reach sale goals in a certain period of time. The contract provided also that all disputes arising out of or connected with the contract shall be settled by negotiations. In case of lack of agreement, the dispute shall be settled by the China International Economic and Trade Arbitration Commission (CIETAC), branch in Shanghai, according to the rules of this Commission in force on the date of filing the request for arbitration. The award shall be final and binding for the parties.

16.33. The contract was concluded in English and its copy (facsimile) was signed by A on December, 27 2007 and then signed by B and faxed back to A. In the place for the signature of B there was a stamp of the company of B and one illegible signature. B filed the following information with the Polish National Court Register (stemming from the deed of partnership): each partner of the company is empowered to represent the company, however at least two partners together or one of them together with a proxy are empowered to make declarations of will and signatures in the name of the company.

16.34. In 2009 the parties took part in a mediation in the Mediation Centre in N., China. B actively took part in the proceedings. Since November, 3 2009, B made 26 payments to A.

16.35. Subsequently, A initiated arbitration under CIETAC. On June, 17 2011 CIETAC filed to A and B an information of accepting the request for arbitration, the list of arbitrators and the rules. However, B did not appoint an arbitrator, did not file an answear to the request and did not appoint any counsel. CIETAC used company Y for mailing services. The confirmation of reception of correspondence is organized in the following manner: the courier scans the number of the mail and the receiver makes a signature on the scanner. Such confirmations of dispatch were made on June, 22 2011 and October, 27 2011.

16.36. On 24 October 2011 a CIETAC tribunal awarded to A from B USD 828.473 with interest from 1 January 2010 to the date of payment, CNY 82.931 for legal costs, CNY 58.525,43 for reimbursement of costs of travel to Poland and CNY 157.344,25 for arbitration fees.

16.37. A filed for a motion for enforcement of the arbitral award in Poland to the Regional Court. B argued that there was no arbitration agreement in the case at hand.

16.38. The Court found that, first, Poland-China Agreement applied in the case, and, second, Poland-China Agreement, as far as the rules on the recognition and enforcement are concerned, directed to the rules set forward in the New York Convention, especially articles II and IV.

16.39. The Regional Court also found that the the contract of December, 27 2007 contained a valid arbitration clause. It is true that the contract was signed by only one partner of B (when under the deed of partnership stipulated for a joint representation), however the arbitration agreement did not set Polish law as the governing law. Even if Polish law applied, under Article 29 k.s.h., on the basis of caselaw, each partner is empowered to act towards third parties on behalf of the company. Consequently, one of the partners of B could sign the contract in the case at hand. Irrespectively of that, Article II New York Convention recognizes both arbitration clause and the submission agreement – both signed by the parties or contained in an exchange of letters or telegrams. Consequently, in the case at hand the arbitral award was issued on the basis of a valid submission agreement, contained in the exchange of facsimile. Moreover, the Regional Court found that B was properly notified in the arbitration proceedings.

16.40. Consequently, the motion for enforcement was granted. The motion for recognition was denied as the award was subject to enforcement.

16.41. B filed a complaint. It underlined, that one partner was not empowered to represent the company, that the arbitration clause cannot be a submission agreement, as it was concluded before the dispute emerged and that it did not receive the notifications during the arbitral proceedings.

[Decision of the Appellate Court]

16.42. In deciding whether the arbitration agreement was valid, the Court underlined that it first needs to establish the proper law to asses the said validity. Under Article 9 § 2 PIL, the legal capacity of a legal entity needs is assessed on the basis of the law of its seat. Relying on caselaw, the Appellate Court indicated that law of the seat of a legal entity decides, i.a. on the issue of representation. The Court therefore decided, on the basis of these conflict of law rules that, B's ability to sign the arbitration agreement needs to be assessed on the basis of Polish law, in particular k.s.h. Under Article 29 § 3 k.s.h. it is true that the right of representation of a partnership may not be limited with effect towards third parties, however the deed of partnership can clearly prescribe for a joint representation of the partners.

16.43. Such a requirement for a joint representation was stipulated in B's deed of partnership and consequently as the contract between A and B was not signed by two partners, it is not valid.

16.44. Furthermore, the arbitration clause included in the contract cannot, by any means, be treated as a submission agreement. A submission agreement is concluded after a certain dispute emerges. In the case at hand, the arbitration agreement was rather a arbitration clause in a contract.

4. In Case of Doubts, a Dispute Arising out of a Tort that Is an Act of Unfair Competition Does Not Fall under an Arbitration Agreement Drafted to Cover Disputes Arising out of or in Connection with Performance of a Contract (Appellate Court of Poznań (*Sąd Apelacyjny w Poznaniu*) 1st Civil Division Decision, Case No. I ACz 2239/12 of January, 10 2013)[22]

Key words:
rejection of statement of claim | arbitration agreement

States Involved:

[POL] - [Poland];

Laws Taken into Account in This Ruling:

➢ Kodeks postępowania cywilnego z dnia 17 listopada 1964 r. [*Code of Civil Procedure of November, 17 1964*] [k.p.c.] [POL], published in: Dziennik Ustaw [*Journal of Laws*] 1964, No. 43, item 296, as amended; Articles: 1161 § 1[23] and Article 1165 § 1;[24]

---

[22] Full text of this Decision available in Polish on the governmental website with collection of decisions of State Courts at: http://orzeczenia.poznan.sa.gov.pl/content/$N/153500000000503_I_ACz_002239_2012_Uz_2013-01-10_001

[23] Article 1161 § 1 k.p.c. [POL] unofficial translation: § 1 Submission of a dispute to the jurisdiction of an arbitral tribunal requires agreement of the parties, in which the following shall be indicated: the subject of the dispute or legal relationship from which the dispute arises or may arose (arbitration agreement).

[24] Article 1165 § 1 k.p.c. [POL] (unofficial translation): § 1. If a party files with the state court a statement of claim concerning a case that regards dispute covered by the arbitration agreement, the court rejects the statement of claim or a motion for initation of non-litigious proceedings, when the defendant of participant of the non-litigious proceedings rises a defense of the arbitration agreement before engaging into the dispute as to its merits.

➢ Ustawa z dnia 16 kwietnia 1993 r. o zwalczaniu nieuczciwej konkurencji [*Act of 4 April 1993 on Combating of Unfair Competition*], published in: Dziennik Ustaw [*Journal of Laws*] 1993, No. 47, item 211, as amended; Article 18 Section 1 Point 4;[25]

16.45. If parties included in a business contract an arbitration agreement which contains a broad wording and stipultes that the arbitration agreement covers all of the parties' disputes arising out of the contract or connected thereto, then disputes stemming under Polish law out of acts of unfair competition do not fall within the arbitration agreement. That is because acts of unfair competition under Polish law are torts and thus claims originating therefrom are not "arising out of contract or connected thereto". That is also true even if a given act of unfair competition was commited alongside performance of the contract.

16.46. An arbitration agreement constitutes an exception to the right to be heard by a state court. As such it should be interpreted narrowly. In case of doubts as to the scope of the arbitration agreement, it should be interpreted to favor the right to be heard by a state court.

[**Description of Facts and Legal Issues**]

16.47. Parties A and B concluded a contract under which A was to supply certain goods to B and B was to resell them at its own shop (hereinafter as: the "Contract"). According to the attachement to this contract A was obligated to grant to B a number of discounts for price of the supplied goods. The contract contained in its § 8 a dispute resolution clause that stipulated: "All disputes arising out of performance of this contract or in connection thereto Parties shall resolve amicably and in absence of a settlement, Parties submit those disputes to the jurisdiction of the Court of Arbitration at the Polish (...) in W (...)".

16.48. Party A sued B before the state court – the Regional Court in Poznań (hereinafter as: the "Regional Court") – for return of value of the discounts that it granted to B under the Contract. A claimed that B by requesting discounts from A for the price of the goods that it later resold B commited an act of unfair competition in the understanding of the u.z.n.k. U.z.n.k. provides that it is an act of unfair competition to obstruct access to the market to other enterpreneurs, in particular by requesting payments (other than reflecting trade margin) for accepting thier goods for resale.

---

[25] Article 18 Section 1 Point 4 u.z.n.k. [POL] (unofficial translation): In case of commiting of act of unfair competition, the enterpreneur whose interest was endangered or impaired, may request: [...] 4) reparing of damage under general principles [...].

16.49. In defence B raised that the parties included in their contract an arbitration agreement that encompassed the claims made by Party A under u.z.n.k. Therefore, B argued, the dispute should be heard in arbitration not before the state court and petitioned the Regional Court for rejection of A's statement of claim under article 1161 § 1 k.p.c.

16.50. The Regional Court granted the motion of B and rejected the statement of claim of A by its decision of November 21, 2012 (hereinafter as: the "Decision of the Regional Court"). The Regional Court stated that parties were bound by arbitration agreement and therefore the disputed belonged in arbitration not in state court.

16.51. Party A filed a complaint from the Decision of the Regional Court to the Appellate Court in Poznań (hereinafter as: the "Appellate Court"). In the complaint A argued that the arbitration agreement did not cover acts of unfair competition. In the opinion of A, Party B commited the act of unfair competition "alongside performing" the Contract not "while performing" the Contract or in connection with its performance. Moreover, Party A stated that while concluding the arbitration agreement the parties did not contemplate it to cover acts of unfair competition.

[Decision of the Appellate Court]

16.52. The Appellate Court began its reasoning with a brief analysis of the nature of claims made by A. The Court stated that claim for return of the value of discounts that A granted to B is its nature a claim for unjust enrichment. For that reason, the Appellate Court explained, the claim of B is not a contractual one, neither did it remain in connection with the Contract.

16.53. The Appellate Court held that generally it is acceptable to submit disputes arising out of acts of unfair competition to jurisdiction of arbitral tribunal. However, in the opinion of the Appellate Court, one cannot assume that while concluding an arbitration agreement to cover disputes "arising out of or in connection of performance of" the Contract the parties contemplated that one of them will commit an act of unfair competition.

16.54. In the assessment of the Appellate Court, the case law clearly states that an arbitration agreement should precisely define what disputes does it cover. If an arbitration agreement is drafted broadly to cover all claims "arising out of or connected with performance" of a contract then it cannot be presumed that it encompasses also tort claims arising out of acts of unfair competition. The Appellate Court stated that conclusion of an arbitration agreement means exclusion of a category of disputes from the jurisdiction of state courts. Due to the fact that it is a right of the parties to be heard by a state court any exclusions therefrom should be interpreted narrowly. As a result, due to doubts as to the scope of the arbitration agreement included in the Contract, the Appellate Court decided that is should be interpreted narrowly as well.

| | |

III. Current Case Law of the Slovak National Courts regarding Arbitration

Martin Magál, Partner, Allen & Overy Bratislava, s.r.o.
e-mail: Martin.Magal@AllenOvery.com

Martina Kasemová, Lawyer, Allen & Overy Bratislava, s.r.o.
e-mail: Martina.Kasemova@AllenOvery.com

Abbreviations

Arbitration Act	Act No. 244/2002 Coll. on arbitration proceedings, as amended *(Zákon č. 244/2002 Z. z. o rozhodcovskom konaní v znení neskorších predpisov)*
Convention	Convention on the Recognition and Enforcement of Foreign Arbitral Awards (New York, 1958)
ICC	International Chamber of Commerce
ICC Rules	Rules of Arbitration of the ICC International Court of Arbitration
SVK	Slovak Republic
UNCITRAL Model Law	Model Law on International Commercial Arbitration (1985), with amendments as adopted in 2006

1. Slovak Courts Do Not Have Jurisdiction to Order an Interim Measure after the Commencement of Arbitral Proceedings. Ruling of the Regional Court in Bratislava [SVK], file No 2 Cob 74/2013, dated 14 March 2013 and Ruling of the Supreme Court of the Slovak Republic, file No 5 Obdo 24/2013, dated 12 June 2013.

Key words:
interim measures | lack of jurisdiction by the court | exclusive jurisdiction of the arbitral tribunal

States Involved:

Chile;

Slovakia

17.01. Slovak courts have no jurisdiction to order interim measures after the initiation of arbitral proceedings even when the arbitral tribunal has not been constituted yet. A court has jurisdiction to issue an interim measure only before the commencement of arbitral proceedings.

[Description of Facts and Legal Issues]

17.02. A Slovak developer involved in the construction of an industrial project in Chile allegedly breached their obligations under the underlying contract and its Chilean counterparty sought payment pursuant to performance bonds issued by a Slovak bank. The respective contract and the performance bonds contained an arbitration clause requiring submission of all disputes to arbitration in Paris under ICC Rules. Facing the request of the Chilean counterparty for payment pursuant to the performance bonds, the Slovak developer initiated arbitral proceedings. In those proceedings, the Slovak developer sought declaratory relief to the effect that they had complied with their contractual obligations and no breach had been committed.

17.03. Pending the outcome of the arbitration, the Slovak developer submitted a request with the Slovak courts to order an interim measure that would prevent the bank from paying under the performance bonds. The Slovak court of first instance issued an interim injunction *ex parte* and the Chilean counterparty filed an appeal with the Regional Court.

[Decision of the Regional Court]

17.04. The Regional Court held that the legislator's intent under the Arbitration Act has to be interpreted in a way that the arbitral tribunal has exclusive jurisdiction to issue interim measures after the commencement of arbitral proceedings. Otherwise, the court argued, the concurrent jurisdiction of courts and the arbitral tribunal could be abused by the parties to arbitral proceedings and result in 'forum shopping'. This could lead to a situation where a party whose request for interim measures has been refused by either the arbitral tribunal or the court could nevertheless attempt to obtain an equivalent measure from the other body.

17.05. On the basis of the above, the Regional Court opined that since ICC arbitration had already commenced, Slovak courts no longer had jurisdiction to order interim measures. This was despite the fact that no arbitral tribunal had been appointed. Consequently, the Regional Court annulled the interim injunction ordered by the court of first instance and terminated proceedings for lack of jurisdiction.

[Decision of the Supreme Court]

17.06. The Slovak developer appealed to the Supreme Court, which affirmed the argumentation of the Regional Court.

[Authors' Note]

17.07. Although article 9 of the UNCITRAL Model Law provides that courts have jurisdiction to order interim measures 'before or during' arbitral proceedings, the respective provision of the Arbitration Act omits the words 'or during'. Therefore, a question regarding the concurrent jurisdiction of courts after the commencement of arbitral proceedings is not surprising in this context.

17.08. There may be reasonable grounds for which a party to arbitral proceedings may seek interim measures from a court even after arbitral proceedings have been initiated. It would appear legitimate in cases when the arbitral tribunal has not yet been constituted or if the intended measure is to bind a third party.

17.09. The Slovak arbitration legislation is to be amended in a way that would achieve full harmonisation of the rules on commercial arbitration with the UNCITRAL Model Law. The proposal is about to enter the legislative process in Q4 of 2013 and its planned entry into force is set for 1 January 2014. The amendment should (among other things) grant Slovak courts concurrent jurisdiction to order interim measures also after the commencement of arbitral proceedings, where the tribunal has not yet been constituted.

2. Incorporation of an Arbitration Clause by Reference to a Separate Document Is Invalid. Ruling of the Supreme Court of the Slovak Republic, file No 2 Cdo 245/2010, dated 30 November 2011.

Key words:
arbitration clause incorporated by reference | general terms and conditions | form of an arbitration agreement

17.10. An arbitration clause incorporated into a written contract by reference to general terms and conditions does not meet the statutory requirement of written form and is therefore invalid.

[Description of Facts and Legal Issues]

17.11. The case relates to a dispute over the applicable interest rate between a bank and its corporate client (i.e. not a consumer). The underlying facility agreement contained specific reference to the bank's general terms and conditions and sought to incorporate those by reference. The general terms and conditions included a standard arbitration clause under which all disputes were submitted to the jurisdiction of the Permanent Arbitration Court of the Slovak Banking Association. The bank sought to rely on the arbitration clause, while the client challenged its validity and requested that the case be heard before a general court.

[Decision of the Supreme Court]

17.12. After conflicting rulings of courts of first and second instances, the dispute over jurisdiction reached the Supreme Court which opined that the arbitration clause was invalid due to the lack of written form. The Supreme Court reasoned that the definition of 'written form' in the Arbitration Act is exhaustive and general principles on incorporation by reference (which under Slovak law are wider than the language used in the Arbitration Act) cannot apply to arbitration agreements. According to the Supreme Court's opinion, the arbitration clause has to be contained in a document signed by the parties or, alternatively, in an exchange of letters, telex, telegrams or other means of telecommunication, but not in a separate document to which the master agreement refers. Therefore, due to the fact that the bank's general terms and conditions were not signed by the parties, they do not satisfy the requirement of written form and, consequently, the arbitration clause included therein is invalid.

[Authors' Note]

17.13. The section of the Arbitration Act governing the form of arbitration agreements lacks a provision enabling an arbitration agreement to be concluded by reference to a document containing an arbitration clause. Unfortunately, the *travaux préparatoires* to the Arbitration Act do not shed light on what the legislator's intent was when omitting this specific provision of the UNCITRAL Model Law. Nevertheless, Slovak law generally recognises the incorporation of contractual terms by reference and the addition of such a provision could have been regarded clear.. This principle has been reflected for the past decade also in the market practice as arbitration clauses have been commonly contained in a party's general terms and conditions and incorporated by reference into a master agreement signed by the parties. This was done without the specific execution of a document containing the general terms and conditions. In addition, Slovak banks and Slovak branches of foreign banks are obliged by law to offer to all clients arbitration clauses referring disputes to the Permanent Arbitration Tribunal of the Slovak Banking Association. A standard business practice used by many banks has been the incorporation of arbitration clauses into their general terms and conditions and a subsequent reference to such terms in the master agreements.

17.14. While the discussed ruling appears very formalistic, it cannot be ignored even taking into account the fact that in Slovakia rulings of the Supreme Court do not constitute precedents and are therefore not binding on other courts in different cases. However, if lower courts decide to follow the decision in this case, it can have far reaching consequences on many arbitration agreements entered into in good faith and effect their validity. If the Supreme Court ruling becomes a generally accepted norm, the risk exists that arbitral awards based on arbitration clauses incorporated by reference will be annulled by courts or their enforcement will be refused.

3. There Is No Jurisdiction of Arbitral Tribunals over Actions for Declaratory Relief. Ruling of the Regional Court in Nitra [SVK], file No 26 Cob 161/2009, dated 21 December 2009. Ruling of the Regional Court in Bratislava [SVK], file No 2 Cob 178/2008, dated 18 December 2008.

Key words:
declaratory relief | limitation of arbitral jurisdiction

17.15. Arbitral tribunals do not have jurisdiction to decide on actions seeking to have a contract declared null and void.

[Decision of the Regional Courts]

17.16. Two Regional Courts have independently ruled that actions for declaratory relief on whether a contract is valid cannot be decided in arbitration. Under the Arbitration Act, one of the pre-conditions for arbitrability is that the issue must be able to be settled by agreement of the parties. The courts opined that invalidity of a contract applies *ab initio* and the parties to a dispute cannot alter by agreement the fact that a contract is either valid or not. Therefore, such a dispute cannot be resolved by settlement and thus cannot be submitted to arbitration.

[Authors' Note]

17.17. Several arguments exist in support of arbitrability of actions for declaratory relief. First, settlements in disputes for declaratory relief are commonly accepted by Slovak courts. Second, arbitral tribunals have jurisdiction to assess the validity of the underlying contracts as a preliminary question in actions for payment. Third, arbitral tribunals are specifically empowered by law to rule on the validity of arbitration agreements.

4. There Is an Interconnection between the Recognition and Enforcement of an Arbitral Award and Public Policy. Ruling of the Regional Court Bratislava [SVK], file No 20 CoE/77/2011 – 2199, dated 12 July 2012.

Key words:
recognition and enforcement of an arbitral award | public policy

17.18. Recognition and enforcement of an arbitral award may be refused if it would contradict the public policy. The public policy exception is to be interpreted restrictively and the refusal of enforcement on this ground is applicable in exceptional circumstances only.

[Decision of the Regional Court]

17.19. The public policy exception is a protective measure granting a state the right to refuse application of provisions of foreign law if these contravene the enforcing state's public policy, even if the application is required by the conflict norms of private international law. The Regional Court ruled that the breach of public policy must entail such a crucial conflict by a foreign arbitral award with the public policy of the Slovak Republic that its recognition and consequent enforcement would manifestly violate social, legal and state principles. These are principles which need to be preserved without any exemption (e.g. right to a fair trial, equality of the parties). Therefore, when deciding on the applicability of the public policy exception, a narrow approach has to be endorsed.

[Authors' Note]

17.20. A court should not be able to disregard a foreign arbitral award by applying an expansive interpretation of the term public policy. Such actions by courts would undermine the arbitral award enforcement process and could lead to weakening of the international commercial arbitration in general.

Book Reviews

Book Reviews

Karl P. Sauvant | Lisa E. Sachs |
Wouter P.F. Schmit Jongbloed, eds.

Sovereign Investment: Concerns and Policy Reactions

Oxford: Oxford University Press, 606 pages, ISBN: 978-0-19-993792-9.

The book under review is a new volume edited by the Vale Columbia Center on Sustainable International Investments (New York) dedicated to focal topics of foreign investment. The volume brings together 21 contributions from experts and scholars in the fields of law, public policy, political science and economics. It is remarkable as a first publication to examine comprehensively the controversy over foreign investment through sovereign investment vehicles such as sovereign wealth funds (SWFs) and state-owned enterprises (SOEs). These two groups of investment vehicles (or sovereign investors) are not new to the world investment map. However, increasing investments during and after the Global Financial Crisis of 2007-2008, especially from Middle Eastern, Chinese and Russian SWFs and SOEs, created completely new concerns and protectionist-like policy reactions in developed countries. The editors collectively name these reactions a 'new mercantilism'. The authors divide such concerns into three main groups: investment motivations, national security of the host state and transparency. These are expressed by host countries in the form of screening procedures (national security review), which may result in prohibition of the transaction or divestment. In the introductory chapter, the volume editors (Karl P. Sauvant, Lisa E. Sachs and Wouter P.F. Schmit Jongbloed) note that while the role of SWFs and SOEs is increasing, the legal definitions of both remain far from unified. The Santiago Principles mentioned in almost every contribution state that SWFs are '[s]pecial-purpose investment funds or arrangements that are owned by general government. Created by the general government for macro-economic purposes, SWFs hold, manage, or administer assets to achieve financial objectives, and employ a set of investment strategies that include investing in foreign financial assets.'[1] However, Edwin M. Truman (chapter 13) argues that faced with any attempt by a country or a group of countries to formally regulate funds falling within a given definition, the home countries of sovereign investment vehicles would either avoid investing in those countries or transform their funds into forms that do not fall under the definition. The latter challenge is only one of those described and analyzed in the 21 chapters of the collection.

The first part of the volume covers in detail SWFs and other sovereign investment vehicles, as well as their history, sources and motives for investment, while the other two parts dwell on the descriptions of regulatory concerns and existing rules for state-owned entities. In chapter 2 Mark Gordon and Sabastian V. Niles dwell on particular investment vehicles – SWFs. They analyze a number of investment transactions performed by SWFs in different countries, and mention several cases when investments by SWFs were either blocked by host governments or revoked by SWFs themselves under political pressure. The chapter provides a brilliant analysis of the existing trends in SWFs' investments with detailed tables summarizing the deals. Talking about existing concerns, the authors note that some SWFs may have non-economic motivations for their investments. They briefly mention screening policies implemented by France, Germany, US, China, Republic of Korea, Japan, Russia, and Canada. They describe the current responses to those concerns and policies by SWFs themselves, in particular by the International Forum of SWFs (IFSWF), a group of 20 of the world's leading SWFs that manages approximately USD 3.437 trillion in assets. The IFSWF's Baku Statement encourages host countries to make their investment regimes more transparent, non-discriminatory and non-protectionist, to assess the application of Santiago Principles by SWFs themselves and to encourage capacity building efforts of all members. Gordon and Niles's conclusion that the vast pools of capital held by SWFs ensure their major role on the global scene contradicts a statement by the editors, who consider SOEs more significant sovereign investment vehicles by virtue of foreign direct investment (FDI) made through them.

In chapter 3 Stephany Griffith-Jones and Jose Antonio Ocampo study SWFs through the prism of the instruments and political economy of foreign exchange asset accumulation. The authors emphasize that developing countries

---

[1] Sovereign Wealth Funds – Generally Accepted Principles and Practices: 'Santiago Principles' (October 2008), available at: http://www.iwg-swf.org/pubs/eng/santiago principles.pdf (accessed on September 18, 2013).

as a group accounted for more than two-thirds of global reserve accumulation from 2001 to 2009. Thus, SWFs' investments in the first phase of the Global Financial Crisis helped stabilize the developed countries banks and softened the impact of the crisis. Paola Sabacchi in chapter 4 focuses on the fact that during the financial crisis, SWFs themselves incurred significant financial losses and only regained their 'appetites for substantial deals' after the recovery. Like Alan M. Rugman (chapter 11), she comments on the distribution of outward investment among SWFs from different regions citing that most Gulf countries SWFs invest in Europe, while Asian funds concentrate on North America and Asia itself. In chapter 5 Daniel M. Shapiro and Steven Globerman make an attempt to analyze governance structures of SOEs, comparing the commercially based SOEs in OECD states and SOEs in emerging markets. They base their analysis on the OECD ownership models using the decentralized model, the dual model and the centralized model, and privatization examples in Central and Eastern Europe compared to privatization in the Commonwealth of Independent States. The authors object to the common statement that SOEs from the emerging and transitional markets are less efficient than their private counterparts in terms of investments , based on the available evidence and an analysis of SOE governance structures. They conclude that the capabilities of those SOE are best exploited in other emerging markets rather than developed countries.

Introducing the reader to regulatory concerns, Katharina Pistor (chapter 6) turns attention to the history of SWFs and notes that famous SWFs' investments in major global banks have roots in past developments in China where banks allowed foreign investors only minority stakes. As a result, Western banks began to develop their relationships with major SWFs offering them deals similar to those in China, where control was out of the question. Pistor raises some painful questions regarding SWFs: should SWFs experiencing financial losses continue to invest in a flagging Western financial sector? Should governments discourage foreign holdings by domestic banks that received government financial help? How should home country governments respond to the actions of domestic banks that prefer to be bailed out by foreign SWFs rather than the home government? She stresses that all these concerns will have to be addressed in the future regulation of the global finance. As noted by the editors in chapter 1, the divergence of approaches to concerns about sovereign investment vehicles as, for example, the national security review, demonstrates the need to contextualize national responses to SOEs and SWFs investments. The national security review is a very controversial topic, as discussed by Mark A. Clodfelter, Francesca M.S. Guerrero (chapter 7), Jose Alvarez (chapter 9), Patrick DeSouza, and W. Michael Reisman (chapter 10), Alan M. Rugman (chapter 11), James Mendenhall (chapter 12), Edwin M. Truman (chapter 13), Clay Lowery (chapter

14), Alan P. Larson, David N. Fagan, Alexander A. Berengaut, and Mark E. Plotkin (chapter 15), A. Edward Safarian (chapter 16), Thomas Jost (chapter 17), Julien Chaise (chapter 18) and is perceived differently by different host countries depending on the source of investment. Above mentioned contributors focus on the US, Canadian and German developments, while Clodfelter and Guerrero (chapter 7) also provide an overview of ownership restrictions in Australia, China, France, Japan, Korea, Russia, and Saudi Arabia. Special mention is made of the US (CFIUS review) and the EU (common investment policy under the Lisbon Treaty). OECD perspectives and concerns are summarized by Kathryn Gordon and David Gaukrodger in chapter 19 and those of the IMF by Udaibir S. Das, Adnan Mazarei, and Alison Stuart in chapter 20.

In chapter 8 Rolando Avendano and Javier Santiso compare SWFs with mutual funds, in an attempt to determine whether SWFs are politically biased, as is claimed in many developed countries that are experiencing more and more inward investments from SWFs and other sovereign investment vehicles. The authors do not hesitate to criticize the growing concern on the part of OECD countries, and the claim that more transparency and good policy are necessary for SWFs activities. They argue that, given the lack of transparency and good practices in some Western central banks, OECD countries do not have the monopoly on best practice; therefore, they cannot dictate their terms to SWFs from emerging economies, many of which have proven that they can generate best practice and be more rigorous in applying sound policy. Although they conclude that SWFs are not much different from mutual funds, the authors leave the political bias question open for future research. Most of the contributors agree that it is detrimental to view foreign ownership of assets as a national threat, as eventually it may harm economic interests of the developed countries; whether developed countries like SWFs or not, they need their money. Various contributions stress that sovereign investors prefer portfolio rather than direct investments and that that alone should alleviate concerns. Various contributors also stress the Global Financial Crisis as a catalyst that reduced the need for special regulations covering SWFs, SOEs and other sovereign investment vehicles. Alan M. Rugman (chapter 11) summarizes how serious the situation with the national security review may become. He speculates that if the US adopts restrictions on SWFs and their investments, it is likely that the EU will continue to welcome these investments and London may eventually replace New York as the leading world financial center. In the view of some contributors, US policies toward SWFs, SOEs and other state-owned investors appear stark. James Mendenhall (chapter 12), for example, provides an excellent historical analysis of the essential security exception in US trade and investment agreements and cites a number of cases that demonstrate the potential for abuse of a self-judging security exception clause. A number of contributors refer to the notorious 2006 Dubai Ports World case, which only strengthened doubts about CFIUS screening procedures as potentially protectionist and biased. Maya Steinitz (chapter 21) concludes the volume with a statement that market intervention by the US government has reached an unprecedented scale since 2008.

Even though the volume does not provide an ultimate answer to the question of what to do with sovereign investments, its value for scholarship cannot be underestimated. The issue of investment by sovereign investment vehicles will no doubt affect the future of international investment law. The volume will become a must-read for national and international policy-makers, arbitrators, representatives of host countries, private sector lobbying against SWFs and SOEs as investors, as well as scholars studying the phenomenon. Any reader interested in the activities of sovereign investment vehicles will find something useful in the volume. If answers to readers' questions are not in the text it will provide them with hints which may transform into answers eventually.

[*Oleksiy Kononov, LL.M., S.J.D.*]
Assistant Professor of Business at the University of Buraimi, Al Buraimi, Sultanate of Oman. Education: Economics & Law Faculty at Donetsk National University in Donetsk, Ukraine – Specialist in Law (2003); Department of Legal Studies at Central European University in Budapest, Hungary – LL.M. (2007), S.J.D. (2010). He is a former legal practitioner in Ukraine.
e-mail: kononov.oleksiy@gmail.com

| | |

News & Reports

News & Reports

Amendments and Additions Included in the New Romanian Code of Civil Procedure in the Matter of Arbitration

The New Romanian Code of Civil Procedure (NRCCP) was adopted through Law 134/2010, published in the Official Monitor no. 485 of 15 July 2010 and republished, pursuant to Article 80 of Law 76/2012 for the enforcement of Law 134/2010 on the Code of Civil Procedure, in the Official Monitor 545 of 3 August 2012. Upon the entry into force of this New Code of Civil Procedure on 15 February 2013, the former Code of Civil Procedure (RCCP) from 1993 and 2010 was repealed.

The New Romanian Code of Civil Procedure (Law no. 134/2010) includes 15 significant changes that impact arbitration procedure.

1. In the wording of the NRCCP, the ability to arbitrate is no longer defined as strictly related to the patrimonial characteristic of the dispute. The rule for disputes concerning rights which can be transacted by arbitration is maintained. On the other hand, disputes related to civil status, an individuals' capacity, inheritance deliberation, family relations and rights on which the parties have not agreed upon by law are excluded from arbitration.[1]

2. The possibility to settle disputes involving parties which are legal state entities by arbitration is now included. Legal state entities whose scope of activity includes economic activities are free to sign arbitration clauses, except when the law or their deed of establishment or organization provides otherwise.[2]

---

[1] Art. 542 of the New Romanian Code of Civil Procedure.

[2] Art. 542 paragraphs (2) and (3) of the New Romanian Code of Civil Procedure – the opportunity for the state, public authorities and legal state entities to sign arbitration

3. The NRCCP, deletes methods of communication such as the telex and the telegram and adds the fax and e-mail. Article 559 sets forth that the means by which documents shall be submitted are: "mail, fax, e-mail and other means ensuring the submittal of the deed content and confirmation of its receipt".

4. There is an element of novelty which is included in the NRCCP, related to the 'arbitration clause.' This new section states that the existence of the arbitration agreement may also derive from the written agreement of the parties made before the arbitral tribunal.[3] At the same time, the lack of a method of appointment of the arbitrators in the agreement becomes a cause for nullity, except when institutionalized arbitration is resorted to, then reference to the institution in question or its rules of procedure is sufficient.[4]

5. With regard to arbitrators, the NRCCP brings about several amendments concerning their citizenship, the number of arbitrators, their appointment, the causes underlying the challenging of arbitrators and their liability. Pursuant to the new regulations, appointed arbitrators are no longer compelled to hold Romanian citizenship. In the NRCCP the citizenship requirement is no longer valid and the possibility to select an arbitrator not holding Romanian citizenship is included.[5] An odd number of arbitrators is an included requirement with regard to the structure of the arbitral tribunal.[6] Article 558 paragraph (5) includes the requirement of proposing a substitute arbitrator together with the nomination of the main arbitrator. Furthermore,there is the obligation to appoint a substitute for the chairman of the arbitral tribunal.[7]

Article 562 paragraph 1 also sets forth additional requirements for challenging an arbitrator. These include:

a) failure to perform the qualification requirements or other requirements concerning arbitrators, as set forth in the arbitration agreement;

b) where the arbitrator is an affiliate or part of the management team of a legal entity that has an interest in the case;

c) if the arbitrator has work or job relations or direct commercial connections, as applicable, with either party, with a company controlled by either party or which is under a joint control with it;

d) when the arbitrator has provided consultancy to either party, has assisted or represented either party or made a testimony in one of the phases prior to the dispute in question.

---

agreements. The state and the public authorities may only sign arbitration agreements if authorized by law or by international conventions of which Romania is a signatory.

[3] Art. 549 para (2) - the Romanian New Code of Civil Procedure.
[4] Art. 550 para (1) - the Romanian New Code of Civil Procedure.
[5] Art 555 - the Romanian New Code of Civil Procedure.
[6] Art.556 para 1 - the Romanian New Code of Civil Procedure.
[7] Art. 560 - the Romanian New Code of Civil Procedure.

Pursuant to Article 562 paragraph 2, a party may not challenge the arbitrator it appointed except for causes occurring or of which it became aware of subsequent to the appointment. The cause for arbitrators' liability is bad faith or the gross negligent breach of their duties.[8]

6. A thorough approach has been added to the Arbitral Tribunal's procedure of checking its own competence. Thus, starting with the first hearing, the Arbitral Tribunal is compelled to check its own competence. Unlike the RCCP,[9] Article 554 paragraph (1) of the NRCCP provide that the court shall declare its lack of competence only if the parties or either party so requests by invoking the arbitration agreement. In such case, the court shall decline its competence in favour of the organization or institution under which institutionalized arbitration operates. Pursuant to the decline decision, the institution shall take all necessary measures for constituting the arbitral tribunal. In the case of ad-hoc arbitration, the court shall reject the request as not being under the jurisdiction of the court.

7. The NRCCP stipulates that any plea concerning the existence and validity of the arbitration agreement, the constitution of the arbitral tribunal, the restrictions on the duties of arbitrators or the performance of the procedure shall be raised before the first hearing where the party has been duly summoned, under the penalty of lapse, unless a shorter term is established. Any requests and any submissions shall be made before the first hearing for which the parties have been duly summoned at the latest.[10]

8. With regard to certain arbitration procedure aspects, Article 582 of the NRCCP regulates the situation where one of the parties does not attend. Absence of such party from the hearing shall not prevent the dispute from proceeding. The requirement for the postponement of the dispute is that an application for postponement of the hearing should be made 3 days prior to the hearing at the latest.This is different from the provisions in the former RCCP, which imposed that the submittal of such an application be made one day before the hearing at the latest. Also, exclusive competence of the arbitral tribunal to find whether one party has solid reasons for its absence is set forth, following which the arbitral tribunal shall adopt a decision which is not subject to any challenging method.

9. Relating to the handling of evidence,[11] Article 588 paragraph (1) provides that the evidentiary issues may be handled by the chairman or, with the agreement of the parties, before an arbitrator of the arbitral tribunal.

---

[8] Art. 565 letter d) of the New Romanian Code of Civil Procedure.

[9] The former Romanian Code of Civil Procedure set forth as follows: Art. 343⁴ paragraph (1) –'Should the parties to the dispute have signed an arbitration agreement which either of them invokes in a court of law, then the latter shall check its own competence.'

[10] Art.592 New Code of Civil Procedure.

[11] Art. 587 New Code of Civil Procedure .

Article 589 paragraph (2) addresses the issue of hearing witnesses and experts, which can be carried out upon their request or with their consent, at their place of residence or at their office. Their obligation to answer to the questions put in writing is also set forth, provided that they comply with a deadline established by the arbitral tribunal.

10. In the NRCCP, the arbitration settlement time is extended from 5 to 6 months.[12] Such deadline may be extended by the arbitral tribunal for solid reasons, expressly mentioning that such measure may only be adopted once. In case of the death of either party, an extension of 2 to 3 months may be granted.

11. When the arbitral award refers to a dispute related to the transfer of the ownership rights and/or the constitution of another real estate right, the arbitral award shall be submitted to the court or the public notary in for the ruling of the court or for acquiring an authentic notary deed, as applicable. Following the scrutiny by the court or the public notary of compliance with the requirements and following the compliance with the procedures as set forth by the law and the payment by the parties of tax related to the transfer of the ownership right, it shall proceed to registration with the land registry and to the actual ownership transfer and/or the constitution of another real estate right.[13]

12. The parties are now entitled to ask for clarification regarding the award,[14] besides completion and adjustment of the award, should there be any need for further clarification concerning the meaning, the scope or enforcement of the award or when the latter comprises contradictory orders.

13. The NRCCP removes the need of vesting the arbitral award with an executory title. As the arbitral award is an executory title, it is executed as a judge's decision. Article 615 provides that the arbitral award is an executory title, unlike the former provisions setting forth that the arbitral award was vested with an executory title upon the request by the winning party.

14. There are several changes concerning the proceedings for an annulment.[15] The Court of Appeal shall judge the action in annulment with the panel for the ruling in first instance as set forth by the law. In other words, if the Arbitral Tribunal rules an award contradictory to the law, then a common law court will have the competence to annul such arbitral award in the cases set forth by the Romanian Code of Civil Procedure. A statement of defence is compulsory. If the proceedings are allowed, then the Court of

---

[12] Art. 567 of the New Romanian Code of Civil Procedure, paragraph 1 provides that the deadline for the ruling of the decision is 6 months after its constitution, subject to the penalty of arbitration caducity. Pursuant toArt. 567 para 4, the arbitral tribunal may order the deadline extension for solid reasons by no longer than 3 months, andonly once.

[13] Art. 603 paragraph 3 New Code of Civil Procedure.

[14] Art. 604 New Code of Civil Procedure.

[15] Art. 613 New Code of Civil Procedure.

Appeal shall annul the arbitral award and, in the cases set forth in Article 608 paragraph (1) letters a), b) and e) , it shall refer the case for trial to the competent court for a settlement under the law. However, should it be necessary to submit new evidence in view of a judgement on the merits, the court shall rule on the merits after handling the evidence. In this latter case, the court shall first rule on the action in annulment and, after handling evidence, the decision on the merits. If the parties made an express agreement that the dispute be settled by an arbitral tribunal in equity, the court of appeal shall settle the case in equity.[16] The judgements of the Court of Appeal, ruled pursuant to the provision of Article 613 paragraph (3), are subject to a second appeal. The requirement of the court determining a guarantee in case of stay of execution of the arbitral award against which the action in annulment was submitted is removed.[17] A new reason underlying an action in annulment is included – the reason occurring when, subsequent to the ruling of an arbitral award, the Constitutional Court decides that a law, an ordinance or an order from a law or ordinance is unconstitutional.[18]

15. Title VII of the NRCCP is dedicated to institutionalized arbitration, i.e. 6 articles regulate the procedure for the appointment of arbitrators, costs of arbitration and the applicable rules of procedure.[19]

In conclusion, the New Romanian Code of Civil Procedure and the law for the enforcement of this New Code comprise substantial amendments in the matter of arbitration. These were absolutely necessary for the law to be in accordance with the current realities, as well as with the need to settle conflicts in a fast, safe way, compliant with the consecrated principles of the Romanian Civil Code.

[*Dr. Alina Mioara Cobuz Bagnaru*]
Attorney-at-law, PhD, Member of the Bucharest Bar, Founding Member of Cobuz si Asociatii, arbitrator with the Bucharest Stock Exchange, FINBAN mediator.
e-mail: alina@cobuz.ro

| | |

---

[16] Art. 613 letter b New Code of Civil Procedure.

[17] Art. 612 New Code of Civil Procedure.

[18] A new cause for nullity of the arbitral award is added, as set forth by Art. 608 paragraph (1) letter i) of the NRCCP if, following the ruling of the arbitral award, the Constitutional Court rules on the plea invoked in the case and declares the law, the ordinance or order from a law or ordinance under whose scope the plea or other orders from the challenged act which, necessarily and clearly, cannot be severed from the provisions mentioned in the notice, was unconstitutional.

[19] Art.616 – 621 New Code of Civil Procedure.

The Development of Arbitration in Romania from 2010-2013 in the Court of International Commercial Arbitration under the Chamber of Commerce and Industry of Romania (CCIR)

The Court of International Commercial Arbitration under the Chamber of Commerce and Industry of Romania (CCIR) is the main arbitration institution in Romania, with over 57 years of experience.It settles disputes under its jurisdiction pursuant to its own Rules of Arbitration Procedure. At the same time, upon the request of the parties, it may also organize *adhoc* arbitration. The average number of cases settled in one year is over 400 domestic disputes and 50 international disputes.[1]

New Court of Arbitration rules of procedure (the Rules) were entered into force on 6 March 2013[2]. These amend and incorporate the arbitration rules adopted in 2010[3] (the former Rules) as a part of the New Romanian Code of Civil Procedure. The changes in the new Rules are consistent with the changes that were made by the entire New Romanian Code of Civil Procedure[4], and differ from the Old Romanian Code of Civil Procedure[5].

As previously, the Rule makes an express distinction between institutionalized arbitration and *ad-hoc* arbitration. Explicit reference is made to the legal provisions completing the regulation for each of the two forms of arbitration. Thus, in the former case, a regulation on the Organization and Operation of the Court of International Commercial Arbitration under the Chamber of Commerce and Industry of Romania is added.

A new element is the provision of Article 1 paragraph (2) of the Regulation, according to which:

> Nomination of the permanent arbitration institution by the arbitration agreement in view of the settlement of disputes determines the

---

[1]   Available at: www.ccir.ro (accessed on 29 October 29 2013).

[2]   Published in the Official Journal, Part I, no. 184 of 02/04/2013.

[3]   Published in the Official Journal, Part I, no. 197 of 29/03/2010; completed by Resolution no. 17/2012 of the CCIR, published in the Official Journal no. 97 of 07/02/2012.

[4]   Adopted by Law no. 134/2010 on the Code of Civil Procedure, published in the Official Journal no. 485 of 15 July 2010 and republished, pursuant to Art. 80 of Law 76/2012 on the enforcement of Law 134/2010 on the Code of Civil Procedure, in the Official Journal no.545 of 3 August 2012.

[5]   Amended and completed by Law no. 59 of 23 July 1993 published in the O.J. no. 177 of 26 July 1993, part I.

exclusive jurisdiction of the respective institution, and the parties, by way of this appointment, make a default option for the application of its rules of procedure, and any waiver of such provision shall be null. For the organization and performance of arbitration, the rules of procedure of the permanent arbitration institution appointed in force upon its notification shall be applied.

Hence, the conclusion of the arbitration agreement precludes the jurisdiction of the courts of law on the dispute falling under its scope.

It is important to note that the Rules makes an express provision for the fact that the New Romanian Code of Civil Procedure is applied to complete the rules of arbitration procedure unless The Code of Civil Procedure comprises provisions to the contrary. [6]

Another change is the removal of the civil-commercial dispute distinction, as the two notions were incorporated within the scope of 'arbitration dispute', thus providing a joint definition.[7]

Also, the definition of international dispute has been amended. Thus, the requirement for the elements of extraneity of a civil juridical relationship raising the issue of applying foreign law is no longer valid, even when the Romanian law is the law effectively applicable.[8]

The definition of institutionalized arbitration is also simplified. The new formula is 'assignment of the Court of Arbitration, by the arbitration agreement, to resolve a determined dispute'.[9]

Concerning the award given by the constituted arbitral tribunal, the intrinsic executory feature of the award is quite unique. In other words, the arbitration agreement is an executory title *per se*, and its vesting with an executory characteristic is no longer necessary.[10]

A new provision is incorporated that attempts to achieve an amicable settlement within a reasonable time limit. Thus, a new regulation sets forth that upon every hearing the parties must be asked whether they have reached an agreement.[11]

The entire text of the Rules attempts to assimilate the arbitration proceedings to the request for arbitration. In order for such a request for arbitration or arbitration proceedings to equal an arbitration agreement, the respondent's acceptance is also necessary in view of the dispute's settlement by the Court of Arbitration. While the former regulations set forth that such acceptance 'can

---

[6]   Art. 3 paragraph 2 of the Rules.
[7]   Art. 4 paragraph 2 of the Rules.
[8]   Art. 4 paragraph 4 of the Rules.
[9]   Art. 6 paragraph 1 of the Rules.
[10] Art. 6 paragraph 3, art. 79 of the Rules.
[11] Art. 11 paragraph 2 of the Rules.

also be implied, however, unambiguous,'[12] the Rules make an amendment: 'acceptance by the respondent shall be express and agreed to in writing'.[13]

The ability to sign arbitration agreements belongs to either the state or the public authorities. The Rules amend and provide for the right of public legal entities operating economic activities to sign arbitration agreements, subject to compliance with their own deed of establishment, organization and the law.[14]

The rule concerning the composition of the arbitral tribunal, providing that it should consist of one sole arbitrator, or two co-arbitrators and one chair remains valid.[15]. Arbitrators, as well as their substitutes, are appointed by the Appointing Authority. The Rulesexpressly provide that it shall be exerted by one member of the Court of Arbitration Panel, pursuant to the provisions of the Regulation on the Organization and Operation of the Court of Arbitration. According to the former Rules, the parties had the opportunity to choose their arbitrator. When they would not exert the right or when they did not select an arbitrator within the provided time limit, the Appointing Authority would intervene and appoint the arbitrators.[16] With regard to this aspect, the major change made by the Rules is that the Appointing Authority must always appoint the arbitrators who shall become members of the arbitral tribunal.[17]

Also incorporated is the express obligation to replace the arbitral chair and/or the appointed arbitrators, in case of a reasonable absence while resolving the dispute. In such a case, there is a provision concerning the susbstitutes' fees.[18]

Changes also occur with regard to the removal and replacement of arbitrators. Thus, one of the reasons for removal set forth by the former Rules is eliminated; i.e. the situation when the arbitrator repeatedly breaches their duties.[19] Also, removal no longer occurs when the award is not given within the time limit provided by the parties' agreement. Currently, such time limit may be determined only pursuant to the provisions of these rules; not giving the award within this time limit is a cause for removing an arbitrator.[20]

As for the replacement of arbitrators, the circumstances when replacement may be ordered remain valid such as abstaining, challenge, renunciation, decease or other reasons for preclusion remain valid.However, this measure can no longer

---

[12]   Art. 14 paragraph 2 of the former Rules.

[13]   Art. 13 paragraph 2 of the Rules.

[14]   Art. 14 of the Rules.

[15]   Art. 15 paragraph 1 of the Rules.

[16]   Art. 18 of the former Rules.

[17]   Art. 18 paragraph 1 of the Rules: 'The Appointing Authority assigns the titular arbitrators and the the substitute arbitrators **to each determined dispute** ...' (emphasis added).

[18]   Art. 18 paragraph 2 si 3 of the Rules.

[19]   Art. 22 B letter f) of the former Rules.

[20]   Art. 20 B letter d) of the Rules.

be taken by the parties, it can only be taken by the Appointing Authority within three days following the date when such circumstances become known.[21]

When it comes to challenging arbitrators, arbitration assistants and experts, the measure is subject to the provisions of the Code of Civil Procedure concerning the challenging of judges andcourt clerks.[22] For the settlement of a challenge request by the arbitral tribunal, the challenged arbitrator is no longer replaced by the President of the Court of Arbitration, by its First Vice President or by an arbitrator appointed by them, pursuant to the former Rules[23], but by a member of the College appointed by the Court of Arbitration President or First Vice President.[24]

Concerning an arbitrator's abstaining, the new Rules elaborate on the former provisions. Thus, Article 24 incorporates two new provisions. These are when an arbitrator or chair arbitrator abstains and when the substitute arbitrator cannot fulfill their mission either.Then, another titular arbitrator/chair and another substitute arbitrator/chair shall be appointed pursuant to these rules. Also, upon the conclusion of settlement of the request for challenge or abstention, the date for resuming the arbitration proceedings is also determined, as applicable.[25]

The arbitration procedure is another area undergoing amendments. First of all, when the request for arbitration or the written submissions are worded in a foreign language, the new Rules provide that the Court of Arbitration Secretariat request the party, of its own motion, to submit a translation of such documents into Romanian.[26] Thus, there is a difference from the former provisions, where the wording 'the arbitral tribunal, of its own motion or upon request, may compel the party to submit a translation into Romanian' (emphasis added) was used.[27] Such wording obviously implies a capacity of the arbitral tribunal, not an obligation on its part. In fact, the new regulation provides, at AArticle 27 paragraph 4, that 'any document not translated is not relevant to the case', which means that an untranslated document lacks any value before the arbitral tribunal. As in the former Rules, there is a possibility for the parties to make a written request for the translation to be made by the Court of Arbitration Secretariat.. However, the costs shall now be borne by the parties.[28]

---

[21] Art. 20 C of the Rules.
[22] Art. 21 paragraph 2 of the Rules.
[23] Art. 24 paragraph 2 of the former Rules.
[24] Art. 22 paragraph 2 of the Rules.
[25] Art. 24 paragraph 3 of the Rules.
[26] Art. 27 paragraph 3 of the Rules.
[27] Art. 29 paragraph 3 of the former Rules.
[28] Art. 27 paragraph 5 of the Rules.

With regard to the registration of the request for arbitration, an element of novelty occurs in the submittal of the request without any proof of payment of the registration fee. According to the new Rules, such failure may be repaired and the request may be submitted again when all requirements are met. When it comes to the submittal of the request by mail, without any proof of payment of the registration fee, non-fulfilment of such requirement within five days following notification of the Court of Arbitration Secretariat triggers the stopage of the processing of the request for arbitration or of the arbitration proceedings.[29]

There are also amendments regarding information notified to the respondent. Thus, explicit provision is made for the elements which should be included in the answer:

- surname and given name, domicile or place of residence of the respondent or, in the case of legal entities, their designation and head office, as well as the personal numeric code or, as applicable, matriculation number with the trade registry or registration in the legal entities' registry, tax code and bank account, the data of the empowered representative of the private legal entity, as per the mentions in the Public Registry where such entity is registered, the address selected by the claimant, as applicable, for notifications related to the proceedings;
- pleas to the proceedings raised by the respondent to the claimant's request;
- the answer to all the *de facto* and *de jure* claims of the request;
- evidence sustaining their pleading against each claim;
- signature.[30]

Also, the respondent is entitled to the right to raise claims against the claimant, by way of a counterclaim, if they are derived from the same legal relation as the request for arbitration.

A new provision is included that addresses these counterclaims.

Claims included in the counterclaim shall be subject to the payment of fees and expenses calculated pursuant to the Rules of arbitration fees and expenses. Payment shall be made within 10 days following the date of receipt of such letter concerning the arbitration fee. The time limit is a time limit for estoppel. Failure to pay such fees triggers the annulment of the counterclaim as unpaid.[31]

---

[29] Art. 28 paragraph 3 of the Rules.
[30] Art. 30 paragraph 2 (a) of the Rules.
[31] Art. 30 paragraph 2 lit. h) of the Rules.

The new regulation makes a major specification concerning the legal characteristic of time limits, namely, that they are limits of incapacity only when the text makes an express provision.[32]

As for the payment of arbitration fees and expenses, the new Rules maintain the provisions concerning the 10-day time limit, starting from the date of receipt of the deed of notification, where the claimant is compelled to include arbitration fees and expenses. The amendment, however, concerns the possibility of extending such limit, currently carried out by substantiated resolution, until the first hearing established for arbitration.[33]

Also, the rules concerning the establishment of arbitration hearings are amended. Thus, starting with the date of the constitution of the arbitral tribunal, the Court of Arbitration has three days to establish the arbitration hearing time on the date when the parties are summoned (unlike the five day term, as provided by the former Rules[34]). Such time limit may not be shorter than 21 days following the date of the submittal of the summons by the parties.[35] We take note that such time limit has been shortened, as the former Rules provided for a 30-day time limit in this respect.

The new Rules do not make any significant amendments regarding the communication of deeds of procedure except as set forth in Article 34 paragraph 10. It states that 'The parties with their domicile/head office abroad shall receive the deeds of procedure in bilingual forms, i.e. in Romanian and an international language.'

Changes have also occurred when it comes to arbitration expenses. The administrative fee, a component of the arbitration fee remunerating the services provided by the Court of Arbitration in the case of *adhoc* arbitration[36], is one such new element. The former Rule, which provided that the amount of fees established under the Rules on arbitration fees and expenses would relate to one arbitrator, remains valid only in the case of institutionalized arbitration. Whereas in the case of *ad-hoc* arbitration 'arbitrators' fees are provided for by and shall be paid pursuant to the agreement of the parties as stipulated to in the arbitration agreement'.[37]

Concerning the constitution of the arbitral tribunal, the new Rules make the most substantial amendments. Thus, the proceedings are visibly amended and simplified, since the parties are no longer allowed to appoint arbitrators. Article 37 and Article 38 of the new Rules establish a new proceeding.

---

[32] Art. 31 paragraph 1 of the Rules.
[33] Art. 32 of the Rules.
[34] Art. 40 of the former Rules.
[35] Art. 33 of the Rules .
[36] Art. 36 paragraph 1 of the Rules.
[37] Art. 36 paragraph 4 of the Rules.

Art. 37. - (1) The arbitral tribunal shall consist in one sole arbitrator or of 3 arbitrators, one of whom shall be chair.

(2) In 24 hours following the receipt of the proof of payment of the claimant's financial obligations towards the Court of Arbitration, the arbitration assistant assigned to the file shall submit, through the Court of Arbitration Secretariat, a report to the Appointment Authority in view of appointing arbitrators.

(3) Within 3 days, the Appointment Authority, after receiving the report and the case file, shall appoint the arbitrator/arbitrators/ chair/substitutes.

Art. 38. - (1) The arbitral tribunal is constituted within 3 days following the appointment of arbitrators/chair, accepted by the latter by signing the Deed of Mission.

(2) Failure of the arbitrator/arbitrators/chair/substitutes to sign the Deed of Mission within the time limit provided for at paragraph (1) shall be deemed a refusal to do so, and replacement is to be made pursuant to the provisions of art. 37 paragraph (3).

In what concerns the deed of mission, the new Rules maintain the former provisions but add just one requirement, the date of acceptance/refusal of the mission, which must be included.[38]

The provisions concerning the taking of guaranteeing measures are more or less the same. The pre-arbitration proceeding implies the taking of guaranteeing and provisional measures or the finding of certain circumstances *de facto* by the competent court of law. We note that the obligation of the party which requested the notification to the arbitral tribunal of consent to such measures before the first hearing is removed.[39]

During arbitration, such measures may be consented to by the arbitral tribunal by way of conclusion. The Rules provide that, in case of refusal, the enforcement of such measures is ordered by the state tribunal under whose jurisdiction arbitration takes place.[40]

The time limit and place of arbitration are major aspects of the rules of arbitration proceedings.. Following the development of regulations in the matter, we note the example of amendments made to the time of ruling of the arbitral award. Originally, the rules adopted in 2010 provided a six-month time limit, which was shortened to five months by way of amendments and completions made in 2012, through Resolution 17 of the CCIR, and then the original six-month time limit was adopted by therules.[41]

---

[38] Art. 39 paragraph 1 of the Rules.
[39] Art. 49 paragraph 2 of the former Rules.
[40] Art. 41 paragraph 2 of the Rules.
[41] Art. 42 of the Rules.

Amendments are also made regarding the circumstances under which the time limit may be suspended. The former Rules provided for the suspension of the limit in three cases. These include during the time of settlement of the exception of unconstitutionality, during the settlement of a related request to the competent court or during the completion of the arbitral tribunal.[42] The first case is removed from the new Rules, and is replaced by the suspension of the time limit during the resolution of the request for challenge. A new circumstance is added and that is the time limit may also be suspended during a judgement of expertise made by the arbitral tribunal in a respective case.[43]

The arbitration time limit may be extended by three months, instead of the two-monthextension provided by the former Rules.[44] A new element is the provision concerning the exceeding of the arbitration time, which triggers a penalty:

> Unless the parties make an express agreement on the extension of the arbitration time and unless a reason occurs which justifies extension, as set forth under this section, delay in settling the dispute shall make the arbitral tribunal members liable and the penalty provided for delay in performing the mission as set forth by these Rules shall be applied.[45]

The provisions on the caducity of arbitration are also elaborated on in the new Rules:

> **Art. 46. - (1)** One reason for caducity is the situation when one of the parties notifies the arbitral tribunal in writing, before the first hearing, that it understands to invoke caducity and it reiterates this exception upon the first hearing following the expiry of the arbitration time.
> **(2)** Lack of an express request within the time limit set forth pursuant to paragraph (1) does not generate any consequence to the deadline for the settlement of the dispute.
> **(3)** When one party, by way of its attitude, frustrates celerity in settling the dispute, it is not a cause for the extension of the dispute settlement time limit, even when such exception is invoked within the estoppel time as set forth at paragraph (1). This finding shall be made by the arbitral tribunal and it is noted in the hearing report.

The place of arbitration shall be the headquarters of the Court of Arbitration. However, the new regulation no longer includes the provisions setting forth

---

[42] Art. 52 of the former Rules.
[43] Art. 43 of the Rules.
[44] Art. 53 paragraph 2 of the former Rules.
[45] Art. 45 of the Rules.

that the parties, by agreement, have the possibility of requesting that the arbitral tribunal carry out the arbitration meetings at another place.[46]

The arbitration proceedings themselves have been amended under various aspects. In relation to the submittal of the answer, provision is made that it should be submitted five days before the date of the first hearing.However, compared to the previous rules, mention is made that the penalty for not meeting such requirements is estoppel related to the submittal of evidence.[47] The penalty of estoppel is also applied when the counterclaim is not submitted, at the latest, before the first hearing.[48]

A completely new provision is incorporated in the Rules. This section states that 'The arbitral tribunal shall judge its own competence to settle the dispute and it shall rule in this respect in the hearing report, which can only be set aside by an action in annulment submitted against the arbitral award.'[49] The arbitral award may only be set aside by an action in annulment (Article 608 of the New Romanian Code of Civil Procedure sets forth nine cases of dissolution of the arbitral award), and the parties cannot waive, through the arbitration clause, the right to submit the action in annulment against the arbitral award. The action in annulment may be submitted within one month following the date of notification of the arbitral decision. The action in annulment can cover the following grounds:

— grounds concerning competence;
— grounds concerning the proceedings;
— grounds concerning the award grounds raising the issue of public order.

The competent court for ruling upon the action in annulment is the Court of Appeal under whose jurisdiction the arbitration proceedings took place.

Other novel elements in the new Rules are the provisions concerning the role of the chair arbitrator during deliberations.

> **Art. 51.** - **(1)** During the performance of the meeting, the arbitrators, the parties and the remainder participants in the deliberations may speak and they may ask questions only through the agency of the chair arbitrator.
>
> **(2)** Arbitrators and the participants in the deliberations communicate, during the meeting, through the chair arbitrator or directly, subject to the chair's consent.

---

[46] Art. 55 paragraph 2 of the former Rules.
[47] Art. 48 paragraph 2 of the Rules.
[48] Art. 48 paragraph 3 of the Rules.
[49] Art. 49 of the Rules.

(3) In view of complying with the meeting discipline, the chair arbitrator may order the suspension of deliberations, by announcing the time of resuming deliberations. Such a situation shall be noted in the hearing report and the reasons underlying the suspension of the meeting shall also be included.

The provisions concerning the meeting reports, which can fall under the scope of the action in annulment, remain the same, with one exception. According to the new Rules, the report related to the unconstitutionality exception of a legal provision may be challenged if the request for acknowledgement of the Constitutional Court is rejected as inadmissible, instead of the unconstitutionality exception.[50] Thus, inadmissibility is appraised in relation to the request for acknowledgement and not to the exception *per se*.

As far as probation is concerned, a new requirement is included concerning the handling of evidence, namely that it should be deemed useful and relevant to the cause.[51] Also, the former provision that the hearing of witnesses and experts should be carried out under oath is removed.[52]

Concerning the arbitral award, no substantial amendments have occurred. However, a new provision is included setting forth that, when the claimant waives arbitration or a claimed right following the constitution of the arbitral tribunal, the arbitration proceedings are terminated by a decision.[53]

The time limits related to the arbitral award are amended in the new regulation. Thus, the time limit related to the postponement of the decision is amended from 15 days, according to the former Rules[54], to 21 days, according to the new ones.[55] Time limits for the request of adjustment of material breaches in the content of the award, the request for clarifications on the decision, as well as the request for its completion, are amended from 15 days according to the former Rules[56] to 10 days according to the new Rules.[57] The date of receiving the award remains the date when such time limits begin to flow.

With regard to the notification of the award, the new Rules elaborate on the previous provisions. A penalty is provided in the case of incompliance with the time limit for drawing up and signing the award. Such penalty is triggered by incompliance or delayed compliance with the obligations arising from the arbitrator position as arbitrator. It is set forth in the Regulation on the

---

[50] Art. 59 paragraph 7 of the Rules.
[51] Art. 60 paragraph 2 of the Rules.
[52] Art. 67 of the former Rules.
[53] Art. 66 paragraph 4 of the Rules.
[54] Art. 75 paragraph 2 of the former Rules.
[55] Art. 68 paragraph 2 of the Rules.
[56] Art. 81 paragraph 1, art. 82 paragraph 1, art. 83 paragraph 1 of the former Rules.
[57] Art. 73 paragraph 1, art. 74 paragraph 1, art. 75 paragraph 1 of the Rules.

Organization and Operation of the Court of International Commercial Arbitration under the Chamber of Commerce and Industry of Romania.[58]
The arbitral award may be dissolved by way of an action in annulment. The new Rules bring two amendments in this respect. The date when the time limit during which the action in annulment may be submitted starts to flow is now the date when the arbitral award is notified[59] and not the date of receipt of the arbitral award, as per the former Rules[60]. This time limit is one month and unlike the former rules, now serves as an estoppel. [61]

The provisions concerning international commercial arbitration have a particular place in the new Rules. The new Rules have made amendments adapted to the pressing needs of the international commerce field. With regard to the determination of the applicable law, the new Rules provide that, in the absence of a written agreement between the parties, the arbitral tribunal may intervene and decide which law applies to the matters of the dispute.[62]

In the field of international arbitration, the duration of time limits set forth in view of settlement of domestic disputes are doubled. According to the new Rules, there is one exception, namely that the 21-day arbitration time limit starting the date of submittal of summons to the parties is not doubled when the party domiciled abroad chooses a domicile in Romania, where all communications concerning the arbitration dispute are to be made.[63] Also, a provision is made showing that, as with international disputes, the Appointing Authority shall mainly appoint international arbitrators included in the List of Arbitrators.[64]

There are also new rules regarding the language of deliberations. Article 88 of the new Rules provides the following:

> **(1)** If the place of arbitration is Romania, then deliberations shall be carried out in Romanian or in an international language, if all arbitrators are from abroad and they have reached a consensus. Otherwise, the provisions of Thesis I shall be applied.
>
> **(2)** If either party is not familiar with the language in which the deliberation is carried out, the arbitral tribunal shall provide it with the services of an interpreter, upon the party's request and at its expense.
>
> **(3)** The parties may take part in the deliberations with an interpreter of their own.

---

[58]   Art. 77 paragraph 4 of the Rules.
[59]   Art. 82 paragraph 1 of the Rules.
[60]   Art. 91 of the former Rules.
[61]   Art. 82 paragraph 2 of the Rules.
[62]   Art. 86 of the Rules.
[63]   Art. 87 paragraph 2 of the Rules.
[64]   Art. 87 paragraph 3 of the Rules.

(4) In any case, the deliberations shall be carried out in the presence of an interpreter appointed by the arbitral tribunal.

Finally, new elements are also included in the matter of *adhoc* arbitration. The definition of arbitration, according to the new Rules, compared to the former ones[65], specifies that the person organizing *ad-hoc* arbitration is a third party, other than an arbitration institution.[66] Also, two new provisions are included in Article 91.

(2) The arbitration agreement concluded by the parties needs to make explicit and express reference to *ad-hoc* arbitration, meaning that the *ad-hoc* arbitration phrase shall be explicitly included in the arbitration agreement.
(3) Any other wording of the will of the parties in the text of the arbitration agreement shall subject the dispute to settlement by institutionalized arbitration pursuant to its own rules and regulations if the claimant notifies the Court of Arbitration by way of a request for arbitration/arbitration proceeding.

Also in the chapter concerning *ad-hoc* arbitration, new provisions are included in the new Rules, which were absent in the former regulations. Thus, express specifications are included concerning the impartiality of arbitrators[67], the individual characteristic of appointing an arbitrator[68] and the appointment of the arbitrator in case of multiple parties.[69] Such provisions currently apply only to *ad-hoc* arbitration, since the parties are no longer allowed to appoint arbitrators as part of institutionalized arbitration, this being a task for the Appointing Authority.

Conclusions

In the past few years, the International Commercial Arbitration Court under the Chamber of Commerce and Industry of Romania has settled disputes dealing with bigger and bigger amounts of money. This is the result of acknowledgement and the trust granted by major Romanian and foreign companies to this manner of settling disputes. The downfalls of the legal system contributed to this development, given the duration of trials, which has extended significantly since 2008, and arbitration was seen as a faster way to

---

[65] Art. 100 of the former Rules.
[66] Art. 91 paragraph 1 of the Rules.
[67] Art. 94 of the Rules.
[68] Art. 95 of the Rules.
[69] Art. 96 of the Rules.

obtain an executory title, as well as the possibility to resort to experienced arbitrators, with vast and complex knowledge in the field; also, celerity in settling disputes and lower costs are significant aspects in settling disputes by arbitration.

[**Dr. Alina Mioara Cobuz Bagnaru**]
Attorney-at-law, PhD, Member of the Bucharest Bar, Founding Member of Cobuz si Asociatii, arbitrator with the Bucharest Stock Exchange, FINBAN mediator.
e-mail: alina@cobuz.ro

| | |

The Creation of the Russian Arbitration Association

I. Why Was It Needed?

According to the study of the ICC National Committee in Russia (ICC Russia), which was conducted in 2011-2012 (the Study),[1] Russia is quite unpopular as a place for arbitrating disputes. Thus, even when such disputes have a connection with Russia, the parties prefer them to be resolved in other jurisdictions that have a reputation for being 'arbitration-friendly'. The factors that contributed to the negative perception of Russia as an arbitration venue included its visa regime and a lack of proper administrative support to the peculiarities of state courts' case law in arbitration-related cases. There was also a clear preference for international arbitral institutions to administer the disputes, even in cases linked to Russia. Therefore, ICC Russia identified a need to improve the arbitration environment in Russia, as well as to radically change the approach employed by arbitration courts in that nation.

The main purpose behind the creation of the Russian Arbitration Association (RAA) is the promotion of both domestic and international arbitration in the Russian Federation and CIS countries, the popularization of Russia as a place for arbitration, the promotion of Russian arbitrators on national and international levels and also the promotion of foreign arbitrators interested in arbitrations directly or indirectly linked with Russia (specialists in Russian law, the Russian language or Russian parties).

The establishment of an institution of this kind was needed to address the growing concern in the professional legal community regarding arbitration in Russia. Although there are somewhere between 500 to 2 000 arbitration institutions in Russia, arbitration still is not really a preferred method of dispute resolution. This is confirmed by the statistics of state arbitrazh (commercial) courts. Thus, the number of challenges of Russian arbitral awards and applications for enforcement submitted to state courts can be measured in the thousands. At the same time, the number of commercial disputes examined by Russian state courts is in the hundreds of thousands. In comparison, the number of arbitral proceedings handled only under the rules of the American Arbitration Association comprises hundreds of thousands per year. The fact that state courts examine hundreds of times more commercial disputes than arbitration courts is a substantial indication of the lack of trust felt by the business community toward arbitration. This is caused by several factors.

---

[1] The results of the Study are available at ICC Russia website at: http://www.iccwbo.ru/news/0/305/

Firstly, there is distrust in the business community regarding the very concept of arbitration. Unfortunately, there are quite a few so-called 'pocket arbitration courts' in Russia, or arbitration courts that employ very dubious procedures or are used to legalize illegal schemes. As a result, for many Russian entrepreneurs arbitration is associated with these kinds of questionable practices.

Secondly, when state courts encounter glaring examples of abuse, they react sometimes with undue severity and create negative case law, restricting the arbitrability of certain kinds of disputes. This has happened, for example, with regard to real estate or corporate disputes.

Thirdly, the quality of dispute resolution by arbitration courts in Russia is unfortunately not the best. There are no special training programs for arbitrators. It is often thought that every able lawyer is capable of being a good arbitrator, but it is not always the case.

In the case of international disputes, the situation is even worse. Russian disputes (even between Russian companies) 'escape' abroad. Moreover, as shown by the ICC statistics, Russian companies, in resolving disputes abroad, do not appoint Russian arbitrators.

The reform of civil legislation is currently being conducted throughout the country, aimed at making the Russian Civil Code friendlier to business. Hopefully this will allow for it to eventually substitute for English law which very often dominates in M&A and financial transactions.

Finally one must take into account that Russian law can be applied adequately only if a dispute based on Russian law is examined, by arbitrators familiar with Russian law. German, Swiss and English arbitrators would never apply Russian law in the same way as Russian lawyers, just as Russian arbitrators would never apply English law in the way it is expected by English lawyers, due to the big gap between the principles of Russian and English law and procedure.

These are the problems the Russian Arbitration Association is called upon to tackle.

II. How Shall This Be Achieved?

First, the RAA will prepare proposals to improve the arbitration climate in Russia, to be addressed to the legislative authorities, the judiciary and the business community. One way is to eliminate the misuse of arbitration for illegal purposes, and, another is to foster the arbitration that meets the highest international standards. This work may materialise in the form of draft laws, as well as establishing certain standards of arbitration proceedings, with the latter including, for example, those regarding the independence of arbitration courts, the transparency of arbitrator appointment procedure and more. These standards will be of recommended nature but there can be no doubt that such standards will be heeded by the judiciary, as well as the business community.

Second, the RAA will organize training for arbitrators in a similar way as is done by the Chartered Institute of Arbitrators (CIArb). This is needed to involve not only trial lawyers in arbitration proceedings but also those lawyers who practice in other areas of law, such as corporate, banking and finance law, or real estate and telecommunications law. Indeed, if two law firms are working on a complex corporate transaction and a dispute arises, it is logical that other corporate lawyers would be resolving this dispute as they have firsthand experience in handling the nuances of such transactions and are thus able to resolve the dispute and issue a commercially sensible award. However, for a corporate lawyer to handle the proceedings and draft the right award they should have at least some knowledge of arbitration and some training how to handle proceedings and draft an award.

Third, information resources of the RAA will play a major role. The RAA website (http://www.arbitrations.ru) will contain not only information about the Russian arbitration community, but also information regarding potential arbitrators (both Russian and foreign) with the possibility of searching by criteria (such as country, language, field of law or practical experience). The website will also have services that could assist in the organization of arbitration proceedings such as venues for hearings, a database of experts or interpreters.

Fourth, the RAA has a membership for young arbitrators (RAA 40) and will develop special programs for young practitioners as well as offering favourable terms for participation in the events of the RAA.

Finally, the RAA itself shall administer arbitrations. The RAA starts with administering disputes under the UNCITRAL Rules, but the relevant regulations are planned for release at the end of the year 2013. In 2014, the RAA plans to develop rules for on-line arbitration.

III. Who Are the Members of the RAA?

The RAA was founded by more than 60 law firms from various regions (international, Russian, Belarusian, Ukrainian etc) and individuals. The names are very impressive, as they include almost all major 'players' in the Russian arbitration market.

The idea to have law firms as a founders came from the fact that law firms objectively have the greatest interest in the development of a trustworthy mechanism for the resolution of disputes, just as all fishermen in one area have a shared interest in the availability of fish in a lake. Should anyone show an inclination to poach, then the professional community will be able to put that poacher in his place.

At the first meeting, the members of the RAA held a competitive election in which they elected the Board and the Nominating Committee.

Out of 17 candidates nominated for the Board, originating from the UK, Belarus, Russia, Ukraine, France and Poland, 11 were elected. The Charter of the Arbitration Association provides that the Board is a permanent, collective managing body whose responsibilities include the development of the Association, working out the rules for resolving disputes, and making decisions on challenges to arbitrators. The voting resulted in the election of a number of prominent arbitration specialists, such as Timur Aitkulov (Clifford Chance, Moscow), David Goldberg (White and Case, London), Alevtina Kamelkova (Alcatel-Lucent, Moscow), Andrei Loboda (Injurservice, Moscow), Yuriy Monastyrsky (Monastyrsky, Zyuba, Stepanov & Partners, Moscow) Ilya Nikiforov (EPAM, Moscow), Noah Rubins (Freshfields, Paris), Vassily Rudomino (Alrud, Moscow) Tatyana Slipachuk (Sayenko Kharenko, Kiev), Vladimir Khvalei (Baker & McKenzie, Moscow) and Alexander Khrapoutski (Sysouev Bondar Khrapoutski, Minsk). The first meeting of the Board elected Vladimir Khvalei as a Chairman and Ilya Nikiforov and Noah Rubins as Vice-chairs of the Board.

The general meeting then selected the Arbitrators' Nominating Committee. This is a body within the Association which will nominate arbitrators for resolving disputes falling under arbitrations administered by the RAA. The voting resulted in the election of the following members to the Arbitrators' Nominating Committee: Tamara Abova (Institute of State and Law of the Russian Academy of Sciences, Moscow), Francesca Albert (Dechert, Moscow), Alexey Dudko (Hogan Lovells, Moscow), Galina Zukova (White and Case, Moscow), Ekaterina Kobrin (Baker & McKenzie, Moscow), Sergei Lebedev (MGIMO, Moscow), and Gleb Sevastyanov (Treteisky Sud Journal, St. Petersburg).

Roman Zykov, an attorney with many years of experience in international arbitration, was elected as the General Secretary of the Russian Arbitration Association.

IV. Conclusion

Overall, the creation of the Russian Arbitration Association is already viewed by many as a step forward in arbitration for Russia. So far it is still early to make definite conclusions on the success of the RAA as the initiative is in its early stages. There is a lot to be done, and time will show whether the initiative of creating a new type of arbitral institution in Russia will withstand the pressures and problems inherent in Russian realities. However, the beginning is very promising and we hope that with the kind of members we have on board, RAA will establish itself among the prominent arbitration institutions.

[***Vladimir Khvalei***]
Vladimir Khvalei is a partner in the Moscow office of Baker & McKenzie heading the firm's CIS Dispute Resolution Practice Group. Mr. Khvalei is a Vice-President of the ICC International Court of Arbitration and a Chairman of the Board of the Russian Arbitration Association.
Mr. Khvalei has wide experience participating in litigation in Russia, Kazakhstan, Belarus and Ukraine, as well as in international arbitration cases in accordance with the arbitration rules of the ICAC, UNCITRAL, ICC, SCC and other arbitration institutions, both as a party counsel and an arbitrator.
e-mail: Vladimir.Khvalei@bakermckenzie.com

| | |

Current Events,
Past & Ongoing CYIL / CYArb® Presentations

I. Current Events

Selected Scientific Conferences, Seminars, Academic Lectures and Other Professional Events and News in the Development of Arbitration and ADR in the Particular Countries[1]

I.1. [CZE] - [CZECH REPUBLIC]

[CZE] **Prague; 11 April 2013**
Czech / Russian Round table jointly held by International Court of Commercial Arbitration Attached to the Chamber of Commerce and Industry Russian Federation and the Court of Arbitration Attached to the Economic Chamber of the Czech Republic and Agrarian Chamber of the Czech Republic.

[CZE] **Prague; 6 – 8 June 2013**
XVIIIth World Forum of Mediation Centers. Organized by **Union Internationale des Avocats (Paris / France) jointly with the Czech Bar Association.**[2]

---

[1] Contributions mentioned herein represent a selection from papers related to arbitration. CYArb editors hereby apologize to the lecturers for omitting some of them and their topics due to the limited space provided for this section. Editors referred especially to published and other accessible information. Readers are specifically warned that the information about papers presented at the individual conferences and other academic and scientific events is only a selection and definitely does not provide a full report on the entire proceedings and the academic scope of each particular event.

[2] Further information available on http://www.uianet.org/en/evenement/type-46996/world-forum-mediation-centres-0 [Last visit 4th April 2013].

[CZE] Olomouc, 27 – 28 September 2013
Second International Scientific Conference, "Mediation 2013. A Way to Cooperation and Consensus." Organized by the Faculty of Law, Palacký University in Olomouc, Czech Republic.

[CZE] Prague, 31 October 2013
"3rd Investment Treaty Arbitration Conference 2013". Organized by the Ministry of Finance of the Czech Republic.

[CZE] Plzeň, 1 November 2013
Third International Conference, Current Issues of Arbitration. Organized by the Dept. of International Law, Faculty of Law, West Bohemia University in Pilsen, Czech Republic, jointly with the Arbitration Court Attached to the Chamber of Economy Czech Republic and Agrarian Chamber Czech Republic.

I.2. [AUT] - [AUSTRIA]

[AUT] Vienna, 25 - 26 January 2013
Vienna Arbitration Days.

[AUT] Vienna, 15 March 2013
Seminar held by the Vienna International Arbitral Centre (VIAC)[3] jointly with the American Bar Association's ILEX on Arbitration in Central and Eastern Europe – "Trends, Developments and Pitfalls".[4]

[AUT] Vienna, 15 March 2013
Seminar held by the Vienna International Arbitral Centre (VIAC)[5] jointly with the American Bar Association's ILEX on Arbitration in Central and Eastern Europe – "Trends, Developments and Pitfalls".[6]

[AUT] Vienna, 21 and 22 March 2013
UNCITRAL / Vienna International Arbitral Centre (VIAC)[7] / YAPP Joint Conference on the following topics (i) Organisation of Arbitral Proceedings

---

[3] The Vienna International Arbitration Centre is partner (cooperating institution) for CYArb.

[4] Further information available on http://news.wko.at/Media/9240a453-6945-44e3-ab00-a41fcf3354ac/2012/Info-3_2013/viac_march_15_2013__cee_seminar_invitation__draft_4_march_2013.pdf [Las visit 6th March 2013].

[5] The Vienna International Arbitration Centre is partner (cooperating institution) for CYArb.

[6] Further information available on http://news.wko.at/Media/9240a453-6945-44e3-ab00-a41fcf3354ac/2012/Info-3_2013/viac_march_15_2013__cee_seminar_invitation__draft_4_march_2013.pdf [Las visit 6th March 2013].

[7] The Vienna International Arbitration Centre is partner (cooperating institution) for CYArb.

from an arbitrator's, the parties'and institutions'perspective, (ii) Arbitrability and public policy – how to reach harmonization? and (iii) Liability of players in arbitration.[8] Presentations done by Corinne Montineri (UNCITRAL), Julia Salasky, Lisa Bench Nieuwveld, Andrew Cannon, Martin Doe, Simon Greenberg, Stefan Kröll, Annette Magnusson, Loukas Mistelis, Ulrike Paukner, Mick Smith and Julia Zagonek.

[AUT] Vienna, 23 March 2013
Young Arbitrators Forum hosted by the Faculty of Law, University Vienna with the support of ICC Austria, on the topics "Young Approaches to Arbitration". Conducted during the Willem C. Vis Moot.

[AUT] Vienna, 25 March 2013
Ninth Annual Leading Arbitrators'Symposium by JurisConferences, under a non-financial sponsorship of the Vienna International Arbitral Centre (VIAC), partnership of CYArb – Czech (& Central) European Yearbook of Arbitration˙ and partnership of further subjects and entities.

[AUT] Vienna, 25 March 2013
Conference on "El Arbitraje en el Mundo Hispano-hablante" organized by the Club Español del Arbitraje, CEA – Capítulo de Alemania y Austria.[9]

[AUT] Vienna, 7 May 2013
Advanced Arbitration Seminar on "The New ICC Arbitration Rules 2012 – Changes & First Experiences" organized by the ICC Austria.

[AUT] [ITA] Milan, 27 June 2013
Vienna International Arbitral Centre (VIAC)[10] / CAM / DIS and SCC Arbitration Institute Conference on **Pathological Arbitration Clauses at the Institutional Level.**[11]

[AUT] Vienna, 11 July 2013
Vienna International Arbitral Centre (VIAC)[12] / UNCITRAL Joint Conference on **Developments in Law and Technology** and **Presentation of the New York**

---

[8]   Detail information available on http://news.wko.at/Media/9240a453-6945-44e3-ab00-a41fcf3354ac/2012/Info-2_2013/2013_programme.pdf [Last visit on 6th March 2013].

[9]   Further information on http://www.arbitration-austria.at/dokumente/FlyerCEA.pdf [Last visit on 6th March 2013].

[10]   The Vienna International Arbitration Centre is partner (cooperating institution) for CYArb.

[11]   See also a similar event in Vienna [AUT] in October 2013.

[12]   The Vienna International Arbitration Centre is partner (cooperating institution) for CYArb.

Convention 1958 Web Platform and draft UNCITRAL Guide on the New York Convention with introduction and auspice by Werner Melis, Honorary President of VIAC. **Panel I**: *Presentation of the New York Convention 1958 web site and of the Guide – How to contribute* (Renaud Sorieul, The Secretary of UNCITRAL) and Yas Banifatemi; **Panel II**: *Enforceability of awards under the New York Convention in the context of investor-State disputes* (Emmanuel Gaillard, Professor at University Paris XII, together with James Castello, Rolf Knieper, Professor emeritus at University of Bremen and John Rooney, Professor at University of Miami); **Panel III**: *Arbitrability and the New York Convention* (George Bermann, Professor at Columbia University, together with Jun Zhao, Associate Professor at Guanghua Law School, Zhejiang University in China, Matthias Neumayr, Judge at the Supreme Court of Austria and Professor at the University of Linz and Reinmal Wolff, Professor at the University of Marburg).[13]

[AUT] **Vienna, 4 September 2013**
Presentation of the Vienna Rules by VIAC (Vienna International Arbitral Centre).

[AUT] **Innsbruck, 13 September 2013**
ArbAut, ASA and LIS Joint Conference on on "Dreiländerkonferenz 2013 – Schiedsverfahren in Österreich, Liechtenstein und der Schweiz" [Three Countries Conference 2013 – Arbitration in Austra, Lichtenstein and Switzerland].

[AUT] **Vienna, 11 October 2013**
Vienna International Arbitral Centre (VIAC) / CEPANI Joint Conference on the following topics: Arbitration landscape in Belgium and in Austria, Arbitration and Confidentiality, Are the new rules carried by Cepani and VIAC suitable for new circumstances? Multiparty arbitration.

I.3. [LVA] - [LATVIA]

[LVA] **Riga, 13 – 14 June 2013**
Conference held by DIS Deutsche Institution für Schiedsgerichtsbarkeit (German Institution for Arbitration) **"Baltic Arbitration Days 2013: Arbitration in Corporate and Finance Disputes"**.[14]

---

[13] Further information on http://news.wko.at/Media/9240a453-6945-44e3-ab00-a41fcf3354ac/2012/Info-6 2013/11 july 2013 conference programme.pdf [Last visit on 31 May 2013].

[14] Further information in English on http://www.dis-arb.de/en/18/events/dis-baltikum-baltic-arbitration-days-2013-arbitration-in-corporate-and-finance-disputes-id182 [Last visit on 20th March 2013].

I.4. [POL] - [POLAND] [15]

[POL] **Warszawa, 25 January 2013**
Seminar *First Polish-Swiss Arbitration and Business Seminar* organized by the Court of Arbitration at the Polish Chamber of Commerce (Sąd Arbitrażowy przy Krajowej Izbie Gospodarczej) and the Swiss Chambers' Arbitration Institution. *Speakers and topics: Welcome Address and Introduction:* Justyna Szpara, Sandra De Vito Bieri, Krzysztof Rączka, Marek Furtek, Rainer Füeg, Jean-Pierre Schneuwly (*Business and cultural relationship between Poland and Switzerland*), Monika Ruggli (*Doing Business in Switzerland*), Sandra De Vito Bieri, Simon Gabriel (*Switzerland: Chocolate, Mountains and... Arbitration: The Swiss Rules of International Arbitration*), Maciej Łaszczuk (*The Polish: Friends of International Arbitration*), Witold Jurcewicz, Rafał Morek, Lukas Wyss, Simon Gabriel (*Roundtable on the Swiss Rules and Polish Arbitration Rules*), *moderated by:* Sandra De Vito Bieri.[16]

[POL] **Warszawa, 13 February 2013**
International conference *Evidence in arbitration* (*Dowody i postępowanie dowodowe w arbitrażu*) organized by the Center of Dispute and Conflict Resolution at the Faculty of Law and Administration of the University of Warsaw (Centrum Rozwiązywania Sporów I Konfliktów przy Wydziale Prawa i Administracji Uniwersytetu Warszawskiego). *Speakers and topics: Welcome Address and Key Note Speech:* Jerzy Rajski, Stavros Brekoulakis. *Panel I. Evidence in Arbitration: General Issues, moderated by:* Sylwester Pieckowski, *speakers:* Olena Perepelynska (*The law and practice of evidence proceedings in court and in arbitration – Similarities and differences*), Joanna Młot (*Burdens of proof, admissibility of evidence, thresholds and weighing of evidence in court proceedings and arbitration*), Wojciech Sadowski (*Legal impediment or privilege – Sensitivity and confidentiality as grounds for exclusion of evidence in international arbitration*), Maria Hauser-Morel (*Scrutiny of awards by the ICC Court: Focus on Evidence*), Michał Pochodyła (*Evidentiary issues as grounds to challenge an arbitral award or refuse its enforcement*). *Panel II. Fact and Expert Witnesses, moderated by:* Piotr Nowaczyk, *speakers:* Bartosz Krużewski (*Preparing of witnesses – Coaching or just familiarization?*), Marcin Asłanowicz (*Credibility of witnesses and experts called by the parties vs. appointed by the arbitration tribunal*), Bartłomiej Niewczas (*Nomination of an external expert in arbitration*), Nils Schmidt-Ahrendts (*Groups of experts: New approach to the*

---

[15] Compiled with the kind assistance of Kubas Kos Gaertner, Law firm (www.kkg.pl). Kubas Kos Gaertner are specialized (among others) in arbitration and ADR.
[16] Detailed information available at: http://www.sakig.pl/en/news/events/first-polish-swiss-arbitration-and-business-seminar (in English); http://www.sakig.pl/pl/aktualnosci/lista/first-polish-swiss-arbitration-and-business-seminar (in Polish).

role of an expert), Tomasz Krawczyk (*Witnesses' written statements in arbitration in the process of control of arbitration rulings by state courts*), Michał Jochemczak (*Procedures for conducting evidence in international commercial arbitration – Observations on witness statements, examination of witnesses and disclosure*). *Panel III. Documentary and Other Evidence, moderated by:* Paweł Pietkiewicz, *speakers:* Volodymyr Yaremko (*Document production: An irreplaceable tool in capable hands*), Wojciech Jaworski, Marek Neumann (*Document production in international arbitration - A few practical remarks*), Katarzyna Michałowska (*Discovery in investment arbitration*), Justyna Szpara (*Forensics in arbitration*).[17]

[POL] Warszawa, 11 March 2013
Conference held by the ICC YAF / ICC International Court of Arbitration on "Time Management and Arbitration Costs: Practical Aspects".[18]
Arbitration workshop *International arbitration without any secrets* (*Międzynarodowy arbitraż bez tajemnic*) led by Maria Hauser-Morel, organized by the Center of Dispute and Conflict Resolution at the Faculty of Law and Administration of the University of Warsaw (Centrum Rozwiązywania Sporów i Konfliktów przy Wydziale Prawa i Administracji Uniwersytetu Warszawskiego).[19]

[POL] Warszawa, 12 March 2013
Meeting of the Polish Arbitration Association.

[POL] Warszawa, 10 April 2013
Conference held by the Arbitration Court Attached to the Polish Economic Chamber to Warsaw [POL] on "Evidence and Evidence Procedure in Arbitration".[20]
Arbitration Workshop: *Evidence and Evidentiary Proceedings in Arbitration* (*Dowody i postępowanie dowodowe w arbitrażu*) organized by Court of Arbitration at the Polish Chamber of Commerce (Sąd Arbitrażowy przy Krajowej Izbie Gospodarczej). *Speakers and topics: Part I. The role of the arbitrator in evidentiary proceedings, moderated by:* Marek Wierzbowski, *speakers:* Andrzej Tynel (*The arbitrator: observer or inquisitor? On the role of*

---

[17] Detailed information available at: http://mediacje.wpia.uw.edu.pl/en/2013/02/04/dowody-i-postepowanie-dowodowe-w-arbitrazu-2/ (in English); http://mediacje.wpia.uw.edu.pl/2013/02/04/dowody-i-postepowanie-dowodowe-w-arbitrazu-2/ (in Polish).
[18] Further information in English on www.iccyaf.org
[Last visit on 4th March 2013].
[19] Detailed information available at: http://mediacje.wpia.uw.edu.pl/2013/03/05/miedzynarodowy-arbitraz-bez-tajemnic-warsztaty-prowadzone-przez-dr-marie-hauser-morel/ (in Polish).
[20] Further information on https://sakig.pl [Last visit on 2nd March 2013].

the arbitrator), Maciej Łaszczuk (*Free evaluation of evidence in arbitration*), Anna Krysiak (*Agreements concerning evidentiary proceedings*), Witold Jurcewicz (*Techniques of managing evidentiary proceedings*). *Part II. Evidence: documents, witnesses and experts, moderated by*: Andrzej Szumański, Bartosz Krużewski (*Witness testimony: witness statements, preparation of witnesses by an attorney and other issues*), Wojciech Sadowski (*Orders for document production in domestic and international arbitration*), Cezary Wiśniewski (*Experts of the parties or experts of the tribunal? Good practices in the admission of evidence from experts*), Paweł Zejer (*Experts – "superarbitrators"?*).[21]

[POL] Warszawa, 11 March 2013
National students and PhD candidates conference *Quo vadis, Arbitration?* (*Quo vadis, Arbitraż?*) organized by the Center of Dispute and Conflict Resolution at the Faculty of Law and Administration of the University of Warsaw (Centrum Rozwiązywania Sporów i Konfliktów przy Wydziale Prawa i Administracji Uniwersytetu Warszawskiego). *Speakers and topics: Welcome Address and Introduction*: Marek Furtek, Sylwester Pieckowski, Justyna Szpara, Rafał Morek. *Different views on the issue of Arbitration, moderated by*: Laura Mazur, *speakers*: Agnieszka Zarówna, Dariusz Kała, Katarzyna Sawicka. *Arbitration and its features, moderated by*: Aleksandra Orzeł, *speakers*: Łukasz Czarnecki, Jacek Zębala, Maciej Troć, Karolina Pasko. *The Rules of Arbitration, moderated by Witold Jurcewicz, speakers*: Magdalena Krawczyk, Maciej Zych, Magdalena Szewczyk, Łukasz Gembiś, Magdalena Rząca, Anna Trocka. *Arbitration in foreign countries – comparative analysis, moderated by*: Aleksandra Orzeł, *speakers*: Jakub Wojas, Katarzyna Szczepańska, Urszula Comi, Łukasz Kuchta, Paula Majcher, Michał Mościcki, Lech Dubiński. *International Arbitration – threats and chances, moderated by*: Piotr Nowaczyk, *speakers*: Maciej Gorgol, Michał Pyka, Magdalena Krzysztoporska, Maciej Kruk, Anita Garnuszek, Wojciech Giemza. *Arbitration in energy disputes, moderated by*: Adam Krenke, *speakers*: Ilona Przybojewska, Łukasz Szmaj-Mroczyński, Magdalena Brodawka, Adam Kowalski. *Arbitration in Internet domain disputes, moderated by*: Michał Nowiński, *speakers*: Marek Porzeżyński, Joanna Kisielińska, Aleksandra Kluczewska, Paweł Dymiński, Tomasz Niedziółka. *Practical and theoretical aspects of arbitration, moderated by*: Laura Mazur, *speakers*: Aleksandra Surma, Paweł Dębowski, Aneta Makowiec, Maksymilian Szeląg-Dylewski, Jakub Zygucki, Wiktor Łoś, Michał Wdowiek, *Arbitration in consumer disputes, moderated by*: Michał Nowiński, *speakers*: Katarzyna Grotkowska, Jagna Pękala, Paweł Michalski. *Miscellaneous, moderated by*: Laura Mazur, *speakers*: Adrian Bielecki, Marcin Alberski, Anna Rak, Karolina

---

[21] Detailed information available at: http://sakig.pl/pl/aktualnosci/lista/dowody-i-postepowanie-dowodowe-w-arbitrazu (in Polish and English).

Alama-Osmólska, Aleksandra Orzeł, Estera Winiarska. *Arbitration in competition disputes, moderated by:* Michał Nowiński, *speakers:* Anna Laszczyk, Dominika Jędrzejczyk. *Arbitration in sport disputes, moderated by:* Stanisław Drozd, *speaker:* Natalia Rutkowska. *Miscellaneous, moderated by:* Andrzej Wiśniewski, *speakers:* Katarzyna Reszczyk, Klaudia Gąsior, Patryk Słowik, Adam Ploszka, Tomasz Pyś, Paweł Kępka, Elżbieta Szulc-Wałecka. *Arbitration in construction disputes, moderated by:* Stanisław Drozd, *speakers:* Patrycja Ryś, Michał Skorupka, Marek Topór. *Miscellaneous, moderated by:* Laura Mazur, *speakers:* Agnieszka Sobecka, Bartłomiej Sasin, Krzysztof Drozdowicz, Tomasz Karwicki.[22]

[POL] Nowy Tomyśl, 19 April 2013
Conference held by the Arbitration Court Attached to the Economic Chamber to Nowy Tomyśl [POL] on "Functioning of permanent arbitral institutions and mediation centers" [Polish title: "Funkcjonowanie stałych sądów polubownych i ośrodków mediacyjnych"].

International conference *Permanent courts of arbitration and mediation centers* (*Funkcjonowanie stałych sądów polubownych i ośrodków mediacyjnych*) organized by the Court of Arbitration at the Chamber of Commerce of Nowy Tomyśl (Sąd Arbitrażowy przy Nowotymyskiej Izbie Gospodarczej). *Speakers and topics: Welcome Address and Introduction:* Włodzimierz Brych. *Panel I, moderated by:* Joachim Hilla, *speakers:* Feliks Zedler (*Settlement before a mediator – legal problems*), Tadeusz Szewioła (*Costs in mediation proceedings*), Katarzyna Zalas-Kamińska (*Promotion of mediation and the functioning of mediation centers*), Maria Ficak (*Mediation in Kaliningrad District*), Medea Demetrashvili (*Mediation in Georgia – perspectives*), Else Mälmeistere (*Mediation in Latvia*), Monika Milosevic (*Mediation in consumer disputes in Serbia*). *Panel II, moderated by:* Agnieszka Rękas, *speakers:* Aleksandra Petrus-Schmidt, Krystian Mularczyk (*People and money – main factors influencing the functioning of permanent courts of arbitration and mediation centers*), Suleymienov Maydan Kuntuarowicz, Asel Duseynova (*Functioning of permanent courts of arbitration and mediation centers in Kazakhstan*), Markian Malskyy (*Practical aspects of dispute resolution with Ukrainian parties*), Yussuf Nazarov (*Functioning of permanent courts of arbitration and mediation centers in Uzbekistan*). *Panel III, moderated by* Andrzej Szumański, *speakers:* Jacek Kaczmarek (*Receptum arbitri – relation between the arbitrator, the parties and the court of arbitration*), Mikhail Savranskyy (*Certain aspects of improving the efficiency of international arbitration*), Alaksandar Ciric (*International commercial arbitration – unification of law applied in international commerce*),

---

[22] Detailed information available at: http://konferencjakomin.wix.com/language (in Polish and English).

Andrzej Kąkolecki (*Modern arbitration rules*), Karl Pörnbacher (*Experience and good practices in managing Polish-German arbitration disputes*), Aleksander Kostenetskyi (*Development of arbitration in Ukraine – interactions with state court system*). *Panel IV, moderated by:* Piotr Nowaczyk, *speakers:* Włodzimierz Brych (*Court of Arbitration at the Chamber of Commerce of Nowy Tomyśl and its functioning*), Maria Hauser-Morel (*Functioning of ICC – New rules of 2012*), Routh Mosh (*German Arbitration Institute and its rules*), Vytautas Nekrošius (*New developments in arbitral law of Lithuania, functioning of the Vilnius Arbitration Court (VCCA) under the new rules of 2013*), Igor Dutka (*Functioning of permanent courts of arbitration in Ukraine*).[23]

[POL] Warszawa, 8 May 2013
Fourth meeting of *the Arbitrators' Club* (*Klub Arbitrów*), organized by the Lewiatan Court of Arbitration (Sąd Arbitrażowy przy Polskiej Konfederacji Pracodawców Prywatnych Lewiatan), entitled *Mediation and arbitration – friends or enemies* (*Mediacja i arbitraż - przyjaciele czy wrogowie*), meeting *moderated by:* Beata Gessel-Kalinowska vel Kalisz, *speakers:* Eligiusz Krześniak, Wojciech Sadowski, Sylwester Pieckowski, Michał Pochodyła, Rafał Morek, Roman Rewald.[24]

[POL] Warszawa, 24 May 2013
National conference *Arbitration: Law, Practice, Institutions* (*ARBITRAŻ: Prawo, Praktyka, Instytucje*) organized by the Court of Arbitration at the Polish Chamber of Commerce (Sąd Arbitrażowy przy Krajowej Izbie Gospodarczej) and the Extraordinary Commission on the Amendments to the Codes. *Speakers: Marek Furtek, Krzysztof Kwiatkowski, Wojciech Popiołek, Bartosz Krużewski.*[25]

[POL] Warszawa, 24 - 25 May 2013
First edition of the Warsaw High School Moot Court organized by the Court of Arbitration at the Polish Chamber of Commerce (Sąd Arbitrażowy przy Krajowej Izbie Gospodarczej) concerning investment arbitration.[26]

---

[23] Detailed information available at: http://www.nig.org.pl/sa/pl/konferencje.html (in Polish).

[24] Detailed information available at: http://www.sadarbitrazowy.org.pl/pl/8maja2013 (in Polish).

[25] Detailed information available at: http://www.sakig.pl/en/news/events/conference-on-arbitration-law-practice-institutions (in English); http://www.sakig.pl/pl/aktualnosci/lista/konferencja-arbitraz-prawo-praktyka-instytucje (in Polish).

[26] Detailed information available at: http://www.sakig.pl/en/news/events/warsaw-high-school-moot-court (in English); http://www.sakig.pl/pl/aktualnosci/lista/warsaw-high-school-moot-court (in Polish).

Czech (& Central European) Yearbook of Arbitration

[POL] Warszawa, 6 – 7 June 2013

International Conference *Dispute Resolution in M&A Transactions 2013* organized by Lewiatan Court of Arbitration (Sąd Arbitrażowy przy Polskiej Konfederacji Pracodawców Prywatnych Lewiatan). *Speakers and topics*: *Welcome and Opening Remarks:* Beata Gessel-Kalinowska vel Kalisz, Artur Nowak-Far, Henryk Orfinger. *Panel I: Hot Topics in M&A Arbitration (e.g. M&A activity worldwide, recent ICC awards), panel moderated by*: Beata Gessel-Kalinowska vel Kalisz, *speakers:* Daniel Busse, Andrea Carlevaris, Nelson Eizirik, Michael Hwang S.C., Penny Madden; *Panel II: To Bifurcate or Not to Bifurcate – This and Other Procedural Issues in M&A Arbitration, panel moderated by:* Mireze Philippe, *speakers:* Philipp Habegger, Paweł Pietkiewicz, Soteris Pittas, Jakob Ragnwaldh. *Panel III: Shareholders Dispute – Case Study under the Patronage of Dechert LLP, panel moderated by*: Krzysztof Stefanowicz, *speakers:* Cecile Amayen, François Hellot, Xavier Nyssen. *Panel IV: Computation of Damages – Panel of Witness Experts, panel moderated by*: Julian Lew, *speakers:* Vladimir Bosiljevac, Anthony Charlton, Nick Andrews, Frank Ilett. *Closing remarks of day I*: Catherine Kessedjian. *BREAKFAST PRESENTATION: M&A and Shareholders Disputes in the CEE Region from the Perspective of Arbitral Institutions, panel moderated by:* Krzysztof Stefanowicz and Małgorzata Surdek, *speakers:* Ziedionic Udris, Daniel Busse, Irina Nazarova, Manfred Heider, Alena Bányaiová, István Varga. *Panel V: Antitrust Law in M&A Disputes, panel moderated by:* Marc Blessing, *speakers:* Gordon Blanke, Mark Kantor, Jean-Claude Najar, Anna Maria Pukszto. *Panel VI: Mandatory Public Law in M&A arbitration, panel moderated by:* Justin Michaelson, *speakers:* Courtenay Griffiths QC, Maciej Jamka, Irina Nazarova, Sulvia Tonova, Stephan Wilske. *Closing remarks of day two:* Tomasz Gizbert-Studnicki.[27]

[POL] Warszawa, 18 June 2013

Young Arbitrators Forum [Arbitrażowe Forum Młodych] **held by the Arbitration Court Attached to the Polish Economic Chamber to Warsaw [POL] on "Evidence and Evidence Procedure in Arbitration".**[28]

[POL] Warszawa, 21 June 2013

Fourth meeting of *the Arbitrators' Club* (*Klub Arbitrów*), organized by the Lewiatan Court of Arbitration (Sąd Arbitrażowy przy Polskiej Konfederacji Pracodawców Prywatnych Lewiatan), entitled *The dream arbitration of*

---

[27] Detailed information available at: http://www.sadarbitrazowy.org.pl/upload/13 Dispute_programme_2013_Stadium.pdf (in English).

[28] Further information in English on https://sakig.pl.

Włodzimierz Kiciński (KGHM), meeting moderated by: Beata Gessel-Kalinowska vel Kalisz, *speaker:* Włodzimierz Kiciński.[29]

[POL] Krakow / Cracow, 21 – 22 June 2013
Conference on the occasion of the tenth anniversary of the LL.M. Programme in American Law at the Jagiellonian University entitled *Legal profession, market of legal services and legal education. A look into the future.* (*Zawody prawnicze, rynek usług prawniczych oraz edukacja prawnicza. Spojrzenie w przyszłość*) organized by the Jagiellonian University (Universytet Jagielloński) and The Catholic University of America.[30]

[POL] Warszawa, 25 June 2013
Polish Kongres of Litigation, Mediation and Arbitration 2013 held by the Institut Allerhanda.[31]
National conference *Allerhand Arbitration & Dispute Resolution Summit 2013 (Polski Kongres Sporów Sądowych, Mediacji I Arbitrażu 2013)* organized by the Allerhand Institute (Instytut Allerhanda). *Speakers and topics: Welcoming:* Mariusz Haładyj. *Session I Class action – summary of experiences after 3 years of its introduction, speakers:* Iwo Gabrysiak, Dominik Gałkowski, Paweł Pietkiewicz, Arkadiusz Radwan, Mikołaj Wild. *Session II Investment arbitration – the protection of Polish investment abroad, speakers:* Marcin Dziurda, Kamil Zawicki. *Session III Development of arbitration and mediation in Poland, speakers:* Włodzimierz Brych, Beata Gessel-Kalinowska vel Kalisz, Sylwester Pieckowski, Andrzej Szumański. *Session IV Can litigation be more expeditious and efficient?, speakers:* Benedykt Fiutowski, Zbigniew Kruczkowski, Paweł Lewandowski, Zbigniew Miczek, Kamil Zawicki. *Session V What do clients expect from litigation lawyers?, speakers:* Łukasz Bendkowski, Michał Kocur, Waldemar Koper, Piotr Marucha, Dominik Wolski.[32]

[POL] Zgierz, 5 – 7 September 2013
National conference *Arbitration in international law (Arbitraż w prawie międzynarodowym)* organised by the Faculty of Law of Cardinal Stefan Wyszyński University in Warsaw (Uniwersytet Kardynała Stefana Wyszyńskiego w Warszawie). *Speakers and topics: General discussion, speakers:* Konrad Marciniak, Marek Jeżewski, Artur Kozłowski, Joanna Połatyńska,

---

[29]   Detailed information available at: http://www.sadarbitrazowy.org.pl/pl/Spotkania-Klubu-Arbitra (in Polish).
[30]   Detailed information available at: http://www.sakig.pl/en/news/events/the-conference-of-the-10-th-anniversary-of-the-ll-m-program-in-american-law (in English); http://www.sakig.pl/pl/aktualnosci/lista/konferencja-z-okazji-x-rocznicy-programu-ll-m (in Polish).
[31]   Further information on www.arbitraz.allerhand.pl [Last visit on 24th April 2013].
[32]   Detailed information available at: http://www.kongresy.allerhand.pl/kongresy/polski-kongres-sporow-sadowych-mediacji-i-arbitrazu-2013/ (in Polish).

Michał Stępień. *Arbitration and development of international law, speakers:* Przemysław Saganek, Cezary Mik, Janusz Symonides, Malgosia Fitzmaurice, Krzysztof Masło. *Arbitration in international investment law, speakers:* Łukasz Kułaga, Barbara Klimek, Ewelina Gruszewska, Elżbieta Morawska, *Arbitration in international practice, speakers:* Joanna Gomuła, Beata Gessel-Kalinowska vel Kalisz, Agnieszka Różalska, Maciej Perkowski.[33]

[POL] **Warszawa, 12 September 2013**
Meeting of *Youth Arbitration Forum* (*Arbitrażowe Forum Młodych*) entitled *Current trends in investment arbitration*, organized by the Court of Arbitration at the Polish Chamber of Commerce (Sąd Arbitrażowy przy Krajowej Izbie Gospodarczej). Special guest: Christoph Schreuer, meeting chaired by Justyna Szpara and Marek Świątkowski.[34]

[POL] **Warszawa, 18 September 2013**
International seminar *Arbitration in London – A Practical Perspective for Polish Companies* organized by the Lewiatan Court of Arbitration (Sąd Arbitrażowy przy Polskiej Konfederacji Pracodawców Prywatnych Lewiatan), Wardyński & Partners and Wragge & Co LLP law firms, *speakers:* Sarah Lancaster, Peter Flint, Tom Price.[35]

[POL] **Warszawa, 11 October 2013**
International seminar *3rd Warsaw Investment Arbitration Debate* organized by the Center of Dispute and Conflict Resolution at the Faculty of Law and Administration of the University of Warsaw (Centrum Rozwiązywania Sporów i Konfliktów przy Wydziale Prawa i Administracji Uniwersytetu Warszawskiego). *Speakers and topics: An appeals mechanism in investment arbitration: is it desirable, is it feasible,* Katarzyna Michałowska, *The ne peius principle in investment arbitration,* Wojciech Sadowski. *Does the system of investment – treaty arbitration need revision?,* moderated by *Rudolf Ostrihansky,* Małgorzata Surdek, Wojciech Jaworski, Bartłomiej Niewczas, Ignacy Janas and Marcin Kałduński.[36]

---

[33] Detailed information available at: http://wpia.uksw.edu.pl/sites/default/files/prawo_ miedzynarodowe_i_europejskie/arbitraz%20w%20pr%20miedz%20program%202.8.13%20 wer%20ost.doc (in Polish).

[34] Detailed information available at: http://www.sakig.pl/en/news/events/young-arbitration-forum-current-trends-in-investment-arbitration (in English); http://www.sakig.pl/pl/ aktualnosci/lista/arbitrazowe-forum-mlodych-trendy-w-arbitrazu-inwestycyjnym (in Polish).

[35] Detailed information available at: http://www.sadarbitrazowy.pl/en/news;id-130 (in English); http://www.sadarbitrazowy.org.pl/pl/news;id-130 (in Polish).

[36] Detailed information available at: http://www.sakig.pl/en/news/events/does-the-system-of-investment-treaty-arbitration-need-revision (in English); http://www.sakig.pl/ pl/aktualnosci/lista/does-the-system-of-investment-treaty-arbitration-need-revision (in Polish).

[POL] Warszawa, 22 October 2013
Joint Conference of VIAC (Vienna International Arbitral Centre) and PSPP on international arbitration.

[POL] Kraków / Cracow, 7 November 2013
Conference held by the **ICC Young Arbitrators Forum (ICCYAF) on "The Selection of Arbitrators – Practical Aspects".**

[POL] Kraków / Cracow, 8 November 2013
Conference held by the **Arbitration Court Attached to the Polish Economic Chamber to Warsaw [POL] jointly with the Department of Economic Law, Faculty of Law and Administration Jagiellonian University in Kraków (Cracow) and jointly with Chamber of Trade and Industry in Kraków (Cracow) on "Arbitral Award".**

Panel I: Binding effects of the arbitral award – chaired by prof. dr hab. A. Szumański, speakers – prof. dr hab. Józef Frąckowiak, prof. dr hab. W. Popiołek, a. Korzeniewski.
Panel II: Form of the Arbitral Award – chaired by prof. dr hab. M. Pazdan, speakers – M. Łaszczuk, dr. W. Jurcewicz, P. Nowaczyk.
Panel III: Effects of an arbitral award to third paries – chaired by prof. dr hab. S. Sołtysiński, speakers – M. Surdek, dr G. Suliński, C. Wiśniewski.
Panel IV: Public policy clause as the reason for set-aside of an arbitral award – chaired by prof. dr hab.T. Ereciński, speakers – dr R. Morek, B. Krużevwski, prof. dr hab. K. Weitz.

I.5. [RUS] - [RUSSIAN FEDERATION]

[RUS] Moscow; 3 – 4 April 2013
Russian Legal Forum "Vedomosti".[37]

[CZE] Prague; 11 April 2013
Czech / Russian Round table jointly held by International Court of Commercial Arbitration Attached to the Chamber of Commerce and Industry Russian Federation and the Court of Arbitration Attached to the Economic Chamber of the Czech Republic and Agrarian Chamber of the Czech Republic

---

[37]   Further informations on http://www.arbitrations.ru/files/calendar/uploaded/Russian_Arbitration_Day_2013.pdf [Last visit 31 May 2013].

[RUS] Moscow; 20 June 2013
Russian Arbitration Day.[38]
The event was followed by the constitutional assembly of the Russian Arbitration Association.

[RUS] St. Petersburg; 27 June 2013
YAS roundtable discussion on "Appointment of arbitrators". Speakers: N. Rubins (Paris), G. Knuts (Helsinki), T. Slipachuk (Kyiv / Kyjev), P. Ewerlöf (Stockholm), and as moderator K. Löf.[39]

[RUS] St. Petersburg; 28 June 2013
IBA Arbitration Committee's "White Nights" Conference on International Arbitration at a Crossroads: Is there a coming backlash?[40]

[RUS] St. Petersburg; 4 – 5 July 2013
All Russia Forum of Arbitration Society - Forum on Innovation of the Law on Arbitration and Law on International Arbitration: Current standards and conducts of leading arbitration institutions.[41] Venue: St. Petersburg's B. N. Jelcin Presidential Library

[RUS] Moscow; 27 September 2013
Conference on "International Commercial Dispute Resolution: CIS Countries. The event was organised by the ICC Russia.

[RUS] Moscow; 10 December 2013
Conference "Russia as a Place for Dispute Resolution: Anticipating the Changes". The event was organised by the ICC Russia.[42]

I.6. [SRB] - [SERBIA]

[SRB] Belgrade / Београд / Beograd [Serbia], 27 September 2013
VIAC [Vienna International Arbitral Centre] and ArbAut [Austrian Arbitration

---

[38] Further informations on http://www.arbitrations.ru/files/calendar/uploaded/Russian_Arbitration_Day_2013.pdf [Last visit 31 May 2013].

[39] Further informations on http://www.arbitrations.ru/files/calendar/uploaded/Invitation_to_YAS_event_in_St_Petersburg_27_June_2013.pdf [Last visit 15 June 2013].

[40] Further informations on www.ibanet.org or on http://www.arbitrations.ru/files/calendar/uploaded/IBA_St_Petersburg_Arbitration_Russia_2013_programme.pdf [Last visit 31 May 2013].

[41] Further informations on www.ibanet.org or on http://www.arbitrations.ru/?i=news/item&id=405 [Last visit 31 May 2013] and on http://arbitrage.spb.ru/misc/konf/info.html [Last visit 15 June 2013].

[42] Further information on http://iccwbo.ru.

Association] joint event on international commercial arbitration in co-operation with leading Serbian arbitration practitioners and academics.[43]

I.7. [SVN] - [SLOVENIA]

[SVN] Portorož, 17 September 2013
Young ICCA [International Council for Commercial Arbitration] Workshop "Opening the doors of international arbitration", in particular on the topic "**Factual & Expert Witnesses**".

I.8. [UKR] - [UKRAINE]

[UKR] Kiev / Kyiv, 26 April 2013
Polish/Ukrainian Twin Conference on International Commercial Arbitration organized by Institute for International Relations (Kyiv National Taras Shevchenko University, Ukraine), Lewiatan Court of Arbitration (Warsaw, Poland) and Committee for ADR of Ukrainian Bar Association (Kyiv, Ukraine). Speakers: **Jur Gruszczyński, Beata Gessel-Kalinowska vel Kalisz, Henryk Litwin, Krzystof Stefanowicz, Ph.D., Małgorzata Podrecka,** PhD., **Paweł Lewandowski, Pavlo Byelousov, Michal Jochemczak, Andriy Dubetsky, Paweł Mazur, Olga Gurgula, Katarzyna Michałowska,** PhD., Yuliya Chernykh, Marcin Olechowski, Darya Rigaud, Przemy**sław P. Krzywosz, Dmytro Marchukov, Henryk Gaertner, Oleksandr Vodyannikov, Markiyan Kliuchovskyi, Paweł Pietkiewicz, Małgorzata Surdek.**[44]

[UKR] Kiev / Kyiv, 25 Mai 2013
One-day international arbitration course "**Introduction to International Commercial Arbitration**" conducted by the the European Branch of the Chartered Institute of Arbitrators (CIArb) supported by ARBITRADE Attorneys at Law. The course has been taught by Bennar Balkaya, MCIArb (Chairman of the European Branch of the Chartered Institute of Arbitrators, partner of Balkaya & Balkaya), Bill McLaughlin, FCIArb (international arbitrator and mediator) and Yuliya Chernykh, FCIArb (partner of ARBITRADE).[45]

---

[43]   Further   information   on   http://news.wko.at/Media/9240a453-6945-44e3-ab00-a41fcf3354ac/2012/Info-12 2013/invitation csb28589 v3 pwiegandt gs.pdf [Last visit on 29th September 2013].
[44]   Further information on http://uba.ua/eng/events/1019/ [Last visit on 14th April 2013].
[45]   Further   information   on   http://www.arbitration-austria.at/dokumente/CiarbKiev.pdf [Last visit on 4th April 2013].

[UKR] Kiev / Kyiv, 14 November 2013
"Kiev Arbitration Days 2013".

[UKR] Kiev / Kyiv, 15 November 2013
"International Arbitration Readings in Memory of Professor Igor Pobirchenko". Organised by the International Commercial Arbitration Court at the Ukrainian Chamber of Commerce and Industry.[46]

II. Past & Ongoing CYIL/CYArb® Presentations

II.1. Past Presentations in 2013

➢ The *Ninth Annual Leading Arbitrators' Symposium on the Conduct of International Arbitration*, Vienna [Austria], 25 March 2013
➢ The *Seventh Annual Investment Treaty Arbitration Conference*, Washington D.C. [USA], 22 April 2013
➢ The *International Conference "Days-of-Law-2013"*, Brno [CZE], 14 - 15 November 2013, organized by the Faculty of Law, Masaryk University, Brno, Czech Republic.
➢ University of International and Public Relations, Prague *Conference on Democratic Peace* under the auspices of Deputy Prime Minister and Minister of Interior Czech Republic, within the program *Prague Legal Autumn*, Prague [CZE], 21 November 2013
➢ *Conference on* **Court Litigation and ADR** under the auspices of the President of the Czech Bar Association, Deputy Mayor of the City of Prague and the CYArb, within

II.2. Selected Ongoing Presentations in 2014

The CYIL and the CYArb® Plan to Hold Presentations (among Others) at the Following 2014 Events:[47]

➢ The *Tenth Annual Leading Arbitrators' Symposium on the Conduct of International Arbitration*, Vienna [Austria]
➢ The *Eighth Annual Investment Treaty Arbitration Conference*, Washington D.C. [USA]
➢ The *Congress of the International Academy of Comparative Law*, Vienna [Austria]

---

[46] Further information on http://www.ucci.org.ua/arb/icac/ru/icac.html.
[47] Further events (international conferences and congresses) scheduled.

Selected Bibliography for 2013

Opening Remarks:
This overview lists only works published in 2013. The individual chapters into which this overview is divided always cover both substantive and procedural issues.
Titles in translations are indicative.

I. [CZE] – [CZECH REPUBLIC] –Titles Published in the Czech Republic

I.1. Monographs

Jozef Zámožík. **III. *Rozhodcovské konanie*** [title in translation – *III. Arbitration*]. In: Jozef Zámožík; Pavol Sojka; Petra Príbelská; Martina Uhliarová; Róbert Dobrovodský. *Civilné právo procesné* [title in translation – *Law of Civil Procedure*].[1] Prague: Aleš Čeněk, 2012, p. 285-333. ISBN :978-80-7380-417-6.

I.2. Periodicals, Collections and Conference Proceedings

Obchodní právo [Commercial Law], Prague: Prospektrum, 2013, Vol. 22, ISSN: 1210-8278[2]

Alexander J. Bělohlávek; Vít Horáček. *Nová pravidla o rozhodčím řízení Mezinárodního rozhodčího soudu ICC* [title in translation – *New Rules of The ICC International Court of Arbitration*]. No. 1, p. 10-19.

---

[1] Book published in Slovak.
[2] Papers published in Czech. Abstracts in English.

Jan Hušek. *Rozhodčí řízení – rozhodčí nález a překážka věci rozsouzené* [title in translation – *Arbitration – Arbitral Award and Res Judicata*]. No. 6, p. 228-230.

Právní rozhledy [*Law Review*], Prague: C. H. Beck, 2013, Vol. 23, ISSN: 1210-6410[3]

Jana Křiváčková; Petr Podrazil. *Řešení procesní situace po zrušení rozhodčího nálezu* [title in translation – *Procedure after Annulment of Arbitral Award*]. No 8, p. 284-287.

Igor Parizek. *K doručování v rozhodčím řízení a (ne)možnosti rozhodce získat údaj z centrální evidence obyvatel* [title in translation – *On Service of Documents in Arbitration and the (Im)Possibility for Arbitrators to Get Information from the Central Register of Inhabitants*]. No. 19, p. 668-670.

Monika Pauknerová; M. *Pfeiffer. Mezinárodní mediace a české právo* [title in translation – *International Mediation and Czech Law*]. No. 1, p. 21-25.

Jan Pichrt. *Alternativní způsoby řešení sporů v pracovněprávních vztazích minulost, současnost a budoucnost* [title in translation – *Alternative Resolution of Disputes from Labour Relations – Past, Present and Future*] No. 21, p. 725-762.

Jiří Spáčil. *Judikatura – Nejvyšší soud České republiky: Rozhodčí řízení. Zásada rovnosti účastníků řízení* [title in translation – *Case Law – Supreme Court of the Czech Republic: Arbitration. Principle of Equality of the Parties*] No. 5, p. 185-186.

Dorota Steinbergerová; Antonín Stanislav. *Nová právní úprava mediace na území České republiky v kontextu právní úpravy mediace ve Spolkové republice Německo a Rakouské republice* [title in translation – *New Law on Mediation in the Territory of the Czech Republic in the Context of the Law on Mediation in the Federal Republic of Germany and the Republic of Austria*]. No. 6, p. 203-208.

Lenka Westphalová. Lenka Holá. *Rodinná mediace, právní a sociální aspekty jejího poskytování* [title in translation – *Family Mediation, Legal and Social Aspects of the Provision Thereof*]. No. 18, pp. 618-626.

Právník [Title in translation - *The Lawyer*], Prague: Ústav státu a práva Akademie věd České republiky [Institute of State and Law of the Academy of Sciences of the Czech Republic], 2013, Vol. 152, ISSN: 0231-6625[4]

---

[3]   Papers published in Czech.

[4] Papers published in Czech with abstracts in a foreign language. The abstract is most often in English (exceptionally in German or French).

Karel Svoboda. *Ke změnám ve vnímání pojmu "právní moci"* [title in translation – *On the Changes in the Perception of the Concept of Legal Power*]. No. 8, p. 826-836.

I.3. Books (Monographs) and Articles by Czech Authors and/or on the Topics regarding Arbitration and ADR in the Czech Republic Published outside the Czech Republic

Monographs

Alexander Bělohlávek. *Arbitration Law of Czech Republic: Practice & Procedure*. Hungtington, New York : JurisNet LLC, 2013, 2270 p. ISBN: 978-1-937518-18-9.

Monika Pauknerová; Jan Brodec; M. Pfeiffer. *Mediation in the Czech Republic*, In: J. L. Igleias; G. Palao (eds.) **Civil and Commercial Mediation in Europe**. Intersentia, 2012, p. 97-130.

Other Publications

Alexander J. Bělohlávek. *Concept of Foreign Arbitral Award in Connection with Recognition and Enforcement and Conflicts of Sources*. in: Revista Română de Arbitraj [title in translation – *Romanian Review of Arbitration*], Bucharest: Arbitration Court attached to the Chamber of Commerce and Industry of Romania, 2013, Vol. 7, Issue No. 2, Total Issue No. 26, Romanian register of publications C.N.C.S.I.S., Code 138, reg. No. 9059/5.11.2008, p. 32-52.[5]

Alexander J. Bělohlávek. *Czech Republic*. In: WEGEN, Gerhard; WILSKE, Stephan (eds.) *Arbitration 2013 – Global Arbitration Review – Eddition Getting the Deal Through*. London : Law Business Research, 2013. ISSN: 1750-9947, p. 159-166.[6]

Alexander J. Bělohlávek. *Importance of the Seat of Arbitration in International Arbitration: Delocalization and Denationalization of Arbitration as an Outdated Myth*. ASA Bulletin. Genève / Alphen aan den Rijn : ASA (Association suisse de l'arbitrage / Schweizerische Vereinigung für Schiedsgerichtsbarkeit / Associatzione svizzera per l'arbitrato / Swiss Arbitration Association) / Kluwer Law International, 2013, Vol. 31, Issue No. 42, p. 262-292, ISSN: 1010-9153.[7]

Alexander J. Bělohlávek. *Arbitration and Basic Rights: Movement from contractual theory to jurisdictional theory*. In: NOCHTA, Tibor,

---

[5] Original language: English.
[6] Country report. Original language: English.
[7] Original language: English, summary both in German and French.

FABÓ, Tibor, MÁRTON, Mária: *Ünnepi tanulmányok Kecskés László Professzor 60. születésnapja tisztteletére* [title in translation – *Liber Amicorum on the occasion of the 60th Anniversary of Professor László Kecskés*], Pécs / Maďarsko [Hungary]: Tudományegyetem Állam- és Jogtudományi Kar [Faculty of Law and Administration, University of Pécs], 2013, p. 47-77, ISBN: 978-963-642-559-3.[8]

II. [SVK] – [SLOVAK REPUBLIC]

Justičná revue [*Judicial Revue*], Bratislava: Ministry of Justice Slovak Republic, 2013, Vol. 65, ISSN: 1335-6461[9]

Katarína Chovancová; *Res iudicata medzinárodného rozhodcovského rozsudku* [title in translation – *Res Judicata of an International Arbitral Award*]. Justičná revue, 2013, Vol. 65, No. 1, p. 1-16. ISSN: 1335-6461.

Právny obzor: časopis Ústavu štátu a práva Slovenskej akademie vied,] *Legal Horizon: The Review of the Institute of State and Law of the Slovak Academy of Science]* **Bratislava, 2013, Vol. 96, ISSN: 0032-6984**

K. Chovancová. *Odstránenie prekážok v prístupe k spravodlivosti prostredníctvom mediácie v Európe* [title in translation – *Elimination of obstacles in access to justice through mediation in Europe*]. No. 2, p. 179-182.

J. Výboch. *Niektoré otázky rozhodcovských doložiek v spotrebiteľských zmluvách z pohľadu posudzovania ich prijateľnosti* [title in translation – *Some issues of arbitration clauses in consumer contracts from the view of assessment of their acceptability*]. No. 3, p. 240-262.

III. [POL] – [POLAND][10]

ADR Arbitraż i Mediacja [*ADR Arbitration and Mediation*], Warszawa: C. H. Beck, 2010, ISSN: 1898-942X[11]

Arkadiusz Bieliński, *Prawnik i jego misja w ramach procedur alternatywnego rozwiązywania sporów w warunkach kryzysu klasycznego wymiaru sprawiedliwości* [A Lawyer and His Mission within the Alternative

---

[8] Original language: English.
[9] Papers published in Czech. Abstracts in English.
[10] Polish bibliography concerning arbitration and ADR for 2013 was compiled with the kind assistance of Kubas Kos Gaertner, Law firm (www.kkg.pl). Kubas Kos Gaertner are specialized (among others) in arbitration and ADR.
[11] Quarterly. Papers published in Polish.

Dispute Resolution Procedures in the Conditions of the Crisis of Classical Judicial System]. No. 2, pp. 25-34.

Adam Bodnar, Adam Płoszka, *Wpływ Europejskiej Konwencji Praw Człowieka na postępowanie polubowne (arbitraż)* [The Influence of the European Convention on Human Rights on Amicable Proceedings (Arbitration)]. No. 3, pp. 5-20.

Elżbieta Kocowska-Siekierka, *Przepisy czeskiej ustawy o arbitrażu. Przekład z wprowadzeniem* [Provisions of the Czech Arbitration Act. Translation with introduction]. No. 3, pp. 117-118.

Michael Leathes, *Dispute Resolution Mules*. No. 2, pp. 57-61.[12]

Katarzyna Michałowska, *Polubowne rozwiązywanie sporów dotyczących inwestycji zagranicznych* [Amicable Resolution of Disputes concerning Foreign Investments]. No. 2, pp. 63-73.

Rafał Morek, *Zasada ugodowego załatwiania spraw w arbitrażu: zarys problematyki* [The Principle of Amicable Resolution of Issues in Arbitration: An Outline of an Issue]. No. 2, pp. 75-86.

Krystian Mularczyk, *Sprawozdanie z konferencji VI. Międzynarodowego Forum „Alternatywne metody rozwiązywania Sporów" we Lwowie (30-31.5.2013 r.)* [Report from the Conference 6th International "Forum Alternative Means of Dispute Resolution" in Lwów (May 30-31, 2013)]. No. 3, pp. 105-107.

Krystian Mularczyk, Dorota Czura-Kalinowska, *Sprawozdanie z konferencji „Arbitraż i mediacja w teorii i praktyce" w Poznaniu (15.1.2013 r.)* [Report from the Conference "Arbitration and Mediation in Theory and in Practice" in Poznań (January 15, 2013)]. No. 1, pp. 111-113.

Krystian Mularczyk, *Sprawozdanie z konferencji z cyklu Arbitraż i mediacja w teorii i praktyce pt. „Funkcjonowanie stałych sądów polubownych i ośrodków mediacyjnych" w Nowym Tomyślu (19.4.2013 r.)* [Report from the Conference from the Series Arbitration and Mediation in Theory and in Practice Entitled "Functioning of Permanent Courts of Arbitration and Mediation Centers" in Nowy Tomyśl (April 19, 2013)]. No. 3, pp. 113-116.

Michał Pyka, *Inwestycja z art. 25 ust. 1 Konwencji waszyngtońskiej w świetle paradygmatu naukowego* [Investment of Article 25 Section 1 of the Washington Convention in the Light of a Scientific Paradigm]. No. 1, 63-75.

Jerzy Rajski, *Polubowne aspekty arbitrażu w sprawach gospodarczych* [Amicable Aspects of Arbitration in Commercial Cases]. No. 2, pp. 7-9.

---

[12] Paper in English.

Karol Ryszkowski, *Klauzula porządku publicznego w postępowaniu przed sądem polubownym a zdatność arbitrażowa* [Public Policy Clause in Arbitration Proceedings and Arbitrability]. No. 1, s. 77-102.

Jakub Rzucidło, Justyna Węgrzyn, *Konstytucja zasada ochrony konsumentów a działalność polubownych sądów konsumenckich na przykładzie Stałego Polubownego Sądu Konsumenckiego przy Dolnośląskim Wojewódzkim Inspektorze Inspekcji Handlowej we Wrocławiu* [Constitutional Principle of Consumer Protection and Functioning of Arbitration Consumer Courts at the Example of the Permanent Arbitration Consumer Court at the Lower-Silesian Commerce Inspector of Commercial Inspection in Wrocław]. No. 3, pp. 55-65.

Alicja Szczęśniak, *Jurysdykcja krajowa sądu państwowego do orzekania w postępowaniu wszczętym skargą o uchylenie wyroku sądu polubownego* [Domestic Jurisdiction of a State Court in Proceedings Initiated by a Motion for Setting Aside of an Arbitral Award]. No. 3, pp. 47-54.

Biuletyn Arbitrażowy [*Bulletin on Arbitration*], Warszawa: LexisNexis Polska Sp. z.o.o. 2011[13]

Maciej Durbas, Michał Pochodyła, *Bifurkacja (podział) postępowania arbitrażowego* [Bifurcation in Arbitral Proceedings]. No. 19, pp. 78-91.

Andrzej Kąkolecki, *Akt misji w postępowaniu według Regulaminu Arbitrażowego Międzynarodowej Izby Handlowej* [Terms of Reference in Proceedings under the Arbitration Rules of the International Chamber of Commerce]. No. 19, pp. 125-128.

Andrzej Kąkolecki, *Nowoczesne regulaminy arbitrażowe* [Modern Arbitration Rules]. No. 20, pp. 88-92.

Zofia Kosteczka, *Zrzeczenie się prawa do wniesienia skargi o uchylenie wyroku sądu polubownego* [Waiver of Right to Challenge of an Arbitral Award]. No. 19, pp. 92-104.

Rafał Morek, *Przegląd orzecznictwa Sądu Najwyższego i sądów apelacyjnych* [Review of the Decisions of the Supreme Court and the Appellate Courts]. No. 20, pp. 93-95.

Piotr Nowaczyk, *Arbitraż i mediacja. Międzykulturowe aspekty mediacji* [Arbitration and Mediation. Inter-Cultural Aspects of Mediation]. No. 19, pp. 71-77.

Piotr Nowaczyk, *Czy moralne jest oVATowanie arbitrażu?* [Is it Morally Right to Charge VAT on Arbitration?]. No. 20, pp. 82-87.

Monika Weingärtner, *Class arbitration – czy forma arbitrażu zbiorowego może zaistnieć w Europie?* [Class Arbitration – Can Form of Group Arbitration Exist in Europe?]. No. 19, pp. 105-119.

---

[13] Issued by Sąd Arbitrażowy przy Krajowej Izbie Gospodarczej [Court of Arbitration attached to the Polish Chamber of Commerce] in LexisNexis Polska.

e-Przegląd Arbitrażowy [*Arbitration e-Review*], Warszawa: Sąd Arbitrażowy przy Polskiej Konfederacji Pracodawców Prywatnych Lewiatan, 2013, ISSN: 2083-8190[14]

Gordon Blanke, *Arbitraż w sprawach o naruszenie zobowiązań unijnych – wprowadzenie* [Arbitration in Cases concerning Violation of European Union Obligations – An Introduction]. No. 1-2, pp. 43-51.

Nelson Eizirik, *Arbitraż w sporach korporacyjnych w Brazylii* [Arbitration in Corporate Disputes in Brazil]. No. 1-2, pp. 35-42.

German Galuschenko, *Wykonywanie na terytorium Ukrainy wyroków wydanych w arbitrażu inwestycyjnym* [Enforcement on the Territory of Ukraine of Arbitral Awards Made in Investment Arbitration]. Special Edition, pp. 32-34.

Courtenay Griffiths, *Bezwzględnie obowiązujące normy publiczno-prawne w arbitrażu w sprawach M&A* [Mandatory Provisions of Public Law in Arbitration concerning M&A Cases]. No. 1-2, pp. 67-73.

Oleksandr Merezhko, *Międzynarodowy arbitraż handlowy z perspektywy psychologicznej teorii prawa* [International Commercial Arbitration from the Perspective of a Psychological Theory of Law]. Special Edition, pp. 6-12.

Ivona Nazarova, *Umowa o arbitraż - w poszukiwaniu zasadnego kompromisu na rozdrożu teorii prawnych?* [Arbitration Agreement – In Search of a Valid Compromise at the Crossroads of Legal Theories?]. Special Edition, pp. 19-23.

Mireze Philippe, *Tryb uproszczony i środki doraźne w toczących się przed ICC postępowaniach arbitrażowych dotyczących fuzji i przejęć oraz wspólnych przedsięwzięć* [Simplified Procedure and Interim Measures in ICC Arbitrations concerning Mergers and Acquisition and Joint-Ventures]. No. 1-2, pp. 6-26.

Jana Planavova-Latanowicz, *Raport z panelu „Arbitraż a Prawo Konkurencji"* [Panel on Arbitration and Competition – Report]. No. 1-2, pp. 74-80.

Witold Rzewuski, Zbigniew Jusis, *Wycena szkody w postępowaniach arbitrażowych dotyczących fuzji i przejęć* [Assessment of Damages in Arbitration Proceedings concerning Mergers and Acquisitions]. No. 1-2, pp. 27-35.

Mykola Selivon, *Wskaźnik cena-jakość-czas w rozstrzyganiu sporów przez Międzynarodowy Handlowy Sąd Arbitrażowy przy Ukraińskiej Izbie Handlowo-Przemysłowej* [The Ratio of Price-Quality-Time in Dispute Resolution by the International Commercial Court of Arbitration at the Ukrainian Chamber of Commerce and Industry]. Special Edition, pp. 24-27.

---

[14] Polish and English editions, available at: http://www.sadarbitrazowy.org.pl/pl/eczasopsima-lista and http://www.sadarbitrazowy.org.pl/en/eczasopisma-lista.

Andrzej Tynel, *Droga Polski i Ukrainy do międzynarodowego arbitrażu* [The Road of Poland and Ukraine to the International Arbitration]. Special Edition, pp. 13-18.

Agnieszka Wolińska, *Sprawozdanie z konferencji „Dispute Resolution in M&A Transactions: Tactics, Challenges, Defenses" 2nd Edition, 6-7.06.2013 w Warszawie* [Report from the Conference "Dispute Resolution in M&A Transactions: Tactics, Challenges, Defenses" 2nd Edition (June 6-7, 2013) in Warsaw]. No. 1-2, pp. 62-66.

Sergei A. Voitovich, *Podział orzekania w przedmiocie właściwości sądu od orzekania co do istoty sporu w sporach inwestycyjnych – uwagi pokonferencyjne w nawiązaniu do Kijowskich Dni Arbitrażu 2012* [Bifurcation of Ruling on the Subject of Jurisdiction of the Court from the Ruling on the Merits in Investment Disputes – Post-Conference Remarks to the Kiev Arbitration Days 2012]. Special Edition, pp. 28-31.

Glosa – Prawo Gospodarcze w Orzeczeniach i Komentarzach [*The Commentary – Commercial Law in Case Law and Commentaries*], Warszawa: Wolters Kluwer Polska Sp. z o. o., 2013, ISSN: 1233-4634[15]

Sebastian Frejowski, *Związanie sądu arbitrażowego orzeczeniem sadu powszechnego, który uznał lub stwierdził wykonalność wcześniejszego wyroku sądu polubownego – glosa do wyroku Sądu Najwyższego z 13.04.2012 r. (I CSK 416/11)* [The Binding of the Court of Arbitration by a Decision of a State Court, which Recognized or Declared Enforceability of a Prior Arbitral Award – A Commentary to the Judgment of the Supreme Court of April 13, 2012 (I CSK 416/11)]. No. 2, pp. 63-67.

Rafał Kos, *O związaniu cesjonariusza zapisem na sąd polubowny – glosa do wyroku Sądu Najwyższego z 3.09.1998 r. (I CKN 822/97)* [About Assignee Being Bound by an Arbitration Agreement – A Commentary to the Judgment of the Supreme Court of September 3, 1998 (I CKN 822/97)]. No. 4, pp. 36-47.

Monitor Prawniczy, 2011

Iga Bałos, *Stosowanie klauzuli porządku publicznego a drażliwe zjawiska społeczne* [Application of Public Policy Clause and Sensitive Social Matters]. No. 3, pp. 135-139.

[15] Quarterly. Papers published in Polish, summaries in English.

Palestra [*The Bar*], Warszawa: Naczelna Rada Adwokacka, 2013, ISSN: 0031-0344[16]

Włodzimierz Brych, *Sprawozdanie z konferencji z cyklu: "Arbitration and mediation in Central and Eastern Europe and Some Asian Countries" pt. "Arbitrators and Mediators in Settling national and international disputes", Baku, Azerbejdżan, 25 października 2012 r.* [Report from Conference from the Series: "Arbitration and Mediation in Central and Eastern Europe and Some Asian Countries" entitled "Arbitrators and Mediators in Settling National and International Disputes", Baku, Azerbaijan, October 25, 2012]. No. 1-2, p. 271.

Włodzimierz Brych, *Międzynarodowa konferencja pt. „Funkcjonowanie stałych sądów polubownych i ośrodków mediacyjnych", Nowy Tomyśl, 19 kwietnia 2013 r.* [International Conference Entitled "Functioning of Permanent Courts of Arbitration and Mediations Centers" in Nowy Tomyśl, April 19, 2013]. No. 7-8, p. 296-297.

Dariusz P. Kała, *Uznanie i stwierdzenie wykonalności wyroku sądu polubownego lub ugody przed nim zawartej (zagadnienia wybrane)* [Recognition and Enforcement of an Arbitral Award or a Settlement Reached before the Arbitration Court]. No. 5-6, pp. 79-84.

Karol Weitz, *Wymaganie przeprowadzenia rozprawy w pierwszej instancji w sprawach o uznanie lub stwierdzenie wykonalności zagranicznych orzeczeń arbitrażowych* [The Requirement of Conducting a Trial in First Instance in Cases for Recognition and Enforcement of Foreign Arbitral Awards]. No. 9-10, pp. 165-169.

Hubert Wysoczański, *Akademia Arbitrażu (International Academy for Arbitration Law), Francja, Paryż, 1-19 lipca 2013 r.* [International Academy for Arbitration Law in Paris, France, (July 1-19, 2013)]. No. 11-12, pp. 291-292.

Polski Proces Cywilny [*Polish Civil Proceedings*], Warszawa: Lexis Nexis Polska Sp. z o. o., Kraków: Towarzystwo Naukowe Procesualistów Cywilnych 2013, ISSN: 2082-1743[17]

Stanisław Sołtysik, *Sprawozdanie z konferencji naukowej p.t. „Arbitraż a osoby trzecie" oraz towarzyszącego jej Seminarium młodych naukowców i praktyków prawa, Katowice, 28 listopada 2012 r.* [A Report from the Conference "Arbitration and Third Parties" and the Accompanying Seminar of Young Law Scholars and Practitioners (Katowice, 28 November 2012)]. No. 2, pp. 288-294.

---

[16] Monthly. Published in Polish.
[17] Quarterly. Papers published in Polish.

Andrzej Wiśniewski, *Skutki wdania się w spór przed arbitrażem za granicą pomimo braku skutecznej umowy o arbitraż. Glosa do postanowienia Sadu Najwyższego z dnia 13 września 2012 r., V CSK 323/11* [The Effects of Engaging in a Dispute in Arbitration Abroad Despite the Lack of Effective Arbitration Agreement. A Commentary to the Decision of the Supreme Court of September 13, 2012, V CSK 323/11]. No. 4, pp. 571-582.

Przegląd Prawa Handlowego [*Commercial Law Review*], Warszawa: Wolters Kluwer Polska Sp. z o. o., 2013, ISSN: 1230-2996[18]

Marcin Asłanowicz, *Zasady i tryb wyłączenia członka zespołu orzekającego w postępowaniu arbitrażowym* [Rules and Procedure for Challenge to a Member of an Arbitral Panel]. No. 8, pp. 11-17.

Beata Gessel-Kalinowska vel Kalisz, *Podstawa normatywna zasady poufności w polskim arbitrażu handlowym* [Legal Basis for the Principle of Confidentiality in Polish Commercial Arbitration]. No. 1, pp. 14-19.

Witold Jurcewicz, *Arbiter jako świadek w postępowaniu sądowym* [Arbitrator as a Witness in State Court Proceedings]. No. 7, pp. 21-26.

Katarzyna Michałowska, *Zasady dostępu do informacji w postępowaniach arbitrażowych w sporach inwestycyjnych (projekt zmian w Regulaminie Arbitrażowym UNCITRAL)* [Rules on Access to Information in Investment Arbitration (Project of Changes in UNCITRAL Arbitration Rules]. No. 8, pp. 8-12.

Jerzy Rajski, *Etos arbitrażu* [Ethos of Arbitration]. No. 5, pp. 4-7.

Izabela Szmit, *Znaczenie dowodu z zeznań świadków w postępowaniu arbitrażowym* [The Role of Witness Testimony as Evidence in Arbitration]. No. 7, pp. 48-52.

Przegląd Ustawodawstwa Gospodarczego [*Commercial Legislation Review*], Warszawa: Polskie Wydawnictwo Ekonomiczne S.A., 2013, ISSN: 0137-5490[19]

Marcin Asłanowicz, *Arbiter doraźny* [Emergency Arbitrator]. No. 8, s. 18-22.

Radca Prawny [*Legal Adviser*], Warszawa: Krajowa Rada Radców Prawnych, 2013, ISSN: 1230-1426[20]

Dariusz P. Kała, *Podstawa odmowy uznania i wykonania wyroku sądu polubownego lub ugody przed nim zawartej (cz. I)* [Grounds for Refusal

---

[18] Monthly. Papers published in Polish, summaries in English.
[19] Monthly. Papers published in Polish, summaries in English.
[20] Monthly. Papers published in Polish.

of Recognition and Enforcement of Arbitral Award or of a Settlement Reached in Arbitration (Part I)]. No. 134, pp. 8-10.

Dariusz P. Kała, *Podstawa odmowy uznania i wykonania wyroku sądu polubownego lub ugody przed nim zawartej (cz. II)* [Grounds for Refusal of Recognition and Enforcement of Arbitral Award or of a Settlement Reached in Arbitration (Part II)]. No. 135, pp. 8-12.

Andrzej Kąkolecki, Andrzej Tynel, *Arbitraż – sukces czy stagnacja* [Arbitration – Success or Stagnation]. No. 141, pp. 26-27.

Rejent [*Notary Public*], Warszawa: Stowarzyszenie Notariuszy Rzeczypospolitej Polskiej, 2013, ISSN: 1230-669X[21]

Anna Wolak-Danecka, *Rozstrzyganie sporów przez sąd polubowny – próba ujęcia zdatności arbitrażowej* [Settlement of Disputes Through Court of Arbitration – An Attempt to Define Eligibility for Arbitration]. No. 4, pp. 123-143.

Dariusz P. Kała, *Wniesienie wniosku o uznanie lub stwierdzenie wykonalności wyroku sądu polubownego lub ugody przed nim zawartej* [Filing a Motion for Legalization or Declaration of Enforcement of an Arbitration Award or a Settlement Reached before the Arbitration Court]. No. 5, pp. 54 – 67.

Studia Prawa Prywatnego [*Private Law Studies*] Warszawa: Wydawnictwo C. H. Beck Sp. z o. o., 2013, ISSN: 1895-1279[22]

Jerzy Poczobut, *Umowa o arbitraż w polskim prawie prywatnym międzynarodowym – z uwagami porównawczymi* [Arbitration Agreement in Polish Private International Law – with Comparative Remarks]. No. 1, pp. 12-33.

IV. [ROU] – [ROMANIA][23]

Monographs

Bogdan Bobei. Domestic and International Arbitration. Text. Commentaries. Mindets. Bucharest: C. H. Beck, 2013.[24]

---

[21] Monthly. Papers published in Polish, abstracts in English.
[22] Quarterly. Papers published in Polish.
[23] For further articles on arbitration in Romania see also *Revista Română de Arbitraj* issued by the International Commercial Arbitration Attached to The Chamber of Commerce and Industry of Romania (see http://arbitration.ccir.ro/engleza/index.htm). The Romanian bibliography prepared also with the kind support of dr. Alina Cobuz, Managing Partner of Cobuz si Asociatii, the Bucharest based law firm.

Revista Română de Arbitraj [title in translation – *Romanian Review of Arbitration*], Bucharest: Arbitration Court Attached to the Chamber of Commerce and Industry of Romania, 2013, Vol. 7, Romanian register of publications C.N.C.S.I.S., Code 138, reg. No. 9059/5.11.2008[25]

Ibrahim Amro. *The liberalization of national laws of arbitration in common law and civil law countries in respect to recognition and enforcement of foreign arbitral awards.* No. 3, p. 84-100.

Crina Baltag. *Arbitrating investment disputes under the Energy Charger Treaty.* No. 3, p. 31-43.

Alexander J. BĚLOHLÁVEK. *Concept of Foreign Arbitral Award in Connection with Recognition and Enforcement and Conflicts of Sources.* No. 2, p. 32-52.

Valentin BEREA; Isabela Delia POPA. *Tehnica definirii termenilor contractuali în cadrul contractelor comerciale: studiu de caz din jurisprudența arbitrală* [Title in translation – *The technique of defining terms within commercial contracts: case study extracted from arbitration jurisprudence*]. Issue No. 2, p. 21-31.

Philippe BILLIET. *Recent collective redress initiatives in Belgium; what is the role of arbitration?* No. 1, p. 59-66.

Christopher Brunner. *The Swiss Rules of International Arbitraiton in their Edition of June 2012.* No. 3, p. 72-83.

Chang-fa Lo. *Constitutional issues for legislative adoption of mandatory arbitration.* No. 2, p. 6-20.

Bernardo M. CREMADES. *Third Party Funding in International Arbitration.* Issue No. 2, p. 1-5.

Ştefan Dundaş. *State Counterclaims in BIT Arbitrations: Can the Tables Be Turned ?* No. 3, p. 11-30.

Alain FARHAD; Matei PURICE. *An introduction to the Dubai International Financial Centre – a jurisdiction within a jurisdiction.* No. 1, p. 67-74.

---

[24] The work is a commentary to art. 541-621 of the New Code of Civil Procedure and to art. 1110-1132 of the same. Private voluntary arbitration is no longer an alternative dispute resolution method. It has become a common dispute resolution means, an interpretation approach to legal texts and, perhaps, a lifestyle. At first sight, the work is exclusively legally-oriented. The reasons substantiating the writing of this work were not exclusively legal. In fact, to write about private voluntary arbitration solely from a legal perspective is to misunderstand the finality of this process. Dispute resolution by arbitration is not a craft, rather it is a piece of art in ongoing progress. This latter perspective is the true scope of writing this work. The novelty of this publication is a pragmatic, but also bookish and exclusive review of Romanian procedural-civil texts on voluntary private arbitration. Presentation text sourced at www.beckshop.ro.

[25] Papers published in English, sometimes in French and exceptionally in Romanian. Abstracts in English. Table of Contents in English, French and Romanian. Published quarterly.

Doug Jones. *Arbitration around the World: Alive or Dead?* No. 3, p. 1-10.

Anna MASSER. *The revised Swiss Rules of International Arbitration.* No. 2, p. 53-61.

Marian NICOLAE. *The limitation and FIDIC Dispute settlement procedures (1999) under the Romanian Private Law.* No. 1, p. 1-38.

Piotr NOWACZYK; Andrzej KĄKOLECKI. *The New ICC Arbitration Rules.* No. 1, p. 50-58.

René Offersen. *An introduction to arbitration in Denmark and some trends.* No. 3, p. 63-71.

Adrian RAȚIU; Gheorghe NĂSTASE. *The intervention of the ordinary courts in the arbitral procedure according to the Romanian Law.* No. 1, p. 39-49.

Mihnea Săraru. *Resolving the conflicts in the hierarchy of norms during arbitral proceedings.* No. 3, p. 44-62.

Irene WELSER. *Arbitration with defaulting parties – a practical approach.* No. 2, p. 62-72.

Important Web Sites

http://www.czechyearbook.org.

Czech Yearbook of International Law® and Czech (& Central European) Yearbook of Arbitration®

The web site is currently available in sixteen languages: English, Bulgarian, Czech, Chinese, Japanese, Korean, Hungarian, German, Polish, Romanian, Russian, Portuguese, Slovenian, Spanish, Ukrainian, Vietnamese. This web site allows access to the annotations of all core articles and to information about the authors of these articles as well as to the entire remaining contents (except core articles) of both yearbooks (CYIL and CYArb®).

I. [CZE] – [CZECH REPUBLIC]

- http://www.cnb.cz.
  Česká národná banka (Czech National Bank as the Central bank of the Czech Republic).[1]

- http://www.compet.cz.
  Office for the protection of competition.[2]

- http://www.concourt.cz.
  The Constitutional Court of the Czech Republic.[3]

- http://www.csesp.cz.
  Czech Society for European and Comparative Law.[4]

- http://www.csmp-csil.org.
  The Czech Society of International Law.[5]

- http://www.czech.cz.
  Portal "Hello Czech Republic". Basic information about the Czech Republic and news interesting for foreigners. Rather a promotional portal.[6]

- http://www.czso.cz.
  Czech Statistical Office.[7]

- http://dtjvcnsp.org.
  Česko-německý spolek právníků. [Czech-German Lawyers Association]. Deutsch-Tschechische Juristenvereinigung e.V.[8]

- http:// ekf.vsb.cz.
  Faculty of Economics, VŠB Technical University of Ostrava.[9]

---

[1]   Web site available in English and Czech.
[2]   Web site available in English and Czech. Basic laws and regulations on the protection of competition in the Czech Republic are also available at the web site, both in Czech and in English (unofficial translation).
[3]   Web site available in English and Czech. Part of the (significant) case law also available in English.
[4]   Web site available in English and Czech.
[5]   Web site available in Czech. In English only a brief summary of the webpages.
[6]   Web site available in English, Czech, French, German, Russian and Spanish.
[7]   Web site available in English and Czech.
[8]   Web site available in German.

- http://ftp.pse.cz/Info.bas/Cz/Predpisy/brs_statut2.pdf.
  Statute of Burzovní rozhodčí soud při Burze cenných papírů Praha, a.s. [Exchange Court of Arbitration at the Prague Stock Exchange][10]

- http://www.hrad.cz.[11]
  Web site of the Office of the President of the Czech Republic.

- http://www.icc-cr.cz.
  ICC National Committee Czech Republic

- http://www.iir.cz.
  Institute of International Relations Prague.[12]

- http://www.ilaw.cas.cz.
  Ústav státu a práva Akademie věd ČR, v.v.i. [Institute of State and Law of the Academy of Sciences of the Czech Republic][13]

- http://www.jednotaceskychpravniku.cz.
  Jednota českých právníků [Czech Lawyers Union]

- http://www.icc-cr.cz.
  ICC National Committee Czech Republic.

- http://justice.cz.
  Czech justice portal including both courts and the Ministry of Justice, prosecution departments, Judicial Academy, Institute of Criminology and Social Prevention, as well as the Probation and Mediation Service and the Prison Service. [14]

---

[9]   Web site available in English and Czech. Some information (regarding post-graduate studies) also available in German. Department of Law see http://en.ekf.vsb.cz/information-about/departments/structure/departments/dept-119 (in English).

[10]   The Statute is available in Czech. One of the three permanent arbitration courts established in the Czech Republic by law (statute), in compliance with Section 13 of Act No. 216/1994 Coll., on Arbitration and Enforcement of Arbitral Awards, as subsequently amended.

[11]   Web site available in English and Czech. This web site also allows access to the personal webpage of the President of the Czech Republic.

[12]   Web site available in English and Czech. This Institute was founded by the Ministry of Foreign Affairs of the Czech Republic.

[13]   Web site available in English and Czech.

[14]   Web site available in Czech. The individual web sites of the institutions covered by this portal also contain pages or summary information in English.

Czech (& Central European) Yearbook of Arbitration

- http://www.law.muni.cz.
  Faculty of Law, Masaryk University, Brno.[15]

- http://www.mzv.cz.
  Ministry of Foreign Affairs of the Czech Republic.[16]

- http://www.nsoud.cz.
  The Supreme Court of the Czech Republic.[17]

- http://www.nssoud.cz.
  The Supreme Administrative Court of the Czech Republic.[18]

- http://www.ochrance.cz.
  Public Defender of Rights (Ombudsman).[19]

- http://www.ok.cz/iksp/en/aboutus.html.
  Institute of Criminology and Social Prevention.[20]

- http://portal.gov.cz.
  Portal of the Public Administration.[21] This web site allows access to the web sites of most supreme public administration authorities (including ministries).

- http://www.prf.cuni.cz.
  Faculty of Law, Charles University in Prague.[22]

- http://www.psp.cz.
  Parliament of the Czech Republic. Chamber of Deputies.[23]

- http://www.rozhodcisoud.cz.
  The Arbitration Court Attached to the Czech-Moravian Commodity Exchange Kladno.[24]

---

[15] Web site available in English and Czech.
[16] Web site available in Czech. Important information from this portal also available in English.
[17] Web site available in Czech. Some basic information also in English and French.
[18] Web site available in English and Czech.
[19] Web site available in English and Czech.
[20] Web site available in English and Czech.
[21] Web site available in English and Czech.
[22] Web site available in Czech. Basic information available in English.
[23] Web site available in English and Czech.

- http://www.senat.cz.
  Parliament of the Czech Republic. Senate.[25]

- http://www.society.cz/wordpress/#awp.
  Common Law Society.[26]

- http://www.soud.cz.
  Arbitration Court attached to the Economic Chamber of the Czech Republic and Agricultural Chamber of the Czech Republic.[27]

- http://www.umpod.cz.
  Office for International Legal Protection of Children.[28]

- http://www.upol.cz/fakulty/pf/.
  Faculty of Law. Palacký University, Olomouc.

- http://www.vse.cz.
  The University of Economics, Prague.[29]

- http://www.zcu.cz/fpr/.
  Faculty of Law, Western Bohemia University in Pilsen.[30]

II. [SVK] – [SLOVAK REPUBLIC]

- http://www.concourt.sk.
  Constitutional Court of the Slovak Republic.[31]

---

[24] Web site available in English and Czech. Web site of one of the three permanent arbitration courts established in the Czech Republic by law (statute), in compliance with Section 13 of Act No. 216/1994 Coll., on Arbitration and Enforcement of Arbitral Awards, as subsequently amended. This arbitration court was established by Act No. 229/1992 Coll., on Commodity Exchanges, as subsequently amended.

[25] Web site available in English and Czech.

[26] Web site available in Czech.

[27] Web site available in English, Czech, German and Russian. Web site of one of the three permanent arbitration courts established in the Czech Republic by law (statute), in compliance with Section 13 of Act No. 216/1994 Coll., on Arbitration and Enforcement of Arbitral Awards, as subsequently amended. This arbitration court was established by Section 19 of Act No. 301/1992 Coll., on the Economic Chamber of the Czech Republic and the Agricultural Chamber of the Czech Republic, as subsequently amended.

[28] The Office is the Central authority responsible for protection of children in civil matters having cross-border implications. Web site available in English and Czech.

[29] Web site available in English and Czech.

[30] Web site available in Czech.

[31] Web site available in English and Slovak.

- http://www.flaw.uniba.sk.
  Faculty of Law, Comenius University in Bratislava (SVK).[32]

- http://iuridica.truni.sk.
  Faculty of Law. Trnava University in Trnava (SVK).[33]

- http://www.justice.gov.sk.
  Ministry of Justice of the Slovak Republic.[34]

- http://www.nbs.sk.
  Národná banka Slovenska (National Bank of Slovakia as the Central bank of Slovak Republic).[35]

- http://www.nrsr.sk.
  National Council of the Slovak Republic (*Slovak Parliament*).[36]

- http://www.prf.umb.sk.
  Faculty of Law. Matej Bel University, Banská Bystrica (SVK).

- http://www.prezident.sk.
  President of the Slovak Republic and Office of the President (SVK).[37]

- http://www.test.sopk.sk.
  The Court of Arbitration of the Slovak Chamber of Commerce and Industry in Bratislava.[38]

- http://www.uninova.sk/pf_bvsp/src_angl/index.php.
  Faculty of Law, Pan European University (SVK).[39]

---

[32] Web site available in English and Slovak.
[33] Web site available in English and Slovak.
[34] Web site available in English and Slovak. This web site also allows access to the following portals: Courts, Slovak Agent before the European Court for Human Rights, Slovak Agent before the Court of Justice of the European Union, The Judicial Academy.
[35] Web site available in English and Slovak.
[36] Web site available in English, French, German and Slovak.
[37] Web site available in English and Slovak.
[38] Web site available in Slovak. Some basic information available in English.

- http://www.upjs.sk/pravnicka-fakulta.
  Faculty of Law, Pavol Jozef Šafárik University in Košice (SVK).[40]

- http://www.usap.sav.sk.
  Institute of State and Law, Slovak Academy of Science.[41]

III. [AUT] – [AUSTRIA]

- http://www.arbitration-austria.at.
  Österreichische Vereinigung für Schiedsgerichtsbarkeit. Austrian Arbitration Association.[42]

- http://www.internationales-schiedsgericht.at/.
  Wiener Internationalen Schiedsgerichts (VIAC). Vienna International Arbitral Centre (VIAC).[43]

IV. [BLR] – [BELARUS]

- http://www.cci.by/ArbitrCourt/AboutCourt_en.aspx.
  International Arbitration Court attached to the Belarusian Chamber of Commerce and Industry.[44]

V. [BGR] – [BULGARIA]

- http://www.bcci.bg/arbitration/index.html.
  Arbitration Court at the Bulgarian Chamber of Commerce and Industry.

- http://www.lex.bg.
  Information server on Bulgarian law.

VI. [EST] – [ESTONIA]

- http://www.koda.ee.
  Arbitration Court Attached to the Estonian Chamber of Commerce and Industry.[45]

---

[39]   Web site available in English, German and Slovak.
[40]   Web site available in English and Slovak.
[41]   Web site available in Slovak.
[42]   Web site available in English and German.
[43]   Web site available in English, Czech, German and Russian.
[44]   Web site available in English and Russian.

VII. [HRV] – [CROATIA]

- http://www2.hgk.hr/en/about_cce.asp?izbor=pac.
  The Permanent Arbitration Court at the Croatian Chamber of Commerce.[46]

VIII. [HUN] – [HUNGARY]

- http://www.mkik.hu/index.php?id=1406.
  Court of Arbitration attached to the Hungarian Chamber of Commerce and Industry.[47]

- http://www.mkik.hu/index.php?id=1409&print=1.
  Act LXXI [Hungary] of 1994 On arbitration. Nonofficial English translation published on the portal of the Hungarian Chamber of Commerce. [**Law on arbitration**].

IX. [LVA] – [LATVIA]

- http://www.chamber.lv.
  The Arbitration Court of the Latvian Chamber of Commerce and Industry LCCI.[48]

X. [LTU] – [LITHUANIA]

- http://www3.lrs.lt/pls/inter3/dokpaieska.showdoc_l?p_id=56461.
  Law on Commercial Arbitration of The Republic of Lithuania No I-1274 as of 2 April 1996.[49] Official translation by Lietuvos Respulikos Seimas (on the portal of the Parliament of the Republic of Lithuania).

- http://www.arbitrazas.lt.
  Vilniaus komercinio arbitražo teismas. Vilnius Court of Commercial Arbitration.[50]

---

[45] Web site available in English, Estonian and Russian.
[46] Web site available in Croatian. Basic information available in English. See the English presentation of the arbitration court at the web site.
[47] Web site available in Hungarian. Basic information available in English.
[48] Web site available in English, Latvian and Russian.
[49] Published in: Parliamentary record, 1998-04-01, Nr. 4 (*Teisės aktą priėmė - Lietuvos Respublikos Seimas*).
[50] Web site available in English, Lithuanian and Polish.

XI. [MKD] – [MACEDONIA]

*   http://www.mchamber.org.mk/%28S%28crtmab45gznlucyny5lvrven%29%29/default.aspx?lId=2&mId=50&smId=0.[51]
    The Permanent Court of Arbitration attached to the Economic Chamber of Macedonia [Стопанската комора на Македонија].

XII. [MDA] – [MOLDOVA]

*   http://www.arbitraj.chamber.md/index.php?id=93.
    Curtea de Arbitraj Comercial International pe linga Camera de Comert si Industrie a Republicii Moldova. The International Commercial Arbitration Court of the Chamber of Commerce and Industry of the Republic of Moldova.[52]

XIII. [POL] – [POLAND][53]

*   http://www.sakig.pl/.
    Sąd Arbitrażowy przy Krajowej Izbie Gospodarczej w Warszawie.[54] Court of Arbitration at the Polish Chamber of Commerce in Warsaw.

*   http://www.iccpolska.pl/
    Polski Komitet Narodowy Międzynarodowej Izby Handlowej. Polish ICC National Committee.

*   http://oirp.bydgoszcz.pl/index.php?page=statut-2.
    Sądu Polubowny przy Okręgowej Izbie Radców Prawnych w Bydgoszczy. Court of Arbitration attached to the Regional Chamber of Legal Advisors in Bydgoscz.[55]

*   http://www.gca.org.pl/x.php/1,392/Arbitraz.html.
    Sąd Arbitrażowy przy Izbie Bawełny w Gdyni. Arbitration Court attached to the Gdynia Cotton Association.[56]

---

[51]   Web site available in English and Macedonian.
[52]   Web site available in English, Moldovan and Russian.
[53]   Operation and accessibility of all web sites were last checked on 17 November 2010.
[54]   Web site available in English, German, French, Polish and Russian.
[55]   Web site available in Polish.
[56]   Web site available in English and Polish.

- http://oirp.gda.pl/portal-dla-przedsiebiorcow/sad-polubowny.
  Stały Sąd Arbitrażowy przy Okręgowej Izbie Radców Prawnych w Gdańsku. Permanent Court of Arbitration attached to the Regional Chamber of Legal Advisers in Gdańsk.[57]

- http://www.igg.pl/1/node/39.
  Sąd Arbitrażowy przy Izbie Gospodarczej Gazownictwa. Court of Arbitration attached to The Chamber of the Natural Gas Industry.[58]

- http://www.ihk.pl/index.html?id=1635.
  Sąd Arbitrażowy przy Polsko-Niemieckiej Izbie Przemysłowo-Handlowej. Court of Arbitration attached to the Polish – German Chamber of Commerce and Industry.[59]

- http://www.iph.krakow.pl/?a=page&id=31.
  Sąd Polubowny przy Izbie Przemysłowo-Handlowej w Krakowie. Court of Arbitration Attached to the Chamber of Industry and Trade in Krakow.[60]

- http://www.iph.torun.pl/index.php?aid=113837484143da38b99fb66.
  Sąd Polubowny przy Izbie Przemysłowo-Handlowej w Toruniu. Court of Arbitration attached to the Chamber of Industry and Trade in Torun.[61]

- http://isap.sejm.gov.pl.
  Legal information (laws and regulations) system on the portal of the Sejm [Parliament] of the Republic of Poland.[62]

- http://www.kigm.pl/index.php?option=com_content&task=view&id=60&Itemid=65&lang=p.
  Międzynarodowy Sąd Arbitrażowy przy Krajowej Izbie Gospodarki Morskiej. International Court of Arbitration Attached to the Polish Chamber of Maritime Commerce in Gdynia.[63]

---

[57] Web site available in English and Polish.

[58] Web site available in Polish. Some basic information, especially about the Chamber, also available in English and German.

[59] Web site available in German and Polish.

[60] Web site available in Polish.

[61] Web site available in Polish. The portal also offers English version which, however, was not available during our last visit [17 November 2010] (we cannot rule out technical problems but we could not verify that before handing over this manuscript to CYArb for printing).

[62] Web site available in Polish. See also http://sejm.gov.pl.

- http://www.knf.gov.pl/regulacje/Sad_Polubowny/index.html.
  Sąd Polubowny przy Komisji Nadzoru Finansowego. Court of Arbitration Attached to the Polish Financial Supervision Authority.[64]

- http://www.liph.com.pl/index.php?body=7.
  Polubowny Sąd Łódzkiej Izby Przemysłowo-Handlowej. Court of Arbitration Attached to the Chamber of Industry and Trade in Łódz.[65]

- http://www.nig.org.pl/sa/pl1.html.
  Sąd Arbitrażowy przy Nowotomyskiej Izbie Gospodarczej w Nowym Tomyślu. Court of Arbitration Attached to the Chamber of Economy in Nowym Tomyśl.[66]

- http://www.nsa.gov.pl/.
  Supreme Administrative Court.[67]

- http://oirp.olsztyn.pl/content/blogsection/23/73/.
  Stały Sąd Arbitrażowy przy Okręgowej Izbie Radców Prawnych w Olsztynie. Permanent Court of Arbitration Attached to the Regional Chamber of Legal Advisors in Olsztyn.[68]

- http://www.piit.org.pl/piit2/index.jsp?layout=1&news_cat_id=62&place=Menu01.
  Sąd Polubowny ds. Domen Internetowych przy Polskiej Izbie Informatyki i Telekomunikacji w Warszawie. Arbitration Court for Internet Domains Attached to the Polish Chamber of Information Technology and Telecommunications.[69]

- http://www.polubowny.org/index.html.
  Centrum Mediacyjne oraz Stały Sąd Polubowny przy Fundacji Adwokatury Polskiej i Ośrodku Badawczym Adwokatury im. adw. W. Bayera. Mediation Center and Permanent Court of Arbitration Attached to the Donation of Polish Bar and Center for Bar Research of W. Bayer.[70]

---

[63] Web site available in Polish. Some basic information available in English.
[64] Web site available in English and Polish.
[65] Web site available in Polish.
[66] Web site available in Polish.
[67] Web site available in Polish.
[68] Web site available in Polish.
[69] Web site available in English and Polish.
[70] Web site available in Polish.

Czech (& Central European) Yearbook of Arbitration

- http://www.pssp.org.pl/index.htm.
  Polskie Stowarzyszenie Sądownictva Polubownego – Polish Arbitration Association.

- http://www.riph.com.pl/index.php/Company/sub32.
  Sąd Arbitrażowy przy Regionalnej Izbie Przemysłowo-Handlowej w Gliwicach. The Permanent Court of Arbitration at the Regional Chamber of Commerce & Industry in Gliwice.[71]

- http://www.sadarbitrazowy.org.pl/.
  Sąd Arbitrażowy przy Polskiej Konfederacji Pracodawców Prywatnych Lewiatan. Court of Arbitration at the Polish Confederation of Private Employers Lewiatan.[72]

- http://www.oirpwarszawa.pl/kategoria/pokaz/idk/612/ida/520/strona/.
  Stały Sąd Polubowny przy Okręgowej Izbie Radców Prawnych w Warszawie. Permanent Court of Arbitration Attached to the Regional Chamber of Legal Advisers in Warszawa.[73]

- http://www.rig.katowice.pl/default.aspx?docId=30.
  Sąd Arbitrażowy przy Regionalnej Izbie Gospodarczej w Katowicach. Court of Arbitration Attached to the Chamber of Economy in Katowice.[74]

- http://www.sa.dig.wroc.pl/sa/index.php?option=com_content&task=iew&id=69&Itemid=28.
  Sąd Arbitrażowy przy Dolnośląskiej Izbie Gospodarczej we Wrocławiu. Court of Arbitration attached to the Lower Silesia Chamber of Economy in Wrocław.[75]

- http://www.sejm.gov.pl.
  Sejm Rzeczypospolitej Polskiej. Sejm [Parliament] of the Republic of Poland.[76,77]

---

[71] Web site available in Polish. Some basic information also available in English and German.

[72] Web site available in English and Polish.

[73] Web site available in Polish.

[74] Web site available in Polish.

[75] Web site available in Polish. Applicable Rules of proceedings available in English and German.

[76] Web site available in English and Polish.

[77] See also http://isap.sejm.gov.pl – legal information system available through the portal of Sejm.

- http://www.senat.gov.pl.
  Senat Rzeczypospolitej polskiej. The Senate of the Republic of Poland.[78]

- http://www.sn.pl/.
  Supreme Court of the Republic of Poland.[79]

- http://www.ssp.piph.pl/.
  Stały Sąd Polubowny przy Pomorskiej Izbie Przemysłowo-Handlowej w Gdańsku. Permanent Court of Arbitration Attached to the See [*Maritime*] Chamber of Industry and Trade in Gdańsk.[80]

- http://www.trybunal.gov.pl.
  Constitutional Court.[81]

- http://www.wib.com.pl/index.php?idkat=11.
  Sąd Arbitrażowy przy Wielkopolskiej Izbie Budownictwa. Court of Arbitration Attached to the Wielkopolska Chamber of Construction.[82]

- http://www.wiph.pl/content/view/69/53/.
  Sąd Arbitrażowy Izb i Organizacji Gospodarczych Wielkopolski. Arbitration Court Attached to the All Polish Chamber of Industry and Trade.[83]

- http://www.zbp.pl/site.php?s=MGM0YzkzYWY1MTc3Nw.
  Sąd Polubowny przy Związku Banków Polskich. Court of Arbitration Attached to the Polish Bank Association (ZBP).[84]

- http://www.ziph.pl/strona,19,polubowny-sad-gospodarczy.
  Polubowny Sąd Gospodarczy przy Zachodniej Izbie Przemysłowo-Handlowej w Gorzowie Wielkopolskim. Court of Arbitration attached to The Western Chamber of Industry and Commerce in Gorzow Wielkopolski.[85]

---

[78] Web site available in English, French, German, Polish and Russian.
[79] Web site available in English and Polish.
[80] Web site available in Polish.
[81] Web site available in English and Polish.
[82] Web site available in Polish. Basic information, especially about the Chamber, available in English.
[83] Web site available in Polish.
[84] Web site available in English and Polish.
[85] Web site available in Polish. Basic information and information about the Chamber also available in English, French, German and Russian.

XIV. [ROM] – [ROMANIA]

- http://arbitration.ccir.ro.
  The Court of International Commercial Arbitration Attached to the Chamber of Commerce and Industry of Romania.[86]

XV. [RUS] – [RUSSIAN FEDERATION]

- http://www.arbitrations.ru.
  Russian Arbitration Association.[87]

- http://www.iccwbo.ru.
  ICC National Committee Russian Federation

- http://www.spbcci.ru/engarbitaltribunal.
  The Arbitration tribunal at Saint-Petersburg Chamber of Commerce and Industry.[88]

XVI. [SVN] – [SLOVENIA]

- http://www.sloarbitration.org.
  The Permanent Court of Arbitration, although attached to the Chamber of Commerce and Industry of Slovenia [CCIS].[89]

- http://www.sloarbitration.org/english/introduction/organization.html.
  Nonofficial English translations of Slovenian law on or related to arbitration published on the portal of the Permanent Court of Arbitration, although attached to the Chamber of Commerce and Industry of Slovenia. (i) Code of Civil Procedure of Slovenia.[90] (ii) Private International Law and Procedure Act.[91] [Law on arbitration].

---

[86] Web site available in English and Romanian.
[87] Web site available in English and Russian.
[88] Web site available in English and Russian.
[89] Web site available in English and Slovenian.
[90] Published in the: Official Gazette of the Republic of Slovenia, No. 26/99.
[91] Published in the: Official Gazette of the Republic of Slovenia, No. 56/99.

Index

A

access to justice
1/8, 10, 12, 14, 15, 18, 19, 21, 22, 23, 24, 25, 26, 27, 29, 31, 33, 34, 35, 36, 37, 38, 40, 46, 49, 50, 69, 70, 85, 95; **4**/27; **9**/22

accountability
1/2, 4, 5, 19, 41, 68, 74, 80, 94, 95

ad hoc arbitration
3/2, 3, 19, 24, 27, 38; **6**/28, 41; **9**/7; **14**/5, 6, 8, 24, 29, 31, 38, 44, 45, 46

adjudication
1/23; **3**/30, 39; **9**/1, 6, 10, 11, 15, 16, 17, 18, 19, 21, 22, 23, 24, 25, 30; **14**/1

alternative dispute resolution
3/20; **5**/15; **9**/2, 16, 18; **12**/2, 17, 72

American Arbitration Association Rules
2/6, 7, 24; **5**/5, 7; **12**/43, 48; **14**/17

annulment
– of an arbitral award
3/32, 33, 38, 39; **4**/11, 13, 17, 18, 19, 21, 22, 24; **8**/23; **14**/21, 28
– procedure
3/33, 37, 38, 39; **4**/11, 13, 32; **8**/23; **14**/7

applicable law
2/23; **4**/3, 5, 6, 28, 29, 30

appointing authority
1/54; **2**/20, 22, 23; **3**/2, 4, 7, 10, 11, 16, 17, 18, 19; **5**/19; **12**/32; **14**/19, 25, 38, 40, 42, 46

arbitral tribunal
1/54, 72, 73, 75, 78, 85, 94; **2**/14, 16, 23, 29, 30, 33, 35, 39, 75, 76, 82, 89; **3**/10, 13, 17, 22, 27, 31, 36, 38; **4**/10, 24, 33; **6**/2, 15, 29; **7**/3, 18; **8**/2, 24, 27, 28; **10**/1; **12**/69; **13**/1, 2, 3, 4, 5, 8, 11, 19, 20, 21, 22, 24, 25, 26, 27, 28, 32, 36, 37, 39, 40; **14**/18, 19, 24, 29, 30, 31

arbitration
– award
2/1, 12, 22, 29, 78, 83, 84, 89, 96; **3**/32, 33, 38, 39; **4**/1, 2, 4, 11, 17, 18, 19, 21, 22, 24, 27, 32, 39; **5**/2, 7, 11, 12, 14; **6**/11, 15, 53; **7**/2, 3, 5, 15, 20, 29; **8**/1, 2, 3, 4, 5, 7, 11, 12, 13, 14, 15, 17, 18, 19, 20, 21, 22, 23, 24, 26, 27, 28; **9**/7, 14; **11**/3, 8, 47; **12**/30, 39, 64, 65, 75; **13**/20, 22, 25, 40; **14**/7, 10, 11, 21, 22, 28

CALL FOR PAPERS FOR VOLUMES 2015/2016/2017

Did you find the articles in the fourth volume of CYArb® interesting?
Would you like to react to a current article
or contribute to future volumes?

We are seeking authors for both
the Czech Yearbook on International Law® and the
Czech (& Central European) Yearbook of Arbitration®.

The general topics for the 2015/2016/2017 volumes are the following:

CYIL 2015
International Transportation

CYArb® 2015
*Interaction of Arbitration
(Arbitrators) and Courts*

CYIL 2016
International Dispute Resolution

CYArb® 2016
*Rights and Duties of Parties in
Arbitration*

CYIL 2017
*Application and Interpretation of
International Treaties*

CYArb® 2017
Conduct of Arbitration

More general and contact information available at:

www.czechyearbook.org

CYIL – Czech Yearbook of International Law®, 2015
International Transportation
International transportation lies at the heart of international business, because no business or even country is self-sufficient. Therefore, this topic is all encompassing and covers as much issues of local or domestic importance as it does those of global importance. From this point of view, the difficulties – to name just a few – associated with transportation of freight or passengers, of import/export customs or of free trade unions and international organizations, fall under the scope of the topic. However, we don't want to limit the breadth of authors' possible interpretation of the theme. Therefore, articles covering the topic from comparative domestic/international perspectives are also very welcome.

CYArb® – Czech (& Central European) Yearbook of Arbitration®, 2015
Interaction of Arbitration (Arbitrators) and Courts
Arbitration proceedings are not self-sustaining. Even if the arbitration lies outside the national court system at the place of arbitration, the local courts play an important role as much during the arbitral proceedings, as they do after the proceedings end. Therefore, this topic invites authors to undertake a full spectrum analysis of the interaction of arbitral tribunals and local courts during enforcement or annulment arbitral proceedings, when the local courts execute their supportive and controlling functions as well as after the arbitral proceedings have come to an end. Again, comparative analyses are very much welcomed, whether they are of the interaction between national arbitration laws with international applicable standards or between international rules. Because this is a general topic, any type of arbitral proceedings (commercial, consumer, investment, sport…) may be covered.

CYIL – Czech Yearbook of International Law®, 2016
International Dispute Resolution
Papers published in the previous editions of the CYIL focused primarily on issues of substantive law. The 2016 volume aims to concentrate on proceedings with an international dimension and the specific features thereof in terms of private law and public law. Hence, our attention will be devoted to purely private disputes, disputes involving states and state agencies, as well as disputes which are the exclusive domain of public law, primarily public international law. Papers should deal with procedural issues, despite the fact that this edition of our yearbook will not be limited to procedural matters. We therefore aim to focus also on the specifics of the application of substantive law in proceedings with an international dimension, the issue of personal status (personal law), etc. We intend to identify and analyse the specific features of proceedings regarding international disputes as well as the current trends in conflict resolution.

CYArb® – Czech (& Central European) Yearbook of Arbitration®, 2016
Rights and Duties of Parties in Arbitration
The 2016 volume of the CYArb® yearbook will concentrate on the status of parties in arbitration, together with the status of the other individuals and entities involved in the proceedings (except arbitrators), such as third parties in the proceedings (intervenor, *amicus curiae*). Papers dealing with the special status of expert witnesses and witnesses among others, primarily as regards their connection to the parties and the rights and duties of the parties, will also be appreciated. However, our editorial team is also expecting essays from academicians as well as practitioners regarding parties' counsels, including their special status in arbitration as opposed to litigation (court proceedings) and as opposed to proceedings conducted by other public authorities.

CYIL – Czech Yearbook of International Law®, 2017
Application and Interpretation of International Treaties
The editorial team and the publisher have intentionally chosen a very broad topic. The application and interpretation of international treaties is dealt with in many publications and within the voluminous international and national case law. Nonetheless, since the topic continues to generate much controversy, an open discussion is indispensable. Our objective is to analyse the day-to-day application of international treaties from the procedural perspective (in various private- and public-law proceedings), in contractual practice and elsewhere. We also welcome articles focusing on international treaties in connection with the rules applied in regional integration organizations, including the European Union, in connection with the interpretation practice employed by international organizations and others.

CYArb® – Czech (& Central European) Yearbook of Arbitration®, 2017
Conduct of Arbitration
This volume of the CYArb® will be devoted to the methods and procedures of hearing disputes, including the examination of evidence. Our aim is to focus primarily but not exclusively on procedural differences between arbitration and litigation. The nature and, above all, the effects of arbitral awards bring arbitration closer to decisions rendered by courts and other public authorities. However, the contractual autonomy of the parties and arbitrators and the variability of the standards used in arbitration offer a great potential that is not always fully exploited. The team of authors therefore wishes to analyse this autonomy and the flexibility of arbitration and include this potential in the broader discussion introduced in the seventh volume of the CYArb®.